BOLLINGEN SERIES XX

THE COLLECTED WORKS

OF

C. G. JUNG

VOLUME 4

EDITORS

SIR HERBERT READ

MICHAEL FORDHAM, M.D., M.R.C.P.

GERHARD ADLER, PH.D.

FREUD AND PSYCHOANALYSIS

C. G. JUNG

TRANSLATED BY R. F. C. HULL

BOLLINGEN SERIES XX

PANTHEON BOOKS

EDITORIAL NOTE

In the Editorial Note to Volume 1 it was pointed out that Jung's interest had gradually transferred itself, over the years, from psychiatry through psychoanalysis and typology to the theory of archetypes, and finally to the psychology of religious motifs. This facilitated the grouping of his published researches under the relevant headings, even though some of the material could equally well fit into any of several volumes. It follows that there is an underlying network linking, in time or subject-matter, each volume with others, and that wide reading among the volumes is required for a thorough grasp of Jung's views on any particular topic. From no single volume, whatever the arrangement, could the continuity of development be seen in historical perspective.

The present volume gives the substance of Jung's published writings on Freud and psychoanalysis between the years 1906 and 1916; two later papers are, however, added for reasons which will become apparent. Anyone familiar with Jung's work will be aware that references to Freud's observations and theories occur frequently throughout his writings; indeed, the discussion of them has engaged his interest from the beginning of the century to the present day. The scientific papers in this volume, while falling short of a complete account of Freud and psychoanalysis, nevertheless give the essential elements in Jung's changing views on this subject.

Between the years 1907 and 1912, when Jung was a psychoanalyst, his association with Freud was very close. Though the personal relationship between the two then became strained, largely owing to the publication of *Wandlungen und Symbole der Libido* in 1911–12, Jung continued to serve as president of the International Psycho-Analytical Association until 1914. Part

I of this volume covers the period of Jung's close and "enthusiastic" collaboration with Freud; the papers in Parts II and III contain the essentials of the criticism that led to the formal rupture. The contents of Part IV are more in need of explanation. "The Significance of the Father in the Destiny of the Individual," having been originally written in 1908, is associated with the material of Part I. It was, however, considerably revised by the author in 1949, and the revisions are sufficiently extensive to warrant its being placed in Part IV. In view of their special interest, the most important differences between the two versions have been indicated by the use of brackets and footnotes (a comparative method applied also to "The Theory of Psychoanalysis" in Part II). The essay "Freud and Jung: Contrasts" was commissioned in 1929 by the editor of the *Kölnische Zeitung* in view of the then current interest in the relation between Freud and Jung. It is included here because it shows the continuity in Jung's thinking from the time he wrote "The Theory of Psychoanalysis" (1912), serving at the same time as an outline of the changes that had taken place in the interim. In particular, it stresses that the element of confession and the personality of the investigator cannot be eradicated from psychological formulations and may even be considered an essential part of them. Jung's estimate of Freud must be seen in this light, not only in the writings in the present volume but in Volume 15, where Freud is viewed in his cultural setting. "Freud and Jung: Contrasts" and the Introduction to Kranefeldt's *Secret Ways of the Mind* (1930) therefore form a basis for further study of Jung's reassessment of psychoanalysis in that and other volumes of this edition.

The concept of personality is closely bound up with the subject of typology, first broached in this volume and elaborated systematically in *Psychological Types* (Volume 6). Indeed, Jung has once again declared (in his British television broadcast, November 1959) that it was the difference between Freud's views and his own that originally impelled him to work out a psychology of types. We can see this very clearly in the publications between the years 1913 and 1921, when *Psychological Types* was published. The break with Freud was followed by a relatively fallow period. Except for a handful of publications chiefly in English only two works appeared during those years, but they are very important indeed: "The Conception of the Unconscious" and "The Psychology of the Unconscious Processes" (a revision of a 1912 work), published in 1916 and 1917. Through periodic revision these ultimately became the celebrated *Two Essays on Analytical Psychology* (Volume 7), and they contain in embryo the whole future development of analytical psychology both as a therapeutic technique and as a method of investigating the unconscious. In these two seminal works and their subsequent revisions, Jung progressively elaborates and clarifies his basic concepts and carefully differentiates his position from that of Freud. They deepen our understanding of Jung's relation to psychoanalysis in that they set his concepts of the collective unconscious, the archetypes, and the individuation process side by side with his assessment of the theories of Freud and Adler. In this respect, they amplify the papers published in Parts I, II, and III of the present volume and form the link between them and Jung's more critical approach to Freud in Part IV.

The combination of scientific with less technical essays illustrates another aspect of editorial policy in this and other volumes. Over the years Jung has responded again and again to the widespread interest which psychoanalysis, and later analytical psychology, aroused. The Editors, therefore, have not hesitated to assemble in the same volume scientific articles with essays of a more popular nature.

TABLE OF CONTENTS

III

IV

I

ARTICLES
1906–1912

FREUD'S THEORY OF HYSTERIA: A REPLY TO ASCHAFFENBURG [1]

1   If I try to answer Aschaffenburg's—on the whole—very moderate and cautious criticism of Freud's theory of hysteria,[2] I do so in order to prevent the baby from being thrown out with the bath-water. Aschaffenburg, of course, does not assert that Freud's importance ends with his theory of hysteria. But the medical public (psychiatrists included) know Freud mainly from this side of his work, and for this reason adverse criticism could easily throw a shadow on Freud's other scientific achievements. I would like to remark at the start that my reply is not directed to Aschaffenburg personally, but to the whole school of thought whose views and aspirations have found eloquent expression in Aschaffenburg's lecture.

2   His criticism is confined exclusively to the role which sexuality, according to Freud, plays in the formation of the psychoneuroses. What he says, therefore, does not affect the wider range of Freud's psychology, that is, the psychology of dreams, jokes, and disturbances of ordinary thinking caused by feeling-toned constellations. It affects only the psychology of sexuality, the determinants of hysterical symptoms, and the methods of psychanalysis.[3] In all these fields Freud has to his credit unique achievements, which can be contested only by one

---

1 [First published as "Die Hysterielehre Freuds: Eine Erwiderung auf die Aschaffenburgsche Kritik," *Münchener medizinische Wochenschrift* (Munich), LIII : 47 (Nov. 1906).—EDITORS.]

2 [Aschaffenburg, "Die Beziehungen des sexuellen Lebens zur Entstehung von Nerven- und Geisteskrankheiten," in the same organ, no. 37 (Sept. 1906). Originally an address (to a congress of neurologists and psychiatrists, Baden-Baden, May 1906) criticizing Freud's "Bruchstück einer Hysterie-analyse," which had been first published in 1905 (i.e., "Fragment of an Analysis of a Case of Hysteria"). See Jones, *Freud: Life and Work*, II, p. 12.—EDITORS.]

3 [The earlier form "psychanalysis" (*Psychanalyse*) is used throughout this and the next paper.—EDITORS.]

who has never taken the trouble to check Freud's thought-processes experimentally. I say "achievements," though this does not mean that I subscribe unconditionally to all Freud's theorems. But it is also an achievement, and often no small one, to propound ingenious problems. This achievement cannot be disputed even by Freud's most vigorous opponents.

3   To avoid being unnecessarily diffuse, I shall leave out of account all those points which are not affected by Aschaffenburg's criticism, and shall confine myself only to those it attacks.

4   Freud maintains that he has found the root of *most* psychoneuroses to be a psychosexual trauma. Is this assertion nonsense?

5   Aschaffenburg takes his stand on the view, generally accepted today, that hysteria is a psychogenic illness. It therefore has its roots in the psyche. It would be a work of supererogation to point out that an essential component of the psyche is sexuality, a component of whose extent and importance we can form absolutely no conception in the present unsatisfactory state of empirical psychology. We know only that one meets sexuality everywhere. Is there any other psychic factor, any other basic drive except hunger and its derivates, that has a similar importance in human psychology? I could not name one. It stands to reason that such a large and weighty component of the psyche must give rise to a correspondingly large number of emotional conflicts and affective disturbances, and a glance at real life teaches us nothing to the contrary. Freud's view can therefore claim a high degree of probability at the outset, in so far as he derives hysteria primarily from psychosexual conflicts.

6   Now what about Freud's particular view that all hysteria is reducible to sexuality?

7   Freud has not examined all the hysterias there are. His proposition is therefore subject to the general limitation which applies to empirical axioms. He has simply found his view confirmed in the cases observed by him, which constitute an infinitely small fraction of all cases of hysteria. It is even conceivable that there are several forms of hysteria which Freud has not yet observed at all. Finally, it is also possible that Freud's material, under the constellation of his writings, has become somewhat one-sided.

8   We may therefore modify his dictum, with the consent of the author, as follows: An indefinitely large number of cases of hysteria derive from sexual roots.

9   Has anyone proved that this is not so? By "prove" I naturally
mean applying Freud's psychanalytic methods and not just carrying out a rigorous examination of the patient and then de-
claring that nothing sexual can be found. All such "proofs" are
of course worthless from the start. Otherwise we would have to
admit that a person who examines a bacterial culture with a
magnifying-glass and asserts that there are no bacteria in it is
right. The application of psychanalytic methods is, logically, a
sine qua non.

10   Aschaffenburg's objection that an entirely traumatic hysteria
contains nothing sexual and goes back to other, very clear traumata seems to me very apt. But the limits of traumatic hysteria,
as Aschaffenburg's example shows (flower-pot falling followed
by aphonia), are very wide. At that rate countless cases of hysteria could be put into the category of "traumatic" hysteria, for
how often does a mild fright produce a new symptom! Aschaffenburg will surely not believe that anyone can be so naïve as to
seek the cause of the symptom in that little affect alone. The
obvious inference is that the patient was hysterical long before.
When for instance a shot is fired and a passing girl gets abasia,
we can safely assume that the vessel, long since full, has merely
overflowed. No special feat of interpretation is needed to prove
this. So these and a legion of similar cases prove nothing against
Freud.

11   It is rather different in the case of physical traumata and
hysterias about insurance money. Here, where the trauma and
the highly affective prospect of money coincide, an emotional
situation arises which makes the outbreak of a specific form of
hysteria appear at least very plausible. It is possible that Freud's
view is not valid in these cases. For lack of other experiences I
incline to this opinion. But if we want to be absolutely fair and
absolutely scientific, we would certainly have to show first that
a sexual constellation really never did pave the way for the hysteria, i.e., that nothing of this sort comes out under analysis. At
any rate the allegation of traumatic hysteria proves, at best,
only that not all cases of hysteria have a sexual root. But this
does not controvert Freud's basic proposition, as modified
above.

12   There is no other way to refute it than by the use of psychanalytic methods. Anyone who does not use them will never
refute Freud; for it must be proved by means of the methods

inaugurated by him that factors can be found in hysteria other than sexual ones, or that these methods are totally unsuited to bringing intimate psychic material to light.

13   Under these conditions, can Aschaffenburg substantiate his criticism?

14   We hear a great deal about "experiments" and "experiences," but there is nothing to show that our critic has used the methods himself and—what is more important—handled them with certainty. He cites a number of—we must admit—very startling examples of Freudian interpretation, which are bound to nonplus the beginner. He himself points out the inadequacy of quotations torn from their context; it should not be too much if I emphasize still further that in psychology the context is everything. These Freudian interpretations are the result of innumerable experiences and inferences. If you present such results naked, stripped of their psychological premises, naturally no one can understand them.

15   When Aschaffenburg says these interpretations are arbitrary and asserts that other interpretations are just as possible, or that there is absolutely nothing behind the facts in question, it is up to him to prove, by his own analyses, that such things are susceptible of altogether different interpretations. Then the matter would be quickly settled, and everyone would thank him for clearing up this question. It is the same with the question of "forgetting" and other symptomatic actions which Aschaffenburg relegates to the realm of mysticism. These phenomena are extraordinarily common; you meet them almost every day. It is therefore not too much to ask a critic to show by means of practical examples how these phenomena can be traced back to other causes. The association experiment would provide him with any amount of material. Again he would be doing constructive work for which one could not thank him enough.

16   As soon as Aschaffenburg meets these requirements, that is to say, publishes psychanalyses with totally different findings, we will accept his criticism, and then the discussion of Freud's theory can be reopened. Till then his criticism hangs in mid air.

17   Aschaffenburg asserts that the psychanalytic method amounts to auto-suggestion on the part of the doctor as well as the patient.

18   Apart from the fact that it is incumbent on a critic to demonstrate his thorough knowledge of the method, we also lack the

proof that the method is auto-suggestion. In earlier writings[4] I have already pointed out that the association experiment devised by me gives the same results in principle, and that psychanalysis is really no different from an association experiment, as Aschaffenburg himself says in his criticism. His assertion that the experiment was used by me in one case only is erroneous; it was used for the purpose of analysis in a great number of cases, as is evident from numerous statements in my own work and from the recent work of Riklin. Aschaffenburg can check my statements and those of Freud at any time, so far as the latter coincide with my own, by experiment, and thereby acquire a knowledge of the exact foundations of psychanalysis.

19   That my experiments have nothing to do with auto-suggestion can easily be seen from their use in the *experimental diagnosis of facts*. The step from the association experiment, which is already pretty complicated, to full psychanalysis is certainly a big one. But, by thorough study of the association experiment —to the development of which Aschaffenburg himself has made outstanding contributions—one can acquire invaluable insights which prove very useful during analysis. (At any rate this has been so with me.) Only when he has gone through this arduous and difficult training can he begin, with some justification, to examine Freud's theory for evidence of auto-suggestion. He will also have a more sympathetic insight into the somewhat apodictic nature of Freud's style. He will learn to understand how uncommonly difficult it is to *describe* these delicate psychological matters. A written exposition will never be able to reproduce the reality of psychanalysis even approximately, let alone reproduce it in such a way that it has an immediately convincing effect on the reader. When I first read Freud's writings it was the same with me as with everybody else: I could only strew the pages with question-marks. And it will be like that for everyone who reads the account of my association

4 *Studies in Word Association.* [Vol. I of *Diagnostische Assoziationsstudien,* which the author actually cited here, was published in 1906, before the present paper. It reprinted Jung's "Psychoanalyse und Assoziationsexperiment" ("Psychoanalysis and Association Experiments," Vol. 2), originally published in the *Journal für Psychologie und Neurologie* (Leipzig), VII (1905). This paper, which discussed Freud's theory of hysteria and commented on the "Fragment of an Analysis" (see n. 2, supra), was Jung's first significant publication on the subject of psychoanalysis.—EDITORS.]

experiments for the first time. Luckily, however, anyone who wants to can repeat them, and so experience for himself what he did not believe before. Unfortunately this is not true of psychanalysis, since it presupposes an unusual combination of specialized knowledge and psychological routine which not everyone possesses, but which can, to a certain extent, be learnt.

20   So long as we do not know whether Aschaffenburg has this practical experience, the charge of auto-suggestion cannot be taken any more seriously than that of arbitrary interpretation.

21   Aschaffenburg regards the exploration of the patient for sexual ideas as, in many cases, immoral.

22   This is a very delicate question, for whenever morals get mixed up with science one can only pit one belief against another belief. If we look at it simply from the utilitarian point of view, we have to ask ourselves whether sexual enlightenment is under all circumstances harmful or not. This question cannot be answered in general terms, because just as many cases can be cited for as against. Everything depends on the individual. Many people can stand certain truths, others not. Every skilled psychologist will surely take account of this fact. Any rigid formula is particularly wrong here. Apart from the fact that there are many patients who are not in the least harmed by sexual enlightenment, there are not a few who, far from having to be pushed towards this theme, guide the analysis to this point of their own accord. Finally, there are cases (of which I have had more than one) that cannot be got at at all until their sexual circumstances are subjected to a thorough review, and in the cases I have known this has led to very good results. It therefore seems to me beyond doubt that there are at least a great many cases where discussion of sexual matters not only does no harm but is positively helpful. Conversely, I do not hesitate to admit that there are cases where sexual enlightenment does more harm than good. It must be left to the skill of the analyst to find out which these cases are. This, it seems to me, disposes of the moral problem. "Higher" moral considerations derive all too easily from some obnoxious schematism, for which reason their application in practice would seem inopportune from the start.

23   So far as the therapeutic effect of psychanalysis is concerned, it makes no difference to the scientific rightness of the hysteria theory or of the analytic method how the therapeutic result

turns out. My personal conviction at present is that Freud's psychanalysis is one of several possible therapies and that in certain cases it achieves more than the others.

24   As to the scientific findings of psychanalysis, nobody should be put off by seeming enormities, and particularly not by sensational quotations. Freud is probably liable to many human errors, but that does not by any means rule out the possibility that a core of truth lies hidden in the crude husk, of whose significance we can form no adequate conception at present. Seldom has a great truth appeared without fantastic wrappings. One has only to think of Kepler and Newton!

25   In conclusion, I would like to utter an urgent warning against the standpoint of Spielmeyer,[5] which cannot be condemned sharply enough. When a person reviles as unscientific not only a theory whose experimental foundations he has not even examined but also those who have taken the trouble to test it for themselves, the freedom of scientific research is imperilled. No matter whether Freud is mistaken or not, he has the right to be heard before the forum of science. Justice demands that Freud's statements should be verified. But to strike them dead and then consign them to oblivion, that is beneath the dignity of an impartial and unprejudiced scientist.

26   To recapitulate:

(1) It has never yet been proved that Freud's theory of hysteria is erroneous in all cases.

(2) This proof can, logically, be supplied only by one who practises the psychanalytic method.

(3) It has not been proved that psychanalysis gives other results than those obtained by Freud.

(4) It has not been proved that psychanalysis is based on false principles and is altogether unsuitable for an understanding of hysterical symptoms.

[5] Untitled note in the *Zentralblatt für Nervenheilkunde und Psychiatrie*, XXIX (1906), 322. [The first review (pub. April) of Freud's "Fragment of an Analysis of a Case of Hysteria"; see n. 2, supra. Jung's paper cited in n. 4, supra, is earlier, however, and is probably the first discussion of the "Dora analysis."—EDITORS.]

THE FREUDIAN THEORY OF HYSTERIA [1]

27   It is always a difficult and ungrateful task to discuss a theory which the author himself has not formulated in any final way. Freud has never propounded a cut-and-dried theory of hysteria; he has simply tried, from time to time, to formulate his theoretical conclusions in accordance with his experience at that moment. His theoretical formulations can claim the status of a working hypothesis that agrees with experience at all points. For the present, therefore, there can be no talk of a firmly-established Freudian theory of hysteria, but only of numerous experiences which have certain features in common. As we are not dealing with anything finished and conclusive, but rather with a process of development, an historical survey will probably be the form best suited to an account of Freud's teachings.

28   The theoretical presuppositions on which Freud bases his investigations are to be found in the experiments of Pierre Janet. Breuer and Freud, in their first formulation of the problem of hysteria, start from the fact of psychic dissociation and unconscious psychic automatisms. A further presupposition is the aetiological significance of affects, stressed among others by Binswanger.[2] These two presuppositions, together with the findings reached by the theory of suggestion, culminate in the now generally accepted view that hysteria is a psychogenic neurosis.

29   The aim of Freud's research is to discover how the mechanism producing hysterical symptoms works. Nothing less is attempted, therefore, than to supply the missing link in the long chain between the initial cause and the ultimate symptom, a

1 [Translated from "Die Freud'sche Hysterietheorie," *Monatsschrift für Psychiatrie und Neurologie* (Berlin), XXIII (1908), 310–22. Originally a report to the First International Congress of Psychiatry and Neurology, Amsterdam, September 1907. Aschaffenburg also addressed the Congress, publishing his paper in the same organ, XXII (1907), 564ff. For an account of this event, see Jones, *Freud: Life and Work*, II, pp. 125ff.—EDITORS.]

2 [Binswanger, "Freud'sche Mechanismen in der Symptomatologie von Psychosen" (1906). Cf. Jones, II, pp. 36f.—EDITORS.]

link which no one had yet been able to find. The fact, obvious enough to any attentive observer, that affects play an aetiologically decisive role in the formation of hysterical symptoms makes the findings of the first Breuer-Freud report, in the year 1893, immediately intelligible. This is especially true of the proposition advanced by both authors, that the hysteric suffers most of all from *reminiscences*, i.e., from feeling-toned complexes of ideas which, in certain exceptional conditions, prevent the initial affect from working itself out and finally disappearing.

30   This view, presented only in broad outline at first, was reached by Breuer, who between the years 1880 and 1882 had the opportunity to observe and treat an hysterical woman patient of great intelligence. The clinical picture was characterized chiefly by a profound splitting of consciousness, together with numerous physical symptoms of secondary importance and constancy. Breuer, allowing himself to be guided by the patient, observed that in her twilight states complexes of reminiscences were reproduced which derived from the previous year. In these states she hallucinated a great many episodes that had had a traumatic significance for her. Further, he noticed that the reliving and retelling of these traumatic events had a marked therapeutic effect, bringing relief and an improvement in her condition. If he broke off the treatment, a considerable deterioration set in after a short time. In order to increase and accelerate the effect of the treatment, Breuer induced, besides the spontaneous twilight state, an artificially suggested one in which more material was "abreacted." In this way he succeeded in effecting a substantial improvement. Freud, who at once recognized the extraordinary importance of these observations, thereupon furnished a number of his own which agreed with them. This material can be found in *Studies on Hysteria*, published in 1895 by Breuer and Freud.

31   On this foundation was raised the original theoretical edifice constructed jointly by the two authors. They start with the symptomatology of affects in normal individuals. The excitation produced by affects is converted into a series of somatic innervations, thus exhausting itself and so restoring the "tonus of the nerve centres." In this way the affect is "abreacted." It is different in hysteria. Here the traumatic experience is followed—to use a phrase of Oppenheim's—by an "abnormal expression of

the emotional impulse." [3] The intracerebral excitation is not discharged directly, in a natural way, but produces pathological symptoms, either new ones or a recrudescence of old ones. The excitation is converted into abnormal innervations, a phenomenon which the authors call "conversion of the sum of excitation." The affect is deprived of its normal expression, of its normal outlet in adequate innervations; it is not abreacted but remains "blocked." The resulting hysterical symptoms can therefore be regarded as manifestations of the retention.

32   This formulates the situation as we see it in the patient; but the important question as to why the affect should be blocked and converted still remains unanswered, and it was to this question that Freud devoted special attention. In "The Defence Neuro-psychoses," published in 1894, he tried to analyse in great detail the psychological repercussions of the affect. He found two groups of psychogenic neuroses, different in principle because in one group the pathogenic affect is converted into somatic innervations, while in the other group it is displaced to a different complex of ideas. The first group corresponds to classic hysteria, the second to obsessional neurosis. He found the reason for the blocking of affect, or for its conversion or displacement, to be the incompatibility of the traumatic complex with the normal content of consciousness. In many cases he could furnish direct proof that the incompatibility had reached the consciousness of the patient, thus causing an active repression of the incompatible content. The patient did not wish to know anything about it and treated the critical complex as "non arrivé." The result was a systematic circumvention or "repression" of the vulnerable spot, so that the affect could not be abreacted.

33   The blocking of affect is due, therefore, not to a vaguely conceived "special disposition" but to a recognizable motive.

34   To recapitulate what has been said: up to the year 1895 the Breuer-Freud investigations yielded the following results. Psychogenic symptoms arise from feeling-toned complexes of ideas that have the effect of a trauma, either

    1. by conversion of the excitation into abnormal somatic innervations, or

[3] ["Thatsächliches und Hypothetisches über das Wesen der Hysterie" (1890). Cf. Breuer and Freud, *Studies on Hysteria*, Standard Edn., p. 203.—EDITORS.]

2. by displacement of the affect to a less significant complex.

35 The reason why the traumatic affect is not abreacted in a normal way, but is retained, is that its content is not compatible with the rest of the personality and must be repressed.

36 The content of the traumatic affect provided the theme for Freud's further researches. Already in the *Studies on Hysteria* and particularly in "The Defence Neuro-psychoses," Freud had pointed out the sexual nature of the initial affect, whereas the first case history reported by Breuer skirts round the sexual element in a striking fashion, although the whole history not only contains a wealth of sexual allusions but, even for the expert, becomes intelligible and coherent only when the patient's sexuality is taken into account. On the basis of thirteen careful analyses Freud felt justified in asserting that the specific aetiology of hysteria is to be found in the sexual traumata of early childhood, and that the trauma must have consisted in a "real irritation of the genitals." The trauma works at first only preparatorily; it develops its real effect at puberty, when the old memory-trace is reactivated by nascent sexual feelings. Thus Freud tried to resolve the vague concept of a special disposition into quite definite, concrete events in the pre-pubertal period. At that time he did not attribute much significance to a still earlier *inborn* disposition.

37 While the Breuer-Freud *Studies* enjoyed a certain amount of recognition (although, despite Raimann's assurances,[4] they have not yet become the common property of science), *this* theory of Freud's met with general opposition. Not that the frequency of sexual traumata in childhood could be doubted, but rather their exclusively pathogenic significance for normal children. Freud certainly did not evolve this view out of nothing, he was merely formulating certain experiences which had forced themselves on him during analysis. To begin with, he found memory-traces of sexual scenes in infancy, which in many cases were quite definitely related to real happenings. Further, he found that though the traumata remained without specific effect in childhood, after puberty they proved to be determinants of hysterical symptoms. Freud therefore felt compelled to grant that the trauma was real. In my personal opinion he

4 [Emil Raimann, Vienna psychiatrist, critic of Freud. See Jones, I, pp. 395f., and II, p. 122.—EDITORS.]

did this because at that time he was still under the spell of the original view that the hysteric "suffers from reminiscences," for which reason the cause and motivation of the symptom must be sought in the past. Obviously such a view of the aetiological factors was bound to provoke opposition, especially among those with experience of hysteria, for the practitioner is accustomed to look for the driving forces of hysterical neurosis not so much in the past as in the present.

38   This formulation of the theoretical standpoint in 1896 was no more than a transitional stage for Freud, which he has since abandoned. The discovery of sexual determinants in hysteria became the starting-point for extensive researches in the field of sexual psychology in general. Similarly, the problem of the determination of associative processes led his inquiry into the field of dream psychology. In 1900 he published his fundamental work on dreams, which is of such vital importance for the development of his views and his technique. No one who is not thoroughly acquainted with Freud's method of dream interpretation will be able to understand the conceptions he has developed in recent years. *The Interpretation of Dreams* lays down the principles of Freudian theory and at the same time its technique. For an understanding of his present views and the verification of his results a knowledge of Freud's technique is indispensable. This fact makes it necessary for me to go rather more closely into the nature of psychanalysis.

39   The original cathartic method started with the symptoms and sought to discover the traumatic affect underlying them. The affect was thus raised to consciousness and abreacted in the normal manner; that is, it was divested of its traumatic potency. The method relied to a certain extent on suggestion—the analyst took the lead, while the patient remained essentially passive. Aside from this inconvenience, however, it was found that there were more and more cases in which no real trauma was present, and in which all the emotional conflicts seemed to derive exclusively from morbid fantasy activity. The cathartic method was unable to do justice to these cases.

40   According to Freud's statements in 1904,[5] much has altered

5 ["Freud's Psycho-Analytic Procedure" and "On Psychotherapy" appear to be the publications Jung referred to. Cf., however, "Fragment of an Analysis of a Case of Hysteria" (1905), Standard Edn., p. 12.—EDITORS.]

in the method since those early days. All suggestion is now discarded. The patients are no longer guided by the analyst; the freest rein is given to their associations, so that it is really the patients who conduct the analysis. Freud contents himself with registering, and from time to time pointing out, the connections that result. If an interpretation is wrong, it cannot be forced on the patient; if it is right, the result is immediately visible and expresses itself very clearly in the patient's whole behaviour.

41   The present psychanalytic method of Freud is much more complicated, and penetrates much more deeply, than the original cathartic method. Its aim is to bring to consciousness all the false associative connections produced by the complex, and in that way to resolve them. Thus the patient gradually gains complete insight into his illness, and also has an objective standpoint from which to view his complexes. The method could be called an educative one, since it changes the whole thinking and feeling of the patient in such a way that his personality gradually breaks free from the compulsion of the complexes and can take up an independent attitude towards them. In this respect Freud's new method bears some resemblance to the educative method of Dubois,[6] the undeniable success of which is due mainly to the fact that the instruction it imparts alters the patient's attitude towards his complexes.

42   Since it has grown entirely out of empirical practice, the theoretical foundations of the psychanalytic method are still very obscure. By means of my association experiments I think I have made at least a few points accessible to experimental investigation, though not all the theorctical difficulties have been overcome. It seems to me that the main difficulty is this. If, as psychanalysis presupposes, free association leads to the complex, Freud logically assumes that this complex is associated with the starting-point or initial idea. Against this it can be argued that it is not very difficult to establish the associative connection between a cucumber and an elephant. But that is to forget, first, that in analysis only the starting-point is given, and not the goal; and second, that the conscious state is not one of directed thinking but of relaxed attention. Here one might object that the *complex* is the point being aimed at and that, because of its

6 [Paul Dubois, of Bern, treated neurosis by "persuasion."—EDITORS.]

independent feeling-tone, it possesses a strong tendency to reproduction, so that it "rises up" spontaneously and then, as though purely by chance, appears associated with the starting-point.

43   This is certainly conceivable in theory, but in practice things generally look different. The complex, in fact, does not "rise up" freely but is blocked by the most intense resistances. Instead, what "rises up" often seems at first sight to be quite incomprehensible intermediate associations, which neither the analyst nor the patient recognizes as belonging in any way to the complex. But once the chain leading to the complex has been fully established, the meaning of each single link becomes clear, often in the most startling way, so that no special work of interpretation is needed. Anyone with enough practical experience of analysis can convince himself over and over again that under these conditions not just *anything* is reproduced, but always something that is related to the complex, though the relationship is, *a priori*, not always clear. One must accustom oneself to the thought that even in these chains of association chance is absolutely excluded. So if an associative connection is discovered in a chain of associations which was not intended—if, that is to say, the complex we find is associatively connected with the initial idea—then this connection has existed from the start; in other words, the idea we took as the starting-point was already constellated by the complex. We are therefore justified in regarding the initial idea as a sign or symbol of the complex.

44   This view is in agreement with already known psychological theories which maintain that the psychological situation at a given moment is nothing but the resultant of all the psychological events preceding it. Of these the most predominant are the affective experiences, that is, the complexes, which for that reason have the greatest constellating power. If you take any segment of the psychological present, it will logically contain all the antecedent individual events, the affective experiences occupying the foreground, according to the degree of their actuality. This is true of every particle of the psyche. Hence it is theoretically possible to reconstruct the constellations from every particle, and that is what the Freudian method tries to do. During this work the probability is that you will come upon just the

affective constellation lying closest to hand, and not merely on one but on many, indeed very many, each according to the degree of its constellating power. Freud has called this fact *over-determination.*

45   Psychanalysis accordingly keeps within the bounds of known psychological facts. The method is extraordinarily difficult to apply, but it can be learnt; only, as Löwenfeld rightly emphasizes, one needs some years of intensive practice before one can handle it with any certainty. For this reason alone all over-hasty criticism of Freud's findings is precluded. It also precludes the method from ever being used for mass therapy in mental institutions. Its achievements as a scientific instrument can be judged only by one who uses it himself.

46   Freud applied his method first of all to the investigation of dreams, refining and perfecting it in the process. Here he found, it appears, all those surprising associative connections which play such an important role in the neuroses. I would mention, as the most important discovery, the significant role which feeling-toned complexes play in dreams and their symbolical mode of expression. Freud attaches great significance to verbal expression—one of the most important components of our thinking—because the double meaning of words is a favourite channel for the displacement and improper expression of affects. I mention this point because it is of fundamental importance in the psychology of neurosis. For anyone who is familiar with these matters, which are everyday occurrences with normal people too, the interpretations given in the "Fragment of an Analysis of a Case of Hysteria," however strange they may sound, will contain nothing unexpected, but will fit smoothly into his general experience. Unfortunately I must refrain from a detailed discussion of Freud's findings and must limit myself to a few hints. These latest investigations are required reading for Freud's present view of hysterical illnesses. Judging by my own experience, it is impossible to understand the meaning of the *Three Essays* and of the "Fragment" without a thorough knowledge of *The Interpretation of Dreams.*

47   By "thorough knowledge" I naturally do not mean the cheap philological criticism which many writers have levelled at this book, but a patient application of Freud's principles to psychic processes. Here lies the crux of the whole problem. Attack and

defence both miss the mark so long as the discussion proceeds only on theoretical ground. Freud's discoveries do not, at present, lend themselves to the framing of general theories. For the present the only question is: do the associative connections asserted by Freud exist or not? Nothing is achieved by thoughtless affirmation or negation; one should look at the facts without prejudice, carefully observing the rules laid down by Freud. Nor should one be put off by the obtrusion of sexuality, for as a rule you come upon many other, exceedingly interesting things which, at least to begin with, show no trace of sex. An altogether harmless but most instructive exercise, for instance, is the analysis of constellations indicating a complex in the association experiment. With the help of this perfectly harmless material a great many Freudian phenomena can be studied without undue difficulty. The analysis of dreams and hysteria is considerably more difficult and therefore less suitable for a beginner. Without a knowledge of the ground-work Freud's more recent teachings are completely incomprehensible, and, as might be expected, they have remained misunderstood.

48   It is with the greatest hesitation, therefore, that I make the attempt to say something about the subsequent development of Freud's views. My task is rendered especially difficult by the fact that actually we have only two publications to go on: they are the above-mentioned *Three Essays on the Theory of Sexuality* and the "Fragment of an Analysis of a Case of Hysteria." There is as yet no attempt at a systematic exposition and documentation of Freud's more recent views. Let us first try to come closer to the argument of the *Three Essays*.

49   These essays are extremely difficult to understand, not only for one unaccustomed to Freud's way of thinking but also for those who have already worked in this special field. The first thing to be considered is that Freud's conception of sexuality is uncommonly wide. It includes not only normal sexuality but all the perversions, and extends far into the sphere of psychosexual derivates. When Freud speaks of sexuality, it must not be understood merely as the sexual instinct.[7] Another concept which Freud uses in a very wide sense is "libido." This concept, originally borrowed from "libido sexualis," denotes in the first

[7] Freud's concept of sexuality includes roughly everything covered by the concept of the instinct for the preservation of the species.

18

place the sexual components of psychic life so far as they are volitional, and then any inordinate passion or desire.

50 Infantile sexuality, as Freud understands it, is a bundle of possibilities for the application or "investment" of libido. A normal sexual goal does not exist at that stage, because the sexual organs are not yet fully developed. But the psychic mechanisms are probably already in being. The libido is distributed among all the possible forms of sexual activity, and also among all the perversions—that is, among all the variants of sexuality which, if they become fixed, later turn into real perversions. The progressive development of the child gradually eliminates the libidinal investment of perverse tendencies and concentrates on the growth of normal sexuality. The investments set free during this process are used as driving-forces for sublimations, that is, for the higher mental functions. At or after puberty the normal individual seizes on an objective sexual goal, and with this his sexual development comes to an end.

51 In Freud's view, it is characteristic of hysteria that the infantile sexual development takes place under difficult conditions, since the perverse investments of libido are much less easily discarded than with normal individuals and therefore last longer. If the real sexual demands of later life impinge in any form on a morbid personality, its inhibited development shows itself in the fact that it is unable to satisfy the demand in the proper way, because the demand comes up against an unprepared sexuality. As Freud says, the individual predisposed to hysteria brings a "bit of sexual repression" with him from his childhood. Instead of the sexual excitation, in the widest sense of the word, being acted out in the sphere of normal sexuality, it is repressed and causes a reactivation of the original infantile sexual activity. This is expressed above all in the fantasy-activity so characteristic of hysterics. The fantasies develop along the line already traced by the special kind of infantile sexual activity. The fantasies of hysterics are, as we know, boundless; hence, if the psychic balance is in some measure to be preserved, equivalent inhibiting mechanisms are needed or, as Freud calls them, resistances. If the fantasies are of a sexual nature, then the corresponding resistances will be shame and disgust. As these affective states are normally associated with physical manifestations, the appearance of physical symptoms is assured.

52   I think a concrete example from my own experience will illustrate the meaning of Freud's teachings better than any theoretical formulations, which, because of the complexity of the subject, are all apt to sound uncommonly ponderous.

53   The case is one of psychotic hysteria in an intelligent young woman of twenty. The earliest symptoms occurred between the third and fourth year. At that time the patient began to keep back her stool until pain compelled her to defecate. Gradually she began to employ the following auxiliary procedure: she seated herself in a crouching position on the heel of one foot, and in this position tried to defecate, pressing the heel against the anus. The patient continued this perverse activity until her seventh year. Freud calls this infantile perversion anal eroticism.

54   The perversion stopped with the seventh year and was replaced by masturbation. Once, when her father smacked her on the bare buttocks, she felt distinct sexual excitement. Later she became sexually excited when she saw her younger brother being disciplined in the same way. Gradually she developed a markedly negative attitude towards her father.

55   Puberty started when she was thirteen. From then on fantasies developed of a thoroughly perverse nature which pursued her obsessively. These fantasies had a compulsive character: she could never sit at table without thinking of defecation while she was eating, nor could she watch anyone else eating without thinking of the same thing, and especially not her father. In particular, she could not see her father's hands without feeling sexual excitement; for the same reason she could no longer bear to touch his right hand. Thus it gradually came about that she could not eat at all in the presence of other people without continual fits of compulsive laughter and cries of disgust, because the defecation fantasies finally spread to all the persons in her environment. If she was corrected or even reproached in any way, she answered by sticking out her tongue, or with convulsive laughter, cries of disgust, and gestures of horror, because each time she had before her the vivid image of her father's chastising hand, coupled with sexual excitement, which immediately passed over into ill-concealed masturbation.

56   At the age of fifteen, she felt the normal urge to form a love relationship with another person. But all attempts in this direction failed, because the morbid fantasies invariably thrust

themselves between her and the very person she most wanted to love. At the same time, because of the disgust she felt, any display of affection for her father had become impossible. Her father had been the object of her infantile libido transference, hence the resistances were directed especially against him, whereas her mother was not affected by them. About this time she felt a stirring of love for her teacher, but it quickly succumbed to the same overpowering disgust. In a child so much in need of affection this emotional isolation was bound to have the gravest consequences, which were not long in coming.

57   At eighteen, her condition had got so bad that she really did nothing else than alternate between deep depressions and fits of laughing, crying, and screaming. She could no longer look anyone in the face, kept her head bowed, and when anybody touched her stuck her tongue out with every sign of loathing.

58   This short history demonstrates the essentials of Freud's view. First we find a fragment of perverse infantile sexual activity—anal eroticism—replaced in the seventh year by masturbation. At this period the administering of corporal punishment, affecting the region of the anus, produced sexual excitement. Here we have the determinants for the later psychosexual development. Puberty, with its physical and spiritual upheavals, brought a marked increase in fantasy activity. This seized on the sexual activity of childhood and modulated it in endless variations. Perverse fantasies of this kind were bound to act as moral foreign bodies, so to speak, in an otherwise sensitive person, and had to be repressed by means of defence mechanisms, particularly shame and disgust. This readily accounts for all those fits of disgust, loathing, exclamations of horror, sticking out the tongue, etc.

59   At the time when the ordinary longings of puberty for the love of other people were beginning to stir, the pathological symptoms increased, because the fantasies were now directed most intensively to the very people who seemed most worthy of love. This naturally led to a violent psychic conflict, which fully explains the deterioration that then set in, ending in hysterical psychosis.

60   We now understand why Freud can say that hysterics bring with them "a bit of sexual repression from childhood." For constitutional reasons they are probably ready for sexual or quasi-

sexual activities earlier than other people. In keeping with their constitutional emotivity, the infantile impressions go deeper and last longer, so that later, at puberty, they have a constellating effect on the trend of the first really sexual fantasies. Again in keeping with their constitutional emotivity, all affective impulses are much stronger than in normal persons. Hence, to counteract the intensity of their abnormal fantasies, correspondingly strong feelings of shame and disgust are bound to appear. When real sexual demands are made, requiring the transference of libido to the love-object, all the perverse fantasies are transferred to him, as we have seen. Hence the resistance against the object of love. The patient could not transfer her libido to him without inhibitions, and this precipitated the great emotional conflict. Her libido exhausted itself in struggling against her feelings of defence, which grew ever stronger, and which then produced the symptoms. Thus Freud can say that the symptoms represent nothing but the sexual activity of the patient.

61   Summing up, we can formulate Freud's present view of hysteria as follows:

a. Certain precocious sexual activities of a more or less perverse nature grow up on a constitutional basis.

b. These activities do not lead at first to real hysterical symptoms.

c. At puberty (which psychologically sets in earlier than physical maturity) the fantasies tend in a direction constellated by the infantile sexual activity.

d. The fantasies, intensified for constitutional (affective) reasons, lead to the formation of complexes of ideas that are incompatible with the other contents of consciousness and are therefore repressed, chiefly by shame and disgust.

e. This repression takes with it the transference of libido to a love-object, thus precipitating the great emotional conflict which then provides occasion for the outbreak of actual illness.

f. The symptoms of the illness owe their origin to the struggle of the libido against the repression; they therefore represent nothing but an abnormal sexual activity.

62   How far does the validity of Freud's view go? This question is exceedingly difficult to answer. Above all, it must be emphatically pointed out that cases which conform exactly to Freud's schema really do exist. Anyone who has learnt the technique

22

knows this. But no one knows whether Freud's schema is applicable to all forms of hysteria (in any case, hysteria in children and the psychotraumatic neuroses form a group apart). For ordinary cases of hysteria, such as the nerve-specialist meets by the dozen, Freud asserts the validity of his views; my own experience, which is considerably less than his, has yielded nothing that would argue against this assertion. In the cases of hysteria which I have analysed, the symptoms were extraordinarily varied, but they all showed a surprising similarity in their psychological structure. The outward appearance of a case loses much of its interest when it is analysed, because one then sees how the same complex can produce apparently very far-fetched and very remarkable symptoms. For this reason it is impossible to say whether Freud's schema applies only to certain groups of symptoms. At present we can only affirm that his findings are true of an indefinitely large number of cases of hysteria which till now could not be delimited as clinical groups.

63   As to the detailed results of Freud's analyses, the violent opposition they have met with is due simply to the fact that practically no one has followed the development of Freud's theory since 1896. Had his dream-analyses been tested and his rules observed, Freud's latest publications, particularly the "Fragment of an Analysis of a Case of Hysteria," would not have been so difficult to understand. The only disconcerting thing about these reports is their frankness. The public can forgive Freud least of all for his sexual symbolism. In my view he is really easiest to follow here, because this is just where mythology, expressing the fantasy-thinking of all races, has prepared the ground in the most instructive way. I would only mention the writings of Steinthal [8] in the 1860's, which prove the existence of a widespread sexual symbolism in the mythological records and the history of language. I also recall the eroticism of our poets and their allegorical or symbolical expressions. No one who considers this material will be able to conceal from himself that there are uncommonly far-reaching and significant analogies between the Freudian symbolisms and the symbols of poetic fantasy in individuals and in whole nations. The Freudian symbol and its interpretation is therefore nothing unheard of, it is

8 [Heymann Steinthal (1823–99), German philologist and philosopher. Cf. *Symbols of Transformation*, index, s.v.—EDITORS.]

merely something unusual for us psychiatrists. But these difficulties should not deter us from going more deeply into the problems raised by Freud, for they are of extraordinary importance for psychiatry no less than for neurology.

THE ANALYSIS OF DREAMS [1]

64　　In 1900, Sigmund Freud published in Vienna a voluminous work on the analysis of dreams. Here are the principal results of his investigations.

65　　The dream, far from being the confusion of haphazard and meaningless associations it is commonly believed to be, or a result merely of somatic sensations during sleep as many authors suppose, is an autonomous and meaningful product of psychic activity, susceptible, like all other psychic functions, of a systematic analysis. The organic sensations felt during sleep are not the cause of the dream; they play but a secondary role and furnish only elements (the material) upon which the psyche works. According to Freud the dream, like every complex psychic product, is a creation, a piece of work which has its motives, its trains of antecedent associations; and like any considered action it is the outcome of a logical process, of the competition between various tendencies and the victory of one tendency over another. Dreaming has a meaning, like everything else we do.

66　　It may be objected that all empirical reality is against this theory, since the impression of incoherence and obscurity that dreams make upon us is notorious. Freud calls this sequence of confused images the *manifest content* of the dream; it is the façade behind which he looks for what is essential—namely, the dream-thought or the *latent content*. One may ask what reason Freud has for thinking that the dream itself is only the façade of a vast edifice, or that it really has any meaning. His supposition is not founded on a dogma, nor on an *a priori* idea, but on empiricism alone—namely, the common experience that no psychic (or physical) fact is accidental. It must have, then, its

1 [Written in French. Translated by Philip Mairet from "L'Analyse des rêves," *Année psychologique* (Paris), XV (1909), 160–67, and revised by R. F. C. Hull. —Editors.]

train of causes, being always the product of a complicated combination of phenomena; for every existing mental element is the resultant of anterior psychic states and ought in theory to be capable of analysis. Freud applies to the dream the same principle that we always instinctively use when inquiring into the causes of human actions.

67   He asks himself, quite simply: why does this particular person dream this particular thing? He must have his specific reasons, otherwise there would be a breakdown in the law of causality. A child's dream is different from an adult's, just as the dream of an educated man differs from that of an illiterate. There is something individual in the dream: it is in agreement with the psychological disposition of the subject. In what does this psychological disposition consist? It is itself the result of our psychic past. Our present mental state depends upon our history. In each person's past there are elements of different value which determine the psychic "constellation." The events which do not awaken any strong emotions have little influence on our thoughts or actions, whereas those which provoke strong emotional reactions are of great importance for our subsequent psychological development. These memories with a strong feeling-tone form complexes of associations which are not only long enduring but are very powerful and closely interlinked. An object which I regard with little interest calls forth few associations and soon vanishes from my intellectual horizon. An object in which, on the contrary, I feel much interest will evoke numerous associations and preoccupy me for a long while. Every emotion produces a more or less extensive complex of associations which I have called the "feeling-toned complex of ideas." In studying an individual case history we always discover that the complex exerts the strongest "constellating" force, from which we conclude that in any analysis we shall meet with it from the start. The complexes appear as the chief components of the psychological disposition in every psychic structure. In the dream, for example, we encounter the emotional components, for it is easy to understand that all the products of psychic activity depend above all upon the strongest "constellating" influences.

68   One does not have to look far to find the complex that sets Gretchen, in *Faust,* singing:

> There was a king in Thule,
> True even to his grave—
> To him his dying mistress
> A golden beaker gave.

69   The hidden thought is Gretchen's doubt about Faust's fidelity. The song, unconsciously chosen by Gretchen, is what we have called the *dream-material,* which corresponds to the secret thought. One might apply this example to the dream, and suppose that Gretchen had not sung but dreamed this romance.[2] In that case the song, with its tragic story of the loves of a far-off king of old, is the "manifest content" of the dream, its "façade." Anyone who did not know of Gretchen's secret sorrow would have no idea why she dreamt of this king. But we, who know the dream-thought which is her tragic love for Faust, can understand why the dream makes use of this particular song, for it is about the "rare faithfulness" of the king. Faust is not faithful, and Gretchen would like his faithfulness to her to resemble that of the king in the story. Her dream—in reality her song—expresses in a disguised form *the ardent desire of her soul.* Here we touch upon the real nature of the feeling-toned complex; it is always a question of *a wish and resistance to it.* Our life is spent in struggles for the realization of our wishes: all our actions proceed from the wish that something should or should not come to pass.

70   It is for this that we work, for this we think. If we cannot fulfil a wish in reality, we realize it at least in fantasy. The religious and the philosophic systems of every people in every age are the best proof of this. The thought of immortality, even in philosophic guise, is no other than a wish, for which philosophy is but the façade, even as Gretchen's song is only the outward form, a beneficent veil drawn over her grief. *The dream represents her wish as fulfilled.* Freud says that *every dream represents the fulfilment of a repressed wish.*

71   Carrying our illustration further, we see that in the dream

---

2 It might be objected that such a supposition is not permissible, as there is a great deal of difference between a song and a dream. But thanks to the researches of Freud we now know that all the products of any dreaming state have something in common. First, they are all variations on the complex, and second, they are only a kind of symbolic expression of the complex. That is why I think I am justified in making this supposition.

Faust is replaced by the king. A transformation has taken place. Faust has become the far-off old king; the personality of Faust, which has a strong feeling-tone, is replaced by a neutral, legendary person. The king is an association by analogy, a *symbol* for Faust, and the "mistress" for Gretchen. We may ask what is the purpose of this arrangement, why Gretchen should dream, so to speak, indirectly about this thought, why she cannot conceive it clearly and without equivocation. This question is easily answered: Gretchen's sadness contains a thought that no one likes to dwell upon; it would be too painful. Her doubt about Faust's faithfulness is repressed and kept down. It makes its reappearance in the form of a melancholy story which, although it realizes her wish, is not accompanied by pleasant feelings. Freud says that the wishes which form the dream-thought are never desires which one openly admits to oneself, but desires that are repressed because of their painful character; and it is because they are excluded from conscious reflection in the waking state that they float up, indirectly, in dreams.

72   This reasoning is not at all surprising if we look at the lives of the saints. One can understand without difficulty the nature of the feelings repressed by St. Catherine of Siena, which reappeared indirectly in the vision of her celestial marriage, and see what are the wishes that manifest themselves more or less symbolically in the visions and temptations of the saints. As we know, there is as little difference between the somnambulistic consciousness of the hysteric and the normal dream as there is between the intellectual life of hysterics and that of normal people.

73   Naturally, if we ask someone why he had such and such a dream, what are the secret thoughts expressed in it, he cannot tell us. He will say that he had eaten too much in the evening, that he was lying on his back; that he had seen or heard this or that the day before—in short, all the things we can read in the numerous scientific books about dreams. As for the dream-thought, he does not and he cannot know it for, according to Freud, the thought is repressed because it is too disagreeable. So, if anyone solemnly assures us that he has never found in his own dreams any of the things Freud talks about, we can hardly suppress a smile; he has been straining to see things it is impossible to see directly. The dream disguises the repressed complex

28

to prevent it from being recognized. By changing Faust into the King of Thule, Gretchen renders the situation inoffensive. Freud calls this mechanism, which prevents the repressed thought from showing itself clearly, the *censor*. The censor is nothing but the resistance which also prevents us, in the daytime, from following a line of reasoning right to the end. The censor will not allow the thought to pass until it is so disguised that the dreamer is unable to recognize it. If we try to acquaint the dreamer with the thought behind his dream, he will always oppose to us the same resistance that he opposes to his repressed complex.

74   We can now ask ourselves a series of important questions. Above all, what must we do to get behind the façade into the inside of the house—that is, beyond the manifest content of the dream to the real, secret thought behind it?

75   Let us return to our example and suppose that Gretchen is an hysterical patient who comes to consult me about a disagreeable dream. I will suppose, moreover, that I know nothing about her. In this case I would not waste my time questioning her directly, for as a rule these intimate sorrows cannot be uncovered without arousing the most intense resistance. I would try rather to conduct what I have called an "association experiment," [3] which would reveal to me the whole of her love-affair (her secret pregnancy, etc.). The conclusion would be easy to draw, and I should be able to submit the dream-thought to her without hesitation. But one may proceed more prudently.

76   I would ask her, for instance: Who is not so faithful as the King of Thule, or who ought to be? This question would very quickly illuminate the situation. In uncomplicated cases such as this, the interpretation or analysis of a dream is limited to a few simple questions.

77   Here is an example of such a case. It concerns a man of whom I know nothing except that he lives in the colonies and happens at present to be in Europe on leave. During one of our interviews he related a dream which had made a profound impression on him. Two years before, he had dreamt that *he was in a wild and desert place, and he saw, on a rock, a man dressed in*

---

[3] Cf. my *Studies in Word Association*.

black covering his face with both hands. Suddenly he set out towards a precipice, when a woman, likewise clothed in black, appeared and tried to restrain him. He flung himself into the abyss, dragging her with him. The dreamer awoke with a cry of anguish.

78   The question, Who was that man who put himself in a dangerous situation and dragged a woman to her doom? moved the dreamer deeply, for that man was the dreamer himself. Two years before, he had been on a journey of exploration across a rocky and desert land. His expedition was pursued relentlessly by the savage inhabitants of that country, who at night made attacks in which several of its members perished. He had undertaken this extremely perilous journey because at that time *life had no value for him.* The feeling he had when engaging in this adventure was that he was *tempting fate.* And the reason for his despair? For several years he had lived alone in a country with a very dangerous climate. When on leave in Europe two and a half years ago, he made the acquaintance of a young woman. They fell in love and the young woman wanted to marry him. He knew, however, that he would have to go back to the murderous climate of the tropics, and he had no wish to take a woman there and condemn her to almost certain death. He therefore broke off his engagement, after prolonged moral conflicts which plunged him into profound despair. It was in such a state of mind that he started on his perilous journey. The analysis of the dream does not end with this statement, for the wish-fulfilment is not yet evident. But as I am only citing this dream in order to demonstrate the discovery of the essential complex, the sequel of the analysis is without interest for us.

79   In this case the dreamer was a frank and courageous man. A little less frankness, or any feeling of unease or mistrust towards me, and the complex would not have been admitted. There are even some who would calmly have asseverated that the dream had no meaning and that my question was completely beside the point. In these cases the resistance is too great, and the complex cannot be brought up from the depths directly into ordinary consciousness. Generally the resistance is such that a direct inquiry, unless it is conducted with great experience, leads to no result. By creating the "psychoanalytic method" Freud has

given us a valuable instrument for resolving or overcoming the most tenacious resistances.

80   This method is practised in the following manner. One selects some specially striking portion of the dream, and then questions the subject about the associations that attach themselves to it. He is directed to say frankly whatever comes into his mind concerning this part of the dream, eliminating as far as possible any criticism. Criticism is nothing but the censor at work; it is the resistance against the complex, and it tends to suppress what is of the most importance.

81   The subject should, therefore, say absolutely everything that comes into his head without paying any attention to it. This is always difficult at first, especially in an introspective examination when his attention cannot be suppressed so far as to eliminate the inhibiting effect of the censor. For it is towards oneself that one has the strongest resistances. The following case demonstrates the course of an analysis against strong resistances.

82   A gentleman of whose intimate life I was ignorant told me the following dream: *"I found myself in a little room, seated at a table beside Pope Pius X, whose features were far more handsome than they are in reality, which surprised me. I saw on one side of our room a great apartment with a table sumptuously laid, and a crowd of ladies in evening-dress. Suddenly I felt a need to urinate, and I went out. On my return the need was repeated; I went out again, and this happened several times. Finally I woke up, wanting to urinate."*

83   The dreamer, a very intelligent and well-educated man, naturally explained this to himself as a dream caused by irritation of the bladder. Indeed, dreams of this class are always so explained.

84   He argued vigorously against the existence of any components of great individual significance in this dream. It is true that the façade of the dream was not very transparent, and I could not know what was hidden behind it. My first deduction was that the dreamer had a strong resistance because he put so much energy into protesting that the dream was meaningless.

85   In consequence, I did not venture to put the indiscreet question: Why did you compare yourself to the Pope? I only asked him what ideas he associated with "Pope." The analysis developed as follows:

31

Pope. "The Pope lives royally . . ." (A well-known students' song.) Note that this gentleman was thirty-one and unmarried.

Seated beside the Pope. "Just in the same way I was seated at the side of a Sheikh of a Moslem sect, whose guest I was in Arabia. The Sheikh is a sort of Pope."

86   The Pope is a celibate, the Moslem a polygamist. The idea behind the dream seems to be clear: "I am a celibate like the Pope, but I would like to have many wives like the Moslem." I kept silent about these conjectures.

The room and the apartment with the table laid. "They are apartments in my cousin's house, where I was present at a large dinner-party he gave a fortnight ago."

The ladies in evening dress. "At this dinner there were also ladies, my cousin's daughters, girls of marriageable age."

87   Here he stopped: he had no further associations. The appearance of this phenomenon, known as a mental inhibition, always justifies the conclusion that one has hit on an association which arouses strong resistance. I asked:

And these young women? "Oh, nothing; recently one of them was at F. She stayed with us for some time. When she went away I went to the station with her, along with my sister."

88   Another inhibition: I helped him out by asking:

What happened then? "Oh! I was just thinking [this thought had evidently been repressed by the censor] that I had said something to my sister that made us laugh, but I have completely forgotten what it was."

89   In spite of his sincere efforts to remember, it was at first impossible for him to recall what this was. Here we have a very common instance of forgetfulness caused by inhibition. All at once he remembered:

"On the way to the station we met a gentleman who greeted us and whom I seemed to recognize. Later, I asked my sister, Was that the gentleman who is interested in —— [the cousin's daughter]?"

90   (She is now engaged to this gentleman, and I must add that the cousin's family was very wealthy and that the dreamer was interested too, but he was too late.)

The dinner at the cousin's house. "I shall shortly have to go to the wedding of two friends of mine."

The Pope's features. "The nose was exceedingly well-formed and slightly pointed."

Who has a nose like that? (Laughing.) "A young woman I'm taking a great interest in just now."

Was there anything else noteworthy about the Pope's face? "Yes, his mouth. It was a very shapely mouth. [Laughing.] Another young woman, who also attracts me, has a mouth like that."

91   This material is sufficient to elucidate a large part of the dream. The "Pope" is a good example of what Freud would call a *condensation*. In the first place he symbolizes the dreamer (celibate life), secondly he is a transformation of the polygamous Sheikh. Then he is the person seated beside the dreamer during a dinner, that is to say, one or rather two ladies—in fact, the two ladies who interest the dreamer.

92   But how comes it that this material is associated with the need to urinate? To find the answer to this question I formulated the situation in this way:

You were taking part in a marriage ceremony and in the presence of a young lady when you felt you wanted to pass water? "True, that did happen to me once. It was very unpleasant. I had been invited to the marriage of a relative, when I was about eleven. In the church I was sitting next to a girl of my own age. The ceremony went on rather a long time, and I began to want to urinate. But I restrained myself until it was too late. I wetted my trousers."

93   The association of marriage with the desire to urinate dates from that event. I will not pursue this analysis, which does not end here, lest this paper should become too long. But what has been said is sufficient to show the technique, the procedure of analysis. Obviously it is impossible to give the reader a comprehensive survey of these new points of view. The illumination that the psychoanalytic method brings to us is very great, not only for the understanding of dreams but for that of hysteria and the most important mental illnesses.

94   The psychoanalytic method, which is in use everywhere, has already given rise to a considerable literature in German. I am persuaded that the study of this method is extremely important,

not only for psychiatrists and neurologists but also for psychologists. The following works are recommended. For normal psychology: Freud, *The Interpretation of Dreams,* and "Jokes and Their Relation to the Unconscious." For the neuroses: Breuer and Freud, *Studies on Hysteria;* Freud, "Fragment of an Analysis of a Case of Hysteria." For the psychoses: Jung, *The Psychology of Dementia Praecox.* The writings of Maeder in the *Archives de psychologie* also give an excellent summary of Freud's ideas.[4]

4 [See the bibliography for fuller data.—EDITORS.]

A CONTRIBUTION TO THE PSYCHOLOGY
OF RUMOUR [1]

95   About a year ago the school authorities in N. asked me to furnish a report on the mental condition of Marie X., a thirteen-year-old school-girl. Marie had recently been expelled from the school because she was instrumental in originating an ugly rumour, spreading gossip about her class-teacher. The punishment hit the child, and especially her parents, very hard, so that the school authorities were inclined to readmit her under the cover of a medical opinion.

96   The facts of the case were as follows. The teacher had heard indirectly that the girls were telling an ambiguous sexual story about him. On investigation, it was found that Marie had one day related a dream to three girl-friends which ran somewhat as follows:

The class was going to the bathing-place. I had to go with the boys because there was no more room.—Then we swam a long way out in the lake. (Asked "Who?" Marie said: "Lina,[2] the teacher, and me.") *A steamer came along. The teacher asked us: "Do you want a ride?" We came to K. A wedding was going on.* ("Whose?" "A friend of the teacher's.") *We were allowed to take part in it. Then we went on a journey.* ("Who?" "Me, Lina, and the teacher.") *It was like a honeymoon trip. We came to Andermatt, and there was no more room in the hotel so we had to spend the night in a barn. There the woman got a child and the teacher became the godfather.*

97   This dream was told me by the child when I examined her. The teacher had also got her to tell the dream in writing. In this earlier version the obvious gap after "Do you want a ride?" was

1 [Originally published as "Ein Beitrag zur Psychologie des Gerüchtes," *Zentralblatt für Psychoanalyse* (Wiesbaden), I (1910/11): 3, 81–90. Previously translated in *Collected Papers on Analytical Psychology* (London, 1916; 2nd edn., London, 1917, and New York, 1922).—EDITORS.]
2 [Her sister. Cf. par. 119.—EDITORS.]

filled in by the words: "We got on it. Soon we felt cold. An old man gave us a blouse which the teacher put on." On the other hand, there was an omission of the passage about finding no room in the hotel and having to spend the night in the barn.

98   The child told the dream immediately not only to her three friends but also to her mother. The mother repeated it to me with only trifling differences from the two readings given above. In his investigations, carried out with the deepest misgivings, the teacher failed, like myself, to discover any other, more dangerous text. It is therefore very probable that the original story could not have been very different. (The passage about the cold and the blouse seems to be an early interpolation, as it tries to establish a logical relationship. Coming out of the water one is wet, has on only a bathing-dress, and therefore cannot take part in a wedding before putting on some clothes.) The teacher would not believe at first that it was simply a dream, he suspected it was an invention. But he had to admit that the innocent telling of the dream was apparently a fact, and that it would be unnatural to credit the child with sufficient guile to make sexual innuendoes in such a veiled form. For a time he wavered between the view that it was a cunning invention and the view that it was really a dream, harmless in itself, which had been given a sexual twist by the other children. When his first indignation wore off he came to see that Marie's guilt could not be so great, and that the fantasies of her friends had contributed to the rumour. He then did something very praiseworthy: he placed Marie's schoolmates under supervision and made them all write out what they had heard of the dream.

99   Before turning our attention to these accounts, let us first consider the dream analytically. To begin with, we must accept the facts and agree with the teacher that it really was a dream and not an invention—the ambiguities are too great for that. Conscious invention tries to create unbroken transitions; the dream takes no account of this, but proceeds regardless of gaps, which, as we have seen, give rise to interpolations during the conscious revision. The gaps are very significant. In the bathing-place there is no picture of undressing, being unclothed, nor any detailed description of being together in the water. The lack of clothes on the steamer is compensated by the above-mentioned interpolation, but only for the teacher, which shows

that his nakedness was most urgently in need of cover. There is no detailed description of the wedding, and the transition from the steamer to the wedding celebration is abrupt. The reason for stopping overnight in the barn at Andermatt is undiscoverable at first. The parallel, however, is the lack of room in the bathing-place, which made it necessary for the girls to go to the men's section; the lack of room at the hotel again prevents the segregation of the sexes. The picture of the barn is very inadequately filled out: the birth follows suddenly and disconnectedly. The teacher as godfather is extremely ambiguous. Marie's role throughout the whole story is of secondary importance; she is no more than a spectator.

100 All this has the appearance of a genuine dream, and those of my readers who have sufficient experience of dreams of girls of this age will certainly confirm this view. The interpretation of the dream is so simple that we can safely leave it to the children themselves, whose statements now follow.

Aural Witnesses

101 (1) Marie dreamt that she and Lina went swimming with our teacher. When they had swum out pretty far in the lake, Marie said she could not swim any further, her foot hurt her so. Our teacher said, she could ride on my back. Marie got on and they swam out together. After a while a steamer came along and they got on it. It seems our teacher had a rope with him with which he tied Marie and Lina together, and so pulled them out into the lake after him. They went as far as Z., where they got out. But now they had no clothes on. The teacher bought a jacket, and Marie and Lina got a long thick veil, and all three walked up the street by the lake. This was when the wedding was going on. Soon they met. The bride had on a blue silk dress but no veil. She asked Marie and Lina if they would be so kind as to give her their veil. Marie and Lina gave it and in return were allowed to go to the wedding. They went to the Sun Inn. Afterwards they made a honeymoon trip to Andermatt, I don't know whether they went to the inn at Andermatt or at Z. There they were given coffee, potatoes, honey, and butter. I must not say any more, only that in the end the teacher became the godfather.

02 Here the roundabout story of lack of room at the bathing-place is missing; Marie goes swimming with the teacher right

away. Their being together in the water is given a more personal relationship by the rope connecting the teacher and the two girls. The ambiguity about the "ride" [3] in the original story has already had consequences here, for the part about the steamer now takes second place, and first place is given to the teacher, who takes Marie on his back. (The delightful little slip "she could ride on my back"—instead of *his*—shows the narrator's inner participation in the scene.) This explains why she brings the steamer into action somewhat abruptly, in order to give the equivocal "ride" a familiar, harmless turn, like the anticlimax in a music-hall song. The passage about the lack of clothes, the ambiguity of which has already been noted, arouses her special interest. The teacher buys a jacket, the girls get a long thick veil, such as is worn only in case of death or at weddings. That the wedding is meant here in a wider sense is shown by the remark that the bride had no veil: the one who has the veil is the bride! The narrator, a good friend of Marie, helps her to dream the dream further: the possession of the veil characterizes Marie and Lina as brides. Anything offensive or immoral in this situation is relieved by the girls' surrendering the veil; the narrator thus gives the story an innocent turn. The same mechanism is followed in the embellishment of the ambiguous situation at Andermatt: there is nothing but nice things, coffee, potatoes, honey, and butter, a reversion to the infantile on the well-known pattern. The conclusion seems to be very abrupt: the teacher becomes a godfather.

103   (2) Marie dreamt that she went bathing with Lina and the teacher. Far out in the lake Marie told the teacher her leg was hurting. The teacher said she could ride on his back. I don't know now whether the last sentence was really told so, but I think it was. As there was a ship on the lake just then, the teacher said she should swim to the ship and then get in. I really don't remember any more how she told it.—Then the teacher or Marie, I don't know which, said they would get out at Z. and run home. So the teacher called to two gentlemen, who had just been bathing, to carry the children ashore. Lina sat on one man's back and Marie on the other fat man,

3 [*Aufsitzen* in the original. The word (usually intransitive) means both to 'sit on a person's back' and to 'mount' a horse or vehicle. As applied to a steamer, its use is quite exceptional. The ambiguity can be preserved in English only by alternating between 'ride' and 'get on.'—TRANS.]

and the teacher held on to the fat man's leg and swam after them. When they landed they ran home.

On the way the teacher met his friend, who had a wedding. Marie said, it was then the fashion to go on foot, not in a carriage. Then the bride said they could come along too. Then the teacher said it would be nice if the two girls gave the bride their black veil, which they had got on the way, I don't know where. The girls gave it to her, and the bride said they were nice generous children. Then they went on further and stopped at the Sun Inn. There they had something to eat, I don't know what. Then they went on the honeymoon trip to Andermatt. They went into a barn and danced. All the men had taken off their coats except the teacher. The bride said he should take off his coat too. The teacher refused, but at last he did. Then the teacher was . . . The teacher said he felt cold. I mustn't tell any more, it is improper. That's all I heard of the dream.

104   The narrator pays special attention to the "ride," but is uncertain whether in the original story it referred to the teacher or the steamer. This uncertainty is amply compensated by the elaborate story of the two strange gentlemen who took the girls on their backs. For her, the piggyback is too valuable a thought to be relinquished, only she is embarrassed at the idea of the teacher as its object. The lack of clothes likewise arouses strong interest. The bridal veil has now become black, like a veil of mourning (naturally in order to conceal anything indelicate). Here the innocent turn has even been given a virtuous accent ("nice generous children"); the immoral wish has surreptitiously changed into something virtuous on which special emphasis is laid, suspect like every accentuated virtue. The narrator has exuberantly filled in the blanks in the scene of the barn; the men take off their coats, the teacher follows suit and is consequently . . . naked, and feels cold. Whereupon it becomes too "improper." She has correctly recognized the parallels we conjectured above when discussing the original story, and has added the undressing scene—which really belongs to the bathing scene—here, for it had to come out in the end that the girls were together with the naked teacher.

105   (3) Marie told me she had dreamt: Once I went bathing but there was no more room. The teacher took me into his cabin. I undressed and went bathing. I swam until I reached the bank. There I met the teacher. He said, wouldn't I like to swim across the lake

39

with him? I went, and Lina also. We swam out and were soon in the middle of the lake. I did not want to swim any further. Now I can't remember it exactly. Soon a ship came along and we got on the ship. The teacher said, "I'm cold," and a sailor gave us an old shirt. Each of us tore a piece off. I tied it round my neck. Then we left the ship and swam on to K.

Lina and I did not want to go any further and two fat men took us on their backs. In K. we got a veil which we put on. In K. we went into the street. The teacher met his friend who invited us to his wedding. We went to the Sun Inn and played games. We also danced the polonaise. Now I don't remember exactly. Afterwards we went on the honeymoon trip to Andermatt. The teacher had no money with him and stole some chestnuts. The teacher told us, "I am so glad I can travel with my two pupils." Now comes something improper which I will not write. Now the dream is finished.

106   Here the undressing together takes place in the bathing-cabin. The lack of clothes on the ship gives rise to a new variant (old shirt torn into three pieces). Because of its uncertainty, the sitting on the teacher is not mentioned. Instead, the girls sit on the backs of two fat men. As "fat" is stressed in this and the previous version, it is worth mentioning that the teacher was more than a little plump. The substitution is typical: each of the girls has a teacher. Duplication or multiplication of personalities expresses their significance, i.e., their investment with libido. The same is true of the repetition of actions.[4] The significance of this multiplication is especially clear in religion and mythology. (Cf. the Trinity and the two mystic formulae of confession: "Isis una quae es omnia," "Hermes omnia solus et ter unus.") Proverbially we say: "He eats, drinks, or sleeps 'for two.' " Also, the multiplication of personality expresses an analogy or comparison: *my friend* has the "same aetiological value" as *myself* (Freud). In dementia praecox, or schizophrenia, to use Bleuler's broader and better term, the multiplication of personality is primarily the expression of libido investment, for it is invariably the person to whom the patient has a transference who is liable to multiplication. ("There are two Professor N's." "Oh, so you are Dr. Jung too. This morning another person came to see me who also called himself Dr. Jung.") It seems

[4] Cf. the duplication of attributes in dementia praecox in my "The Psychology of Dementia Praecox."

that, in keeping with the general tendency of schizophrenia, this splitting is an analytical depotentiation for the purpose of preventing too powerful impressions. A further significance of the multiplication of personality, though it does not come exactly into this category, is the raising of some attribute to a living figure. A simple example is Dionysus and his companion Phales, Phales (*phallos*) being the personification of the penis of Dionysus. The so-called Dionysian train (satyrs, tityrs, Sileni, maenads, Mimallones, etc.) consists of personifications of Dionysian attributes.

107   The scene in Andermatt is portrayed with a nice wit, or more correctly, is dreamt further. "The teacher stole some chestnuts" is equivalent to saying that he did something prohibited. By chestnuts is meant roast chestnuts, which because of the split are known to be female sexual symbols. Hence the teacher's remark that he was "so glad to travel with his two pupils," following directly on the theft of the chestnuts, becomes understandable. The theft of the chestnuts is certainly a personal interpolation, for it occurs in no other account. It shows how intense was the inner participation of her schoolmates in Marie's dream, i.e., it had the "same aetiological value" for them.

108   This is the last of the aural witnesses. The story of the veil and the pain in the foot or leg are items which may well have been mentioned in the original narrative. Other interpolations are altogether personal and are based on inner participation in the meaning of the dream.

Hearsay Evidence

109   (1) The whole school went bathing with the teacher. Only Marie had no room to undress in the bathing-place. So the teacher said, "You can come into my room and undress with me." She must have felt very uncomfortable. When both were undressed they went into the lake. The teacher took a long cord and tied it round Marie. Then they both swam far out. But Marie got tired, so the teacher took her on his back. Then Marie saw Lina, she called out, "Come with me," and Lina came. They all swam out still further. They met a ship. Then the teacher asked, "May we get in? These girls are tired." The ship stopped and they all got in. I don't know exactly how they came ashore at K. Then the teacher got an old night-shirt. He put it on. Then he met a friend who was having a wedding.

Teacher, Marie, and Lina were invited. The wedding was celebrated at the Crown in K. They wanted to dance the polonaise. The teacher said he would not do it. But the others said he might as well. He did it with Marie. Teacher said, "I will not go home any more to my wife and children. I love you best, Marie." She was very pleased. After the wedding there was a honeymoon trip. Teacher, Marie, and Lina were allowed to go with them. The trip was to Milan. Afterwards they went to Andermatt, where they could find no place to sleep. They went to a barn, where they could stop the night all together. I must not tell any more because it becomes very indecent.

110   The undressing scene at the bathing-place is fully developed. The swim undergoes a simplification for which the story of the rope had paved the way: the teacher ties himself to Marie, but Lina is not mentioned here, she comes only later when Marie was already sitting on the teacher's back. Here the clothing is a night-shirt. The wedding celebrations are given a very direct interpretation: the teacher does not want to go home any more to his wife and children, he loves Marie best. In the barn they found a place "all together" and then it "became very indecent."

111   (2) They said she had gone with the school to the bathing-place to bathe. But as the bathing-place was too full, the teacher called her to come with him. Then we swam out in the lake and Lina followed us. Then the teacher took a cord and tied us together. I don't know exactly how they got separated again. But after a long time they suddenly arrived at Z. There a scene is said to have taken place which I would rather not tell, for if it was true it would be too shameful. Also I don't know exactly what is supposed to have happened as I was very tired. Only I have heard that Marie said she was always to remain with the teacher now, and that he hugged her again and again as his best pupil. If I knew exactly I would also tell the other thing, but my sister only said something about a little child that was born there, and the teacher was said to be the godfather.

112   Note that in this story the indecent scene is inserted at the wedding festivities, where it is just as appropriate as at the end, for the attentive reader will long ago have observed that it could also have taken place in the bathing-cabin. Actually, things have happened as they usually do in dreams: the final thought in a long series of dream-images contains precisely what the first

image in the series was trying to represent. The censor pushes the complex away as long as possible by means of ever-renewed symbolical disguises, displacements, bowdlerizations, etc. Nothing happens in the bathing-cabin, there is no piggyback in the water, on landing it is not on the teacher's back that the girls sit, it is another pair who get married, another girl has a child in the barn, and the teacher is only—godfather. But all these situations and images lend themselves to representing the wish for coitus. Behind all these metamorphoses the action nevertheless takes place, and the result is the birth staged at the end.

113   (3) Marie said: the teacher had a wedding with his wife, and afterwards they went to the Crown and danced together. Marie said all sorts of other wild things which I must not tell or write about, it is too embarrassing.

114   - Here pretty well everything is too improper to be told. Note that the wedding takes place with the "wife."

115   (4) The teacher and Marie went bathing, and he asked Marie if she wanted to come along too. She said yes. When they had gone out together they met Lina, and the teacher asked if she wanted to come with them. And they went further out. Then I heard that she said the teacher said that Lina and she were his favourite pupils. She also told us that the teacher was in his bathing-dress. Then they went to a wedding and the bride got a little child.

116   The personal relationship to the teacher is strongly emphasized ("favourite pupils"), likewise the inadequate clothing ("bathing-dress").

117   (5) Marie and Lina went bathing with the teacher. When Marie and Lina and the teacher had swum a little way, Marie said, "Teacher, I can't go any further, my foot hurts me." The teacher told her to sit on his back and Marie did so. Then a little steamer came along and the teacher got into the ship. The teacher had two ropes with him and tied the children to the ship. Then they all went to Z. and got out there. The teacher bought himself a night-shirt and put it on and the children put a towel over them. Teacher had a bride and they were in a barn. The two children were also with the teacher and his bride in the barn and they danced. I must not write the other thing for it is too awful.

118   Here Marie sits on the teacher's back. The teacher fastens the two children to the ship with ropes, from which it can be

seen how easily "ship" is substituted for "teacher." The night-shirt again emerges as the article of clothing. It was the teacher's own wedding, and what is improper comes after the dance.

119   (6: Lina.) The teacher went bathing with the whole school. Marie could not find any room, and she cried. The teacher then told Marie she could come into his cabin.

"I must leave out something here and there," said my sister, "for it is a long story." But she told me something more which I must tell in order to speak the truth. When they were in the water the teacher asked Marie if she would like to swim across the lake with him. She answered that if I came she would come too. Then we swam about halfway. Marie got tired and the teacher pulled her by a cord. At K. they went on shore and from there to Z. All this time the teacher is supposed to have been dressed as for swimming. There we met a friend who was having a wedding. We were invited to it by this friend. After the feast there was a honeymoon trip, and we went to Milan. We had to sleep one night in a barn and there something happened which I must not tell. The teacher said we were his favourite pupils, and he also kissed Marie.

120   The excuse "I must leave out something here and there" re-places the undressing scene. Special emphasis is laid on the teacher's inadequate clothing. The journey to Milan is a typical honeymoon trip. This passage likewise seems to be an independ-ent fantasy due to inner participation. Marie clearly figures as the loved one.

121   (7) The whole school and teacher went bathing. They all went into a room. Teacher also. Only Marie could find no room, so the teacher said to her, "I still have room." She went. Then the teacher said, "Lie on my back, I will swim out into the lake with you." I must not write any more, for it is so improper that I can hardly even say it. Except for the improper part which followed I know nothing more of the dream.

122   This narrator is getting down to the facts. Already at the bathing-place Marie was to lie on the teacher's back. Logically enough the narrator does not know anything of the rest of the dream except the improper part.

123   (8) The whole school went bathing. Marie had no room and was invited into his cabin by the teacher. The teacher swam out with her and told her, straight, she was his darling or something like

that. When they came ashore at Z. a friend had just had a wedding and this friend invited them both in their bathing-costume. The teacher had found an old night-shirt and put it on over his swimming-pants. He also kissed Marie a lot and said he would not go home to his wife any more. They were both invited on the honeymoon trip. The journey went through Andermatt, where they could not find any place to sleep, and so had to sleep in the hay. A woman was there too, now comes the dreadful part, and it is not at all right to laugh and joke about something so serious. This woman got a little child, but I will not say any more for it is too dreadful.

124   The narrator is very downright ("he told her, straight, she was his darling," "he kissed her a lot" etc.). Her obvious indignation over the silly tattling tells us something special about her character. Subsequent investigations showed that this girl was the only one of all the witnesses who had been sexually enlightened by her mother.

Summary

125   So far as the interpretation of the dream is concerned, there is nothing for me to add; the children themselves have done all that is necessary, leaving practically nothing over for psychoanalytic interpretation. *The rumour has analysed and interpreted the dream.* So far as I know, rumour has not been investigated in this capacity up to now. Our case certainly makes it appear worth while to fathom the psychology of rumour from the psychoanalytic side. In presenting the material I have purposely restricted myself to the psychoanalytic point of view, though I do not deny that my material offers numerous openings for the invaluable researches of the followers of Stern, Claparède, and others.

126   The material enables us to understand the structure of the rumour, but psychoanalysis cannot rest satisfied with that. We need to know more about the why and the wherefore of the whole phenomenon. As we have seen, the teacher was greatly affected by the rumour and was left puzzled by the problem of its cause and effect. How can a dream, which is notoriously harmless and never means anything (teachers, as we know, also have a training in psychology), produce such effects, such malicious gossip? Faced with this question, the teacher seems to me to have hit instinctively on the right answer. The effect of the

45

dream can only be explained by its being "le vrai mot de la situation"; that is to say, it gave suitable expression to something that was already in the air. It was the spark which fell into the powder-barrel. Our material affords all the necessary proofs of this view. Throughout, I have drawn attention to the inner participation of Marie's schoolmates in her dream, and to the points of special interest where some of them have added their own fantasies or day-dreams. The class consisted of girls between the ages of twelve and thirteen, who were therefore in the midst of the prodromata of puberty. The dreamer herself was almost fully developed sexually and in this respect ahead of her class; she was the leader who gave the watchword for the unconscious and so detonated the sexual complexes lying dormant in her companions.

127   As can easily be understood, the whole affair was most distressing for the teacher. The supposition that this, precisely, was what the girls secretly intended is justified by the psychoanalytic axiom that actions are to be judged more by their results than by their conscious motives.[5] Accordingly, we would conjecture that Marie had been especially troublesome to her teacher. At first she liked this teacher most of all. In the course of the last six months, however, her position had changed. She had become dreamy and inattentive, she was afraid to go into the streets after dark because of bad men. On several occasions she talked about sex to her companions in a rather obscene way; her mother asked me anxiously how she was to explain the approaching menstruation to her daughter. Because of her behaviour she had forfeited the good opinion of her teacher, as was clearly evidenced for the first time by a bad report which she and some of her friends received a few days before the outbreak of the rumour. Their disappointment was so great that the girls indulged in all sorts of vengeful fantasies about the teacher; for instance, they might push him on to the rails so that the train would run over him. Marie was especially to the fore in these murderous fantasies. On the night following this great outburst of anger, when her former love for her teacher seemed quite forgotten, that repressed part of herself rose up in the dream, and fulfilled its wish for sexual union with the

5 Cf. my "Psychic Conflicts in a Child."

teacher—as compensation for the hate which had filled the day.[6] On waking, the dream became a subtle instrument of her hatred, because its wishful thinking was also that of her companions, as it always is in rumours of this kind. Revenge certainly had its triumph, but the recoil upon Marie herself was even more severe. Such is the rule when our impulses are given over to the unconscious. Marie was expelled from school, but on my report was allowed to return.

128   I am well aware that this short report is inadequate and unsatisfactory from the point of view of exact science. Had the original story been accurately verified we could have demonstrated quite clearly what we have now only been able to suggest. This case, therefore, merely poses a question, and it remains for more fortunate observers to collect really convincing evidence in this field.

6 [It may be not without significance that, used transitively, the word *aufsitzen*— literally, 'sit a person up'—means 'to deceive,' 'to make a fool of,' someone, or, as we might say today in this context, 'to take him for a ride.'—TRANS.]

ON THE SIGNIFICANCE OF NUMBER DREAMS [1]

129   The symbolism of numbers, which greatly engaged the philosophic fantasy of earlier centuries, has acquired a fresh interest from the analytical researches of Freud and his school. In the material of number dreams we no longer discover conscious speculations on the symbolic connections between numbers, but rather the unconscious roots of number symbolism. As there is nothing fundamentally new to be offered in this field since the researches of Freud, Adler, and Stekel, we must content ourselves with corroborating their experience by citing parallel cases. I have under observation a few cases of this kind which may be worth reporting for their general interest.

130   The first three examples are from a middle-aged man whose conflict of the moment was an extramarital love-affair. The dream-fragment from which I take the symbolical number is:
. . . *the dreamer shows his season ticket to the conductor. The conductor protests at the high number on the ticket. It was 2477.*

131   The analysis of the dream brought out a rather ungentlemanly reckoning up of the expenses of this love-affair, which was foreign to the dreamer's generous nature. His unconscious made use of this in order to resist the affair. The most obvious interpretation would be that this number had a financial significance and origin. A rough estimate of the expenses so far involved led to a number which in fact approached 2477 francs; a more careful calculation gave 2387 francs, a number which could only arbitrarily be translated into 2477. I then left the number to the free association of the patient. It occurred to him that in the dream the number appeared divided: 24 77. Perhaps it was a telephone number. This conjecture proved incorrect. The next association was that it was the sum of various

1 [Originally published as "Ein Beitrag zur Kenntnis des Zahlentraumes," *Zentralblatt für Psychoanalyse* (Wiesbaden), I (1910/11), 567–72. Previously translated by M. D. Eder in *Collected Papers on Analytical Psychology* (London, 1916; 2nd edn., London, 1917, and New York, 1922).—EDITORS.]

other numbers./At this point the patient remembered telling me earlier that he had just celebrated the hundredth birthday of his mother and himself, since she was sixty-five and he was thirty-five. (Their birthdays fell on the same day.) In this way he arrived at the following series of associations:

He was born on	26. II [2]
His mistress	28. VIII
His wife	1. III
His mother (his father was long dead)	26. II
His two children	29. IV
	13. VII
He was born	II. 75 [3]
His mistress	VIII. 85
He was now	36
His mistress	25

132   If this series of associations is written down in the usual figures, we get the following sum:

$$
\begin{array}{r}
262 \\
288 \\
13 \\
262 \\
294 \\
137 \\
275 \\
885 \\
36 \\
25 \\
\hline
2477
\end{array}
$$

133   This series, which includes all the members of his family, thus gives the number 2477. Its composition led to a deeper layer of the dream's meaning. The patient was greatly attached to his family but on the other hand very much in love with his mistress. This caused him severe conflicts. The details of the "conductor's" appearance (omitted here for the sake of brevity) pointed to the analyst, from whom the patient both feared and wished firm control as well as sharp censure of his dependent state.

2 [Day and month.]   3 [Month and year.]

134   The dream that followed shortly afterwards ran (much abbreviated): *The analyst asked the patient what he actually did when he was with his mistress. The patient said he gambled, and always on a very high number: 152. The analyst remarked: "You are sadly cheated."*

135   Analysis once more revealed a repressed tendency to reckon up the costs of the affair. The monthly expenses amounted to close on 152 francs (actually between 148 and 158). The remark that he was being cheated alluded to the point at issue between himself and his mistress. She asserted that he deflowered her, but he was quite convinced that she was not a virgin and had already been deflowered by someone else at a time when he was seeking her favours and she was refusing him. The word "number" led to the association "size in gloves," "size of calibre." From there it was but a short step to the fact that he had noted at the first coitus a remarkable width of the opening instead of the expected resistance of the hymen. This seemed to him proof of deception. The unconscious naturally used this discovery as a most effective means of resistance against the relationship. The number 152 proved refractory at first to further analysis. But on a later occasion it led to the not so distant idea of a "house number," followed by these associations: when he first knew her the lady lived at 17 X Street, then at 129 Y Street, then at 48 Z Street.

136   Here the patient realized that he had already gone far beyond 152, for the total was 194. It then occurred to him that, for certain reasons, the lady had left 48 Z Street at his instigation, so the total must be $194 - 48 = 146$. She was now living at 6 A Street, hence it was $146 + 6 = 152$.

137   Later in the analysis he had the following dream: *He received a bill from the analyst charging him interest of 1 franc on a sum of 315 francs for delay in payment from the 3rd to the 29th September.*

138   This reproach of meanness and avariciousness levelled at the analyst covered, as analysis proved, a strong unconscious envy. There were several things in the analyst's life that might arouse the envy of the patient. One thing in particular had made an impression on him: the analyst had lately had an addition to his family. The disturbed relations between the patient and his wife unfortunately permitted no such expectation in his case.

There was therefore ample ground for invidious comparisons.

139   As before, the analysis started by dividing the number 315 into 3 1 5. The patient associated 3 with the fact that the analyst had 3 children, with the recent addition of another 1. He himself would have had 5 children if all were living, as it was he had 3 — 1 = 2, for 3 children were stillborn. But these associations were far from exhausting the number symbolism of the dream.

140   The patient remarked that the period from the 3rd to the 29th September comprised 26 days. His next thought was to add this and the remaining numbers together: 26 + 315 + 1 = 342. He then carried out the same operation on 342 as on 315, dividing it into 3 4 2. Whereas before it came out that the analyst had 3 children, with 1 in addition, and the patient would have had 5, now the meaning was: the analyst had 3 children, now has 4, but the patient only 2. He remarked that the second number sounded like a rectification of the wish-fulfilment of the first.

141   The patient, who had discovered this explanation for himself without my help, declared himself satisfied. His analyst, however, was not; to him it seemed that the above revelations did not exhaust the possibilities determining the unconscious products. In connection with the number 5, the patient had carefully noted that, of the 3 stillborn children, 1 was born in the 9th and 2 in the 7th month. He also emphasized that his wife had had 2 miscarriages, 1 in the 5th week and 1 in the 7th. If we add these figures together we get the determination of the number 26:

1 child	7 months
1 "	7 "
1 "	9 "
2 miscarriages (5 + 7 weeks) =	3 "
	26

142   It seems as if 26 were determined by the number of lost periods of pregnancy. In the dream the period of 26 days denoted a delay for which the patient was charged 1 franc interest. Owing to the lost pregnancies he did in fact suffer a delay, for during the time in which the patient knew him the analyst got

ahead by 1 child. 1 franc may therefore mean 1 child. We have already noted the patient's tendency to add together all his children, including the dead ones, in order to outdo his rival. The thought that his analyst had outdone him by 1 child might influence even more strongly the determination of the number 1. We shall therefore follow up this tendency of the patient and continue his number game by adding to 26 the 2 successful pregnancies of 9 months each: $26 + 18 = 44$.

143   Dividing the numbers again into integers we get $2 + 6$ and $4 + 4$, two groups of figures which have only one thing in common, that each gives 8 by addition. It is to be noted that these figures are composed entirely of the months of pregnancy accruing to the patient. If we compare them with the figures indicating the progenitive capacity of the analyst, namely 315 and 342, we observe that the latter, added crosswise, each gives a total of 9. Now $9 - 8 = 1$. Again it seems as if the thought of the difference of 1 were asserting itself. The patient had remarked earlier that 315 seemed to him a wish-fulfilment and 342 a rectification. Letting our fantasy play round them, we discover the following difference between the two numbers:

$$3 \times 1 \times 5 = 15 \qquad 3 \times 4 \times 2 = 24 \qquad 24 - 15 = 9$$

144   Once more we come upon the significant figure 9, which fits very aptly into this calculus of pregnancies and births.

145   It is difficult to say where the borderline of play begins—necessarily so, for an unconscious product is the creation of sportive fantasy, of that psychic impulse out of which play itself arises. It is repugnant to the scientific mind to indulge in this kind of playfulness, which tails off everywhere in inanity. But we should never forget that the human mind has for thousands of years amused itself with just this kind of game, so it would be no wonder if those tendencies from the distant past gained a hearing in dreams. Even in his waking life the patient gave free rein to his number-fantasies, as the fact of celebrating the 100th birthday shows. Their presence in his dreams is therefore beyond question. For a single example of unconscious determination exact proofs are lacking, only the sum of our experiences can corroborate the accuracy of the individual discoveries. In investigating the realm of free creative fantasy we have to rely,

more almost than anywhere else, on a broad empiricism; and though this enjoins on us a high degree of modesty with regard to the accuracy of individual results, it by no means obliges us to pass over in silence what has happened and been observed, simply from fear of being execrated as unscientific. There must be no parleying with the superstition-phobia of the modern mind, for this is one of the means by which the secrets of the unconscious are kept veiled.

146   It is particularly interesting to see how the problems of the patient were mirrored in the unconscious of his wife. His wife had the following dream: she dreamt—and this is the whole dream—*Luke 137.* Analysis of this number showed that she associated as follows: the analyst has got 1 more child. He had 3. If all her children (counting the miscarriages) were living, she would have 7; now she has only $3 - 1 = 2$. But she wants $1 + 3 + 7 = 11$ (a twin number, 1 and 1), which expresses her wish that her two children had been pairs of twins, for then she would have had the same number of children as the analyst. Her mother once had twins. The hope of getting a child by her husband was very precarious, and this had long since implanted in the unconscious the thought of a second marriage.

147   Other fantasies showed her as "finished" at 44, i.e., when she reached the climacteric. She was now 33, so there were only 11 more years to go till she was 44. This was a significant number, for her father died in his 44th year. Her fantasy of the 44th year thus contained the thought of her father's death. The emphasis on the death of her father corresponded to the repressed fantasy of the death of her husband, who was the obstacle to a second marriage.

148   At this point the material to "Luke 137" comes in to help solve the conflict. The dreamer, it must be emphatically remarked, was not at all well up in the Bible, she had not read it for an incredible time and was not in the least religious. It would therefore be quite hopeless to rely on associations here. Her ignorance of the Bible was so great that she did not even know that "Luke 137" could refer only to the Gospel according to St. Luke. When she turned up the New Testament she opened it instead at the Acts of the Apostles.[4] As Acts 1 has only 26

---

4 [Sometimes called in German *Apostelgeschichte St Lucae.*—TRANS.]

verses, she took the 7th verse: "It is not for you to know the times or the seasons, which the Father hath put in his own power." But if we turn to Luke 1 : 37, we find the Annunciation of the Virgin:

35. The Holy Ghost shall come upon thee, and the power of the Highest shall overshadow thee: therefore also that holy thing which shall be born of thee shall be called the Son of God.

36. And, behold, thy cousin Elisabeth, she hath also conceived a son in her old age: and this is the sixth month with her, who was called barren.

37. For with God nothing shall be impossible.

149   The logical continuation of the analysis of "Luke 137" requires us also to look up Luke 13 : 7. There we read:

6. A certain man had a fig tree planted in his vineyard; and he came and sought fruit thereon, and found none.

7. Then said he unto the dresser of his vineyard, Behold, these three years I come seeking fruit on this fig tree, and find none: cut it down; why cumbereth it the ground?

150   The fig-tree, since ancient times a symbol of the male genitals, must be cut down on account of its unfruitfulness. This passage is in complete accord with the numerous sadistic fantasies of the dreamer, which were concerned with cutting off or biting off the penis. The allusion to her husband's unfruitful organ is obvious. It was understandable that the dreamer withdrew her libido from her husband, for with her he was impotent,[5] and equally understandable that she made a regression to her father (". . . which the Father hath put in his own power") and identified with her mother, who had twins. By thus advancing her age she put her husband in the role of a son or boy, of an age when impotence is normal. We can also understand her wish to get rid of her husband, as was moreover confirmed by her earlier analysis. It is therefore only a further confirmation of what has been said if, following up the material to "Luke 137," we turn to Luke 7 : 13:

12. Now when he came nigh to the gate of the city, behold, there was a dead man carried out, the only son of his mother, and she was a widow . . .

[5] The husband's principal trouble was a pronounced mother complex.

13. And when the Lord saw her, he had compassion on her, and said unto her, Weep not.

14. And he came and touched the bier: and they that bare him stood still. And he said, Young man, I say unto thee, Arise.

151   In the particular psychological situation of the dreamer the allusion to the raising up of the dead man acquires a pretty significance as the curing of her husband's impotence. Then the whole problem would be solved. There is no need for me to point out in so many words the numerous wish-fulfilments contained in this material; the reader can see them for himself.

152   Since the dreamer was totally ignorant of the Bible, "Luke 137" must be regarded as a cryptomnesia. Both Flournoy [6] and myself [7] have already drawn attention to the important effects of this phenomenon. So far as one can be humanly certain, any manipulation of the material with intent to deceive is out of the question in this case. Those familiar with psychoanalysis will know that the whole nature of the material rules out any such suspicion.

153   I am aware that these observations are floating in a sea of uncertainties, but I think it would be wrong to suppress them, for luckier investigators may come after us who will be able to put them in the right perspective, as we cannot do for lack of adequate knowledge.

[6] From India to the Planet Mars (1900); "Nouvelles Observations sur un cas de somnambulisme avec glossolalie" (1901).
[7] Cf. Psychiatric Studies, pp. 81ff. and 95ff.

MORTON PRINCE, "THE MECHANISM AND INTERPRETATION OF DREAMS": A CRITICAL REVIEW [1]

154   I hope that all colleagues and fellow workers who, following in Freud's footsteps, have investigated the problem of dreams, and have been able to confirm the basic principles of dream-interpretation, will forgive me if I pass over their corroborative work and speak instead of another investigation which, though it has led to less positive results, is for that reason the more suited to public discussion. A fact especially worth noting is that Morton Prince, thanks to his previous work and his deep insight into psychopathological problems, is singularly well equipped to understand the psychology inaugurated by Freud. I do not know whether Morton Prince has sufficient command of German to read Freud in the original, though this is almost a *sine qua non* for understanding him. But if he must rely only on writings in English, the very clear presentation of dream-analysis by Ernest Jones, in "Freud's Theory of Dreams," [2] would have given him all the necessary knowledge. Apart from that, there are already a large number of articles and reports by Brill and Jones, and recently also by Putnam,[3] Meyer, Hoch, Scripture, and others, which shed light on the various aspects of psycho-

1 [Originally published in the *Jahrbuch für psychoanalytische und psychopathologische Forschungen*, III (1911), 309–28. The article by Prince (1854–1929) was published in the *Journal of Abnormal Psychology* (Boston), V (1910), 139–95. For Prince's relations with the early psychoanalytical movement, see Jones, *Life and Work*, II, passim.—EDITORS.]

2 *American Journal of Psychology*, XXI (1910), 283ff.

3 I should not omit to mention that James J. Putnam, professor of neurology in Harvard Medical School, has tested and made medical use of psychoanalysis. (See Putnam, "Persönliche Erfahrungen mit Freuds psychoanalytischer Methode," 1911.) [And Putnam's "Personal Impressions of Sigmund Freud and His Work" (1909–10). Adolf Meyer, August Hoch, and Edward Wheeler Scripture also practised in America.—EDITORS.]

analysis (or "depth psychology," as Bleuler calls it). And, for full measure, there have been available for some time not only Freud's and my lectures at Clark University,[4] but several translations of our works as well, so that even those who have no knowledge of German would have had ample opportunity to familiarize themselves with the subject.

155   It was not through personal contact, of whose suggestive influence Professor Hoche [5] has an almost superstitious fear very flattering to us, but presumably through reading that Morton Prince acquired the necessary knowledge of analysis. As the German-speaking reader may be aware, Morton Prince is the author of a valuable book, *The Dissociation of a Personality,* which takes a worthy place beside the similar studies of Binet, Janet, and Flournoy.[6] Prince is also, of course, the editor of the *Journal of Abnormal Psychology,* in almost every issue of which questions of psychoanalysis are discussed without bias.

156   From this introduction the reader will see that I am not saying too much when I represent Morton Prince as an unprejudiced investigator with a firmly established scientific reputation and undisputed competence in judging psychopathological problems. Whereas Putnam is chiefly concerned with the therapeutic aspect of psychoanalysis and has discussed it with admirable frankness, Morton Prince is interested in a particularly controversial subject, namely, dream-analysis. It is here that every follower of Freud has lost his honourable name as a man of science in the eyes of German scientists. Freud's fundamental

4 [The lectures were first published (in English translation) in the *American Journal of Psychology,* XXI (1910). For Freud's, see "Five Lectures on Psycho-Analysis," Standard Edn., XI. The three lectures by Jung, entitled "The Association Method," were republished in *Collected Papers on Analytical Psychology* (1916). For the first two, "The Association Method" and "The Familial Constellations," see Vol. 2 in the *Collected Works;* the third, "Psychic Conflicts in a Child," appears in Vol. 17 in its later, revised form of 1946.—EDITORS.]

5 As is well known, Professor Hoche, of Freiburg im Breisgau, described Freud and his school as afflicted with epidemic insanity. Participants in the congress accepted this diagnosis without rebuttal and with applause. [Alfred E. Hoche, "Eine psychische Epidemie unter Ärzten," Versammlung Süd-West Deutscher Irrenärzte, Baden-Baden, May 1910. See Jones, *Life and Work,* II, 131.—EDITORS.]

6 It is especially to be regretted that the learned men—or to be more accurate, the men who today go in for learning—all too often have an interest which is merely national and stops at the frontier. It would be a great relief to psychoanalysts if more Binet, Janet, and Flournoy were read in Germany.

contribution, *The Interpretation of Dreams,* has been treated with irresponsible levity by the German critics. As usual, they were ready to hand with glib phrases like "brilliant mistake," "ingenious aberration," etc. But that any of the psychologists, neurologists, and psychiatrists should really get down to it and try out his wit on Freud's dream-interpretation was too much to expect.[7] Perhaps they did not dare to. I almost believe they did not dare, because the subject is indeed very difficult—less, I think, for intellectual reasons than on account of personal, subjective resistances. For it is just here that psychoanalysis demands a sacrifice which no other science demands of its adherents: ruthless self-knowledge. It needs to be repeated again and again that *practical and theoretical understanding of psychoanalysis is a function of analytical self-knowledge.* Where self-knowledge fails, psychoanalysis cannot flourish. This is a paradox only so long as people think that they know themselves. And who does not think that? In ringing tones of deepest conviction everyone assures us that he does. And yet it is simply not true, a childish illusion which is indispensable to one's self-esteem. There can be no doubt whatever that a doctor who covers up his lack of knowledge and ability with increased self-confidence will never be able to analyse, for otherwise he would have to admit the truth to himself and would become impossible in his own eyes.

157 We must rate it all the higher, then, when a scientist of repute, like Morton Prince, courageously tackles the problem and seeks to master it in his own way. We are ready to meet at any time the objections that spring from honest work of this kind. We have no answer only for those who are afraid of real work and are satisfied with making cheap academic speeches. But before taking up Prince's objections, we shall have a look at his field of inquiry and at his—in our sense—positive results. Prince worked through six dreams of a woman patient who was capable of different states of consciousness and could be examined in several of these states. He used interrogation under hypnosis as well as "free association." We learn that he had already analysed

---

[7] Those who did so were the ones who openly sided with Freud. Isserlin, on the other hand, contented himself with criticizing the method *a priori,* having no practical knowledge of the matter. Bleuler did what he could, under the circumstances, to answer him ("Die Psychoanalyse Freuds," 1910).

several dozen dreams.[8] Prince found that the method of free association "enables us by the examination of a large number of dreams in the same person to search the whole field of the unconscious, and by comparison of all the dreams to discover certain persistent, conserved ideas which run through and influence the psychical life of the individual." [9] Using the "insane" psychoanalytic method, therefore, the American investigator was able to discover, in the realm of the unconscious, something that perceptibly influences psychic life. For him the "method" is a method after all, he is convinced that there is an unconscious and all the rest of it, without being in any way hypnotized by Freud personally.

158   Prince admits, further, that we must consider as dream-material "certain subconscious ideas of which the subject had not been aware" (p. 150), thus recognizing that the sources of dreams can lie in the unconscious. The following passage brings important and emphatic confirmation of this:

It was a brilliant stroke of genius that led Freud to the discovery that dreams are not the meaningless vagaries that they were previously supposed to be, but when interpreted through the method of psychoanalysis may be found to have a logical and intelligible meaning. This meaning, however, is generally hidden in a mass of symbolism which can only be unraveled by a searching investigation into the previous mental experiences of the dreamer. Such an investigation requires, as I have already pointed out, the resurrection of all the associated memories pertaining to the elements of the dream. When this is done the conclusion is forced upon us, I believe, that even the most fantastic dream may express some intelligent idea, though that idea may be hidden in symbolism. My own observations confirm those of Freud, so far as to show that running through each dream there is an intelligent *motive;* so that the dream can be interpreted as expressing some idea or ideas which the dreamer previously has entertained. At least all the dreams I have subjected to analysis justify this interpretation.

8 In order to give the reader some idea of the experience the psychoanalyst possesses of dream analysis I would mention that, on average, I analyse eight dreams per working day. That makes about two thousand a year. Similar figures probably hold good for most psychoanalysts. Freud himself has immense experience in analysing dreams.

9 "The Mechanism and Interpretation of Dreams," p. 145.

159   Prince is thus in a position to admit that dreams have a meaning, that the meaning is hidden in symbols, and that in order to find the meaning one needs the memory-material. All this confirms essential portions of Freud's dream interpretation, far more than the *a priori* critics have ever admitted. As a result of certain experiences Prince has also come to conceive hysterical symptoms "as possible symbolisms of hidden processes of thought." In spite of the views expressed in Binswanger's *Die Hysterie*, which might have prepared the ground, this has still not penetrated the heads of German psychiatrists.

160   I have, as I said, begun with Prince's affirmative statements. We now come to the deviations and objections (p. 151):

> I am unable to confirm [Freud's view] that every dream can be interpreted as "the imaginary fulfillment of a wish," which is the motive of the dream. That sometimes a dream can be recognized as the fulfillment of a wish there can be no question, but that every dream, or that the majority of dreams are such, I have been unable to verify, even after subjecting the individual to the most exhaustive analysis. On the contrary I find, if my interpretations are correct, that some dreams are rather the expression of the non-fulfillment of a wish; some seem to be that of the fulfillment of a fear or anxiety.

161   In this passage we have everything that Prince cannot accept. It should be added that the wish itself often seems to him not to be "repressed" and not to be so unconscious or important as Freud would lead us to expect. Hence Freud's theory that a repressed wish is the real source of the dream, and that it fulfils itself in the dream, is not accepted by Prince, because he was unable to see these things in his material. But at least he tried to see them, and the theory seemed to him worth a careful check, which is definitely not the case with many of our critics. (I should have thought that this procedure would be an unwritten law of academic decency.) Fortunately, Prince has also presented us with the material from which he drew his conclusions. We are thus in a position to measure our experience against his and at the same time to find the reasons for any misunderstanding. He has had great courage in exposing himself in this commendable way, for we now have an opportunity to compare our divergencies openly with his material, a procedure which will be instructive in every respect.

162   In order to show how it is that Prince was able to see only the formal and not the dynamic element of the dreams, we must examine his material in more detail. One gathers, from various indications in the material, that the dreamer was a lady in late middle age, with a grown-up son who was studying, and apparently that she was unhappily married (or perhaps divorced or separated). For some years she had suffered from an hysterical dissociation of personality, and, we infer, had regressive fantasies about two earlier love-affairs, which the author, perhaps owing to the prudery of the public, is obliged to hint at rather too delicately. He succeeded in curing the patient of her dissociation for eighteen months, but now things seem to be going badly again, for she remained anxiously dependent on the analyst, and he found this so tiresome that he twice wanted to send her to a colleague.

163   Here we have the well-known picture of an unanalysed and unadmitted transference, which, as we know, consists in the anchoring of the patient's erotic fantasies to the analyst. The six dreams are an illustrative excerpt from the analyst's struggle against the clinging transference of the patient.

164   *Dream 1:* C [the patient's dream-ego] was somewhere and saw an old woman who appeared to be a *Jewess.* She was holding a *bottle* and a *glass* and seemed to be drinking *whiskey;* then this woman changed into her own *mother,* who had the bottle and glass, and appeared likewise to be drinking whiskey; then the door opened and her *father* appeared. He had on her *husband's dressing-gown,* and he was holding two *sticks of wood* in his hand. [Pp. 147ff.]

165   Prince found, on the basis of copious and altogether convincing material,[10] that the patient regarded the temptation to drink, and also the temptations of "poor people" in general, as something very understandable. She herself sometimes took a little whiskey in the evening, and so did her mother. But there might be something wrong in it. "The dream scene is therefore the symbolical representation and justification of her own belief and answers the doubts and scruples that beset her mind" (p. 154). The second part of the dream, about the sticks, is certainly, according to Prince, a kind of wish-fulfilment, but he says it tells us nothing, since the patient had ordered fire-

10 For the practised analyst the dream itself is so clear that it can be read directly.

wood the evening before. Despite the trouble expended on it (eight pages of print) the dream has not been analysed thoroughly enough, for the two most important items—the whiskey-drinking and the sticks—remain unanalysed. If the author would follow up those "temptations," he would soon discover that the patient's scruples are at bottom of a far more serious nature than a spoonful of whiskey and two bundles of wood. Why is the father who comes in, condensed with the husband? How is the Jewess determined other than by a memory of the previous day? Why are the two sticks significant and why are they in the hand of the father? And so on. The dream has not been analysed. Unfortunately its meaning is only too clear to the psychoanalyst. It says very plainly: "If I were this poor Jewess, whom I saw on the previous day, I would not resist temptation (just as mother and father don't—a typical infantile comparison!), and then a man would come into my room with firewood—naturally to warm me up." This, briefly, would be the meaning. The dream contains all that, only the author's analysis has discreetly stopped too soon. I trust he will forgive me for indiscreetly breaking open the tactfully closed door, so that it may clearly be seen what kind of wish-fulfilments, which "one cannot see," hide behind conventional discretion and medical blindness to sex.

166   *Dream 2:* A hill—she was toiling up the hill; one could hardly get up; had the sensation of some one, or thing, following her. She said, *"I must not show that I am frightened, or this thing will catch me."* Then she came where it was lighter, and she could see two clouds or *shadows,* one black and one red, and she said, "My God, it is *A and B*! If I don't have help I am lost." (She meant that she would change again—i.e., relapse into dissociated personalities.) She began to call "Dr. Prince! Dr. Prince!" and you were there and laughed, and said, "Well, you will have to fight the damned thing yourself." Then she woke up *paralysed* with fright. [P. 156.]

167   As the dream is very simple, we can dispense with any further knowledge of the analytical material. But Prince cannot see the wish-fulfilment in this dream, on the contrary he sees in it the "fulfilment of a fear." He commits the fundamental mistake of once again confusing the manifest dream-content with the unconscious dream-thought. In fairness to the author it should be remarked that in this case the repetition of the mistake was the

more excusable since the crucial sentence ("Well, you will have to fight the damned thing yourself") is really very ambiguous and misleading. Equally ambiguous is the sentence "I must not show that I am frightened," etc., which, as Prince shows from the material, refers to the thought of a relapse into the illness, since the patient was *frightened* of a relapse.

168   But what does "frightened" mean? We know that it is far more convenient for the patient to be ill, because recovery brings with it a great disadvantage: she would lose her analyst. The illness reserves him, as it were, for her needs. With her interesting illness, she has obviously offered the analyst a great deal, and has received from him a good deal of interest and patience in return. She certainly does not want to give up this stimulating relationship, and for this reason she is afraid of remaining well and secretly hopes that something weird and wonderful will befall her so as to rekindle the analyst's interest. Naturally she would do anything rather than admit that she really had such wishes. But we must accustom ourselves to the thought that in psychology there are things which the patient simultaneously knows and does not know. Things which are apparently quite unconscious can often be shown to be conscious in another connection, and actually to have been known. Only, they were not known in their true meaning. Thus, the true meaning of the wish which the patient could not admit was not directly accessible to her consciousness, which is why we call this true meaning not conscious, or "repressed." Put in the brutal form "I will have symptoms in order to re-arouse the interest of the analyst," it cannot be accepted, true though it is, for it is too hurtful; but she could well allow a few little associations and half-smothered wishes to be discerned in the background, such as reminiscences of the time when the analysis was so interesting, etc.

169   The sentence "I must not show that I am frightened" therefore means in reality "I must not show that I would really like a relapse because keeping well is too much trouble." "If I don't have help, I am lost" means "I hope I won't be cured too quickly or I cannot have a relapse." Then, at the end, comes the wishfulfilment: "Well, you will have to fight the damned thing yourself." The patient keeps well only out of love for the analyst. If he leaves her in the lurch she will have a relapse, and it will

be his fault for not helping her. But if she has a relapse she will have a renewed and more intense claim on his attention, and this is the point of the whole manœuvre. It is altogether typical of dreams that the wish-fulfilment is always found where it seems most impossible to the conscious mind. The fear of a relapse is a symbol that needs analysing, and this the author has forgotten, because he took the fear, like the whiskey-drinking and the sticks, at its face value, instead of examining it sceptically for its genuineness. His colleague Ernest Jones's excellent work *On the Nightmare* [11] would have informed him of the wishful character of these fears. But, as I know from my own experience, it is difficult for a beginner to remain conscious of all the psychoanalytic rules all the time.

170   *Dream 3:* She was in the rocky path of Watts's,[12] barefooted, stones hurt her feet, few clothes, cold, could hardly climb that path; she saw you there, and she called on you to help her, and you said, "I cannot help you, you must help yourself." She said, "I can't, I can't." "Well, you have got to. Let me see if I cannot hammer it into your head." You picked up a stone and hammered her head, and with every blow you said, "I can't be bothered, I can't be bothered." And every blow sent a weight down into her heart so she felt heavy-hearted. She woke and I saw you pounding with a stone; you looked cross. [Pp. 159f.]

171   As Prince again takes the dream literally, he can see in it merely the "non-fulfillment of a wish." Once again it must be emphasized that Freud has expressly stated that the true *dream-thoughts are not identical with the manifest dream-contents.* Prince has not discovered the true dream-thought simply because he stuck to the wording of the dream. Now, it is always risky to intervene without knowing the material oneself; one can make enormous blunders. But it may be that the material brought out by the author's analysis will be sufficient to give us a glimpse of the latent dream-thought. (Anyone who has experience will naturally have guessed the meaning of the dream long ago, for it is perfectly clear.)

172   The dream is built up on the following experience. On the previous morning the patient had begged the author for medical help and had received the answer by telephone: "I cannot

11 [Orig. 1910.—Editors.]   12 See Dream 5.

possibly come to see you today. I have engagements all the day and into the evening. I will send Dr. W, you must not depend on me" (p. 160). An unmistakable hint, therefore, that the analyst's time belonged also to others. The patient remarked: "I didn't say anything about it, but it played ducks and drakes with me the other night." She therefore had a bitter morsel to swallow. The analyst had done something really painful, which she, as a reasonable woman, understood well enough—but not with her heart. Before going to sleep she had thought: "I must not bother him; I should think I would get that *into my head* after a while" (p. 161). (In the dream it is actually hammered into her head.) "If my heart was not like a *stone*, I should weep." (She was hammered with a stone.)

173   As in the previous dream, it is stated that the analyst will not help her any more, and he hammers this decision of his into her head so that at every blow her heart became heavier. The situation that evening, therefore, is taken up too clearly in the manifest dream-content. In such cases we must always try to find where a new element has been added to the situation of the previous day; at this point we may penetrate into the real meaning of the dream. The painful thing is that the analyst will not treat the patient any more, but in the dream she *is* treated, though in a new and remarkable way. When the analyst hammers it into her head that he cannot let himself be tormented by her chatter, he does it so emphatically that his psychotherapy turns into an extremely intense form of physical treatment or torture. This fulfils a wish which is far too shocking to be recognized in the decent light of day, although it is a very natural and simple thought. Popular humour and all the evil tongues that have dissected the secrets of the confessional and the consulting-room know it.[13] Mephistopheles, in his famous speech about Medicine,[14] guessed it too. It is one of those imperishable thoughts which nobody knows and everybody has.

13 Analysis by rumour. Cf. supra, "A Contribution to the Psychology of Rumour."
14 ["Learn how to handle women, that make sure,
   Since all the aches and sighs that come to vex
   The tender sex
   The doctor knows one little place to cure.
   A bedside manner sets their hearts at ease,
   And then they're yours for treatment as you please."
                    —*Faust*, Part One, trans. by Wayne, p. 98.]

65

174   When the patient awoke she saw the analyst still carrying out that movement: pounding [15] with a stone. To name an action for a second time is to give it special prominence.[16] As in the previous dream, the wish-fulfilment lies in the greatest disappointment.

175   It will no doubt be objected that I am reading my own corrupt fantasies into the dream, as is customary with the Freudian school. Perhaps my esteemed colleague, the author, will be indignant at my attributing such impure thoughts to his patient, or at least will find it quite unjustified of me to draw such a far-reaching conclusion from these scanty hints. I am well aware that this conclusion, seen from the standpoint of yesterday's science, looks almost frivolous. But hundreds of parallel experiences have shown me that the above data are really quite sufficient to warrant my conclusion, and with a certainty that meets the most rigorous requirements. Those who have no experience of psychoanalysis can have no idea how very probable is the presence of an erotic wish and how extremely improbable is its absence. The latter illusion is naturally due to moral sex-blindness on the one hand, but on the other to the disastrous mistake of thinking that consciousness is the whole of the psyche. This does not, of course, apply to our esteemed author. I therefore beg the reader: no moral indignation, please, but calm verification. This is what science is made with, and not with howls of indignation, mockery, abuse, and threats, the weapons which the spokesmen of German science use in arguing with us.

176   It would really be incumbent on the author to present all the interim material which would finally establish the erotic meaning of the dream. Though he has not done it for this dream, everything necessary is said indirectly in the following dreams, so that my above-mentioned conclusion emerges from its isolation and will prove to be a link in a consistent chain.

177   *Dream 4:* [Shortly before the last dream the subject] dreamt that she was in a great *ballroom*, where everything was very *beautiful*. She was walking about, and a man came up to her and asked, "Where is your escort?" She replied, "I am *alone*." He then said, "You cannot stay here, we do not want any *lone women*." In the

15 A pounder is a pestle or club.
16 Cf. "A Contribution to the Psychology of Rumour," par. 106.

next scene she was in a *theater* and was going to sit down, when someone came and said the same thing to her: "You can't stay here, we do not want any *lone women* here." Then she was in ever so many different places, but wherever she went she had to leave because she was *alone;* they would not let her stay. Then she was in the street; there was a great crowd, and she saw her husband a little way ahead, and struggled to get to him through the crowd. When she got quite near she saw . . . [what we may interpret as a symbolical representation of happiness, says Prince.] Then sickness and nausea came over her and she thought there was no place for her there either. [P. 162.]

178   The gap in the dream is a praiseworthy piece of discretion and will certainly please the prudish reader, but it is not science. Science admits no such considerations of decency. Here it is simply a question of whether Freud's maligned theory of dreams is right or not, and not whether dream-texts sound nice to immature ears. Would a gynaecologist suppress the illustration of the female genitalia in a textbook of midwifery on grounds of decency? On p. 164 of this analysis we read: "The analysis of this scene would carry us too far into the intimacy of her life to justify our entering upon it." Does the author really believe that in these circumstances he has any scientific right to speak about the psychoanalytic dream-theory, when he withholds essential material from the reader for reasons of discretion? By the very fact of reporting his patient's dream to the world he has violated discretion as thoroughly as possible, for every analyst will see its meaning at once: what the dreamer instinctively hides most deeply cries out loudest from the unconscious. For anyone who knows how to read dream-symbols all precautions are in vain, the truth will out. We would therefore request the author, if he doesn't want to strip his patient bare the next time, to choose a case about which he can say everything.

179   Despite his medical discretion this dream too, which Prince denies is a wish-fulfilment, is accessible to understanding. The end of the dream betrays, despite the disguise, the patient's violent resistance to sexual relations with her husband. The rest is all wish-fulfilment: she becomes a "lone woman" who is socially somewhat beyond the pale. The feeling of loneliness ("she feels that she cannot be alone any more, that she must have company") is fittingly resolved by this ambiguous situation: there

are "lone women" who are not so alone as all that, though certainly they are not tolerated everywhere. This wish-fulfilment naturally meets with the utmost resistance, until it is made clear that in case of necessity the devil, as the proverb says, eats even flies—and this is in the highest degree true of the libido. This solution, so objectionable to the conscious mind, seems thoroughly acceptable to the unconscious. One has to know what the psychology of a neurosis is in a patient of this age; psychoanalysis requires us to take people as they really are and not as they pretend to be. Since the great majority of people want to be what they are not, and therefore believe themselves identical with the conscious or unconscious ideal that floats before them, the individual is blinded by mass suggestion from the start, quite apart from the fact that he himself feels different from what he really is. This rule has the peculiarity of being true of everybody else, but never of the person to whom it is being applied.

180   I have set forth the historical and general significance of this fact in a previous work,[17] so I can spare myself the trouble of discussing it here. I would only remark that, to practise psychoanalysis, one must subject one's ethical concepts to a total revision. It is a requirement which explains why psychoanalysis becomes intelligible to a really serious person only gradually and with great difficulty. It needs not only intellectual but, to an even greater extent, moral effort to understand the meaning of the method, for it is not just a medical method like vibromassage or hypnosis, but something of much wider scope, that modestly calls itself "psychoanalysis."

181   *Dream 5:* She dreamt that she was in a dark, gloomy, rocky place, and she was walking with difficulty, as she always does in her dreams, over this rocky path, and all at once the place was filled with cats. She turned in terror to go back, and there in her path was a frightful creature like a wild man of the woods. His hair was hanging down his face and neck; he had a sort of skin over him for covering; his legs and arms were bare and he had a club. A wild figure. Behind him were hundreds of men like him—the whole place was filled with them, so that in front were cats and behind were wild men. The man said to her that she would have to go forward

17 *Symbols of Transformation.* [The first part of the original, *Wandlungen und Symbole der Libido,* appeared in the same issue of the *Jahrbuch* as the present article.—EDITORS.]

through those cats, and that if she made a sound they would all come down on her and smother her, but if she went through them without making a sound she would never again feel any regret about the past . . . [mentioning certain specific matters which included two particular systems of ideas known as the Z and Y complexes, all of which had troubled her, adds the author]. She realized that she must choose between death from the wild men and the journey over the cats, so she started forward. Now, in her dream of course she had to step on the cats [the subject here shivers and shudders], and the horror of knowing that they would come on her if she screamed caused her to make such an effort to keep still that the muscles of her throat contracted in her dream [they actually did contract, I could feel them, says Prince]. She waded through the cats without making a sound, and then she saw her mother and tried to speak to her. She reached out her hands and tried to say "O mamma!" but she could not speak, and then she woke up feeling nauseated, frightened, and fatigued, and wet with perspiration. Later, after waking, when she tried to speak, she could only whisper. [Pp. 164f. A footnote adds: "She awoke with complete aphonia, which persisted until relieved by appropriate suggestion."]

182   Prince sees this dream partly as a wish-fulfilment, because the dreamer did after all walk over the cats. But he thinks: "The dream would rather seem to be principally a symbolical representation of her idea of life in general, and of the moral precepts with which she has endeavoured to inspire herself, and which she has endeavoured to live up to in order to obtain happiness" (p. 168).

183   That is not the meaning of the dream, as anyone can see who knows anything of dreams. The dream has not been analysed at all. We are merely told that the patient had a phobia about cats. What that means is not analysed. The treading on the cats is not analysed. The wild man wearing the skin is not analysed, and there is no analysis of the skin and the club. The erotic reminiscences Z and Y are not described. The significance of the aphonia is not analysed. Only the rocky path at the beginning is analysed a little: It comes from a painting by Watts, "Love and Life." A female figure (Life) drags herself wearily along the rocky path, accompanied by the figure of Love. The initial image in the dream corresponds exactly to this picture, "minus the figure of Love," as Prince remarks. Instead there are the cats, as the dream shows and as we remark. This means

that the cats symbolize love. Prince has not seen this; had he studied the literature he would have discovered from one of my earlier publications that I have dealt in detail with the question of cat phobia.[18] There he would have been informed of this conclusion and could have understood the dream and the cat phobia as well.

184   For the rest, the dream is a typical anxiety dream which, in consequence, *must* be regarded from the standpoint of the sexual theory, unless Prince succeeds in proving to us that the sexual theory of anxiety is wrong. Owing to the complete lack of any analysis I refrain from further discussion of the dream, which is indeed very clear and pretty. I would only point out that the patient has succeeded in collecting a symptom (aphonia) which captured the interest of the analyst, as she reckoned it would. It is evident that one cannot criticize the dream-theory on the basis of analyses which are not made; this is merely the method of our German critics.

185   *Dream 6:* This dream occurred twice on succeeding nights. She dreamed she was in the same rocky, dark path she is always in—Watts's path—but with trees besides (there are always trees, or a hillside, or a canyon). The *wind* was blowing very hard, and she could hardly walk on account of something, as is always the case. Someone, a *figure,* came rushing past her with his hand over his (or her) eyes. This figure said, *"Don't look, you will be blinded."* She was at the entrance of a great *cave;* suddenly it *flashed light* in the cave like a flashlight picture, and there, down on the ground *you* were lying, and you were *bound round and round* with bonds of some kind, and your clothes were torn and dirty, and your face was covered with blood, and you looked terribly anguished; and all over you there were just hundreds of little gnomes or pigmies or brownies, and they were *torturing you.* Some of them had axes, and were chopping on your legs and arms, and some were sawing you. Hundreds of them had little things like joss-sticks, but shorter, which were red hot at the ends, and they were jabbing them into you. It was something like Gulliver and the little creatures running over him. You saw C, and you said, "O Mrs. C, for heaven's sake get me out of this damned hole." (You always swear in C's dreams.) She was horrified, and said, "O Dr. Prince, I am coming," but she *could not move,* she was rooted to the spot; and then it all went away,

18 ["Association, Dream, and Hysterical Symptoms" (orig. 1906) (1918 edn., pp. 378f.)—EDITORS.]

everything became black, as if she were *blinded,* and then it would flash again and illuminate the cave, and she would see again. This happened three or four times in the dream. She kept saying, "I am coming," and *struggled to move,* and she woke up saying it. In the same way *she could not move when she woke up, and she could not see.* [Pp. 170f.]

186   The author does not report the details of the analysis of this dream, "in order not to weary the reader." He gives only the following résumé:

The dream proved to be a symbolic representation of the subject's conception of life (the rocky path), of her dread of the future, which for years she has said she dared not face; of her feeling that the future was "blind," in that she could not "see anything ahead"; of the thought that she would be overwhelmed, "lost," "swept away" if she looked into and realized this future, *and she must not look.* And yet there are moments in life when she realizes vividly the future; and so in the dream one of these moments is when she looks into the cave (the future), and in the flash of light the realization comes—she sees her son (metamorphosed through substitution of another person) tortured, as she has thought of him tortured, and handicapped (bound) by the moral "pin pricks" of life. Then follows the symbolic representation (paralysis) of her utter "helplessness" to aid either him or anyone else or alter the conditions of her own life. Finally follow the prophesied consequences of this realization. She is overcome by blindness and to this extent the dream is a fulfillment of a fear. [P. 171.]

187   The author says in conclusion: "In this dream, as in the others, we find no 'unacceptable' and 'repressed wish,' no 'conflict' with 'censoring thoughts,' no 'compromise,' no 'resistance' and no 'disguise' in the dream-content to deceive the dreamer —elements and processes fundamental in the Freud school of psychology" (p. 173).

188   From this devastating judgment we shall delete the words "as in the others," for the other dreams are analysed so inadequately that the author has no right to pronounce such a judgment on the basis of the preceding "analyses." Only the last dream remains to substantiate this judgment, and we shall therefore look at it rather more closely.

189   We shall not linger over the constantly recurring symbol of

the painting by Watts, in which the figure of Love is missing and was replaced by the cats in dream 5. Here it is replaced by a figure who warns the patient not to look or she will be "blinded." Now comes another very remarkable image: the analyst bound round and round with bonds, his clothes torn and dirty, his face covered with blood—the Gulliver situation. Prince remarks that it is the patient's son who is in this agonizing situation, but withholds further details. Where the bonds, the bloody face, the torn clothes come from, what the Gulliver situation means—of all this we learn nothing. Because the patient "must not look into the future," the cave signifies the future, remarks Prince. But why is the future symbolized by a cave? The author is silent. How comes it that the analyst is substituted for the son? Prince mentions the patient's helplessness with regard to the situation of the son, and observes that she is just as helpless with regard to the analyst, for she does not know how to show her gratitude. But these are, if I may say so, two quite different kinds of helplessness, which do not sufficiently explain the condensation of the two persons. An essential and unequivocal *tertium comparationis* is lacking. All the details of the Gulliver situation, especially the red-hot joss-sticks, are left unanalysed. The highly significant fact that the analyst himself suffers hellish tortures is passed over in complete silence.

190   In Dream 3 the analyst pounded the patient on the head with a stone, and this torture seems to be answered here, but swelled out into a hellish fantasy of revenge. Without doubt these tortures were thought up by the patient and intended for her analyst (and perhaps also for her son); that is what the dream says. This fact needs analysing. If the son is really "tortured by the moral pin pricks of life," we definitely require to know why in the dream the patient multiplies this torture a hundred-fold, brings the son (or the analyst) into the Gulliver situation and then puts Gulliver in the "damned hole." Why must the analyst swear in the dreams? Why does the patient step into the analyst's shoes and say she is unable to bring help, when really the situation is the other way round?

191   Here the way leads down into the wish-fulfilling situation. But the author has not trodden this path; he has either omitted to ask himself any of these questions or answered them much too

superficially, so that this analysis too must be disqualified as "unsatisfactory." [19]

192   With this the last prop for a criticism of the dream-theory collapses. We must require of a critic that he carry out his investigations just as thoroughly as the founder of the theory, and that he should at least be able to explain the main points of the dream. But in the author's analyses, as we have seen, the most important items are brushed aside. You cannot produce psychoanalysis out of a hat, as everyone knows who has tried; *unumquemque movere lapidem* is nearer the truth.

*

193   Only after the conclusion of this review did I see the criticism which Ernest Jones [20] lavished on Morton Prince's article. We learn from Prince's reply that he *does not claim to have used the psychoanalytic method.* In that case he might fairly have refrained from criticizing the findings of psychoanalysis, it seems to me. His analytical methods, as the above examples show, are so lacking in scientific thoroughness that the conclusions he reaches offer no basis for a serious criticism of Freud's dream-theory. The rest of his remarks, culminating in the admission that he will never be able to see eye to eye with the psychoanalytic school, do not encourage me to make further efforts to explain the problems of dream-psychology to him or to discuss his reply. I confine myself to expressing my regret that he has even gone to the length of denying the scientific training and scientific thinking of his opponents.

19 The dream is a typical fantasy of revenge for scorned love and contains in the torture (as in the pounding) scene the boundless gratitude of the patient. Hence the mysterious scene in the cave, which is so scandalous that she will be struck blind at the sight of it. Proof of this can be found in the details of the cave scene.
20 "Remarks on Dr. Morton Prince's article, 'The Mechanism and Interpretation of Dreams'" (1910–11).

ON THE CRITICISM OF PSYCHOANALYSIS [1]

194   It is a well-known fact to the psychoanalyst that laymen, even those with relatively little education, are able to understand the nature and rationale of psychoanalysis without undue intellectual difficulty. It is the same with educated people, be they scholars, business-men, journalists, artists, or teachers. They can all understand the truths of psychoanalysis. They also understand very well why psychoanalysis cannot be expounded in the same convincing way as a mathematical proposition. Everyone of common sense knows that a psychological proof must necessarily be different from a physical one, and that each branch of science can only offer proofs that are suited to its material. It would be interesting to know just what kind of empirical proof our critics expect, if not proof on the evidence of the empirical facts. Do these facts exist? We point to our observations. Our critics, however, simply say No. What, then, are we to offer if our factual observations are flatly denied? Under these circumstances we would expect our critics to study the neuroses and psychoses as thoroughly as we have done (quite independently of the method of psychoanalysis), and to put forward facts of an essentially different kind concerning their psychological determination. We have waited for this for more than ten years. Fate has even decreed that all investigators in this field who have worked independently of the discoverer of the new theory, but as thoroughly, have arrived at the same results as Freud; and that those who have taken the time and trouble to acquire the necessary knowledge under a psychoanalyst have also gained an understanding of these results.

195   In general, we must expect the most violent resistance from medical men and psychologists, chiefly because of scientific

1 [Translated from "Zur Kritik über Psychoanalyse," *Jahrbuch für psychoanalytische und psychopathologische Forschungen* (Leipzig), II (1910), 743–46.—EDITORS.]

74

prejudices based on a different way of thinking to which they obstinately adhere. Our critics, unlike earlier ones, have progressed inasmuch as they try to be more serious and to strike a more moderate note. But they commit the mistake of criticizing the psychoanalytic method as though it rested on *a priori* principles, whereas in reality it is purely empirical and totally lacking in any final theoretical framework. All we know is that it is simply the quickest way to find facts which are of importance for our psychology, but which, as the history of psychoanalysis shows, can also be discovered in other more tedious and complicated ways. We would naturally be happy if we possessed an analytical technique which led us to the goal even more quickly and reliably than the present method. Our critics, however, will scarcely be able to help us towards a more suitable technique, and one that corresponds better to the assumptions of psychology up till now, merely by contesting our findings. So long as the question of the facts is not settled, all criticism of the method hangs in the air, for concerning the ultimate secrets of the association process our opponents know as little as we do. It should be obvious to every thinking person that what matters is simply and solely the empirical facts. If criticism confines itself to the method, it may easily come one day to deny the existence of facts merely because the method of finding them betrays certain theoretical defects—a standpoint that would carry us happily back to the depths of the Middle Ages. In this respect our critics commit grave mistakes. It is the duty of intelligent people to point them out, for to err is human.

196   Occasionally, however, the criticism assumes forms which arouse the interest of the psychological worker in the highest degree, since the scientific endeavour of the critic is thrust into the background in the most surprising way by symptoms of personal participation. Such critics make a valuable contribution to the knowledge of the personal undercurrents beneath so-called scientific criticism. We cannot deny ourselves the pleasure of making such a *document humain* accessible to a wider public.

*

Review by Kurt Mendel [2] of an Exposition of the Freudian Standpoint

The present reviewer, who has read many works of Freud and his followers, and has *himself had practical experience of psychoanalysis,*[3] must admit that he finds many things in this doctrine utterly repugnant, especially the latest additions concerning anal eroticism and the sexuality of children. After perusing the work under review,[4] he stepped up to his youngest child, lying there innocently in his cot, and spoke as follows: "Poor little boy! I fancied you were pure and chaste, but now I know that you are depraved and full of sin! 'From the first day of your existence you have led a sexual life' (p. 184); now you are an exhibitionist, a fetishist, a sadist, a masochist, an anal-erotic, an onanist—in short, you are 'polymorphous-perverse' (p. 185). 'There is scarcely a Don Juan among grown-ups whose erotic fantasies could be compared with the products of your infant brain' (p. 185). How, indeed, could it be otherwise? For you are corrupt from birth. Your father has the reputation of being unusually tidy and economical, and the Freudians say he is stubborn because he won't give full acceptance to their teachings. Unusually tidy, economical, and stubborn! A hopeless anal-erotic, therefore! (Cf. Freud, "Charakter und Analerotik," *Psych.-neur. Wochenschr.* IX: 51.) As for your mother, she cleans out the house every four weeks. 'Cleaning, and particularly spring-cleaning, is the specific female reaction to suppressed anal eroticism' (Sadger, "Analerotik und Analcharakter," *Die Heilkunde,* Feb. 1910). You are a congenital anal-erotic from your father's and your mother's side! And a little while ago, before going to bed, you would not 'empty the bowels when you were put on the pot, because you want to derive extra pleasure from defecation and therefore enjoy holding back your stool.' Previously your father simply told your mother on such occasions: 'The boy is constipated, give him a pill!' Pfui! How shamelessly perverse I was then, a regular pimp and corrupter of youth! You'll get no good-night kiss from me any more, for a caress like that would only 'arouse your sexuality' (p. 191). And don't say your evening prayer to me again: 'I am small, my heart is pure';[5] that would be a lie; you are dissipated, an exhibitionist, fetishist, sadist, mas-

---

[2] In *Neurologisches Centralblatt* (Leipzig), XXIX : 6 (March 16, 1910).
[3] My italics.—C. G. J.
[4] J. A. Haslebacher, "Psychoneurosen und Psychoanalyse," *Correspondenzblatt für Schweizer Ärzte* (Basel), XL:7 (March 1, 1910), 184–96.
[5] "Ich bin klein, mein Herz ist rein."

ochist, anal-erotic, onanist, 'polymorphous-perverse'—through me, through your mother, and through yourself! Poor little boy!"

Freudians! I have repeatedly asserted that your teachings have opened up many new and valuable perspectives. But for heaven's sake make an end of your boundless exaggerations and nonsensical fantasies! Instead of puns, give us proofs! Instead of books that read like comics, give us serious works to be taken seriously! Prove to me the truth of your squalid and slanderous statement (p. 187): "There is but one form of love, and that is erotic love"! Do not plunge our most sacred feelings, our love and respect for our parents and our happy love for our children, into the mire of your fantasies by the continual imputation of sordid sexual motives! Your whole argument culminates in the axiom: "Freud has said it, therefore it is so!" But I say with Goethe, the son of an anal-erotic (Sadger, op. cit.):

"A man who speculates
Is like a beast upon a barren heath
Led round in circles by an evil sprite,
While all around lie pastures green and bright."

CONCERNING PSYCHOANALYSIS [1]

Küsnacht, 28 January 1912

To the Editor.

Sir,

197   Thank you for kindly inviting me to publish in your columns an epilogue to the series of articles in the *Neue Zürcher Zeitung*. Such an epilogue could only be a defence either of the scientific truth which we think we can discern in psychoanalysis, and which has been so heavily attacked, or of our own scientific qualities. The latter defence offends against good taste, and is unworthy of anyone dedicated to the service of science. But a defence of the first kind can be carried out only if the discussion takes an objective form, and if the arguments used arise from a careful study of the problem, practical as well as theoretical. I am ready to argue with opponents like this, though I prefer to do so in private; I have, however, also done it in public, in a scientific journal.[2]

198   I shall not reply, either, to scientific criticism the essence of which is: "The method is morally dangerous, therefore the theory is wrong," or: "The facts asserted by the Freudians do not exist but merely spring from the morbid fantasy of these so-called researchers, and the method used for discovering these facts is in itself logically at fault." No one can assert *a priori* that certain facts do not exist. This is a scholastic argument, and it is superfluous to discuss it.

---

1 [Translated from "Zur Psychoanalyse," *Wissen und Leben* (Zurich; former title of the *Neue Schweizer Rundschau*), V (1912), 711–14. An introductory editorial note stated: "A series of communications pro and con Freudian theories in the *Neue Zürcher Zeitung* seems to prove that remarkable misunderstanding and prejudice with respect to modern psychology are the rule with the general public. Since all this impassioned wrangling was more likely to confuse than to enlighten, we have asked Dr. Karl Jung (*sic*) for a few closing words, which should be the more welcome for calming ruffled tempers."—Editors.]

2 [See the preceding article.—Editors.]

199   It is repugnant to me to make propaganda for the truth and to defend it with slogans. Except in the Psychoanalytical Society and in the Swiss Psychiatric Society I have never yet given a public lecture without first having been asked to do so; similarly, my article in Rascher's Yearbook [3] was written only at the request of the editor, Konrad Falke. I do not thrust myself upon the public. I shall therefore not enter the arena now in order to engage in barbarous polemics on behalf of a scientific truth. Prejudice and the almost boundless misunderstanding we are faced with can certainly prevent progress and the spread of scientific knowledge for a long time, and this is perhaps a necessity of mass psychology to which one has to submit. If this truth does not speak for itself, it is a poor truth and it is better for it to perish. But if it is an inner necessity, it will make its way, even without battle-cries and the martial blast of trumpets, into the hearts of all straight-thinking and realistic persons and so become an essential ingredient of our civilization.

200   The sexual indelicacies which unfortunately occupy a necessarily large place in many psychoanalytic writings are not to be blamed on psychoanalysis itself. Our very exacting and responsible medical work merely brings these unlovely fantasies to light, but the blame for the existence of these sometimes repulsive and evil things must surely lie with the mendaciousness of our sexual morality. No intelligent person needs to be told yet again that the psychoanalytic method of education does not consist merely in psychological discussions of sex, but covers *every department of life.* The goal of this education, as I have expressly emphasized in Rascher's Yearbook, is not that a man should be delivered over helplessly to his passions but that he should attain the necessary self-control. In spite of Freud's and my assurances, our opponents want us to countenance "licentiousness" and then assert that we do so, regardless of what we ourselves say. It is the same with the theory of neurosis—the sexual or libido theory, as it is called. For years I have been pointing out, both in my lectures and in my writings, that the concept of libido is taken in a very general sense, rather like the instinct of preservation of the species, and that in psycho-

---

[3] [*Neue Bahnen der Psychologie,* published in *Raschers Jahrbuch für Schweizer Art und Kunst* (Zurich), 1912. Trans. as "New Paths in Psychology," *Two Essays on Analytical Psychology,* pp. 243ff.—EDITORS.]

analytic parlance it definitely does not mean "localized sexual excitation" but all striving and willing that exceed the limits of self-preservation, and that this is the sense in which it is used. I have also recently expressed my views on these general questions in a voluminous work,[4] but our opponents wishfully decree that our views are as "grossly sexual" as their own. Our efforts to expound our psychological standpoint are quite useless, as our opponents want this whole theory to resolve itself into unspeakable banality. I feel powerless in the face of this overwhelming demand. I can only express my sincere distress that, through a misunderstanding which confuses day with night, many people are preventing themselves from employing the extraordinary insights afforded by psychoanalysis for the benefit of their own ethical development. Equally I regret that, by thoughtlessly ignoring psychoanalysis, many people are blinding themselves to the profundity and beauty of the human soul.

201   No sensible person would lay it at the door of scientific research and its results that there are clumsy and irresponsible people who use it for purposes of hocus-pocus. Would anybody of intelligence lay the blame for the faults and imperfections in the execution of a method designed for the good of mankind on the method itself? Where would surgery be if one blamed its methods for every lethal outcome? Surgery is very dangerous indeed, especially in the hands of a fool. No one would trust himself to an unskilled surgeon or let his appendix be removed by a barber. So it is with psychoanalysis. That there are not only unskilled psychiatrists but also laymen who play about in an irresponsible way with psychoanalysis cannot be denied, any more than that there are, today as always, unsuitable doctors and unscrupulous quacks. But this fact does not entitle anyone to lump together science, method, researcher, and doctor in a wholesale condemnation.

202   I regret, Sir, having to bore you and the readers of your paper with these self-evident truths, and I therefore hasten to a conclusion. You must forgive me if my manner of writing is

[4] [Presumably *Wandlungen und Symbole der Libido*, Part I of which appeared in the *Jahrbuch* in 1911. Part II, the second chapter of which is devoted to the concept and the genetic theory of the libido, appeared early in 1912.—EDITORS.]

at times a little heated; but no one, perhaps, is so far above public opinion as not to be painfully affected by the frivolous discrediting of his honest scientific endeavours.

Yours, etc.,

Dr. Jung

II

THE THEORY OF PSYCHOANALYSIS

[Written originally in German under the title *Versuch einer Darstellung der psychoanalytischen Theorie* and translated (by Dr. and Mrs. M. D. Eder and Miss Mary Moltzer) for delivery as a series of lectures under the present title at the medical school of Fordham University, New York, in September 1912. The German text was published in the *Jahrbuch für psychoanalytische und psychopathologische Forschungen* (Vienna and Leipzig), V (1913; reprinted as a book the same year); the English, in five issues of the *Psychoanalytic Review* (New York): I (1913/14): 1–4 and II (1915): 1. The latter was then republished in the Nervous and Mental Disease Monograph Series, No. 19 (New York, 1915). The analysis of a child in the last chapter had been previously presented as "Über Psychoanalyse beim Kinde" at the First International Congress of Pedagogy, Brussels, August 1911, and printed in the proceedings of the Congress (Brussels, 1912), II, 332–43.

[A second edition of the German text, with no essential alterations, was published in 1955 (Zurich). The present translation is made from this edition in consultation with the previous English version.

[The text of the 1913 and 1955 editions in German is uninterrupted by headings, but at the author's request the original division into nine lectures (ascertained from an examination of the manuscript) has here been preserved. This arrangement differs from that of the previous English version, which is divided into ten lectures; the chapter and section headings there introduced have in general been retained, with some modifications. A number of critical passages inserted at a later stage into the original manuscript and included in the German editions were omitted from the previous English version, together with the footnotes. In the present version these passages are given in pointed brackets 〈 〉. —Editors.]

FOREWORD TO THE FIRST EDITION

In these lectures I have attempted to reconcile my practical experiences in psychoanalysis with the existing theory, or rather, with the approaches to such a theory. It is really an attempt to outline my attitude to the guiding principles which my honoured teacher Sigmund Freud has evolved from the experience of many decades. Since my name is associated with psychoanalysis, and for some time I too have been the victim of the wholesale condemnation of this movement, it will perhaps be asked with astonishment how it is that I am now for the first time defining my theoretical position. When, some ten years ago, it came home to me what a vast distance Freud had already travelled beyond the bounds of contemporary knowledge of psychopathological phenomena, especially the psychology of complex mental processes, I did not feel in a position to exercise any real criticism. I did not possess the courage of those pundits who, by reason of their ignorance and incompetence, consider themselves justified in making "critical" refutations. I thought one must first work modestly for years in this field before one might dare to criticize. The unfortunate results of premature and superficial criticism have certainly not been lacking. Yet the great majority of the critics missed the mark as much with their indignation as with their technical ignorance. Psychoanalysis continued to flourish undisturbed and did not trouble itself about the unscientific chatter that buzzed around it. As everyone knows, this tree has waxed mightily, and not in one hemisphere only, but alike in Europe and America. Official critics meet with no better success than the Proktophantasmist in *Faust,* who laments in the Walpurgisnacht:

> Preposterous! You still intend to stay?
> Vanish at once! You've been explained away.

The critics have omitted to take it to heart that everything that exists has sufficient right to its own existence, and that this

85

holds for psychoanalysis as well. We will not fall into the error of our opponents, neither ignoring their existence nor denying their right to exist. But this enjoins upon us the duty of applying a just criticism ourselves, based on a proper knowledge of the facts. To me it seems that psychoanalysis stands in need of this weighing-up from inside.

It has been wrongly suggested that my attitude signifies a "split" in the psychoanalytic movement. Such schisms can only exist in matters of faith. But psychoanalysis is concerned with knowledge and its ever-changing formulations. I have taken as my guiding principle William James's pragmatic rule: "You must bring out of each word its practical cash-value, set it at work within the stream of your experience. It appears less as a solution, then, than as a program for more work, and more particularly as an indication of the ways in which existing realities may be changed. *Theories thus become instruments, not answers to enigmas, in which we can rest.* We don't lie back upon them, we move forward, and, on occasion, make nature over again by their aid." [1]

In the same way, my criticism does not proceed from academic arguments, but from experiences which have forced themselves on me during ten years of serious work in this field. I know that my own experience in no wise approaches Freud's quite extraordinary experience and insight, but nonetheless it seems to me that certain of my formulations do express the observed facts more suitably than Freud's version of them. At any rate I have found, in my teaching work, that the conceptions I have put forward in these lectures were of particular help to me in my endeavours to give my pupils an understanding of psychoanalysis. I am far indeed from regarding a modest and temperate criticism as a "falling away" or a schism; on the contrary, I hope thereby to promote the continued flowering and fructification of the psychoanalytic movement, and to open the way to the treasures of psychoanalytic knowledge for those who, lacking practical experience or handicapped by certain theoretical preconceptions, have so far been unable to master the method.

For the opportunity to deliver these lectures I have to thank my friend Dr. Smith Ely Jelliffe, of New York, who kindly in-

[1] [*Pragmatism* (1907), p. 53.]

vited me to take part in the Extension Course at Fordham University, in New York. The nine lectures were given in September 1912. I must also express my best thanks to Dr. Gregory, of Bellevue Hospital, for his ready assistance at my clinical demonstrations.

Only after the preparation of these lectures, in the spring of 1912, did Alfred Adler's book *Über den nervosen Charakter* [*The Nervous Constitution*] become known to me, in the summer of that year. I recognize that he and I have have reached similar conclusions on various points, but here is not the place to discuss the matter more thoroughly. This should be done elsewhere.

C. G. J.

Zurich, autumn 1912

FOREWORD TO THE SECOND EDITION

Since the appearance of the first edition in 1913 so much time has elapsed, and so many things have happened, that it is quite impossible to rework a book of this kind, coming from a long-past epoch and from one particular phase in the development of knowledge, and bring it up to date. It is a milestone on the long road of scientific endeavour, and so it shall remain. It may serve to call back to memory the constantly changing stages of the search in a newly discovered territory, whose boundaries are not marked out with any certainty even today, and thus to make its contribution to the story of an evolving science. I am therefore letting this book go to press again in its original form and with no essential alterations.

C. G. J.

October 1954

1. A REVIEW OF THE EARLY HYPOTHESES

203   It is no easy task to lecture on psychoanalysis at the present time. I am not thinking so much of the fact that this whole field of research raises—I am fully convinced—some of the most difficult problems facing present-day science. Even if we put this cardinal fact aside, there remain other serious difficulties which interfere considerably with the presentation of the material. I cannot offer you a well-established, neatly rounded doctrine elaborated from the practical and the theoretical side. Psychoanalysis has not yet reached that point of development, despite all the labour that has been expended upon it. Nor can I give you a description of its growth *ab ovo,* for you already have in your country, dedicated as always to the cause of progress, a number of excellent interpreters and teachers who have spread a more general knowledge of psychoanalysis among the scientifically-minded public. Besides this, Freud, the true discoverer and founder of the movement, has lectured in your country and given an authentic account of his views. I, too, have already had the great honour of lecturing in America, on the experimental foundation of the theory of complexes and the application of psychoanalysis to education.[1]

204   In these circumstances you will readily appreciate that I am afraid of repeating what has already been said or already been published in scientific journals. Another difficulty to be considered is the fact that quite extraordinary misconceptions prevail in many quarters concerning the nature of psychoanalysis. At times it is almost impossible to imagine what exactly these erroneous conceptions might be. But sometimes they are so preposterous that one is astonished that anyone with a scientific background could ever arrive at ideas so remote from reality. Obviously it would not be worth while to cite examples of these curiosities. It will be better to devote time and energy to discussing those problems of psychoanalysis which by their very nature give rise to misunderstandings.

1 [The Clark Lectures. See par. 154, n. 4, supra.—EDITORS.]

THE TRAUMA THEORY

205   Although it has been pointed out on any number of occasions before, many people still do not seem to know that the theory of psychoanalysis has changed considerably in the course of the years. Those, for instance, who have read only the first book, *Studies on Hysteria*,[2] by Breuer and Freud, still believe that, according to psychoanalysis, hysteria and the neuroses in general are derived from a so-called trauma in early childhood. They continue senselessly to attack this theory, not realizing that it is more than fifteen years since it was abandoned and replaced by a totally different one. This change is of such great importance for the whole development of the technique and theory of psychoanalysis that we are obliged to examine it in rather more detail. So as not to weary you with case histories that by now are well known, I shall content myself with referring to those mentioned in Breuer and Freud's book, which I may assume is known to you in its English translation. You will there have read that case of Breuer's to which Freud referred in his lectures at Clark University,[3] and will have discovered that the hysterical symptom did not derive from some unknown anatomical source, as was formerly supposed, but from certain psychic experiences of a highly emotional nature, called traumata or psychic wounds. Nowadays, I am sure, every careful and attentive observer of hysteria will be able to confirm from his own experience that these especially painful and distressing occurrences do in fact often lie at the root of the illness. This truth was already known to the older physicians.

206   So far as I know, however, it was really Charcot who, probably influenced by Page's theory of "nervous shock," [4] first made theoretical use of this observation. Charcot knew, from his experience of the new technique of hypnotism, that hysterical symptoms can be produced and also be made to disappear by

2 [First published 1895; partially trans. by A. A. Brill in *Selected Papers on Hysteria and Other Neuroses* (New York, 1909; later edns.); trans. in Standard Edn. of Freud, II (1955).—EDITORS.]
3 ["Five Lectures on Psycho-Analysis"; see par. 154, n. 4, supra.—EDITORS.]
4 [Probably Herbert W. Page, British psychiatrist, who published on this subject; see Bibliography.—EDITORS.]

suggestion. He believed something of the kind could be observed in those increasingly common cases of hysteria caused by accidents. The traumatic shock would be comparable, in a sense, to the moment of hypnosis, since the emotion it produced would cause, temporarily, a complete paralysis of the will during which the trauma could become fixed as an auto-suggestion.

shock to realization

207   This conception laid the foundations for a theory of psychogenesis. It was left for later aetiological researches to find out whether the same mechanism, or a similar one, existed in cases of hysteria which could not be called traumatic. This gap in our knowledge of the aetiology of hysteria was filled by the discoveries of Breuer and Freud. They showed that even in cases of ordinary hysteria which had not been regarded as traumatically conditioned the same traumatic element could be found, and that it seemed to have an aetiological significance. So it was very natural for Freud, himself a pupil of Charcot, to see in this discovery a confirmation of Charcot's views. Consequently, the theory elaborated out of the experience of that period, mainly by Freud, bore the imprint of a traumatic aetiology. It was therefore fittingly called the trauma theory.

208   The new thing about this theory, apart from the truly admirable thoroughness of Freud's analysis of hysterical symptoms, is the abandonment of the concept of auto-suggestion, which was the dynamic element in the original theory. It was replaced by a more detailed conception of the psychological and psychophysical effects produced by the shock. The shock or trauma causes an excitation which, under normal conditions, is got rid of by being expressed ("abreacted"). In hysteria, however, the trauma is incompletely abreacted, and this results in a "retention of the excitation," or a "blocking of affect." The energy of the excitation, always lying ready *in potentia,* is transmuted into the physical symptoms by the mechanism of conversion. According to this view, the task of therapy was to release the accumulated excitation, thereby discharging the repressed and converted affects from the symptoms. Hence it was aptly called the "cleansing" or "cathartic" method, and its aim was to "abreact" the blocked affects. That stage of the analysis was therefore bound up fairly closely with the symptoms—one analysed the symptoms, or began the work of analysis with the symptoms, very much in contrast to the psychoanalytical tech-

nique employed today. The cathartic method and the theory on which it is based have, as you know, been taken over by other professional people, so far as they are interested in psychoanalysis at all, and have also found appreciative mention in the text-books.

209   Although the discoveries of Breuer and Freud are undoubtedly correct in point of fact, as can easily be proved by any case of hysteria, several objections can nevertheless be raised against the trauma theory. The Breuer-Freud method shows with wonderful clearness the retrospective connection between the actual symptom and the traumatic experience, as well as the psychological consequences which apparently follow of necessity from the original traumatic situation. All the same, some doubt arises as to the *aetiological* significance of the trauma. For one thing, the hypothesis that a neurosis, with all its complications, can be related to events in the past—that is, to some factor in the patient's predisposition—must seem doubtful to anyone who knows hysteria. It is the fashion nowadays to regard all mental abnormalities not of exogenous origin as consequences of hereditary degeneration, and not as essentially conditioned by the psychology of the patient and his environment. But this is an extreme view which fails to do justice to the facts. We know very well how to find the middle course in dealing with the aetiology of tuberculosis. There are undoubtedly cases of tuberculosis where the germ of the disease proliferates from early childhood in soil predisposed by heredity, so that even under the most favourable conditions the patient cannot escape his fate. But there are also cases where there is no hereditary taint and no predisposition, and yet a fatal infection occurs. This is equally true of the neuroses, where things will not be radically different from what they are in general pathology. An extreme theory about predisposition will be just as wrong as an extreme theory about environment.

THE CONCEPT OF REPRESSION

210   Although the trauma theory gave distinct prominence to the predisposition, even insisting that some past trauma is the *conditio sine qua non* of neurosis, Freud with his brilliant em-

piricism had already discovered, and described in the Breuer-Freud *Studies,* certain elements which bear more resemblance to an "environment theory" than to a "predisposition theory," though their theoretical importance was not sufficiently appreciated at the time. Freud had synthesized these observations in a concept that was to lead far beyond the limits of the trauma theory. This concept he called "repression." As you know, by "repression" we mean the mechanism by which a conscious content is displaced into a sphere outside consciousness. We call this sphere the unconscious, and we define it as the psychic element of which we are not conscious. The concept of repression is based on the repeated observation that neurotics seem to have the capacity for forgetting significant experiences or thoughts so thoroughly that one might easily believe they had never existed. Such observations are very common and are well known to anyone who enters at all deeply into the psychology of his patients.

211   As a result of the Breuer-Freud *Studies,* it was found that special procedures were needed to call back into consciousness traumatic experiences that had long been forgotten. This fact, I would mention in passing, is astonishing in itself, inasmuch as we are disinclined from the start to suppose that things of such importance could ever be forgotten. For this reason it has often been objected that the reminiscences brought back by hypnotic procedures are merely "suggested" and bear no relation to reality. Even if this doubt were justified, there would certainly be no justification for denying repression in principle on that account, for there are plenty of cases where the actual existence of repressed memories has been verified objectively. Quite apart from numerous proofs of this kind, it is possible to demonstrate this phenomenon experimentally, by the association test. Here we discover the remarkable fact that associations relating to feeling-toned complexes are much less easily remembered and are very frequently forgotten. As my experiments were never checked, this finding was rejected along with the rest. It was only recently that Wilhelm Peters, of the Kraepelin school, was able to confirm my earlier observations, proving that "painful experiences are very rarely reproduced correctly." [5]

[5] ("Gefühl und Erinnerung," in Kraepelin, *Psychologische Arbeiten,* VI, pt. 2, p. 237.)

212   As you see, then, the concept of repression rests on a firm empirical basis. But there is another side of the question that needs discussing. We might ask if the repression is due to a conscious decision of the individual, or whether the reminiscences disappear passively, without his conscious knowledge? In Freud's writings you will find excellent proofs of the existence of a conscious tendency to repress anything painful. Every psychoanalyst knows dozens of cases showing clearly that at some particular moment in the past the patient definitely did not want to think any longer of the content to be repressed. One patient told me, very significantly: "Je l'ai mis de côté." On the other hand, we must not forget that there are any number of cases where it is impossible to show, even with the most careful examination, the slightest trace of "putting aside" or of conscious repression, and where it seems as if the process of repression were more in the nature of a passive disappearance, or even as if the impressions were dragged beneath the surface by some force operating from below. Patients of the first type give us the impression of being mentally well-developed individuals who seem to suffer only from a peculiar cowardice in regard to their own feelings. But among the second you may find cases showing a more serious retardation of development, since here the process of repression could be compared rather to an automatic mechanism. This difference may be connected with the question discussed above, concerning the relative importance of predisposition and environment. Many factors in cases of the first type appear to depend on the influence of environment and education, whereas in the latter type the factor of predisposition seems to predominate. It is pretty clear where the treatment will be more effective.

213   As I have indicated, the concept of repression contains an element which is in intrinsic contradiction with the trauma theory. We saw, for instance, in the case of Miss Lucy R., analysed by Freud,[6] that the aetiologically significant factor was not to be found in the traumatic scenes but in the insufficient readiness of the patient to accept the insights that forced themselves upon her. And when we think of the later formulation in the

6 [*Studies on Hysteria*, pp. 106ff.]

Schriften zur Neurosenlehre,[7] where Freud's experience obliged him to recognize certain traumatic events in early childhood as the source of the neurosis, we get a forcible impression of the incongruity between the concept of repression and that of the trauma. The concept of repression contains the elements of an aetiological theory of environment, while the trauma concept is a theory of predisposition.

214   At first the theory of neurosis developed entirely along the lines of the trauma concept. In his later investigations Freud came to the conclusion that no positive validity could be attributed to the traumatic experiences of later life, as their effects were conceivable only on the basis of a specific predisposition. It was evidently there that the riddle had to be solved. In pursuing the roots of hysterical symptoms, Freud found that the analytical work led back into childhood; the links reached backwards from the present into the distant past. The end of the chain threatened to get lost in the mists of earliest infancy. But it was just at that point that reminiscences appeared of certain sexual scenes—active or passive—which were unmistakably connected with the subsequent events leading to the neurosis. For the nature of these scenes you must consult the works of Freud and the numerous analyses that have already been published.

THE THEORY OF SEXUAL TRAUMA IN CHILDHOOD

215   Hence arose the theory of sexual trauma in childhood, which provoked bitter opposition not because of theoretical objections against the trauma theory in general, but against the element of sexuality in particular. In the first place, the very idea that children might be sexual, and that sexual thoughts might play any part in their lives, aroused great indignation. In the second place, the possibility that hysteria had a sexual basis was most unwelcome, for the sterile position that hysteria either was a uterine reflex-neurosis or arose from lack of sexual satisfaction

7 [By 1912, two volumes of Freud's *Sammlungen kleiner Schriften zur Neurosenlehre* had appeared, in 1906 and 1909 (another in 1913). The various contents of these volumes were trans., regrouped, in the *Collected Papers* (1924 ff.), and, further rearranged, in the Standard Edn. The precise reference here is unavailable.—EDITORS.]

had just been given up. Naturally, therefore, the validity of Freud's observations was contested. Had the critics confined themselves to that question, and not embellished their opposition with moral indignation, a calm discussion might have been possible. In Germany, for example, this method of attack made it impossible to gain any credit at all for Freud's theory. As soon as the question of sexuality was touched, it aroused universal resistance and the most arrogant contempt. But in reality there was only one question at issue: were Freud's observations true or not? That alone could be of importance to a truly scientific mind. I daresay his observations may seem improbable at first sight, but it is impossible to condemn them *a priori* as false. Wherever a really honest and thorough check has been carried out, the existence of the psychological connections established by Freud has been absolutely confirmed, but not the original hypothesis that it is always a question of real traumatic scenes.

216   Freud himself had to abandon that first formulation of his sexual theory of neurosis as a result of increasing experience. He could no longer retain his original view as to the absolute reality of the sexual trauma. Those scenes of a decidedly sexual character, the sexual abuse of children, and premature sexual activity in childhood were later on found to be to a large extent unreal. You may perhaps be inclined to share the suspicion of the critics that the results of Freud's analytical researches were therefore based on suggestion. There might be some justification for such an assumption if these assertions had been publicized by some charlatan or other unqualified person. But anyone who has read Freud's works of that period with attention, and has tried to penetrate into the psychology of his patients as Freud has done, will know how unjust it would be to attribute to an intellect like Freud's the crude mistakes of a beginner. Such insinuations only redound to the discredit of those who make them. Ever since then patients have been examined under conditions in which every possible precaution was taken to exclude suggestion, and still the psychological connections described by Freud have been proved true in principle. We are thus obliged to assume that many traumata in early infancy are of a purely fantastic nature, mere fantasies in fact, while others do have objective reality.

217   With this discovery, somewhat bewildering at first sight, the

aetiological significance of the sexual trauma in childhood falls to the ground, as it now appears totally irrelevant whether the trauma really occurred or not. Experience shows us that fantasies can be just as traumatic in their effects as real traumata. As against this, every doctor who treats hysteria will be able to recall cases where violent traumatic impressions have in fact precipitated a neurosis. This observation is only in apparent contradiction with the unreality, already discussed, of the infantile trauma. We know very well that there are a great many more people who experience traumata in childhood or adult life without getting a neurosis. Therefore the trauma, other things being equal, has no absolute aetiological significance and will pass off without having any lasting effect. From this simple reflection it is perfectly clear that the individual must meet the trauma with a quite definite inner predisposition in order to make it really effective. This inner predisposition is not to be understood as that obscure, hereditary disposition of which we know so little, but as a psychological development which reaches its climax, and becomes manifest, at the traumatic moment.

THE PREDISPOSITION FOR THE TRAUMA

218   I will now show you, by means of a concrete example, the nature of the trauma and its psychological preparation. It concerns the case of a young woman who suffered from acute hysteria following a sudden fright.[8] She had been to an evening party and was on her way home about midnight in the company of several acquaintances, when a cab came up behind them at full trot. The others got out of the way, but she, as though spellbound with terror, kept to the middle of the road and ran along in front of the horses. The cabman cracked his whip and swore; it was no good, she ran down the whole length of the road, which led across a bridge. There her strength deserted her, and to avoid being trampled on by the horses she would, in her desperation, have leapt into the river had not the passers-by restrained her. Now, this same lady had happened to be in St. Petersburg on the bloody 22nd of January [1905], in the very street which

8 [This case is fully reported in *Two Essays on Analytical Psychology*, pars. 8ff., 417ff.—EDITORS.]

was being cleared by the volleys of the soldiers. All round her people were falling to the ground dead or wounded; she, however, quite calm and clear-headed, espied a gate leading into a yard, through which she made her escape into another street. These dreadful moments caused her no further agitation. She felt perfectly well afterwards—indeed, rather better than usual.

219   This failure to react to an apparent shock is often observed. Hence it necessarily follows that the intensity of a trauma has very little pathogenic significance in itself; everything depends on the particular circumstances. Here we have a key to the "predisposition." We have therefore to ask ourselves: what are the particular circumstances of the scene with the cab? The patient's fear began with the sound of the trotting horses; for an instant it seemed to her that this portended some terrible doom —her death, or something as dreadful; the next moment she lost all sense of what she was doing.

220   The real shock evidently came from the horses. The patient's predisposition to react in so unaccountable a way to this unremarkable incident might therefore be due to the fact that horses have some special significance for her. We might conjecture, for instance, that she once had a dangerous accident with horses. This was actually found to be the case. As a child of about seven she was out for a drive with the coachman, when suddenly the horses took fright and at a wild gallop made for the precipitous bank of a deep river-gorge. The coachman jumped off and shouted to her to do likewise, but she was in such deadly fear that she could hardly make up her mind. Nevertheless she managed to jump in the nick of time, while the horses crashed with the carriage into the depths below. That such an event would leave a very deep impression hardly needs proof. Yet it does not explain why at a later date such an insensate reaction should follow a perfectly harmless stimulus. So far we know only that the later symptom had a prelude in childhood. The pathological aspect of it still remains in the dark.

221   This anamnesis, whose continuation we shall find out later,[9] shows very clearly the discrepancy between the so-called trauma and the part played by fantasy. In this case fantasy must predominate to a quite extraordinary degree in order to produce

9 [See infra, pars. 297ff. and 355ff.—EDITORS.]

such a great effect from so insignificant a stimulus. At first one is inclined to adduce that early childhood trauma as an explanation—not very successfully, it seems to me, because we still do not understand why the effects of that trauma remained latent so long, and why they manifested themselves precisely on this occasion and on no other. The patient must surely have had opportunities enough during her lifetime of getting out of the way of a carriage going at full speed. The moment of deadly peril she experienced earlier in St. Petersburg did not leave behind the slightest trace of neurosis, despite her being predisposed by the impressive event in her childhood. Everything about this traumatic scene has still to be explained, for, from the standpoint of the trauma theory, we are left completely in the dark.

222   You must forgive me if I return so persistently to this question of the trauma theory. I do not think it superfluous to do so, because nowadays so many people, even those closely connected with psychoanalysis, still cling to the old standpoint, and this gives our opponents, who mostly never read our writings or do so only very superficially, the impression that psychoanalysis still revolves round the trauma theory.

223   The question now arises: what are we to understand by this "predisposition," through which an impression, insignificant in itself, can produce such a pathological effect? This is a question of fundamental importance, and, as we shall see later, it plays a very important role in the whole theory of neurosis. We have to understand why apparently irrelevant events of the past still have so much significance that they can interfere in a daemonic and capricious way with our reactions in actual life.

THE SEXUAL ELEMENT IN THE TRAUMA

224   The early school of psychoanalysis, and its later disciples, did all they could to find in the special quality of those original traumatic experiences the reason for their later effectiveness. Freud went deepest: he was the first and only one to see that some kind of sexual element was mingled with the traumatic event, and that this admixture, of which the patient was generally unconscious, was chiefly responsible for the effect of the

trauma. The unconsciousness of sexuality in childhood seemed to throw a significant light on the problem of the long-lasting constellation caused by the original traumatic experience. The real emotional significance of that experience remains hidden all along from the patient, so that, not reaching consciousness, the emotion never wears itself out, it is never used up. We might explain the long-lasting constellative effect of the experience as a kind of *suggestion à échéance,* for this, too, is unconscious and develops its effect only at the appointed time.

225   It is hardly necessary to give detailed examples showing that the real character of sexual activities in infancy is not recognized. Doctors are aware, for instance, that open masturbation right up to adult life is not understood as such, especially by women. From this it is easy to deduce that a child would be even less conscious of the character of certain actions; hence the real meaning of these experiences remains hidden from consciousness even in adult life. In some cases the experiences themselves are completely forgotten, either because their sexual significance is quite unknown to the patient, or because their sexual character, being too painful, is not admitted, in other words, is repressed.

226   As already mentioned, Freud's observation that the admixture of a sexual element in the trauma is a characteristic concomitant having a pathological effect led to the theory of the infantile sexual trauma. This hypothesis means that the pathogenic experience is a sexual one.

INFANTILE SEXUAL FANTASY

227   At first this hypothesis was countered by the widespread opinion that children have no sexuality at all in early life, thus making such an aetiology unthinkable. The modification of the trauma theory already discussed, that the trauma is generally not real at all but essentially just fantasy, does not make things any better. On the contrary, it obliges us to see in the pathogenic experience a positive sexual manifestation of infantile fantasy. It is no longer some brutal accidental impression coming from outside, but a sexual manifestation of unmistakable clearness actually created by the child. Even real traumatic

experiences of a definitely sexual character do not happen to the child entirely without his co-operation; it was found that very often he himself prepares the way for them and brings them to pass. Abraham has furnished valuable proofs of great interest in support of this, which in conjunction with many other experiences of the same kind make it seem very probable that even real traumata are frequently aided and abetted by the psychological attitude of the child. Medical jurisprudence, quite independently of psychoanalysis, can offer striking parallels in support of this psychoanalytic assertion.

228   The precocious manifestations of sexual fantasy, and their traumatic effect, now seemed to be the source of the neurosis. One was therefore obliged to attribute to children a much more developed sexuality than was admitted before. Cases of precocious sexuality had long been recorded in the literature, for instance of a two-year-old girl who was menstruating regularly, or of boys between three and five years old having erections and therefore being capable of cohabitation. But these cases were curiosities. Great was the astonishment, therefore, when Freud began to credit children not only with ordinary sexuality but even with a so-called "polymorphous-perverse" sexuality, and moreover on the basis of the most exhaustive investigations. People were far too ready with the facile assumption that all this had merely been suggested to the patients and was accordingly a highly debatable artificial product.

229   In these circumstances, Freud's *Three Essays on the Theory of Sexuality* [10] provoked not only opposition but violent indignation. I need hardly point out that the progress of science is not furthered by indignation and that arguments based on the sense of moral outrage may suit the moralist—for that is his business—but not the scientist, who must be guided by truth and not by moral sentiments. If matters really are as Freud describes them, all indignation is absurd; if they are not, indignation will avail nothing. The decision as to what is the truth must be left solely to observation and research. In consequence of this misplaced indignation the opponents of psychoanalysis, with a few honourable exceptions, present a slightly comic picture of pitiful backwardness. Although the psychoanalytic school

[10] [First published in 1905.]

was unfortunately unable to learn anything from its critics, as the critics did not trouble to examine our actual conclusions, and although it could not get any useful hints, because the psychoanalytic method of investigation was and still is unknown to them, it nevertheless remains the duty of our school to discuss very thoroughly the discrepancies between the existing views. It is not our endeavour to put forward a paradoxical theory contradicting all previous theories, but rather to introduce a certain category of new observations into science. We therefore consider it our duty to do whatever we can from our side to promote agreement. True, we must give up trying to reach an understanding with all those who blindly oppose us, which would be a waste of effort, but we do hope to make our peace with men of science. This will now be my endeavour in attempting to sketch the further conceptual development of psychoanalysis, up to the point where it reached the *sexual theory of neurosis.*[11]

11 [See Ch. 4.—EDITORS.]

2. THE THEORY OF INFANTILE SEXUALITY

230   As you have heard in the last lecture, the discovery of precocious sexual fantasies, which seemed to be the source of the
neurosis, forced Freud to assume the existence of a richly developed infantile sexuality. As you know, the validity of this
observation has been roundly contested by many, who argue
that crude error and bigoted delusion have misled Freud and his
whole school, alike in Europe and in America, into seeing things
that never existed. We are therefore regarded as people in the
grip of an intellectual epidemic. I must confess that I have no
way of defending myself against this sort of "criticism." For the
rest, I must remark that science has no right to start off with
the idea that certain facts do not exist. The most one can say is
that they appear to be very improbable, and that more confirmation and more exact study are needed. This is also our reply to
the objection that nothing reliable can be learnt from the psychoanalytic method, as the method itself is absurd. No one believed in Galileo's telescope, and Columbus discovered America
on a false hypothesis. The method may for all I know be full of
errors, but that should not prevent its use. Chronological and
geographical observations were made in the past with quite inadequate instruments. The objections to the method must be
regarded as so many subterfuges until our opponents come to
grips with the facts. It is there that the issue should be decided
—not by a war of words.

231   Even our opponents call hysteria a psychogenic illness. We
believe we have discovered its psychological determinants and
we present, undaunted, the results of our researches for public
criticism. Anyone who does not agree with our conclusions is at
liberty to publish his own analyses of cases. So far as I know,
this has never yet been done, at least in the European literature.
Under these circumstances, critics have no right to deny our
discoveries *a priori*. Our opponents have cases of hysteria just
as we have, and these are just as psychogenic as ours, so there is
nothing to prevent them from finding the psychological deter-

minants. It does not depend on the method. Our opponents content themselves with attacking and vilifying our researches, but they do not know how to find a better way.

232   Many of our critics are more careful and more just, and admit that we have made many valuable observations and that the psychic connections revealed by the psychoanalytic method very probably hold good, but they maintain that our conception of them is all wrong. The alleged sexual fantasies of children, with which we are here chiefly concerned, must not be taken, they say, as real sexual functions, being obviously something quite different, since the specific character of sexuality is acquired only at the onset of puberty.

233   This objection, whose calm and reasonable tone makes a trustworthy impression, deserves to be taken seriously. It is an objection that has given every thoughtful analyst plenty of cause for reflection.

THE CONCEPT OF SEXUALITY

234   The first thing to be said about this problem is that the main difficulty resides in the concept of sexuality. If we understand sexuality as a fully developed function, then we must restrict this phenomenon to the period of maturity and are not justified in speaking of infantile sexuality. But if we limit our conception in this way, we are faced with a new and much greater difficulty. What name are we then to give to all those biological phenomena correlated with the sexual function in the strict sense, such as pregnancy, birth, natural selection, protection of offspring, and so on? It seems to me that all this belongs to the concept of sexuality, although a distinguished colleague did once say that childbirth is not a sexual act. But if these things do pertain to the concept of sexuality, then countless psychological phenomena must come into it too, for we know that an incredible number of purely psychological functions are connected with this sphere. I need only mention the extraordinary importance of fantasy in preparing and perfecting the sexual function. Thus we arrive at a highly biological conception of sexuality, which includes within it a series of psychological functions as well as a series of physiological phenomena. Availing

ourselves of an old but practical classification, we might identify sexuality with the instinct for the preservation of the species, which in a certain sense may be contrasted with the instinct of self-preservation.

235   Looking at sexuality from this point of view, we shall no longer find it so astonishing that the roots of the preservation of the species, on which nature sets such store, go much deeper than the limited conception of sexuality would ever allow. Only the more or less grown-up cat catches mice, but even the very young kitten at least plays at catching them. The puppy's playful attempts at copulation begin long before sexual maturity. We have a right to suppose that man is no exception to this rule. Even though we do not find such things on the surface in our well-brought-up children, observation of children of primitive peoples proves that they are no exceptions to the biological norm. It is really far more probable that the vital instinct for preservation of the species begins to unfold in early infancy than that it should descend at one fell swoop from heaven, fully-fledged, at puberty. Also, the organs of reproduction develop long before the slightest sign of their future function can be discerned.

236   So when the psychoanalytic school speaks of "sexuality," this wider concept of the preservation of the species should be associated with it, and it should not be thought that we mean merely the physical sensations and functions which are ordinarily connoted by that word. It might be said that in order to avoid misunderstandings one should not call the preliminary phenomena of early infancy "sexual." But this demand is surely not justified, since anatomical nomenclature is taken from the fully-developed system and it is not usual to give special names to the more or less rudimentary stages.

IMPORTANCE OF THE NUTRITIVE FUNCTION

237   Now although no fault can be found with Freud's sexual terminology as such, since he logically gives all the stages of sexual development the general name of sexuality, it has nevertheless led to certain conclusions which in my view are untenable. For if we ask ourselves how far the first traces of sexuality

go back into childhood, we have to admit that though sexuality exists implicity *ab ovo* it only manifests itself after a long period of extra-uterine life. Freud is inclined to see even in the infant's sucking at its mother's breast a kind of sexual act. He was bitterly attacked for this view, yet we must admit that it is sensible enough if we assume with Freud that the instinct for the preservation of the species, i.e., sexuality, exists as it were separately from the instinct of self-preservation, i.e., the nutritive function, and accordingly undergoes a special development *ab ovo*. But this way of thinking seems to me inadmissible biologically. It is not possible to separate the two modes of manifestation or functioning of the hypothetical life-instinct and assign each of them a special path of development. If we judge by what we see, we must take into consideration the fact that in the whole realm of organic nature the life-process consists for a long time only in the functions of nutrition and growth. We can observe this very clearly indeed in many organisms, for instance in butterflies, which as caterpillars first pass through an asexual stage of nutrition and growth only. The intra-uterine period of human beings, as well as the extra-uterine period of infancy, belong to this stage of the life process.

238   *This period is characterized by the absence of any sexual function,* so that to speak of manifest sexuality in infancy would be a contradiction in terms. The most we can ask is whether, among the vital functions of the infantile period, there are some that do not have the character of nutrition and growth and hence could be termed sexual. Freud points to the unmistakable excitement and satisfaction of the infant while sucking, and he compares these emotional mechanisms with those of the sexual act. This comparison leads him to assume that the act of sucking has a sexual quality. Such an assumption would be justifiable only if it were proved that the tension of a physical need, and its release by gratification, is a sexual process. But the fact that sucking has this emotional mechanism proves just the contrary. Consequently we can only say that this emotional mechanism is found both in the nutritive function and in the sexual function. If Freud derives the sexual quality of the act of sucking from the analogy of the emotional mechanism, biological experience would also justify a terminology qualifying the sexual act as a function of nutrition. This is exceeding the bounds in both

directions. What is quite evident is that the act of sucking cannot be qualified as sexual.

239   We know, however, of other functions at the infantile stage which apparently have nothing to do with the function of nutrition, such as sucking the finger and its numerous variants. Here is rather the place to ask whether such things belong to the sexual sphere. They do not serve nutrition, but produce pleasure. Of that there can be no doubt, but it nevertheless remains disputable whether the pleasure obtained by sucking should be called by analogy a sexual pleasure. It could equally well be called a nutritive pleasure. This latter qualification is the more apt in that the form of pleasure and the place where it is obtained belong entirely to the sphere of nutrition. The hand which is used for sucking is being prepared in this way for the independent act of feeding in the future. That being so, surely no one will beg the question by asserting that the first expressions of human life are sexual.

240   Yet the formula we hit on just now, that pleasure is sought in sucking the finger without serving any nutritive purpose, leaves us feeling doubtful whether it does belong entirely to the sphere of nutrition. We notice that the so-called bad habits of a child as it grows up are closely connected with early infantile sucking, like putting the finger in the mouth, biting the nails, picking the nose, ears, etc. We see, too, how easily these habits pass over into masturbation later on. The conclusion that these infantile habits are the first stages of masturbation or of similar activities, and therefore have a distinctly sexual character, cannot be denied: it is perfectly legitimate. I have seen many cases in which an indubitable correlation existed between these childish habits and masturbation, and if masturbation occurs in late childhood, before puberty, it is nothing but a continuation of the infantile bad habits. The inference from masturbation that other infantile habits have a sexual character appears natural and understandable from this point of view, in so far as they are acts for obtaining pleasure from one's own body.

241   From here it is but a short step to qualifying the infant's sucking as sexual. Freud, as you know, took that step and you have just heard me reject it. For here we come upon a contradiction which is very hard to resolve. It would be fairly easy if we could assume two separate instincts existing side by side.

Then the act of sucking the breast would be a nutritive act and at the same time a sexual act, a sort of combination of the two instincts. This seems to be Freud's conception. The obvious co-existence of the two instincts, or rather their manifestation in the form of hunger and the sexual drive, is found in the life of adults. But at the infantile stage we find *only* the function of nutrition, which sets a premium on pleasure and satisfaction. Its sexual character can be argued only by a *petitio principii,* for the facts show that the act of sucking is the first to give pleasure, not the sexual function. *Obtaining pleasure is by no means identical with sexuality.* We deceive ourselves if we think that the two instincts exist side by side in the infant, for then we project into the psyche of the child an observation taken over from the psychology of adults. The co-existence or separate manifestation of the two instincts is *not* found in the infant, for one of the instinctual systems is not developed at all, or is quite rudimentary. If we take the attitude that the striving for pleasure is something sexual, we might just as well say, paradoxically, that hunger is a sexual striving, since it seeks pleasure by satisfaction. But if we juggle with concepts like that, we should have to allow our opponents to apply the terminology of hunger to sexuality. This kind of one-sidedness appears over and over again in the history of science. I am not saying this as a reproach: on the contrary, we must be glad that there are people who are courageous enough to be immoderate and one-sided. It is to them that we owe our discoveries. What is regrettable is that each should defend his one-sidedness so passionately. Scientific theories are merely suggestions as to how things might be observed.

242   The co-existence of two instinctual systems is an hypothesis that would certainly facilitate matters, but unfortunately it is impossible because it contradicts the observed facts and, if pursued, leads to untenable conclusions.

THE POLYMORPHOUS-PERVERSE SEXUALITY OF INFANCY

243   Before I try to resolve this contradiction, I must say something more about Freud's sexual theory and the changes it has undergone. As I explained earlier, the discovery of a sexual

fantasy-activity in childhood, which apparently had the effect of a trauma, led to the assumption that the child must have, in contradiction to all previous views, an almost fully developed sexuality, and even a polymorphous-perverse sexuality. Its sexuality does not seem to be centred on the genital function and on the other sex, but is occupied with the child's own body, whence it is said to be autoerotic. If its sexual interest is directed outwards to another person, it makes but little difference to the child what that person's sex is. Hence the child may very easily be "homosexual." Instead of the non-existent, localized sexual function there are a number of so-called bad habits, which from this point of view appear as perverse actions since they have close analogies with subsequent perversions.

244   As a result of this conception sexuality, ordinarily thought of as a unity, was decomposed into a plurality of separate drives; and since it was tacitly assumed that sexuality originates in the genitals, Freud arrived at the conception of "erogenous zones," by which he meant the mouth, skin, anus, etc.

245   The term "erogenous zone" reminds us of "spasmogenic zone." At all events the underlying idea is the same: just as the spasmogenic zone is the place where a spasm originates, the erogenous zone is the place from which comes an afflux of sexuality. On the underlying model of the genitals as the anatomical source of sexuality, the erogenous zones would have to be conceived as so many genital organs out of which sexuality flows. This state is the polymorphous-perverse sexuality of children. The term "perverse" appeared justified by the close analogy with later perversions which are, so to speak, simply a new edition of certain "perverse" interests in early infancy. They are frequently connected with one or other of the erogenous zones and cause those sexual anomalies which are so characteristic of children.

SEXUAL COMPONENTS AS ENERGIC MANIFESTATIONS

246   From this point of view the later, normal, "monomorphic" sexuality is made up of several components. First it falls into a homo- and a heterosexual component, then comes the autoerotic component, and then the various erogenous zones. This concep-

tion can be compared with the position of physics before Robert Mayer, when only separate fields of phenomena existed, each credited with elementary qualities whose correlation was not properly understood. The law of the conservation of energy brought order into the relationship of forces to one another, at the same time abolishing the conception of those forces as having an absolute, elementary character and making them manifestations of the same energy. The same thing will have to happen with this splitting of sexuality into the polymorphous-perverse sexuality of childhood.

247   Experience compels us to postulate a constant interchange of individual components. It was recognized more and more that perversions, for instance, exist at the expense of normal sexuality, and that increased application of one form of sexuality follows a decrease in the application of another form. To make the matter clearer I will give an example. A young man had a homosexual phase lasting for some years, during which time he had no interest in girls. This abnormal condition gradually changed towards his twentieth year, and his erotic interests became more and more normal. He began to take an interest in girls, and soon he had overcome the last traces of homosexuality. This lasted for several years, and he had a number of successful love-affairs. Then he wanted to marry. But here he suffered a severe disappointment, as the girl he adored threw him over. During the ensuing phase he gave up all idea of marriage. After that he experienced a dislike of all women, and one day he discovered that he had become homosexual again, for young men once more had a peculiarly irritating effect upon him.

248   If we regard sexuality as consisting of a fixed heterosexual and a fixed homosexual component we shall never explain this case, since the assumption of fixed components precludes any kind of transformation. In order to do justice to it, we must assume a great mobility of the sexual components, which even goes so far that one component disappears almost completely while the other occupies the foreground. If nothing but a change of position took place, so that the homosexual component lapsed in full force into the unconscious, leaving the field of consciousness to the heterosexual component, modern scientific knowledge would lead us to infer that equivalent effects would then arise from the unconscious sphere. These effects would have to

be regarded as resistances to the activity of the heterosexual component, that is, as resistances against women. But in our case there is no evidence of this. Though faint traces of such influences existed, they were of such slight intensity that they could not be compared with the previous intensity of the homosexual component.

249   On the existing theory, it remains incomprehensible how the homosexual component, regarded as so firmly fixed, could disappear without leaving any active traces behind it. ⟨Further, it would be very difficult to conceive how these transformations come about. One could, at a pinch, understand the development passing through a homosexual stage in the pubertal period in order to lay the foundation for normal heterosexuality later, in a fixed, definite form. But how are we then to explain that the product of a gradual development, to all appearances bound up very closely with organic processes of maturation, is suddenly abolished under the impact of an impression, so as to make room for an earlier stage? Or, if two active components are postulated as existing simultaneously side by side, why is only one of them active and not the other as well? One might object that the homosexual component in men does in fact show itself most readily in a peculiar irritability, a special sensitiveness in regard to other men. According to my experience the apparent reason for this characteristic behaviour, of which we find so many examples in society today, is an invariable disturbance in the relationship with women, a special form of dependence on them. This would constitute the "plus" that is counterbalanced by the "minus" in the homosexual relationship. (Naturally this is not the real reason. The real reason is the infantile state of the man's character.)⟩

250   It was, therefore, urgently necessary to give an adequate explanation of such a change of scene. For this we need a dynamic hypothesis, since these permutations of sex can only be thought of as dynamic or energic processes. Without an alteration in the dynamic relationships, I cannot conceive how a mode of functioning can disappear like this. Freud's theory took account of this necessity. His conception of components, of separate modes of functioning, began to be weakened, at first more in practice than in theory, and was eventually replaced by a conception of energy. The term chosen for this was *libido*.

3. THE CONCEPT OF LIBIDO

251   Freud had already introduced the concept of libido in his
Three Essays on the Theory of Sexuality, where he says:

> The fact of the existence of sexual needs in human beings and ani-
> mals is expressed in biology by the assumption of a "sexual instinct,"
> on the analogy of the instinct of nutrition, that is of hunger. Every-
> day language possesses no counterpart to the word "hunger," but
> science makes use of the word "libido" for that purpose.[1]

252   In Freud's definition the term *libido* connotes an exclusively
sexual need, hence everything that Freud means by libido must
be understood as sexual need or sexual desire. In medicine the
term *libido* is certainly used for sexual desire, and specifically
for sexual lust. But the classical use of the word as found in
Cicero, Sallust, and others was not so exclusive; there it is used
in the more general sense of passionate desire.[2] I mention this
fact now, because further on it will play an important part in
our argument, and because it is important to know that the term
libido really has a much wider range of meaning than it has in
medicine.

253   The concept of libido—whose sexual meaning in the Freudian sense we shall try to retain as long as possible—represents
that dynamic factor which we were seeking in order to explain
the shifting of the psychological scenery. This concept makes it
much easier to formulate the phenomena in question. Instead of
the incomprehensible exchanging of the homosexual component for the heterosexual component, we can now say that the
libido was gradually withdrawn from its homosexual application and that it passed over in the same measure to a heterosexual application. In the process the homosexual component
disappeared almost completely. It remained only an empty possibility, signifying nothing in itself. Its very existence is quite

1 [Standard Edn., VII, p. 135.]
2 [Cf. the definition of libido in *Symbols of Transformation*, pars. 185f.]

rightly denied by the layman, just as he would deny the possibility that he is a murderer. The libido concept also helps to explain the reciprocal relationships between the various modes of sexual functioning. At the same time, it does away with the original idea of a plurality of sexual components, which savoured too much of the old philosophical notion of psychic faculties. Their place is taken by libido, which is capable of the most varied applications. The earlier "components" represent only possible modes of action. The libido concept puts in the place of a divided sexuality split into many roots a dynamic unity, lacking which these once-significant components remain nothing but potential activities. This conceptual development is of the greatest importance; it accomplishes for psychology the same advance that the concept of energy introduced into physics. Just as the theory of the conservation of energy deprived the various forces of their elementary character and made them manifestations of a single energy, so the theory of libido deprives the sexual components of their elementary significance as psychic "faculties" and gives them a merely phenomenological value.

THE ENERGIC THEORY OF LIBIDO

254   This view is a far better reflection of reality than the theory of components. With the libido theory we can easily explain the case of the young man cited earlier. The disappointment he met with at the moment he wanted to marry drove his libido away from its heterosexual mode of application, with the result that it assumed a homosexual form again and thus reinduced the earlier homosexuality. Here I cannot refrain from remarking that the analogy with the law of the conservation of energy is very close. In both cases one has to ask, when one sees that a quantum of energy has disappeared, where this energy has re-emerged in the meantime? If we apply this point of view as an explanatory principle to the psychology of human conduct, we shall make the most surprising discoveries. We can then see that the most heterogeneous phases in an individual's psychological development are connected with one another in an energic relationship. Every time we come across a person who has a "bee in his bonnet," or a morbid conviction, or some extreme

attitude, we know that there is too much libido, and that the excess must have been taken from somewhere else where, consequently, there is too little. From this point of view psychoanalysis is a method which helps us to discover those places or functions where there is too little libido, and to restore the balance. Thus the symptoms of a neurosis must be regarded as exaggerated functions over-invested with libido.[3] The energy used for this purpose has been taken from somewhere else, and it is the task of the psychoanalyst to discover the place it was taken from or where it was never applied.

255   The question has to be reversed in the case of those syndromes characterized mainly by lack of libido, for instance apathetic states. Here we have to ask, where did the libido go? The patient gives us the impression of having no libido, and there are many doctors who take him at his face value. Such doctors have a primitive way of thinking, like a savage who, seeing an eclipse of the sun, believes that the sun has been swallowed and killed. But the sun is only hidden, and so it is with these patients. The libido is there, but it is not visible and is inaccessible to the patient himself. Superficially, we have here a lack of libido. It is the task of psychoanalysis to search out that hidden place where the libido dwells and where the patient himself cannot get at it. The hidden place is the "non-conscious," which we may also call the "unconscious" without attributing to it any mystical significance.

UNCONSCIOUS FANTASY SYSTEMS

256   Psychoanalysis has taught us that there are non-conscious psychological systems which, by analogy with conscious fantasies, can be described as unconscious fantasy systems. In states of neurotic apathy these unconscious fantasy systems are the objects of libido. We are fully aware that when we speak of unconscious fantasy-systems we are speaking only figuratively. By this we mean no more than that we accept as a necessary postulate the conception of psychic entities outside consciousness. Experience teaches us, we might say daily, that there are non-conscious

3 We meet with a similar view in Janet.

psychic processes which perceptibly influence the libido economy. Those cases known to every psychiatrist, in which a complicated system of delusions breaks out with comparative suddenness, prove that there must be unconscious psychic developments that have prepared the ground, for we can hardly suppose that such things come into being just as suddenly as they enter consciousness.

257   I have allowed myself to make this digression concerning the unconscious in order to point out that, with regard to the changing localization of libidinal investments, we have to reckon not merely with the conscious but with another factor, the unconscious, into which the libido sometimes disappears. We can now resume our discussion of the further consequences resulting from the adoption of the libido theory.

THE CONSERVATION OF LIBIDO

258   Freud has taught us, and we see it in the everyday practice of psychoanalysis, that there exist in early childhood, instead of the later normal sexuality, the beginnings of many tendencies which in later life are called "perversions." We have had to admit Freud's right to apply a sexual terminology to these tendencies. Through the introduction of the libido concept, we see that in adults those elementary components which seemed to be the origin and source of normal sexuality lose their importance and are reduced to mere potentialities. Their operative principle, their vital force, so to speak, is the libido. Without libido these components mean practically nothing. Freud, as we saw, gives the libido an unquestionably sexual connotation, something like "sexual need." It is generally assumed that libido in this sense comes into existence only at puberty. How, then, are we to explain the fact that children have a polymorphous-perverse sexuality, and that the libido activates not merely one perversion but several? If the libido, in Freud's sense, comes into existence only at puberty, it cannot be held accountable for earlier infantile perversions—unless we regard them as "psychic faculties," in accordance with the theory of components. Quite apart from the hopeless theoretical confusion this would lead to, we would be sinning against the methodological axiom

that "explanatory principles are not to be multiplied beyond the necessary."

259   There is no alternative but to assume that before and after puberty it is the same libido. Hence the infantile perversions arise in exactly the same way as in adults. Common sense will object to this, as obviously the sexual needs of children cannot possibly be the same as those of sexually mature persons. We might, however, compromise on this point and say with Freud that though the libido before and after puberty is the same it is different in its intensity. Instead of the intense sexual need after puberty there would be only a slight sexual need in childhood, gradually diminishing in intensity until, at about the first year, it is nothing but a trace. We could declare ourselves in agreement with this from the biological point of view. But we should also have to assume that everything that comes within the realm of the wider concept of sexuality discussed in the previous lecture is already present in miniature, including all those emotional manifestations of psychosexuality, such as need for affection, jealousy, and many other affective phenomena, and by no means least the neuroses of childhood. It must be admitted, however, that these affective phenomena in children do not at all give the impression of being "in miniature"; on the contrary, they can rival in intensity those of an adult. Nor should we forget that, as experience has shown, the perverse manifestations of sexuality in childhood are often more glaring, and even seem to be more richly developed, than in adults. In an adult showing a similar state of richly developed perversion we could rightly expect a total extinction of normal sexuality and of many other important forms of biological adaptation, as is normally the case with children. An adult is rightly called perverse when his libido is not used for normal functions, and the same can reasonably be said of a child: he is polymorphous-perverse because he does not yet know the normal sexual function.

260   These considerations suggest that perhaps the amount of libido is always the same and that no enormous increase occurs at sexual maturity. This somewhat audacious hypothesis leans heavily, it is clear, on the law of the conservation of energy, according to which the amount of energy remains constant. It is conceivable that the peak of maturity is reached only when the infantile, subsidiary applications of libido gradually discharge

themselves into one definite channel of sexuality and are extinguished in it. For the moment we must content ourselves with these suggestions, for we must next pay attention to one point of criticism concerning the nature of the infantile libido.

261   Many of our critics do not concede that the infantile libido is simply less intense but of essentially the same nature as the libido of adults. The libidinal impulses of adults are correlated with the genital function, those of children are not, or only in exceptional cases, and this gives rise to a distinction whose importance must not be underestimated. It seems to me that this objection is justified. There is indeed a considerable difference between immature and fully developed functions, just as there is between play and seriousness, between shooting with blank and with loaded cartridges. This would give the infantile libido that undeniably harmless character which is demanded by common sense. But neither can one deny that blank-shooting is shooting. We must get accustomed to the idea that sexuality really exists, even before puberty, right back into early childhood, and we have no grounds for not calling the manifestations of this immature sexuality sexual.

262   This naturally does not invalidate the objection which, while admitting the existence of infantile sexuality in the form we have described, nevertheless contests Freud's right to designate as "sexual" early infantile phenomena such as sucking. We have already discussed the reasons which may have induced Freud to stretch his sexual terminology so far. We mentioned, too, how this very act of sucking could be conceived just as well from the standpoint of the nutritive function and that, on biological grounds, there was actually more justification for this derivation than for Freud's view. It might be objected that these and similar activities of the oral zone reappear in later life in an undoubtedly sexual guise. This only means that these activities can be used later for sexual purposes, but proves nothing about their originally sexual character. I must, therefore, admit that I can find no ground for regarding the pleasure-producing activities of the infantile period from the standpoint of sexuality, but rather grounds to the contrary. It seems to me, so far as I am capable of judging these difficult problems correctly, that from the standpoint of sexuality it is necessary to divide human life into three phases.

THE THREE PHASES OF LIFE

263   The first phase embraces the first years of life; I call this period the *presexual stage*.[4] It corresponds to the caterpillar stage of butterflies, and is characterized almost exclusively by the functions of nutrition and growth.

264   The second phase embraces the later years of childhood up to puberty, and might be called the *prepubertal stage*. Germination of sexuality takes place at this period.

265   The third phase is the adult period from puberty on, and may be called the period of *maturity*.

266   It will not have escaped you that the greatest difficulty lies in assigning limits to the presexual stage. I am ready to confess my great uncertainty in regard to this problem. When I look back on my own psychoanalytic experiences with children—insufficiently numerous as yet, unfortunately—at the same time bearing in mind the observations made by Freud, it seems to me that the limits of this phase lie between the third and fifth year, subject, of course, to individual variation. This age is an important one in many respects. The child has already outgrown the helplessness of a baby, and a number of important psychological functions have acquired a reliable hold. From this period on, the profound darkness of the early infantile amnesia, or discontinuity of consciousness, begins to be illuminated by the sporadic continuity of memory. It seems as if, at this stage, an essential step forward is taken in the emancipation and centring of the new personality. So far as we know, the first signs of interests and activities which may fairly be called sexual also fall into this period, even though these indications still have the infantile characteristics of harmlessness and naïveté.

THE SEXUAL TERMINOLOGY

267   I think I have sufficiently explained why a sexual terminology cannot be applied to the presexual stage, so we may now consider the other problems from the standpoint we have just

4 [Cf. *Symbols of Transformation*, par. 206.]

reached. You will remember that we dropped the problem of decreased libido in childhood because it was impossible in that way to reach any clear conclusion. We now take up this question once again, if only to see whether the energic conception fits in with our present formulations.

268   We saw that the difference between infantile and mature sexuality can be explained, according to Freud, by the diminishing intensity of sexuality in childhood. But we have just advanced reasons why it seems doubtful that the life-processes of a child, with the exception of sexuality, are any less intense than those of adults. We could say that, sexuality excepted, the affective phenomena, and the nervous symptoms if there are any, are quite as intense as in adults. Yet, on the energic view, they are all manifestations of libido. It is therefore difficult to believe that the intensity of libido can make the difference between mature and immature sexuality. Rather the difference seems to be conditioned by a change in the localization of libido (if such an expression be permitted). In contradistinction to its medical definition, the libido of a child is occupied far more with subsidiary functions of a mental and physical nature than with local sexual functions. This being so, one is tempted to withdraw the predicate "sexualis" from the term "libido" and to strike out the sexual definition of libido given in Freud's *Three Essays on the Theory of Sexuality*. The necessity for this becomes really urgent when we ask ourselves whether the intense joys and sorrows of a child in the first years of his life, that is, *at the presexual stage,* are conditioned solely by his sexual libido.

269   Freud has pronounced himself in favour of this supposition. There is no need for me to repeat here the reasons which compelled me to postulate a presexual stage. The caterpillar stage possesses an alimentary libido but no sexual libido; we have to put it like that if we want to retain the energic view which the libido theory offers us. I think there is nothing for it but to abandon the sexual definition of libido, or we shall lose what is valuable in the libido theory, namely the energic point of view. For a long time now the need to give the concept of libido breathing-space and to remove it from the narrow confines of the sexual definition has forced itself on the psychoanalytical school. One never wearied of insisting that sexuality was not to

be taken too literally but in a wider sense; yet exactly *how* remained obscure and so could not satisfy the serious critics.

270   I do not think I am going astray if I see the real value of the concept of libido not in its sexual definition but in its energic view, thanks to which we are in possession of an extremely valuable heuristic principle. We are also indebted to the energic view for dynamic images and correlations which are of inestimable value to us in the chaos of the psychic world. Freudians would be wrong not to listen to those critics who accuse our libido theory of mysticism and unintelligibility. We were deceiving ourselves when we believed that we could make the *libido sexualis* the vehicle of an energic conception of psychic life, and if many of Freud's school still believe that they are in possession of a well-defined and, so to speak, concrete conception of libido, they are not aware that this concept has been put to uses which far exceed the bounds of any sexual definition. Consequently the critics are right when they object that the libido theory purports to explain things which do not properly belong to its sphere. This really does evoke the impression that we are operating with a mystical entity.

THE PROBLEM OF LIBIDO IN DEMENTIA PRAECOX

271   In my book *Wandlungen und Symbole der Libido* I tried to furnish proof of these transgressions and at the same time to show the need for a new conception of libido which took account only of the energic view. Freud himself was forced to admit that his original conception of libido might possibly be too narrow when he tried to apply the energic view consistently to a famous case of dementia praecox—the so-called Schreber case.[5] This case is concerned among other things with that well-known problem in the psychology of dementia praecox, the loss of adaptation to reality, a peculiar phenomenon consisting in the special tendency of these patients to construct an inner fantasy world of their own, surrendering for this purpose their adaptation to reality.

272   One aspect of this phenomenon, the absence of emotional

5 ["Psycho-Analytic Notes on an Autobiographical Account of a Case of Paranoia (Dementia Paranoides)."]

rapport, will be well known to you, as this is a striking disturbance of the reality function. By dint of much psychoanalytic work with these patients we established that this lack of adaptation to reality is compensated by a progressive increase in the creation of fantasies, which goes so far that the dream world becomes more real for the patient than external reality. Schreber found an excellent figurative description for this phenomenon in his delusion about the "end of the world." He thus depicts the loss of reality in a very concrete way. The dynamic explanation is simple: we say that libido has withdrawn more and more from the external world into the inner world of fantasy, and there had to create, as a substitute for the lost world, a so-called reality equivalent. This substitute is built up piece by piece, so to speak, and it is most interesting to see out of what psychological material this inner world is constructed.

273   This way of looking at the displacement of libido is based on the everyday use of the term, its original, purely sexual connotation being very rarely remembered. In actual practice we speak simply of *libido,* and this is understood in so innocuous a sense that Claparède once remarked to me that one could just as well use the word "interest." The customary use of the term has developed, quite naturally and spontaneously, into a usage which makes it possible to explain Schreber's end of the world simply as a withdrawal of libido. On this occasion Freud remembered his original sexual definition of libido and tried to come to terms with the change of meaning that had quietly taken place in the meantime. In his paper on Schreber he asks himself whether *what the psychoanalytic school calls libido and conceives as "interest from erotic sources" coincides with interest in general.* You see that, putting the problem in this way, Freud asks himself the question which Claparède had already answered in practice.

274   Freud thus broaches the question of whether the loss of reality in schizophrenia, to which I drew attention in my "Psychology of Dementia Praecox," [6] is due entirely to the withdrawal of erotic interest, or whether this coincides with objective interest in general. We can hardly suppose that the normal "fonction du réel" (Janet) is maintained solely by erotic interest. The fact

[6] [The first paper in *The Psychogenesis of Mental Disease,* Collected Works, Vol. 3.]

is that in very many cases reality disappears altogether, so that not a trace of psychological adaptation can be found in these patients. (In these states reality is replaced by complex contents.) We are therefore compelled to admit that not only the erotic interest, but all interest whatsoever, has got lost, and with it the whole adaptation to reality.

275   Earlier, in my "Psychology of Dementia Praecox," I tried to get round this difficulty by using the expression "psychic energy," because I could not base the theory of dementia praecox on the theory of displacements of libido sexually defined. My experience—at that time chiefly psychiatric—did not permit me to understand this latter theory: only later did I come to realize its partial correctness as regards the neuroses, thanks to increased experiences in the field of hysteria and obsessional neurosis. Abnormal displacements of libido, quite definitely sexual, do in fact play a great role in these illnesses. But although very characteristic repressions of sexual libido do take place in the neuroses, the loss of reality so typical of dementia praecox never occurs. In dementia praecox the loss of the reality function is so extreme that it must involve the loss of other instinctual forces whose sexual character must be denied absolutely, for no one is likely to maintain that reality is a function of sex, Moreover, if it were, the withdrawal of erotic interest in the neuroses would necessarily entail a loss of reality comparable to that which occurs in dementia praecox. But, as I said before, this is not the case.

276   ⟨Another thing to be considered—as Freud also pointed out in his work on the Schreber case—is that the introversion of sexual libido leads to an investment of the ego which might conceivably produce that effect of loss of reality. It is indeed tempting to explain the psychology of the loss in this way. But when we examine more closely the various things that can arise from the withdrawal and introversion of sexual libido, we come to see that though it can produce the psychology of an ascetic anchorite, it cannot produce dementia praecox. The anchorite's whole endeavour is to exterminate every trace of sexual interest, and this is something that cannot be asserted of dementia praecox.[7]⟩

7 ⟨It might be objected that dementia praecox is characterized not only by the introversion of sexual libido but also by a regression to the infantile level, and

277   These facts have made it impossible for me to apply Freud's libido theory to dementia praecox. I am also of the opinion that Abraham's essay on this subject [8] is theoretically untenable from the standpoint of Freud's conception of libido. Abraham's belief that the paranoid system, or the schizophrenic symptomatology, is produced by the withdrawal of sexual libido from the outside world cannot be justified in terms of our present knowledge. For, as Freud has clearly shown, a mere introversion or regression of libido invariably leads to a neurosis and not to dementia praecox. It seems to me impossible simply to transfer the libido theory to dementia praecox, because this disease shows a loss of reality which cannot be explained solely by the loss of erotic interest.

THE GENETIC CONCEPTION OF LIBIDO

278   The attitude of reserve which I adopted towards the ubiquity of sexuality in my foreword to "The Psychology of Dementia Praecox," despite the fact that I recognized the psychological mechanisms pointed out by Freud, was dictated by the position of the libido theory at that time. Its sexual definition did not permit me to explain functional disturbances which affect the indefinite sphere of the hunger drive just as much as that of sex solely in the light of a sexual libido theory. Freud's libido theory had long seemed to me inapplicable to dementia praecox. In my analytical work I noticed that, with growing experience, a slow change in my conception of libido had taken place. Instead of the descriptive definition set forth in Freud's *Three Essays*, there gradually took shape a genetic definition of libido, which enabled me to replace the expression "psychic energy" by "libido." I had to tell myself: if the reality function consists nowadays to only a very small extent of sexual libido

that this constitutes the difference between the anchorite and the schizophrenic. This is certainly correct, but it would still have to be proved that in dementia praecox it is regularly and exclusively the erotic interest which goes into a regression. It seems to me rather difficult to prove this, because erotic interest would then have to be understood as the "Eros" of the old philosophers. But that can hardly be meant. I know cases of dementia praecox where all regard for self-preservation disappears, but not the very lively erotic interests.)

[8] ["The Psycho-Sexual Differences between Hysteria and Dementia Praecox."]

and to a far greater extent of other instinctual forces, then it is very important to consider whether, phylogenetically speaking, the reality function is not, at least very largely, of sexual origin. It is impossible to answer this question directly, but we can seek to approach it by a circuitous route.

279   A cursory glance at the history of evolution suffices to show that numerous complicated functions, which today must be denied all trace of sexuality, were originally nothing but offshoots of the reproductive instinct. As we know, an important change occurred in the principles of reproduction during the ascent through the animal kingdom: the vast numbers of gametes which chance fertilization made necessary were progressively reduced in favour of assured fertilization and effective protection of the young. The decreased production of ova and spermatozoa set free considerable quantities of energy for conversion into the mechanisms of attraction and protection of offspring, etc. Thus we find the first stirrings of the artistic impulse in animals, but subservient to the reproductive instinct and limited to the breeding season. The original sexual character of these biological phenomena gradually disappears as they become organically fixed and achieve functional independence. Although there can be no doubt that music originally belonged to the reproductive sphere, it would be an unjustified and fantastic generalization to put music in the same category as sex. Such a terminology would be tantamount to treating of Cologne cathedral in a text-book of mineralogy, on the ground that it consisted very largely of stones.

280   Up to now we have spoken of libido as the instinct for propagation or for the preservation of the species, and have kept within the confines of a view which contrasts libido with hunger in the same way as the instinct for the preservation of the species is contrasted with the instinct for self-preservation. In nature, of course, this artificial distinction does not exist. There we see only a continuous life-urge, a will to live, which seeks to ensure the continuance of the whole species through the preservation of the individual. Thus far our conception of libido coincides with Schopenhauer's Will, inasmuch as a movement perceived from the outside can only be grasped as the manifestation of an inner will or desire. Once we have arrived at the bold conjecture that the libido which was originally employed in the

production of ova and spermatozoa is now firmly organized in the function of nest-building, for instance, and can no longer be employed otherwise, we are compelled to include every striving and every desire, as well as hunger, in this conception. There is no longer any justification for differentiating in principle between the desire to build nests and the desire to eat.[9]

281   I think you will already see where our argument is leading us. We are in the process of carrying through the energic point of view consistently, putting the energic mode of action in the place of the purely formal functioning. Just as the older sciences were always talking of reciprocal actions in nature, and this old-fashioned point of view was replaced by the law of the conservation of energy, so here too, in the realm of psychology, we are seeking to replace the reciprocal action of co-ordinated psychic faculties by an energy conceived to be homogeneous. We thus take cognizance of the justified criticism that the psychoanalytic school is operating with a mystical conception of libido.

282   For this reason I must dispel the illusion that the whole psychoanalytic school has a clearly understood and concrete conception of libido. I maintain that the libido with which we operate is not only not concrete or known, but is a complete X, a pure hypothesis, a model or counter, and is no more concretely conceivable than the energy known to the world of physics. Only in this way can we escape those violent transgressions of the proper boundaries, which happen time and again when we try to reduce co-ordinated forces to one another. ⟨We shall never be able to explain the mechanics of solid bodies or of electromagnetic phenomena in terms of a theory of light, for mechanics and electromagnetism are not light. Moreover, strictly speaking, it is not physical forces that change into one another, but the energy that changes its outward form. Forces are phenomenal manifestations; what underlies their relations with one another is the hypothetical idea of energy, which is, of course, entirely psychological and has nothing to do with so-called objective reality.⟩ This same conceptual achievement that has taken place in physics we seek to accomplish for the libido theory. We want to give the concept of libido the position that really belongs to it, which is a purely energic one, so that we can conceive the

9 [Pars. 278–80 and 274–75 reappear with certain modifications and additions in *Symbols of Transformation*, pars. 192ff.—EDITORS.]

life-process in terms of energy and replace the old idea of reciprocal action by relations of absolute equivalence. We shall not
be disturbed if we are met with the cry of vitalism. We are as
far removed from any belief in a specific life-force as from any
other metaphysical assertion. Libido is intended simply as a
name for the energy which manifests itself in the life-process and
is perceived subjectively as conation and desire. It is hardly necessary to defend this view. It brings us into line with a powerful
current of ideas that seeks to comprehend the world of appearances energically. Suffice it to say that everything we perceive
can only be understood as an effect of force.

283   In the diversity of natural phenomena we see desire—libido
—taking the most variegated forms. In early childhood it appears
at first wholly in the form of the nutritive instinct which builds
up the body. As the body develops, new spheres of activity are
opened up successively for the libido. A definitive and extremely
important sphere of activity is sexuality, which to begin with
appears closely bound up with the function of nutrition (one
has only to think of the influence of nutritional factors on propagation in the lower animals and plants). In the sphere of sexuality the libido acquires a form whose tremendous importance
gives us the justification for using the ambiguous term "libido"
at all. Here it appears at first in the form of an undifferentiated,
primary libido, as the energy of growth that causes cell-division,
budding, etc. in individuals.

284   Out of this primary, sexual libido, which produces from one
small organism millions of ova and spermatozoa, there developed, by a tremendous restriction of fertility, offshoots whose
function is maintained by a specifically differentiated libido.
This differentiated libido is now "desexualized" by being divested of its original function of producing eggs and sperm, nor
is there any possibility of restoring it to its original function.
Thus the whole process of development consists in a progressive
absorption of the primary libido, which produced nothing but
gametes, into the secondary functions of attraction and protection of offspring. This development presupposes a quite different and much more complicated relation to reality, a genuine
reality function which is inseparably connected with the needs
of reproduction. In other words, the altered mode of reproduction brings with it, as a correlate, a correspondingly enhanced

125

adaptation to reality. This, of course, does not imply that the reality function owes its existence exclusively to the differentiation in reproduction. I am fully aware of the indefinitely large role played by the nutritive function.

285   In this way we gain some insight into the factors originally conditioning the reality function. It would be a fundamental error to say that its driving force is a sexual one. It *was* in large measure a sexual one originally, but even then not exclusively so.

286   The process of absorption of primary libido into secondary functions probably always occurred in the form of "libidinal affluxes," that is to say sexuality was diverted from its original destination and part of it used for the mechanisms of attraction and protection of the young—functions which gradually increase the higher you go in the phylogenetic scale. This transfer of sexual libido from the sexual sphere to subsidiary functions is still taking place. (Malthusianism, for instance, is an artificial continuation of the natural tendency.) Wherever this operation occurs without detriment to the adaptation of the individual we call it "sublimation," and "repression" when the attempt fails.

287   The descriptive standpoint of psychoanalysis views the multiplicity of instincts, among them the sexual instinct, as partial phenomena, and, in addition, recognizes certain affluxes of libido to nonsexual instincts.

288   The genetic standpoint is different. It regards the multiplicity of instincts as issuing from a relative unity, the libido; it sees how portions of libido continually split off from the reproductive function, add themselves as libidinal affluxes to the newly formed functions, and finally merge into them.

289   From this point of view we can rightly say that the schizophrenic withdraws his libido from the outside world and in consequence suffers a loss of reality compensated by an increase in fantasy activity.

INFANTILE PERVERSIONS

290   We shall now try to fit this new conception of libido into the theory of infantile sexuality, which is so very important for the

theory of neurosis. In infants we find that libido as energy, as a vital activity, first manifests itself in the nutritional zone, where, in the act of sucking, food is taken in with a rhythmic movement and with every sign of satisfaction. With the growth of the individual and development of his organs the libido creates for itself new avenues of activity. The primary model of rhythmic movement, producing pleasure and satisfaction, is now transferred to the zone of the other functions, with sexuality as its ultimate goal. A considerable portion of the "alimentary libido" has to convert itself into "sexual libido." This transition does not take place quite suddenly at puberty, but only very gradually during the course of childhood. The libido can free itself only with difficulty and quite slowly from the modality of the nutritive function in order to pass over into the sexual function.

291   In this transitional stage there are, so far as I am able to judge, two distinct phases: the phase of sucking, and the phase of displaced rhythmic activity. Sucking belongs by its very nature to the sphere of the nutritive function, but outgrows it by ceasing to be a function of nutrition and becoming a rhythmic activity aiming at pleasure and satisfaction without intake of nourishment. At this point the hand comes in as an auxiliary organ. It appears even more clearly as an auxiliary organ in the phase of displaced rhythmic activity for pleasure, which then leaves the oral zone and turns to other regions. As a rule, it is the other body-openings that become the first objects of libidinal interest; then the skin, or special parts of it. The activities carried out in these places, taking the form of rubbing, boring, picking, pulling, and so forth, follow a certain rhythm and serve to produce pleasure. After lingering for a while at these stations, the libido continues its wanderings until it reaches the sexual zone, where it may provide occasion for the first attempts at masturbation. In the course of its migrations the libido carries traces of the nutritional phase into its new field of operations, which readily accounts for the many intimate connections between the nutritive and the sexual function.[10] This migration of libido takes place during the presexual stage, whose special distinguishing-mark is that the libido gradually sloughs off the

10 [Pars. 290–91 likewise recur with small changes in *Symbols of Transformation*, par. 206.—EDITORS.]

character of the nutritive instinct and assumes that of the sexual instinct.[11] At the stage of nutrition, therefore, we cannot yet speak of a true sexual libido.

292   In consequence, we are obliged to qualify the so-called polymorphous-perverse sexuality of early infancy. The polymorphism of libidinal strivings at this period can be explained as the gradual migration of libido, stage by stage, away from the sphere of the nutritive function into that of the sexual function. Thus the term "perverse," so bitterly attacked by our critics, can be dropped, since it creates a false impression.

293   When a chemical substance breaks up into its elements, these elements are, under those conditions, products of disintegration. But it is not permissible to describe all elements whatsoever as products of disintegration. Perversions are disturbed products of a developed sexuality. They are never the initial stages of sexuality, although there is an undoubted similarity between the initial stage and the product of disintegration. As sexuality develops, its infantile stages, which should no longer be regarded as "perverse" but as rudimentary and provisional, resolve themselves into normal sexuality. The more smoothly the libido withdraws from its provisional positions, the more quickly and completely does the formation of normal sexuality take place. It is of the essence of normal sexuality that all those early infantile tendencies which are not yet sexual should be sloughed off as much as possible. The less this is so, the more perverse will sexuality become. Here the expression "perverse" is altogether appropriate. The basic conditioning factor in perversion, therefore, is an infantile, insufficiently developed state of sexuality. The expression "polymorphous-perverse" has been borrowed from the psychology of neurosis and projected backwards into the psychology of the child, where of course it is quite out of place.

11 (I must ask the reader not to misunderstand my figurative way of speaking. It is, of course, not libido as energy that gradually frees itself from the function of nutrition, but libido as a function, which is bound up with the slow changes of organic growth.)

4. NEUROSIS AND AETIOLOGICAL FACTORS IN CHILDHOOD

294   Now that we have ascertained what is to be understood by infantile sexuality, we can follow up the discussion of the theory of neurosis, which we began in the first lecture and then dropped. We followed the theory of neurosis up to the point where we ran up against Freud's statement that the predisposition which makes traumatic experiences pathogenically effective is a sexual one. Helped by our reflections since then, we can now understand how that sexual predisposition is to be conceived: it is a retardation, a check in the process of freeing the libido from the activities of the presexual stage. The disturbance must be regarded in the first place as a temporary fixation: the libido lingers too long at certain stations in the course of its migration from the nutritive function to the sexual function. This produces a state of disharmony because provisional and, as it were, outworn activities still persist at a period when they should have been given up. This formula can be applied to all those infantile features which are so prevalent in neurotics that no attentive observer can have failed to notice them. In dementia praecox the infantilism is so striking that it has even given a telltale name to one particular syndrome—*hebephrenia* (literally, 'adolescent mind').

295   The matter is not ended, however, by saying that the libido lingers too long in the preliminary stages. For while the libido is lingering, time does not stand still, and the development of the individual is proceeding apace. Physical maturation heightens the discrepancy between the perseverating infantile activity and the demands of later years with their changed conditions of life. In this way the foundation is laid for a dissociation of the personality, and hence for a conflict, which is the real basis of a neurosis. The more the libido is engaged in retarded activities, the more intense will the conflict be. The particular experience

best suited to make this conflict manifest is a traumatic or pathogenic one.

296   As Freud has shown in his early writings, one can easily
imagine a neurosis arising in this way. It was a conception that
fitted in quite well with the views of Janet, who attributed a
neurosis to some kind of defect. From this standpoint one could
regard neurosis as a product of retarded affective development,
and I can easily imagine that this conception must seem self-
evident to anyone who is inclined to derive the neuroses more
or less directly from a hereditary taint or congenital degeneracy.
Unfortunately the real state of affairs is much more complicated. In order to give you some idea of these complications, I
shall cite a very ordinary example of hysteria, which I hope will
show you how characteristic and how extremely important they
are theoretically.

297   You will probably remember the case of the young hysteric
I mentioned earlier, who, surprisingly enough, did not react to
a situation which might have been expected to make a profound
impression on her, and yet displayed an unexpected and patho-
logically violent reaction to a quite ordinary occurrence. We
took this occasion to express our doubt as to the aetiological
significance of the trauma, and to investigate more closely the
so-called predisposition which rendered the trauma effective.
The result of that investigation led to the conclusion just mentioned, that it is by no means improbable that the origin of a
neurosis is due to a retardation of affective development.

298   You will now ask in what way the patient's affective development was retarded. The answer is that she lived in a world of
fantasy which can only be described as infantile. It is unnecessary for me to give you a description of these fantasies, for, as
neurologists or psychiatrists, you undoubtedly have a daily opportunity to listen to the childish prejudices, illusions, and emotional demands of neurotics. The disinclination to face stern
reality is the distinguishing feature of these fantasies; there is a
lack of seriousness, a playfulness in them, which sometimes
frivolously disguises real difficulties, at other times makes mountains out of molehills, always thinking up fantastic ways of
evading the demands of real life. We immediately recognize in
them the intemperate psychic attitude of the child to reality, his
precarious judgment, his lack of orientation, his dislike of un-

pleasant duties. With such an infantile mentality all manner of wishful fantasies and illusions can grow luxuriantly, and this is where the danger comes in. By means of these fantasies people can easily slip into an unreal and completely unadapted attitude to the world, which sooner or later must lead to catastrophe.

THE TRAUMA THEORY CRITICIZED

299   If we follow the patient's infantile fantasy-life back into earliest childhood, we find, it is true, many obviously outstanding scenes which might well serve to provide fresh food for this or that fantastic variation, but it would be vain to search for the so-called traumatic elements from which something pathological, for instance her abnormal fantasy activity, might have originated. There were plenty of "traumatic" scenes, but they did not lie in early childhood; and the few scenes of early childhood which were remembered did not appear to be traumatic, being more like accidental experiences which passed by without having any effect worth mentioning on her fantasies. The earliest fantasies consisted of all sorts of vague and half-understood impressions she had received of her parents. All sorts of special feelings clustered round the father, fluctuating between fear, horror, aversion, disgust, love, and ecstasy. The case was like so many other cases of hysteria for which no traumatic aetiology can be found; they are rooted instead in a peculiar, premature fantasy activity which permanently retains its infantile character.

300   You will object that it is just that scene with the bolting horses that represents the trauma, and that this was obviously the model for that nocturnal scene eighteen years later, when the patient could not get out of the way of the horses trotting along behind her and wanted to throw herself into the river, following the model of the horses and carriage plunging down the ravine. From this moment on she also suffered from hysterical twilight states. But, as I tried to show you in my earlier lecture, we find no trace of any such aetiological connection in the development of her fantasy system. It is as though the danger of losing her life, that first time with the bolting horses, passed by without noticeable effect. In all the years following

that experience there was no discernible trace of that fright. It was as though it had never happened. In parenthesis let me add that perhaps it never happened at all. There is nothing to prevent it from being sheer fantasy, for here I have only the statements of the patient to rely on.[1]

301   Suddenly, after eighteen years, this experience becomes significant, is reproduced and acted out in all its details. The old theory says: the previously blocked affect has suddenly forced its way to the surface. This assumption is extremely unlikely and becomes still more inconceivable when we consider that the story of the bolting horses may not even be true. Be that as it may, it is almost inconceivable that an affect should remain buried for years and then suddenly explode at an unsuitable opportunity.

302   It is very suspicious, too, that patients often have a pronounced tendency to account for their ailments by some long-past experience, ingeniously drawing the analyst's attention away from the present to some false track in the past. This false track was the one pursued by the first psychoanalytical theory. But to this false hypothesis we owe an insight into the determination of neurotic symptoms which we should never have reached if the investigators had not trodden this path, guided into it, really, by the tendency of the patient to mislead. I think that only those who regard the happenings in this world as a concatenation of errors and accidents, and who therefore believe that the pedagogic hand of the rationalist is constantly needed to guide us, can ever imagine that this path was an aberration from which we should have been warned off with a signboard. Besides the deeper insight into psychological determination, we owe to this "error" a method of inquiry of incalculable importance. It is for us to rejoice and be thankful that Freud had the courage to let himself be guided along this path. Not thus is the progress of science hindered, but rather by blind adherence to insights once gained, by the typical conservatism of authority, by the childish vanity of the savant and his fear of making mistakes. This lack of courage is considerably more injurious to the name of science than an honest error. When

1 (It may not be superfluous to remark that there are still people who believe that psychologists swallow the lies of their patients. That is quite impossible. Lies are fantasies, and we deal in fantasies.)

will there be an end to the incessant squabbling about who is right? One has only to look at the history of science: how many have *been* right, and how few have *remained* right!

THE PARENTAL COMPLEX

303   But to return to our case. The question that now arises is this: if the old trauma is not of aetiological significance, then the cause of the manifest neurosis is obviously to be sought in the retardation of affective development. We must therefore regard the patient's statement that her hysterical twilight states were caused by the fright she got with the horses as null and void, although that fright was the starting-point for her manifest illness. This experience merely *seems* to be important without being so in reality, a formulation which is true of most other traumata. They merely *seem* to be important because they provide occasion for the manifestation of a condition that has long been abnormal. The abnormal condition, as we have already explained, consists in the anachronistic persistence of an infantile stage of libido development. The patients continue to hang on to forms of libido activity which they should have abandoned long ago. It is almost impossible to catalogue these forms, so extraordinarily varied are they. The commonest, which is scarcely ever absent, is an excessive fantasy activity characterized by a thoughtless overvaluation of subjective wishes. Excessive fantasy activity is always a sign of faulty application of libido to reality. Instead of being used for the best possible adaptation to the actual circumstances, it gets stuck in fantastic applications. We call this state one of partial introversion when libido is used for the maintenance of fantasies and illusions instead of being adapted to the actual conditions of life.

304   A regular concomitant of this retardation of affective development is the *parental complex*. When the libido is not used for purposes of real adaptation it is always more or less introverted.[2] The material content of the psychic world consists of

2 (Introversion does not mean that libido simply accumulates inactively. But it is used for the creation of fantasies and illusions when the introversion results in regression to an infantile mode of adaptation. Introversion can also lead to action on a rational plane.)

memories, that is, of material from the individual's past (aside from actual perceptions). If the libido is partially or totally introverted, it invests to a greater or lesser degree large areas of memory, with the result that these reminiscences acquire a vitality that no longer properly belongs to them. The patients then live more or less entirely in the world of the past. They battle with difficulties which once played a role in their lives but which ought to have faded out long ago. They still worry, or rather are forced to worry, about things which should long since have ceased to be important. They amuse or torment themselves with fancies which, in the normal course of events, were once significant but no longer have any significance for adults.

305   Among the things that were of the utmost significance at the infantile period the most influential are the personalities of the parents. Even when the parents have long been dead and have lost, or should have lost, all significance, the situation of the patient having perhaps completely changed since then, they are still somehow present and as important as if they were still alive. The patient's love, admiration, resistance, hatred, and rebelliousness still cling to their effigies, transfigured by affection or distorted by envy, and often bearing little resemblance to the erstwhile reality. It was this fact that compelled me to speak no longer of "father" and "mother" but to employ instead the term "imago," because these fantasies are not concerned any more with the real father and mother but with subjective and often very much distorted images of them which lead a shadowy but nonetheless potent existence in the mind of the patient.

306   The complex of the parental imagos, that is, the whole tissue of ideas relating to the parents, provides an important field of activity for the introverted libido. I should mention in passing that the complex in itself leads but a shadowy existence if it is not invested with libido. In accordance with the earlier usage worked out in my *Studies in Word Association,* the word "complex" denoted a system of ideas already invested with libido and activated by it. But this system also exists *in potentia,* ready for possible action, even when not temporarily or permanently invested with libido.

PARENTAL INFLUENCES ON CHILDREN

307   At the time when psychoanalytic theory was still dominated by the trauma concept and, in conformity with that view, was inclined to look for the *causa efficiens* of the neurosis in the past, it seemed to us that the parental complex was, as Freud called it, the "nuclear complex" of neurosis. The role of the parents seemed to be so powerful a factor that we were apt to blame them for all the subsequent complications in the life of the patient. Some years ago I discussed this in my paper, "The Significance of the Father in the Destiny of the Individual." [3] Once again we had allowed ourselves to be guided by the tendency of the patient to revert to the past, following the direction of his introverted libido. This time, certainly, it was no longer an external, accidental experience or event which seemed to produce the pathogenic effect; it was rather a psychological effect apparently arising out of the individual's difficulties in adapting to the conditions of the family milieu. The disharmony between the parents on the one hand and between the parents and the child on the other seemed especially liable to produce psychic currents in the child which were incompatible with his individual way of life.

308   In the paper just alluded to I cited a number of instances, taken from a wealth of material on this subject, which show these effects particularly clearly. The effects apparently emanating from the parents are not limited to the endless recriminations of their neurotic offspring, who constantly lay the blame for their illness on their family circumstances or bad upbringing, but extend even to actual events in the life of the patients, where no such determining influence could have been expected. The lively imitativeness which we find in primitives as well as in children can give rise, in particularly sensitive children, to a peculiar inner identification with the parents, to a mental attitude so similar to theirs that effects in real life are sometimes produced which, even in detail, resemble the personal experiences of the parents.[4]

3 [See infra, pars. 670ff.]

4 ⟨I am discounting the inherited organic similarity which is naturally responsible for many things but by no means all.⟩

309   For the empirical material on this subject, I must refer you to the literature, but should just like to remind you that one of my pupils, Dr. Emma Fürst, has adduced valuable experimental proofs in regard to this problem. I have already referred to her researches in my lectures at Clark University.[5] By applying the association test to whole families, Dr. Fürst established the great conformity of reaction type among all members of one family. These experiments show that very often there exists an unconscious concordance of association between parents and children, which can only be explained as an intensive imitation or identification. The results of these researches indicate a far-reaching parallelism of biological tendencies that readily explains the sometimes astonishing similarity in the destinies of parents and children. Our destinies are as a rule the outcome of our psychological tendencies.

310   These facts enable us to understand why not only the patients themselves, but the theories that have been built on these researches, tend to assume that neurosis is the result of the characterological influence of the parents on the children. This assumption is, moreover, supported by the experience which lies at the base of all education, namely, the plasticity of the child's mind, which is commonly compared with soft wax, taking up and preserving all impressions. We know that the first impressions of childhood accompany us inalienably throughout life, and that, just as indestructibly, certain educational influences can keep people all their lives within those limits. In these circumstances it is not surprising that conflicts break out between the personality moulded by educational and other influences of the infantile milieu and one's own individual style of life. It is a conflict which all those must face who are called upon to live a life that is independent and creative.

311   Owing to the enormous influence which childhood has on the later development of character, you will readily understand why one would like to attribute the cause of a neurosis directly to the influences of the infantile environment. I must confess

5 [Fürst, "Statistical Investigations on Word-Associations and on Familial Agreement in Reaction Type among Uneducated Persons" (orig. 1905). Jung's discussion of her work occurred in the second of the Clark Lectures under the title "Familial Constellations," and it appears as the latter part of "The Association Method" in Vol. 2.—EDITORS.]

that I have known cases in which any other explanation seemed to me less plausible. There are indeed parents whose own contradictory nature causes them to treat their children in so unreasonable a fashion that the children's illness would appear to be unavoidable. Hence it is almost a rule among nerve specialists to remove neurotic children, whenever possible, from the dangerous family atmosphere and place them among more healthy influences, where, even without any medical treatment, they thrive much better than at home. There are many neurotic patients who were clearly neurotic as children and so have never been free from illness since childhood. In such cases the view outlined above seems generally valid.

THE INFANTILE MENTALITY

312   This knowledge, which for the time being seemed to us definitive, was considerably deepened by the researches of Freud and the psychoanalytic school. The parent-child relationship was studied in all its details, since it was just this relationship which was considered aetiologically important. It was soon noticed that these patients really did live partly or entirely in their childhood world, although themselves quite unconscious of this fact. On the contrary, it was the arduous task of psychoanalysis to investigate the psychological mode of adaptation so thoroughly that one could put one's finger on the infantile misunderstandings. As you know, a striking number of neurotics were spoiled as children. Such cases offer the best and clearest examples of the infantilism of their psychological mode of adaptation. They start out in life expecting the same friendly reception, tenderness, and easy success to which they were accustomed by their parents in their youth. Even very intelligent patients are incapable of seeing that from the very beginning they owe the complications of their lives as well as their neurosis to dragging their infantile emotional attitude along with them. The small world of the child, the family milieu, is the model for the big world. The more intensely the family sets its stamp on the child, the more he will be emotionally inclined, as an adult, to see in the great world his former small world. Of course this must not be taken as a conscious intellectual process. On the contrary,

the patient feels and sees the difference between now and then, and tries as well as he can to adapt himself. Perhaps he will even believe himself perfectly adapted, since he may be able to grasp the situation intellectually, but that does not prevent his emotions from lagging far behind his intellectual insight.

313   It is scarcely necessary to give you examples of this phenomenon, for it is an everyday experience that our emotions never come up to the level of our insight. It is exactly the same with the neurotic, but greatly intensified. He may perhaps believe that, except for his neurosis, he is a normal person, fully adapted to the conditions of life. It never crosses his mind that he has still not given up certain infantile demands, that he still carries with him, in the background, expectations and illusions of which he has never made himself conscious. He indulges in all sorts of pet fantasies, of which he is seldom, if ever, so conscious that he knows that he has them. Very often they exist only as emotional expectations, hopes, prejudices, and so forth. In this case we call them unconscious fantasies. Sometimes they appear on the fringe of consciousness as fleeting thoughts, only to vanish again the next moment, so that the patient is unable to say whether he had such fantasies or not. It is only during psychoanalytic treatment that most patients learn to retain and observe these fugitive thoughts. Although most fantasies were once conscious, for a moment, as fleeting thoughts, it would not do to call them *conscious,* because most of the time they are practically *unconscious.* It is therefore right to call them unconscious fantasies. Of course there are also infantile fantasies which are perfectly conscious and can be reproduced at any time.

5. THE FANTASIES OF THE UNCONSCIOUS

314   The realm of unconscious infantile fantasies has become the real object of psychoanalytic research, for it seems to offer the key to the aetiology of neurosis. Here, quite otherwise than with the trauma theory, we are forced by all the reasons we have mentioned to assume that the roots of the psychological present are to be found in the family history of the patient.

315   The fantasy systems which patients present on being questioned are mostly of a composite nature and are elaborated like a novel or a drama. But, despite their elaboration, they are of relatively little value in investigating the unconscious. Just because they are conscious, they defer too much to the demands of etiquette and social morality. They have been purged of all painful personal details, and also of everything ugly, thereby becoming socially presentable and revealing very little. The more valuable and evidently more influential fantasies are not conscious, in the sense previously defined, and so have to be dug out by the psychoanalytic technique.

316   Without wishing to enter fully into the question of technique, I must here meet an objection that is constantly heard. It is that the so-called unconscious fantasies are merely suggested to the patient and exist only in the mind of the analyst. This objection is on the same vulgar level as those which impute to us the crude mistakes of beginners. Only people with no psychological experience and no knowledge of the history of psychology are capable of making such accusations. No one with the faintest glimmering of mythology could possibly fail to see the startling parallels between the unconscious fantasies brought to light by the psychoanalytic school and mythological ideas. The objection that our knowledge of mythology has been suggested to the patient is without foundation, because the psychoanalytic school discovered the fantasies first and only then became acquainted with their mythology. Mythology, as we know, is something quite outside the ken of the medical man.

317   As these fantasies are unconscious, the patient is naturally unaware of their existence, and to question him about them directly would be quite pointless. Nevertheless it is said over and over again, not only by patients but by so-called normal persons: "But if I had such fantasies, surely I would know it!" But what is unconscious is in truth something that we do *not* know. Our opponents, too, are firmly convinced that such things do not exist. This *a priori* judgment is pure scholasticism and has no grounds to support it. We cannot possibly rest on the dogma that consciousness alone is the psyche, for we have daily proof that our consciousness is only a part of the psychic function. When the contents of our consciousness appear they are already in a highly complex state; the constellation of our thoughts from the material contained in our memory is a predominantly unconscious process. We are therefore obliged to assume, whether we like it or not, the existence of a non-conscious psychic sphere, even if only as a "negative borderline concept," like Kant's *Ding an sich*. Since we perceive effects whose origin cannot be found in consciousness, we are compelled to allow hypothetical contents to the sphere of the non-conscious, which means presupposing that the origin of those effects lies in the unconscious precisely because it is not conscious. This conception of the unconscious can hardly be accused of "mysticism." We do not pretend to know or to assert anything positive about the state of psychic elements in the unconscious. Instead, we have formulated symbolical concepts in a manner analogous to our formulation of conscious concepts, and this terminology has proved its value in practice.

THE CONCEPT OF THE UNCONSCIOUS

318   This way of thinking is the only possible one if we accept the axiom that "principles are not to be multiplied beyond the necessary." We therefore speak about the effects of the unconscious just as we do about the phenomena of consciousness. Great objection was taken to Freud's statement: "The unconscious can only wish." This was regarded as an unheard-of metaphysical assertion, something like a tenet from von Hartmann's *Philosophy of the Unconscious*. The indignation was

due simply to the fact that these critics, unknown to themselves, evidently started from a metaphysical conception of the unconscious as an *ens per se,* and naïvely projected their epistemologically unclarified ideas on to us. For us the unconscious is not an entity in this sense but a mere term, about whose metaphysical essence we do not permit ourselves to form any idea. In this we are unlike those arm-chair psychologists who are not only perfectly informed about the localization of the psyche in the brain and the physiological correlates of mental processes, but can assert positively that beyond consciousness there are nothing but "physiological processes in the cortex."

319   Such naïvetés should not be imputed to us. When Freud says that the unconscious can only wish, he is describing in symbolical terms effects whose source is not conscious, but which from the standpoint of conscious thinking can only be regarded as analogous to wishes. The psychoanalytic school is, moreover, aware that the discussion as to whether "wishing" is a suitable analogy or not can be reopened at any time. Anybody who knows a better one will be welcome. Instead of which, our opponents content themselves with denying the existence of these phenomena or else, if certain phenomena have to be admitted, they abstain from all theoretical formulations. This last point is understandable enough, since it is not everyone's business to think theoretically.

320   Once one has succeeded in freeing oneself from the dogma of the psyche's identity with consciousness, thus admitting the possible existence of extra-conscious psychic processes, one cannot, *a priori,* either assert or deny anything about the potentialities of the unconscious. The psychoanalytic school has been accused of making assertions without sufficient grounds. It seems to us that the abundant, perhaps too abundant case-material contained in the literature offers enough and more than enough grounds, yet it does not seem sufficient for our opponents. There must be a good deal of difference as to the meaning of the word "sufficient" in regard to the validity of these grounds. So we must ask: Why does the psychoanalytic school apparently demand far less exacting proofs of its formulations than its opponents?

321   The reason is simple. An engineer who has built a bridge and calculated its load needs no further proof of its holding

capacity. But a sceptical layman, who has no notion how a bridge is built, or what is the strength of the material used, will demand quite different proofs of its holding capacity, since he can have no confidence in it. It is chiefly the profound ignorance of our opponents about what we are doing that screws their demands up to such a pitch. In the second place, there are the countless theoretical misunderstandings: it is impossible for us to know them all and to clear them up. Just as we find in our patients new and ever more astounding misconceptions about the ways and aims of psychoanalysis, so our critics display an inexhaustible ingenuity in misunderstanding. You can see from our discussion of the concept of the unconscious just what kind of false philosophical assumptions can vitiate understanding of our terminology. Obviously a person who thinks of the unconscious as an absolute entity is bound to require proofs of a totally different kind, utterly beyond our power to give, as our opponents in fact do. Had we to offer proof of immortality, mountains of proofs of the weightiest nature would have to be furnished, very different from what would be required to demonstrate the existence of plasmodia in a malaria patient. Metaphysical expectations still bedevil scientific thinking far too much for the problems of psychoanalysis to be seen in their own frame of reference.

322   But, in fairness to our critics, I must admit that the psychoanalytic school has itself given rise to plenty of misunderstandings, even though in all innocence. One of the principal sources is the confusion that reigns in the theoretical sphere. Regrettable though it is, we have no presentable theory. You would understand this if you could see in concrete instances the enormous difficulties we have to wrestle with. Contrary to the opinion of nearly all the critics, Freud is anything rather than a theorist. He is an empiricist, as anyone must admit who is willing to go at all deeply into Freud's writings and to try to see his cases as he sees them. Unfortunately, our critics are not willing. As we have repeatedly been told, it is "repulsive and disgusting" to see them as Freud does. But how can anyone learn the nature of Freud's method if he allows himself to be put off by disgust? Just because people make no effort to accommodate themselves to Freud's point of view, adopted perhaps as a necessary working hypothesis, they come to the absurd conclusion

that he is a theorist. They readily assume that *Three Essays on the Theory of Sexuality* is simply a theory, invented by a speculative brain, and that everything is put into the patient's head by suggestion. But that is turning things upside down. This makes it easy for the critics, which is just what they want. They pay no attention at all to the "couple of case-histories" with which the psychoanalyst conscientiously documents his theoretical statements, but only to the theory and the formulation of technique. The weak spots of psychoanalysis are not to be found here—for psychoanalysis is essentially empirical—though here, undoubtedly, is a large and insufficiently cultivated field where the critics can romp to their heart's content. In the field of theory there are many uncertainties and not a few contradictions. We were conscious of this long before our learned critics began to honour us with their attentions.

THE DREAM

323   After this digression we will return to the question of unconscious fantasies which occupied us before. Nobody, as we have seen, has the right to assert their existence or define their qualities unless effects of unconscious origin are observed which can be expressed in terms of conscious symbolism. The only question is whether effects can in fact be found that comply with this expectation. The psychoanalytic school believes it has discovered such effects. I will mention the principal phenomenon at once: the dream.

324   Of this it may be said that it enters consciousness as a complex structure compounded of elements whose connection with each other is not conscious. Only afterwards, by adding a series of associations to the individual images in the dream, can we show that these images had their origin in certain memories of the recent past. We ask ourselves: Where have I seen or heard that? And then, by the ordinary process of association, comes the memory that certain parts of the dream have been consciously experienced, some the day before, some earlier. So far there will be general agreement, for these things have been known for a long time. To that extent the dream presents itself to us as a more or less unintelligible jumble of elements not at

first conscious and only recognized afterwards through their associations.[1] It should be added that not all parts of the dream have a recognizable quality from which their conscious character can be deduced; they are often, and indeed mostly, unrecognizable at first. Only afterwards does it occur to us that we have consciously experienced this or that part of the dream. From this standpoint alone we may regard the dream as a product of unconscious origin.

325   The technique for exploring the unconscious origin is the one I have just mentioned, used as a matter of course long before Freud by every dream-investigator. We simply try to remember where the parts of the dream came from. The psychoanalytic technique of dream elucidation is based on this very simple principle. It is a fact that certain parts of the dream are derived from our waking life, from events which, on account of their obvious unimportance, would have fallen into oblivion and were already on the way to becoming definitely unconscious. It is just these parts that are the effects of "unconscious ideas." Exception has been taken to this expression too. Naturally we do not take things nearly so concretely, not to say ponderously, as our critics. Certainly this expression is nothing more than conscious symbolism—we were never in any doubt on that point. But it is perfectly clear and serves very well as a sign for an unknown psychic fact. As I have said before, we have no alternative but to conceive the unconscious by analogy with the conscious. We do not pretend that we understand a thing merely because we have invented a sonorous and all-but-incomprehensible name for it.

THE METHOD OF DREAM-ANALYSIS

326   The principle of psychoanalytic elucidation is, therefore, extraordinarily simple and has actually been known for a long time. The subsequent procedure follows logically along the

---

1 ⟨This might be disputed on the ground that it is an *a priori* assertion. I must remark, however, that this view conforms to the one generally accepted working hypothesis concerning the origin of dreams: that they are derived from the experiences and thoughts of the recent past. We are, therefore, moving on known ground.⟩

same lines. If we get really absorbed in a dream—which naturally never happens outside analysis—we shall succeed in discovering still more reminiscences about the individual dream-parts. But we are not always successful in finding reminiscences about some of them. These must be put aside for the time being. ⟨When I say "reminiscences" I do not mean only memories of actual experiences; I also mean the reproduction of meaningful associations and connections.⟩ The reminiscences so gathered are called the "dream-material." We treat this material in accordance with a generally accepted scientific principle. If you have any experimental material to work up, you compare its individual parts and classify them according to their similarities. You proceed in exactly the same way with dream-material; you look for the common features, whether of form or content.

327   In doing this one has to get rid, so far as possible, of certain prejudices. I have observed that the beginner is always looking for some special feature and then tries to force his material to conform to his expectations. I have noticed this particularly with colleagues who, because of the well-known prejudices and misunderstandings, were once passionate opponents of psychoanalysis. If it was my fate to analyse them, and they at last obtained real insight into the method, the first mistake they generally made in their psychoanalytic work was to do violence to the material by their own preconceived opinions. That is, they now vented their previous attitude to psychoanalysis on their material, which they could not assess objectively but only in terms of their subjective fantasies.

328   Once embarked on the task of examining the dream-material, you must not shrink from any comparison. The material usually consists of very disparate images, from which it is sometimes very difficult to extract the *tertium comparationis*. I must refrain from giving detailed examples, as it is quite impossible to discuss such voluminous material in a lecture. I would, however, like to call your attention to a paper by Rank on "a dream which interprets itself." [2] There you will see how extensive is the material that must be taken into account for purposes of comparison.

329   Hence, in exploring the unconscious, we proceed in the

[2] "Ein Traum, der sich selbst deutet" (1910).

usual way when conclusions are to be drawn by the comparative method. It has often been objected: Why should a dream have any unconscious content at all? This objection is in my view about as unscientific as it could possibly be. Every psychological element has its special history. Every sentence I utter has, besides the meaning consciously intended by me, its historical meaning, which may turn out to be quite different from its conscious meaning. I am expressing myself somewhat paradoxically on purpose: I do not mean that I could explain the historical meaning of every individual sentence. That is easier in the case of larger and more complex structures. Thus, it will be clear to everyone that, apart from the manifest content of a poem, the poem itself is especially characteristic of the poet in regard to its form, content, and manner of origin. While the poet merely gave expression in his poem to the mood of the moment, the literary historian will see things in it and behind it which the poet would never have suspected. The analysis which the literary historian makes of the poet's material is exactly comparable with the method of psychoanalysis, not excluding the mistakes that may creep in.

330   The psychoanalytic method can be compared with historical analysis and synthesis in general. Suppose, for instance, we did not understand the meaning of the baptismal rite practised in our churches today. The priest tells us: baptism means the admission of the child into the Christian community. But this does not satisfy us. Why is the child sprinkled with water? In order to understand this ceremony, we must gather together from the whole history of ritual, that is, from mankind's memories of the relevant traditions, a body of comparative material culled from the most varied sources:

1. Baptism is clearly a rite of initiation, a consecration. Therefore we have to collect all memories in which any initiation rites are preserved.

2. The act of baptism is performed with water. For this special form another series of memories must be collected, namely, of rites in which water is used.

3. The person to be baptized is sprinkled with water. Here we have to collect all those rites in which the neophyte is sprinkled, immersed, etc.

4. All reminiscences from mythology, folklore, as well as

146

superstitious practices, etc., have to be recalled, in so far as they run in any way parallel to the symbolism of the baptismal act.

331   In this way we build up a comparative study of the act of baptism. We discover the elements out of which the baptismal act is formed; we ascertain, further, its original meaning, and at the same time become acquainted with the rich world of myths that have laid the foundation of religions and help us to understand the manifold and profound meanings of baptism. The analyst proceeds in the same way with a dream. He collects the historical parallels to every part of the dream, even the remotest, and tries to reconstruct the psychological history of the dream and its underlying meanings. Through this monographic elaboration we obtain, just as in the analysis of baptism, a profound insight into the marvellously delicate and meaningful network of unconscious determination—an insight that may legitimately be compared with the historical understanding of an act which we had hitherto regarded in a very superficial and one-sided way.

332   This excursus seemed to me unavoidable. In view of the numerous misunderstandings of all those who constantly seek to discredit the psychoanalytic method, I felt obliged to give you a very general account of the method and its position within the methodology of science. I do not doubt that there are superficial and improper applications of this method. But an intelligent critic should not allow this to detract from the method itself, any more than a bad surgeon should be used to discredit the value of surgery in general. I do not doubt, either, that not all the expositions of dream-psychology by psychoanalysts are entirely free from misunderstandings and distortions. But much of this is due to the fact that, precisely because of his training in the natural sciences, it is difficult for the medical man to get an intellectual grasp of a very subtle psychological method, even though he instinctively handles it correctly.

333   The method I have described is the one I adopt and the one to which I hold myself scientifically responsible. To give advice about dreams and to make direct attempts at interpretation is, in my opinion, absolutely wrong and scientifically inadmissible. It is not a methodological but a quite arbitrary proceeding which defeats itself by the sterility of its results, like every false method.

334   If I have made the attempt to illustrate the principles of the psychoanalytic method by means of dream-analysis it is because the dream is one of the clearest examples of psychic contents whose composition eludes direct understanding. When someone knocks in a nail with a hammer in order to hang something up, we can understand every detail of the action; it is immediately evident. It is otherwise with the act of baptism, where every phase is problematic. We call these actions, whose meaning and purpose are not immediately evident, symbolic actions, or symbols. On the basis of this reasoning we call a dream symbolic, because it is a psychological product whose origin, meaning, and purpose are obscure, and is therefore one of the purest products of unconscious constellation. As Freud aptly says, the dream is the *via regia* to the unconscious.

THE ASSOCIATION EXPERIMENT

335   There are many products of unconscious constellation besides dreams. In the association experiment we have a means of determining exactly the influence of the unconscious. We see these effects in the disturbances which I have called "complex indicators." The task which the association test sets the subject of the experiment is so extraordinarily simple that even children can accomplish it without difficulty. It is all the more surprising that, despite this, so many disturbances of the intended action should be registered. The only things that can regularly be shown to be causes of these disturbances are the partly conscious, partly unconscious constellations caused by complexes. In the majority of cases the connection of these disturbances with feeling-toned complexes can be demonstrated without difficulty. But very often we must have recourse to the psychoanalytic method in order to explain the connection; that is, we must ask the patient what associations he can give to the disturbed reactions.

336   In this way we obtain the historical material on which to base our judgment. It has been objected that the patient could then say whatever he liked—in other words, any old nonsense. This objection is made, I believe, on the unconscious assumption that the historian who gathers material for his monograph

is an imbecile, incapable of distinguishing real parallels from apparent ones and authentic reports from crude falsifications. The professional has means at his disposal for avoiding clumsy mistakes with certainty and more subtle ones with some probability. For anyone who understands psychoanalytic work it is a well-known fact that it is not so very difficult to see where there is coherence and where there is none. In addition, fraudulent statements are in the first place very significant of the person who makes them, and secondly they are easily recognized as fraudulent.

137   ⟨There is, however, another objection to be considered, which is more worth mentioning. One can ask oneself whether the reminiscences subsequently produced were really the basis of a dream. If, in the evening, I read an interesting account of a battle, and at night dream of the Balkan War, and then during analysis remember by association certain details in the account of the battle, even the most rigorous critic will fairly assume that my retrospective association is right and true. As I mentioned earlier, this is one of the most firmly entrenched hypotheses regarding the origin of dreams. All we have done is to apply this working hypothesis consistently to all the remaining associations relating to all other parts of the dream. Ultimately, we are saying no more than that this dream-element is linked with this association, that it therefore has something to do with it, that there is a connection between the two things. When a distinguished critic once remarked that, by means of psychoanalytic interpretations, one could even connect a cucumber with an elephant, this worthy showed us, by the very fact of associating "cucumber" with "elephant," that these two things somehow have an associative connection in his mind. One must have a lot of nerve and a magisterial judgment to declare that the human mind produces entirely meaningless associations. In this instance, only a little reflection is needed to understand the meaning of the association.⟩

138   In the association experiment we can ascertain the extraordinarily intense effects emanating from the unconscious precisely through the interference of complexes. The slips and faults in the experiment are nothing but prototypes of the mistakes we make in everyday life, the majority of which must be regarded as due to the interference of complexes. Freud has gathered

this material together in his book *The Psychopathology of Everyday Life*. It includes the so-called symptomatic actions—which from another point of view might equally well be called "symbolic actions"—and real slips like lapses of memory, slips of the tongue, and so on. All these phenomena are effects of unconscious constellations and are therefore so many gateways to the realm of the unconscious. When they are cumulative, we have to call them a neurosis, which from this point of view looks like a dysfunction and must be understood as the effect of an unconscious constellation.

339   Thus the association experiment is, not infrequently, a means of unlocking the unconscious directly, although mostly it is simply a technique for obtaining a wide selection of faulty reactions which can then be used for exploring the unconscious by psychoanalysis. At least, this is its most reliable form of application at present. However, it is possible that it will furnish other, especially valuable facts which would give us direct glimpses of the unconscious, but I do not consider this question sufficiently ripe to speak about yet.

6. THE OEDIPUS COMPLEX

340 After what I have told you about our method you may have gained rather more confidence in its scientific character, and will be inclined to agree that the fantasies which have been brought to light by psychoanalytic research are not just the arbitrary suppositions and illusions of psychoanalysts. Perhaps you will even be willing to listen patiently to what these products of unconscious fantasy can tell us.

341 The fantasies of adults are, in so far as they are conscious, immensely varied and take the most strongly individual forms. It is therefore impossible to give a general description of them. But it is very different when we enter by means of analysis into the world of unconscious fantasies. The diversity of the fantasy-material is indeed very great, but we do not find nearly so many individual peculiarities as in the conscious realm. We meet here with more typical material which is not infrequently repeated in similar form in different individuals. Constantly recurring in these fantasies are ideas which are variations of those found in religion and mythology. This fact is so striking that we may say we have discovered in these fantasies the forerunners of religious and mythological ideas.

342 I should have to enter into very much more detail to give you any adequate examples. For these problems I must refer you to my book *Symbols of Transformation*. Here I will only mention that the central symbol of Christianity—sacrifice—plays an important part in the fantasies of the unconscious. The Viennese school knows this phenomenon under the ambiguous name of "castration complex." This paradoxical use of the term follows from the special attitude of the Viennese school towards the question of sexuality, which I discussed earlier. I have devoted special attention to the problem of sacrifice in the above-mentioned book. I must content myself with this passing reference and will now proceed to say something about the origin of unconscious fantasies.

343   In a child's unconscious the fantasies are very much simpler, as if scaled to the childish milieu. Thanks to the concerted efforts of the psychoanalytic school, we have discovered that the most frequent fantasy of childhood is the so-called Oedipus complex. This term, too, seems the most unsuitable one possible. We all know that the tragic fate of Oedipus consisted in his marrying his mother and slaying his father. This tragic conflict of adult life appears far removed from the psyche of a child, and to the layman it seems quite inconceivable that a child should suffer from this conflict. But, with a little reflection, it will become clear that the *tertium comparationis* lies precisely in the *narrow restriction of the fate of Oedipus to his two parents*. This restriction is characteristic of the child, for the fate of the adult is not limited to the parents. To that extent Oedipus is the exponent of an infantile conflict magnified to adult proportions. The term "Oedipus complex" naturally does not mean conceiving this conflict in its adult form, but rather on a reduced scale suitable to childhood. All it means, in effect, is that the childish demands for love are directed to mother and father, and to the extent that these demands have already attained a certain degree of intensity, so that the chosen object is jealously defended, we can speak of an "Oedipus complex."

344   This weakening and reduction in scale of the Oedipus complex should not be understood as a diminution of the total sum of affect, but as indicating the smaller share of sexual affect characteristic of a child. To make up for this, childish affects have that peculiar intensity which is characteristic of the sexual affect in adults. The little son would like to have his mother all to himself and to be rid of his father. As you know, small children can sometimes force themselves between the parents in the most jealous way. In the unconscious these wishes and intentions assume a more concrete and more drastic form. Children are small primitive creatures and are therefore quickly ready to kill—a thought which is all the easier in the unconscious, because the unconscious is wont to express itself very dramatically. But as a child is, in general, harmless, this seemingly dangerous wish is as a rule harmless too. I say "as a rule," for we know that children can occasionally give way to their murderous impulses, not only indirectly, but in quite direct fashion. But just as the child is incapable of making systematic plans, so his intention to murder

is not all that dangerous. The same is true of his Oedipal intention towards the mother. The faint hints of this fantasy in the child's consciousness can easily be overlooked; all parents are therefore convinced that their children have no Oedipus complex. Parents, like lovers, are mostly blind. If I now say that the Oedipus complex is in the first place only a formula for childish desires in regard to the parents and for the conflict which these desires evoke—as every selfish desire must—the matter may seem more acceptable.

345   The history of the Oedipus fantasy is of special interest because it teaches us a great deal about the development of unconscious fantasies in general. People naturally think that the Oedipus problem is the problem of the son. But this, remarkably enough, is an illusion. Under certain conditions, the sexual libido reaches its final differentiation, corresponding to the sex of the individual, only relatively late in puberty. Before this time it has a sexually undifferentiated character, which could also be termed bisexual. It is therefore not surprising if little girls have an Oedipus complex too. So far as we know, the first love of a child, regardless of sex, belongs to the mother. If the love for the mother is intense at this stage, the father is jealously kept away as a rival. Of course, for the child itself, the mother at this early stage of childhood has no sexual significance worth mentioning, and to that extent the term "Oedipus complex" is not really suitable. At this period the mother still has the significance of a protecting, enfolding, nourishing being, who for this reason is a source of pleasure.

346   ⟨It is characteristic, too, that the babyish word for mother, "mamma," is the name for the maternal breast. As Dr. Beatrice Hinkle has informed me, interrogation of small children elicited the fact that they defined "mother" as the person who gives food, chocolate, etc. One could hardly assert that for children of this age food is only a symbol for sex, though this is sometimes true of adults. A superficial glance at the history of civilization will show just how enormous the nutritive source of pleasure is. The colossal feasts of Rome in its decadence were an expression of anything you like, only not of repressed sexuality, for that is the last thing one could accuse the Romans of in those days. There is no doubt that these excesses were some kind of substitute, but not for sexuality; they were far more a

substitute for neglected moral functions, which we are too prone to regard as laws forced on man from outside. Men have the laws which they make for themselves.)

347   As I explained earlier, I do not identify the feeling of pleasure *eo ipso* with sexuality. Sexuality has an increasingly small share in pleasure-sensations the further back we go in childhood. Nevertheless, jealousy can play a large role, for it too is something that does not belong entirely to the sexual sphere, since the desire for food has itself much to do with the first stirrings of jealousy—one has only to think of animals! Certainly it is reinforced by a budding eroticism relatively early. This element gains in strength as the years go on, so that the Oedipus complex soon assumes its classical form. The conflict takes on a more masculine and therefore more typical form in a son, whereas a daughter develops a specific liking for the father, with a correspondingly jealous attitude towards the mother. We could call this the Electra complex. As everyone knows, Electra took vengeance on her mother Clytemnestra for murdering her husband Agamemnon and thus robbing her—Electra—of her beloved father.

348   Both these fantasy complexes become more pronounced with increasing maturity, and reach a new stage only in the post-pubertal period, when the problem arises of detachment from the parents. This stage is characterized by the symbol we have already mentioned: the symbol of sacrifice. The more sexuality develops, the more it drives the individual away from his family and forces him to achieve independence. But the child has become closely attached to the family by his whole previous history, and especially to the parents, so that it is often only with the greatest difficulty that the growing individual can free himself inwardly from his infantile milieu. If he does not succeed in this, the Oedipus (or Electra) complex will precipitate a conflict, and then there is the possibility of neurotic disturbances. The libido, already sexually developed, pours into the Oedipal "mould" and gives rise to feelings and fantasies which prove beyond doubt the effectiveness of the complex, which till then had been unconscious and more or less inoperative.

349   The first consequence is the formation of intense resistances against the "immoral" impulses stemming from the now active complex. This affects the conscious behaviour in two ways.

Either the consequences are direct, in which case the son displays violent resistances against his father and a particularly affectionate and dependent attitude towards his mother; or they are indirect, that is to say compensated: instead of resistance to the father there is marked submissiveness coupled with an irritated, antagonistic attitude towards the mother. Direct and compensated consequences can sometimes alternate. All this is true also of the Electra complex. If the sexual libido were to get stuck in this form, the Oedipus and Electra conflict would lead to murder and incest. This naturally does not happen with normal people, nor in so-called "amoral" primitive communities, otherwise the human race would have perished long ago. On the contrary, it is in the natural order of things that familiar objects lose their compelling charm and force the libido to seek new objects; and this acts as an important regulative factor which prevents parricide and incest. The continuous development of libido towards objects outside the family is perfectly normal and natural, and it is an abnormal and pathological phenomenon if the libido remains, as it were, glued to the family. Nevertheless, it is a phenomenon that can sometimes be observed in normal people.

THE PROBLEM OF INCEST

350   ⟨The unconscious fantasy of sacrifice, occurring some time after puberty, is a direct outcome of the infantile complexes. Of this I have given a circumstantial example in my book *Symbols of Transformation*. The fantasy of sacrifice means the giving up of infantile wishes. I have shown this in my book and at the same time have pointed out the parallels in the history of religion. It is not surprising that this problem plays an important role in religion, for religion is one of the greatest helps in the psychological process of adaptation. The chief obstacle to new modes of psychological adaptation is conservative adherence to the earlier attitude. But man cannot leave his previous personality and his previous objects of interest simply as they are, otherwise his libido would stagnate in the past, and this would be an impoverishment for him. Here religion is a great help because, by the bridge of the symbol, it leads his

libido away from the infantile objects (parents) towards the symbolic representatives of the past, i.e., the gods, thus facilitating the transition from the infantile world to the adult world. In this way the libido is set free for social purposes.)

351   Freud has a special conception of the incest complex which has given rise to heated controversy. He starts from the fact that the Oedipus complex is usually unconscious, and he conceives this to be the consequence of a moral repression. It is possible that I am not expressing myself quite correctly if I give you Freud's view in these words. At any rate, according to him the Oedipus complex seems to be repressed, that is, displaced into the unconscious through the reactive effect of conscious tendencies. It almost looks as if the Oedipus complex would rise to consciousness if the child's development were uninhibited and were not affected by cultural influences.[1]

352   Freud calls the barrier that prevents this acting out of the Oedipus complex the "incest barrier." He seems to believe, so far as one can gather from his writings, that the incest barrier is formed by the backwash of experience, that it is a correction by reality, since the unconscious strives for boundless and immediate satisfaction without regard for others. In this he agrees with Schopenhauer, who says of the egoism of the blind World-Will that it is so strong that a man could slay his brother merely to grease his boots with his brother's fat. Freud considers that the psychological incest barrier can be compared with the incest prohibitions found even among primitives. He further considers that these prohibitions are a proof that men really do desire incest, for which reason laws were framed against it even on the primitive level. He therefore takes the tendency towards incest to be an absolutely concrete sexual wish, for he calls this complex the root-complex, or nucleus, of the neuroses and is inclined, viewing this as the original one, to reduce practically the whole psychology of the neuroses, as well as many other phenomena in the realm of the mind, to this one complex.

---

[1] A view expressed most strongly by Stekel.

7. THE AETIOLOGY OF NEUROSIS

353   With this new conception of Freud's we come back to the question of the aetiology of neurosis. We have seen that psychoanalytic theory started from a traumatic experience in childhood, which later on was found to be partly or wholly unreal. In consequence, the theory made a change of front and sought the aetiologically significant factor in the development of abnormal fantasies. The investigation of the unconscious, continued over a period of ten years with the help of an increasing number of workers, gradually brought to light a mass of empirical material which showed that the incest complex was a highly important and never-failing element in pathological fantasy. But it was found that the incest complex was not a special complex of neurotic people; it proved to be a component of the normal infantile psyche. We cannot tell from its mere existence whether this complex will give rise to a neurosis or not. To become pathogenic, it must precipitate a conflict; the complex, which in itself is inactive, must be activated and intensified to the point where a conflict breaks out.

354   This brings us to a new and important question. If the infantile "nuclear complex" is only a general form, not in itself pathogenic but requiring special activation, then the whole aetiological problem is altered. In that case we would dig in vain among the reminiscences of earliest childhood, since they give us only the general forms of later conflicts but not the actual conflict. ⟨It makes no difference that there were already conflicts in childhood, for the conflicts of childhood are different from the conflicts of adults. Those who have suffered ever since childhood from a chronic neurosis do not suffer now from the same conflict they suffered from then. Maybe the neurosis broke out when they first had to go to school as children. Then it was the conflict between indulgence and duty, between love for their parents and the necessity of going to school. But now it is the conflict between, say, the joys of a

comfortable bourgeois existence and the strenuous demands of professional life. It only seems to be the same conflict. It is just as if the "Teutschen" of the Napoleonic wars were to compare themselves with the old Germans who rebelled against the Roman yoke.⟩

UNCONSCIOUS DETERMINATION

355   I think I can best make my meaning clear if I describe the subsequent development of the theory by using the example of the young lady whose story you have heard in the earlier lectures. As you will probably remember, we found in the anamnesis that the fright with the horses led to the reminiscence of a similar scene in childhood, in which connection we discussed the trauma theory. We found that we had to look for the real pathological element in her exaggerated fantasies, which arose from her retarded psychosexual development. We now have to apply the theoretical insight we have thus gained to the genesis of this particular illness if we want to understand how, just at that moment, that childhood experience was constellated so effectively.

356   The simplest way to find an explanation for that nocturnal occurrence would be to make an exact inquiry into the circumstances of the moment. The first thing I did, therefore, was to question the patient about the company she had been keeping at the time. From this I learnt that she knew a young man to whom she thought of getting engaged; she loved him and hoped to be happy with him. At first nothing more could be discovered. But it would never do to be deterred from investigation by the negative results of the preliminary questioning. There are indirect ways of reaching the goal when the direct way fails. We therefore return to that singular moment when the lady ran headlong in front of the horses. We inquire about her companions and the sort of festive occasion she had just taken part in. It had been a farewell party for her best friend, who was going abroad to a health-resort on account of her nerves. This friend was married and, we are told, happily; she was also the mother of a child. We may take leave to doubt the statement that she was happy; for, were she really so, she would

presumably have no reason to be "nervous" and in need of a cure.

357   Shifting my angle of approach, I learnt that after her friends had caught up with her they took the patient back to the house of her host, as this was the nearest shelter. There she was hospitably received in her exhausted state. At this point the patient broke off her narrative, became embarrassed, fidgeted, and tried to change the subject. Evidently some disagreeable recollection had suddenly bobbed up. After the most obstinate resistance had been overcome, it appeared that yet another very remarkable incident had occurred that night: the amiable host had made her a fiery declaration of love, thus precipitating a situation which, in the absence of the lady of the house, might well be considered both difficult and distressing. Ostensibly this declaration of love came to her like a bolt from the blue. A modicum of criticism teaches us, however, that these things never drop from the skies but always have their history. It was now the task of the next few weeks to dig out bit by bit a long love-story, until at last a complete picture emerged which I attempt to outline as follows:

358   As a child the patient had been a regular tomboy, caring only for wild boys' games, scorning her own sex and avoiding all feminine ways and occupations. After puberty, when the erotic problem might have come too close, she began to shun all society, hated and despised everything that even remotely reminded her of the biological destiny of woman, and lived in a world of fantasy which had nothing in common with rude reality. Thus, until about her twenty-fourth year, she evaded all those little adventures, hopes, and expectations which ordinarily move a girl's heart at this age. Then she got to know two men who were destined to break through the thorny hedge that had grown up around her. Mr. A was her best friend's husband, and Mr. B was his bachelor friend. She liked them both. Nevertheless it soon began to look as though she liked Mr. B a vast deal better. An intimacy quickly sprang up between them and before long there was talk of a possible engagement. Through her relations with Mr. B and through her friend she often came into contact with Mr. A, whose presence sometimes disturbed her in the most unaccountable way and made her nervous.

359   About this time the patient went to a large party. Her friends were also there. She became lost in thought and was dreamily playing with her ring when it suddenly slipped off her finger and rolled under the table. Both gentlemen looked for it and Mr. B succeeded in finding it. He placed the ring on her finger with an arch smile and said, "You know what that means!" Overcome by a strange and irresistible feeling, she tore the ring from her finger and flung it through the open window. A painful moment ensued, as may be imagined, and soon she left the party in deep dejection.

360   Not long after this, so-called chance brought it about that she should spend her summer holidays at a health resort where Mr. and Mrs. A were also staying. Mrs. A then began to grow visibly nervous, and frequently stayed indoors because she felt out of sorts. The patient was thus in a position to go out for walks alone with Mr. A. On one occasion they went boating. So boisterous was she in her merriment that she suddenly fell overboard. She could not swim, and it was only with great difficulty that Mr. A pulled her half-unconscious into the boat. And then it was that he kissed her. With this romantic episode the bonds were tied fast. To excuse herself in her own eyes she tried all the more energetically to get herself engaged to Mr. B, telling herself every day that it was Mr. B whom she really loved. Naturally this curious little game had not escaped the keen glances of wifely jealousy. Mrs. A, her friend, had guessed the secret and fretted accordingly, so that her nerves only got worse. Hence it became necessary for Mrs. A to go abroad for a cure.[1]

361   The farewell party presented a dangerous opportunity. The patient knew that her friend and rival was going off the same evening, and that Mr. A would be alone in the house. Of course she did not think this out logically and clearly, for some women have a remarkable capacity for thinking purely with their feelings, and not with their intellects, so that it seems to them as if they had never thought certain things at all. At any rate she had a very queer feeling all the evening. She felt extraordinarily nervous, and when Mrs. A had been accompanied to the station and had gone, the hysterical twilight state came over her on the

1 [Cf. *Two Essays*, pars. 11f. and 420. For the first two instalments of the story see supra, pars. 218ff. and 297ff.—EDITORS.]

way back. I asked her what she had been thinking or feeling at the actual moment when she heard the horses coming along behind her. Her answer was that she had only a feeling of panic, the feeling that something dreadful was approaching which she could no longer escape. The consequence was, as you know, that she was brought back exhausted to the house of her host, Mr. A.

362   To the simple mind this dénouement seems perfectly obvious. Every layman will say, "Well, that is clear enough, she only intended to return by one way or another to Mr. A's house." But the psychologist would reproach the layman for his incorrect way of expressing himself, and would tell him that the patient was not conscious of the motives of her behaviour, and that we cannot therefore speak of her *intention* to return to Mr. A's house. There are, of course, learned psychologists who could find any number of theoretical reasons for disputing the purposiveness of her action—reasons based on the dogma of the identity of consciousness and psyche. But the psychology inaugurated by Freud recognized long ago that the purposive significance of psychological acts cannot be judged by conscious motives but only by the objective criterion of their psychological result. Today it can no longer be contested that there are unconscious tendencies which have a great influence on a person's reactions and on the effect he has on others.

363   What happened at Mr. A's house bears out this observation. Our patient made a sentimental scene, and Mr. A felt obliged to react to it with a declaration of love. Looked at in the light of these concluding events, the whole previous history seems to be very ingeniously directed towards precisely this end, though consciously the patient was struggling against it all the time.

364   The theoretical gain from this story is the clear recognition that an unconscious "intention" or tendency stage-managed the fright with the horses, very probably using for this purpose the infantile reminiscence of the horses galloping irresistibly towards disaster. Seen in the light of the whole material, the nocturnal scene with the horses—the starting point of the illness —seems to be only the keystone of a planned edifice. The fright and the apparently traumatic effect of the childhood experience are merely staged, but staged in the peculiar way characteristic of hysteria, so that the *mise en scène* appears almost exactly

like a reality. We know from hundreds of experiences that hysterical pains are staged in order to reap certain advantages from the environment. Nevertheless these pains are entirely real. The patients do not merely think they have pains; from the psychological point of view the pains are just as real as those due to organic causes, and yet they are stage-managed.

THE REGRESSION OF LIBIDO

365   This utilization of reminiscences for staging an illness or an ostensible aetiology is called a *regression of libido*. The libido goes back to these reminiscences and activates them, with the result that an apparent aetiology is simulated. In this instance, according to the old theory, it might seem as if the fright with the horses were due to the old trauma. The resemblance between the two scenes is unmistakable, and in both cases the patient's fright was very real. At all events, we have no reason to doubt her assertions in this respect, as they fully accord with our experiences of other patients. The nervous asthma, the hysterical anxiety-attacks, the psychogenic depressions and exaltations, the pains, the cramps, etc. are all quite real, and any doctor who has himself suffered from a psychogenic symptom will know how absolutely real it feels. Regressively reactivated reminiscences, however fantastic they may be, are as real as recollections of events which have actually happened.

366   As the term "regression of libido" indicates, we understand by this retrograde mode of application a reversion to earlier stages. From our example we can see very clearly how the process of regression takes place. At that farewell party, which presented a good opportunity for her to be alone with her host, the patient shrank from the idea of turning this opportunity to her advantage, but let herself be overpowered by desires which hitherto she had never admitted. The libido was not used consciously for that purpose, nor was this purpose ever acknowledged. In consequence, the libido had to carry it out by means of the unconscious, under the cover of panic in face of overwhelming danger. Her feelings at the moment when the horses approached illustrate our formulation very clearly: she felt as if something inescapable now had to happen.

367   The process of regression is beautifully illustrated in an image used by Freud. The libido can be compared with a river which, when it meets with an obstruction, gets dammed up and causes an inundation. If this river has previously, in its upper reaches, dug out other channels, these channels will be filled up again by reason of the damming below. They appear to be real river-beds, filled with water as before, but at the same time they have only a provisional existence. The river has not permanently flowed back into the old channels, but only for as long as the obstruction lasts in the main stream. The subsidiary streams carry the water not because they were independent streams from the beginning, but because they were once stages or stations in the development of the main river-bed, passing possibilities, traces of which still exist and can therefore be used again in times of flood.

368   This image can be applied directly to the development of the uses of libido. The final direction, the main river-bed, has not yet been found at the time of the infantile development of sexuality. Instead, the libido branches out into all sorts of subsidiary streams, and only gradually does the final form appear. But when the river has dug out its main bed, all the subsidiary streams dry up and lose their importance, leaving only traces of their former activity. Similarly, the importance of the child's preliminary exercises at sexuality disappears almost completely as a rule, except for a few traces. If later an obstruction occurs, so that the damming up of libido reactivates the old channels, this state is properly speaking a new and at the same time an abnormal one. The earlier, infantile state represents a normal application of libido, whereas the reversion of libido to infantile ways is something abnormal. I am therefore of the opinion that Freud is not justified in calling the infantile sexual manifestations "perverse," since a normal manifestation should not be designated by a pathological term. This incorrect usage has had pernicious consequences in confusing the scientific public. Such a terminology is a misapplication to normal people of insights gained from neurotic psychology, on the assumption that the abnormal by-path taken by the libido in neurotics is still the same phenomenon as in children.

369   The so-called "amnesia of childhood," which I would like to mention in passing, is a similar illegitimate "retrograde" appli-

cation of terms from pathology. Amnesia is a pathological condition, consisting in the repression of certain conscious contents, and this cannot possibly be the same as the anterograde amnesia of children, which consists in an incapacity for intentional memory-reproduction, such as is also found among primitives. This incapacity for memory-reproduction dates from birth and can be understood on quite obvious biological grounds. It would be a remarkable hypothesis if we were to assume that this totally different quality of infantile consciousness could be reduced to sexual repressions on the analogy of a neurosis. A neurotic amnesia is punched out, as it were, from the continuity of memory, whereas memory in early childhood consists of single islands in the continuum of non-memory. This condition is in every sense the opposite of the condition found in neurosis, so that the expression "amnesia" is absolutely incorrect. The "amnesia of childhood" is an inference from the psychology of neurosis, just as is the "polymorphous-perverse" disposition of the child.

THE PERIOD OF SEXUAL LATENCY

370   This error in theoretical formulation comes to light in the peculiar doctrine of the so-called "period of sexual latency" in childhood. Freud observed that the early infantile sexual manifestations, which I call phenomena of the presexual stage, disappear after a time and reappear only much later. What Freud calls "infantile masturbation"—that is, all those quasi-sexual activities which we spoke about before—is said to return later as real masturbation. Such a process of development would be biologically unique. In conformity with this theory we would have to assume, for instance, that when a plant forms a bud from which a blossom begins to unfold, the blossom is taken back again before it is fully developed, and is again hidden within the bud, to reappear later on in a similar form. This impossible supposition is a consequence of the assertion that the early infantile activities of the presexual stage are sexual phenomena, and that the quasi-masturbational acts of that period are genuine acts of masturbation. Here the incorrect terminology and the boundless extension of the concept of sexuality take their

revenge. Thus it was that Freud was compelled to assume that there is a disappearance of sexuality, in other words, a period of sexual latency. What he calls a disappearance is nothing other than the *real beginning of sexuality,* everything preceding it being but a preliminary stage to which no real sexual character can be attributed. The impossible phenomenon of sexual latency is thus explained in a very simple way.

371   The theory of the latency period is an excellent example of the incorrectness of the conception of infantile sexuality. But there has been no error of observation. On the contrary, the hypothesis of the latency period proves how exactly Freud observed the apparent recommencement of sexuality. The error lies in the conception. As we have already seen, the prime error consists in a somewhat old-fashioned conception of a plurality of instincts. As soon as we accept the idea of two or more instincts existing side by side, we must necessarily conclude that, if one instinct is not yet manifest, it is still present *in nuce,* in accordance with the old theory of encasement.[2] Or, in physics, we should have to say that when a piece of iron passes from the condition of heat to the condition of light, the light was already present *in nuce* (latently) in the heat. Such assumptions are arbitrary projections of human ideas into transcendental regions, contravening the requirements of the theory of cognition. We have therefore no right to speak of a sexual instinct existing *in nuce,* as we would then be giving an arbitrary interpretation of phenomena which can be explained otherwise, in a much more suitable manner. We can only speak of the manifestation of the nutritive function, of the sexual function, and so on, and then only when that function has come to the surface with unmistakable clarity. We speak of light only when the iron is visibly glowing, but not when the iron is merely hot.

372   Freud as an observer sees quite clearly that the sexuality of neurotics cannot really be compared with infantile sexuality, just as there is a great difference, for instance, between the uncleanliness of a two-year-old child and the uncleanliness of a forty-year-old catatonic. The one is normal, the other exceedingly

2 [*Einschachtelung:* "An old theory of reproduction which assumed that when the first animal of each species was created, the germs of all other individuals of the same species which were to come from it were encased in its ova."—*Century Dictionary* (1890).—TRANS.]

pathological. Freud inserted a short passage in his *Three Essays*,[3] stating that the infantile form of neurotic sexuality is either wholly, or at any rate partly, due to regression. That is, even in those cases where we can say that it is still the same old infantile by-path, the function of this by-path is intensified by the regression. Freud thus admits that the infantile sexuality of neurotics is for the greater part a regressive phenomenon. That this must be so is evidenced by the researches of recent years, showing that the observations concerning the childhood psychology of neurotics hold equally true of normal people. At any rate we can say that the historical development of infantile sexuality in a neurotic is distinguished from that of normal people only by minimal differences which completely elude scientific evaluation. Striking differences are exceptional.

THE AETIOLOGICAL SIGNIFICANCE OF THE ACTUAL PRESENT

373　　The more deeply we penetrate into the heart of the infantile development, the more we get the impression that as little of aetiological significance can be found there as in the infantile trauma. Even with the acutest ferreting into their respective histories we shall never discover why people living on German soil had just such a fate, and why the Gauls another. The further we get away, in analytical investigations, from the epoch of the manifest neurosis, the less can we expect to find the real *causa efficiens,* since the dynamics of the maladjustment grow fainter and fainter the further we go back into the past. In constructing a theory which derives the neurosis from causes in the distant past, we are first and foremost following the tendency of our patients to lure us as far away as possible from the critical present. *For the cause of the pathogenic conflict lies mainly in the present moment.* It is just as if a nation were to blame its miserable political conditions on the past; as if the Germany of the nineteenth century had attributed her political dismemberment and incapacity to her oppression by the Romans, instead of seeking the causes of her difficulties in the actual present. It is mainly in the present that the effective causes lie, and here alone are the possibilities of removing them.

3 Standard Edn., p. 232.

374   The greater part of the psychoanalytic school is still under the spell of the conception that infantile sexuality is the *sine qua non* of neurosis. It is not only the theorist, delving into childhood simply from scientific interest, but the practising analyst also, who believes that he has to turn the history of infancy inside out in order to find the fantasies conditioning the neurosis. A fruitless enterprise! In the meantime the most important factor escapes him, namely, the conflict and its demands in the present. In the case we have been describing, we should not understand any of the motives which produced the hysterical attacks if we looked for them in earliest childhood. Those reminiscences determine only the form, but the dynamic element springs from the present, and insight into the significance of the actual moment alone gives real understanding.

375   It may not be out of place to remark here that it would never occur to me to blame Freud personally for the innumerable misunderstandings. I know very well that Freud, being an empiricist, always publishes only provisional formulations to which he certainly does not attribute any eternal value. But it is equally certain that the scientific public is inclined to make a creed out of them, a system which is asserted as blindly on the one hand as it is attacked on the other. I can only say that from the sum total of Freud's writings certain average conceptions have crystallized out, which both sides treat far too dogmatically. These views have led to a number of undoubtedly incorrect technical axioms the existence of which cannot be postulated with any certainty in Freud's own work. We know that in the mind of a creator of new ideas things are much more fluid and flexible than they are in the minds of his followers. They do not possess his vital creativity, and they make up for this deficiency by a dogmatic allegiance, in exactly the same way as their opponents, who, like them, cling to the dead letter because they cannot grasp its living content. My words are thus addressed less to Freud, who I know recognizes to some extent the final orientation of the neuroses, than to his public, who continue to argue about his views.

376   From what has been said it should be clear that we gain insight into the history of a neurosis only when we understand that each separate element in it serves a purpose. We can now understand why that particular element in the previous history

of our case was pathogenic, and we also understand why it was chosen as a symbol. Through the concept of regression, the theory is freed from the narrow formula of the importance of childhood experiences, and the actual conflict acquires the significance which, on the empirical evidence, implicitly belongs to it. Freud himself introduced the concept of regression, as I have said, in his *Three Essays,* rightly acknowledging that experience does not permit us to seek the cause of a neurosis exclusively in the past. If it is true, then, that reminiscences become effective again chiefly because of regressive activation, we have to consider whether the apparently determining effects of the reminiscences can be traced back solely to the regression of libido.

377 As you have heard already, Freud himself in the *Three Essays* gives us to understand that the infantilism of neurotic sexuality is for the most part due to regression. This statement deserves considerably more emphasis than it received there. (Actually Freud did give it due emphasis in his later works.) The point is that the *regression of libido abolishes to a very large extent the aetiological significance of childhood experiences.* It had seemed to us very peculiar anyway that the Oedipus or Electra complex should have a determining influence in the formation of a neurosis, since these complexes are actually present in everyone, even in people who have never known their father and mother and were brought up by foster-parents. I have analysed cases of this kind, and found that the incest complex was as well developed in them as in other patients. This seems to me a good proof that the incest complex is much less a reality than a purely regressive fantasy formation, and that the conflicts resulting from it must be reduced rather to an anachronistic clinging to the infantile attitude than to real incestuous wishes, which are merely a cover for regressive fantasies. Looked at from this point of view, childhood experiences have a significance for neurosis only when they are made significant by a regression of libido. That this must be so to a very large extent is shown by the fact that neither the infantile sexual trauma nor the incest complex present in everyone causes hysteria. Neurosis occurs only when the incest complex is activated by regression.

FAILURE OF ADAPTATION

378   This brings us to the question: why does the libido become regressive? In order to answer this, we must examine more closely the conditions under which a regression arises. In discussing this problem with my patients I generally give the following example: A mountain-climber, attempting the ascent of a certain peak, happens to meet with an insurmountable obstacle, for instance a precipitous rock-face whose ascent is a sheer impossibility. After vainly seeking another route, he will turn back and regretfully abandon the idea of climbing that peak. He will say to himself: "It is not in my power to get over this difficulty, so I will climb an easier mountain."

379   Here we see a normal utilization of libido: the man turns back when he meets an insurmountable difficulty, and uses his libido, which could not attain its original goal, for the ascent of another mountain.

380   Now let us imagine that the rock-face was not really unclimbable so far as the man's physical abilities were concerned, but that he shrank back from this difficult undertaking from sheer funk. In this case two possibilities are open:

1. The man will be annoyed by his own cowardice and will set out to prove himself less timid on another occasion, or perhaps he will admit that with his timidity he ought never to undertake such daring ascents. At any rate, he will acknowledge that his moral capacity is not sufficient to overcome the difficulties. He therefore uses the libido which did not attain its original aim for the useful purpose of self-criticism, and for evolving a plan by which he may yet be able, with due regard to his moral capacity, to realize his wish to climb a mountain.

2. The second possibility is that the man does not admit his cowardice, and flatly asserts that the rock face is physically unclimbable, although he can very well see that, with sufficient courage, the obstacle could be overcome. But he prefers to deceive himself. This creates the psychological situation which is of significance for our problem.

381   At bottom the man knows perfectly well that it would be physically possible to overcome the difficulty, and that he is simply morally incapable of doing so. But he pushes this thought

aside because of its disagreeable character. He is so conceited that he cannot admit his cowardice. He brags about his courage and prefers to declare that things are impossible rather than that his own courage is inadequate. In this way he falls into contradiction with himself: on the one hand he has a correct appreciation of the situation, on the other he hides this knowledge from himself, behind the illusion of his bravery. He represses his correct insight and tries to force his subjective illusions on reality. The result of this contradiction is that his libido is split and the two halves fight one another. He pits his wish to climb the mountain against the opinion, invented by himself and supported by artificial arguments, that the mountain is unclimbable. He draws back not because of any real impossibility but because of an artificial barrier invented by himself. He has fallen into disunion with himself. From this moment on he suffers from an internal conflict. Now the realization of his cowardice gains the upper hand, now defiance and pride. In either case his libido is engaged in a useless civil war, and the man becomes incapable of any new enterprise. He will never realize his wish to climb a mountain, because he has gone thoroughly astray in the estimation of his moral qualities. His efficiency is reduced, he is not fully adapted, he has become—in a word—neurotic. The libido that retreated in face of the difficulty has led neither to honest self-criticism nor to a desperate struggle to overcome the difficulty at any price; it has been used merely to maintain the cheap pretence that the ascent was absolutely impossible and that even heroic courage would have availed nothing.

REVERSION TO THE INFANTILE LEVEL

382   This kind of reaction is called *infantile*. It is characteristic of children, and of naïve minds generally, not to find the mistake in themselves but in things outside them, and forcibly to impose on things their own subjective judgment.

383   This man, therefore, solves the problem in an infantile way; he substitutes for the adapted attitude of the first climber a mode of adaptation characteristic of the child's mind. That is what we mean by regression. His libido retreats before the ob-

stacle it cannot surmount and substitutes a childish illusion for real action.

384   Such cases are a daily occurrence in the treatment of neurosis. I would only remind you of all those young girls who suddenly become hysterically ill the moment they have to decide whether to get engaged or not. As an example, I will present the case of two sisters. The two girls were separated by only a year in age. In talents and also in character they were very much alike. They had the same education and grew up in the same surroundings under the same parental influences. Both were ostensibly healthy, neither showed any noticeable nervous symptoms. An attentive observer might have discovered that the elder daughter was rather more the darling of her parents than the younger. Her parents' esteem was due to the special kind of sensitiveness which this daughter displayed. She demanded more affection than the younger one, was somewhat more precocious and forthcoming than she. Besides, she showed some delightfully childish traits—just those things which, because of their contradictory and slightly unbalanced character, make a person specially charming. No wonder father and mother had great joy in their elder daughter.

385   When the two sisters became of marriageable age, they both made the acquaintance of two young men, and the possibility of their marriages soon drew near. As is generally the case, there were certain difficulties in the way. Both girls were quite young and had very little experience of the world. The men were fairly young too, and in positions which might have been better; they were only at the beginning of their careers, nevertheless both were capable young men. The two girls lived in social surroundings which gave them the right to certain expectations. It was a situation in which doubts as to the suitability of either marriage were permissible. Moreover, both girls were insufficiently acquainted with their prospective husbands, and were not quite sure of their love. Hence there were many hesitations and doubts. It was noticed that the elder sister always showed greater waverings in all her decisions. On account of these hesitations there were some painful moments with the two young men, who naturally pressed for a definite answer. At such moments the elder sister showed herself much more agitated than the younger one. Several times she went weeping to her mother, bemoaning

her own uncertainty. The younger one was more decided, and put an end to the unsettled situation by accepting her suitor. She thus got over her difficulty and thereafter events ran smoothly.

386 As soon as the admirer of the elder sister heard that the younger one had given her word, he rushed to his lady and begged passionately for her final acceptance. His tempestuous behaviour irritated and rather frightened her, although she was really inclined to follow her sister's example. She answered in a haughty and rather offhand way. He replied with sharp reproaches, causing her to answer still more tartly. At the end there was a tearful scene, and he went away in a huff. At home, he told the story to his mother, who expressed the opinion that the girl was obviously not the right one for him and that he had better choose someone else. The quarrel had made the girl profoundly doubtful whether she really loved him. It suddenly seemed to her impossible to leave her beloved parents and follow this man to an unknown destiny. Matters finally went so far that the relationship was broken off altogether. From then on the girl became moody; she showed unmistakable signs of the greatest jealousy towards her sister, but would neither see nor admit that she was jealous. The former happy relationship with her parents went to pieces too. Instead of her earlier child-like affection she put on a sulky manner, which sometimes amounted to violent irritability; weeks of depression followed. While the younger sister was celebrating her wedding, the elder went to a distant health-resort for nervous intestinal catarrh. I shall not continue the history of the illness; it developed into an ordinary hysteria.

387 In the analysis of this case great resistance was found to the sexual problem. The resistance was due to numerous perverse fantasies whose existence the patient would not admit. The question as to where these perverse fantasies, so unexpected in a young girl, could come from led to the discovery that once, as a child of eight years old, she had found herself suddenly confronted in the street by an exhibitionist. She was rooted to the spot by fright, and for a long time afterwards the ugly image pursued her in her dreams. Her younger sister had been with her at the time. The night after the patient told me about this, she dreamt of a man in a grey suit, who started to do in front of

her what the exhibitionist had done. She awoke with a cry of terror.

388   Her first association to the grey suit was a suit of her father's, which he had been wearing on an excursion she had made with him when she was about six years old. This dream, without any doubt, connects the father with the exhibitionist. There must be some reason for this. Did something happen with the father that might possibly call forth such an association? This question met with violent resistance from the patient, but it would not let her alone. At the next interview she reproduced some very early reminiscences, in which she had watched her father undressing; and one day she came, terribly embarrassed and shaken, to tell me that she had had an abominable vision, absolutely distinct. In bed at night, she suddenly felt herself once again a child of two or three years old, and she saw her father standing by her bed in an obscene attitude. The story was gasped out bit by bit, obviously with the greatest internal struggle. Then followed wild lamentations about how dreadful it was that a father should do such a terrible thing to his child.

389   Nothing is less probable than that the father really did this. It is only a fantasy, presumably constructed in the course of the analysis from that same need for causality which once misled the analysts into supposing that hysteria was caused merely by such impressions.

390   This case seems to me perfectly designed to demonstrate the importance of the regression theory, and to show at the same time the sources of the previous theoretical errors. Originally, as we saw, there was only a slight difference between the two sisters, but from the moment of their engagement their ways became totally divided. They now seemed to have two entirely different characters. The one, vigorous in health, and enjoying life, was a fine courageous girl, willing to submit to the natural demands of womanhood; the other was gloomy, ill-tempered, full of bitterness and malice, unwilling to make any effort to lead a reasonable life, egotistical, quarrelsome, and a nuisance to all around her. This striking difference was brought out only when one of the sisters successfully got over the difficulties of the engagement period, while the other did not. For both, it hung by a hair whether the affair would be broken off. The younger, somewhat more placid, was the more decided, and she

was able to find the right word at the right moment. The elder was more spoiled and more sensitive, consequently more influenced by her emotions, so that she could not find the right word, nor had she the courage to sacrifice her pride to put things straight afterwards. This little cause had a great effect, as we shall see. Originally the conditions were exactly the same for both sisters. It was the greater sensitiveness of the elder that made all the difference.

SENSITIVENESS AND REGRESSION

391   The question now is, whence came this sensitiveness which had such unfortunate results? Analysis demonstrated the existence of an extraordinarily well-developed sexuality with an infantile, fantastic character; further, of an incestuous fantasy about the father. Assuming that these fantasies had long been alive and active in the patient, we have here a quick and very simple solution of the problem of sensitiveness. We can easily understand why the girl was so sensitive: she was completely shut up in her fantasies and had a secret attachment to her father. In these circumstances it would have been a miracle if she had been willing to love and marry another man.

392   The further we pursue the development of these fantasies back to their source, following our need for causality, the greater become the difficulties of analysis, that is, the greater become the "resistances," as we called them. Finally we reach that impressive scene, that obscene act, whose improbability has already been established. This scene has exactly the character of a later fantasy-formation. Therefore, we have to conceive these difficulties, these "resistances," not—at least in this stage of the analysis—as defences against the conscious realization of a painful memory, but as a struggle against the construction of this fantasy.

393   You will ask in astonishment: But what is it that compels the patient to weave such a fantasy? You will even be inclined to suggest that the analyst forced the patient to invent it, otherwise she would never have produced such an absurd idea. I do not venture to doubt that there have been cases where the analyst's need to find a cause, especially under the influence of the

trauma theory, forced the patient to invent a fantasy of this kind. But the analyst, in his turn, would never have arrived at this theory had he not followed the patient's line of thought, thus taking part in that retrograde movement of libido which we call regression. He is simply carrying out to its logical conclusion what the patient is afraid to carry out, that is, a regression, a retreat of libido with all the consequences that this entails.

394   Hence, in tracing the libido regression, the analysis does not always follow the exact path marked out by the historical development, but often that of a subsequently formed fantasy, based only in part on former realities. In our case, too, the events were only partly real, and they got their enormous significance only afterwards, when the libido regressed. Whenever the libido seizes upon a certain reminiscence, we may expect it to be elaborated and transformed, for everything that is touched by the libido revives, takes on dramatic form, and becomes systematized. We have to admit that by far the greater part of the material became significant only later, when the regressing libido, seizing hold of anything suitable that lay in its path, had turned all this into a fantasy. Then that fantasy, keeping pace with the regressive movement of libido, came back at last to the father and put upon him all the infantile sexual wishes. Even so has it ever been thought that the golden age of Paradise lay in the past!

395   As we know that the fantasy material brought out by analysis became significant only afterwards, we are not in a position to use this material to explain the onset of the neurosis; we should be constantly moving in a circle. The critical moment for the neurosis was the one when the girl and the man were both ready to be reconciled, but when the inopportune sensitiveness of the patient, and perhaps also of her partner, allowed the opportunity to slip by.

IS SENSITIVENESS PRIMARY?

396   It might be said—and the psychoanalytic school inclines to this view—that the critical sensitiveness arose from a special psychological history which made this outcome a foregone conclu-

sion. We know that in psychogenic neuroses sensitiveness is always a symptom of disunion with oneself, a symptom of the struggle between two divergent tendencies. Each of these tendencies has its psychological prehistory, and in our case it can clearly be shown that the peculiar resistance at the bottom of the patient's critical sensitiveness was in fact bound up historically with certain infantile sexual activities, and also with that so-called traumatic experience—things which may very well cast a shadow on sexuality. This would be plausible enough, were it not that the patient's sister had experienced pretty much the same things—including the exhibitionist—without suffering the same consequences, and without becoming neurotic.

397   We would therefore have to assume that the patient experienced these things in a special way, perhaps more intensely and enduringly than her sister, and that the events of early childhood would have been more significant to her in the long run. If that had been true in so marked a degree, some violent effect would surely have been noticed even at the time. But in later youth the events of early childhood were as much over and done with for the patient as they were for her sister. Therefore, yet another conjecture is conceivable with regard to that critical sensitiveness, namely, that it did not come from her peculiar prehistory but had existed all along. An attentive observer of small children can detect, even in early infancy, any unusual sensitiveness. I once analysed a hysterical patient who showed me a letter written by her mother when the patient was two years old. Her mother wrote about her and her sister: she—the patient—was always a friendly and enterprising child, but her sister had difficulties in getting along with people and things. The first one in later life became hysterical, the other catatonic. These far-reaching differences, which go back into earliest childhood, cannot be due to accidental events but must be regarded as innate. From this standpoint we cannot assert that our patient's peculiar prehistory was to blame for her sensitiveness at the critical moment; it would be more correct to say that this sensitiveness was inborn and naturally manifested itself most strongly in any unusual situation.

398   This excessive sensitiveness very often brings an enrichment of the personality and contributes more to its charm than to the undoing of a person's character. Only, when difficult and un-

usual situations arise, the advantage frequently turns into a very great disadvantage, since calm consideration is then disturbed by untimely affects. Nothing could be more mistaken, though, than to regard this excessive sensitiveness as in itself a pathological character component. If that were really so, we should have to rate about one quarter of humanity as pathological. Yet if this sensitiveness has such destructive consequences for the individual, we must admit that it can no longer be considered quite normal.

399   We are driven to this contradiction when we contrast the two views concerning the significance of the psychological prehistory as sharply as we have done here. In reality, it is not a question of either one or the other. A certain innate sensitiveness produces a special prehistory, a special way of experiencing infantile events, which in their turn are not without influence on the development of the child's view of the world. Events bound up with powerful impressions can never pass off without leaving some trace on sensitive people. Some of them remain effective throughout life, and such events can have a determining influence on a person's whole mental development. Dirty and disillusioning experiences in the realm of sexuality are especially apt to frighten off a sensitive person for years afterwards, so that the mere thought of sex arouses the greatest resistances.

400   As the trauma theory shows, we are too much inclined, knowing of such cases, to attribute the emotional development of a person wholly, or at least very largely, to accidents. The old trauma theory went too far in this respect. We must never forget that the world is, in the first place, a subjective phenomenon. *The impressions we receive from these accidental happenings are also our own doing.* It is not true that the impressions are forced on us unconditionally; our own predisposition conditions the impression. A man whose libido is blocked will have, as a rule, quite different and very much more vivid impressions than one whose libido is organized in a wealth of activities. A person who is sensitive in one way or another will receive a deep impression from an event which would leave a less sensitive person cold.

401   Therefore, in addition to the accidental impression, we have to consider the subjective conditions seriously. Our previous

reflections, and in particular our discussion of an actual case, have shown that the most important subjective condition is regression. The effect of regression, as practical experience shows, is so great and so impressive that one might be inclined to attribute the effect of accidental occurrences solely to the mechanism of regression. Without any doubt, there are many cases where everything is dramatized, where even the traumatic experiences are pure figments of the imagination, and the few real events among them are afterwards completely distorted by fantastic elaboration. We can safely say that there is not a single case of neurosis in which the emotional value of the antecedent experience is not intensified by libido regression, and even when large tracts of infantile development seem to be extraordinarily significant (as for instance the relationship to the parents), it is almost always a regression that gives them this value.

402   The truth, as always, lies in the middle. The previous history certainly has a determining value, and this is intensified by regression. Sometimes the traumatic significance of the previous history comes more to the forefront, sometimes only its regressive meaning. These considerations naturally have to be applied to infantile sexual experiences as well. Obviously there are cases where brutal sexual experiences justify the shadow thrown on sexuality and make the later resistance to sex thoroughly comprehensible. (I would mention, by the way, that frightful impressions other than sexual can leave behind a permanent feeling of insecurity which may give the individual a hesitating attitude to reality.) Where real events of undoubted traumatic potency are absent—as is the case in most neuroses—the mechanism of regression predominates.

403   It might be objected that we have no criterion by which to judge the potential effect of a trauma, since this is an extremely relative concept. That is not altogether true; we have such a criterion in the average normal person. Something that is likely to make a strong and abiding impression on a normal person must be considered as having a determining influence for neurotics also. But we cannot attribute determining importance, in neurosis either, to impressions which normally would disappear and be forgotten. In most cases where some event has had an unexpected traumatic effect, we shall in all probability find a regression, that is to say, a secondary fantastic dramatization.

The earlier in childhood an impression is said to have arisen, the more suspect is its reality. Primitive people and animals have nothing like that capacity for reviving memories of unique impressions which we find among civilized people. Very young children are not nearly as impressionable as older children. The higher development of the mental faculties is an indispensable prerequisite for impressionability. We can therefore safely assume that the earlier a patient places some impressive experience in his childhood, the more likely it is to be a fantastic and regressive one. Deeper impressions are to be expected only from experiences in late childhood. At any rate, we generally have to attribute only regressive significance to the events of early infancy, that is, from the fifth year back. In later years, too, regression can sometimes play an overwhelming role, but even so one must not attribute too little importance to accidental events. In the later course of a neurosis, accidental events and regression together form a vicious circle: retreat from life leads to regression, and regression heightens resistance to life.

THE TELEOLOGICAL SIGNIFICANCE OF REGRESSION

404   ⟨Before pursuing our argument further, we must turn to the question of what teleological significance should be attributed to regressive fantasies. We might be satisfied with the hypothesis that these fantasies are simply a substitute for real action and therefore have no further significance. That can hardly be so. Psychoanalytic theory inclines to see the reason for the neurosis in the fantasies (illusions, prejudices, etc.), as their character betrays a tendency which is often directly opposed to reasonable action. Indeed, it often looks as if the patient were really using his previous history only to prove that he cannot act reasonably, whereupon the analyst, who, like everyone else, is easily inclined to sympathize with the patient (i.e., to identify with him unconsciously), gets the impression that the patient's arguments constitute a real aetiology. In other cases the fantasies have more the character of wonderful ideals which put beautiful and airy phantasms in the place of crude reality. Here a more or less obvious megalomania is always present, aptly compensating for the patient's indolence and deliberate incompetence. But the

decidedly sexual fantasies often reveal their purpose quite clearly, which is to accustom the patient to the thought of his sexual destiny, and so help him to overcome his resistance.

405   If we agree with Freud that neurosis is an unsuccessful attempt at self-cure, we must allow the fantasies, too, a double character: on one hand a pathological tendency to resist, on the other a helpful and preparatory tendency. With a normal person the libido, when it is blocked by an obstacle, forces him into a state of introversion and makes him reflect. So, too, with a neurotic under the same conditions: an introversion ensues, with increased fantasy activity. But he gets stuck there, because he prefers the infantile mode of adaptation as being the easier one. He does not see that he is exchanging his momentary advantage for a permanent disadvantage and has thus done himself a bad turn. In the same way, it is much easier and more convenient for the civic authorities to neglect all those troublesome sanitary precautions, but when an epidemic comes the sin of omission takes bitter revenge. If, therefore, the neurotic claims all manner of infantile alleviations, he must also accept the consequences. And if he is not willing to do so, then the consequences will overtake him.

406   It would, in general, be a great mistake to deny any teleological value to the apparently pathological fantasies of a neurotic. They are, as a matter of fact, the first beginnings of spiritualization, the first groping attempts to find new ways of adapting. His retreat to the infantile level does not mean only regression and stagnation, but also the possibility of discovering a new life-plan. Regression is thus in very truth the basic condition for the act of creation. Once again I must refer you to my oft-cited book *Symbols of Transformation*.⟩

8. THERAPEUTIC PRINCIPLES
OF PSYCHOANALYSIS

407   With the concept of regression, psychoanalysis made probably one of the most important discoveries in this field. Not only were the earlier formulations of the genesis of neurosis overthrown or at least considerably modified, but the *actual conflict* received, for the first time, its proper valuation.

408   In our earlier case of the lady and the horses, we saw that the symptomatological dramatization could only be understood when it was seen as an expression of the actual conflict. Here psychoanalytic theory joins hands with the results of the association experiments, of which I spoke in my lectures at Clark University. The association experiment, when conducted on a neurotic person, gives us a number of pointers to definite conflicts in his actual life, which we call complexes. These complexes contain just those problems and difficulties which have brought the patient into disharmony with himself. Generally we find a love-conflict of a quite obvious character. From the standpoint of the association experiment, neurosis appears as something quite different from what it seemed to be from the standpoint of earlier psychoanalytic theory. From that standpoint, neurosis seemed to be a formation having its roots in earliest infancy and overgrowing the normal psychic structure; considered from the standpoint of the association experiment, neurosis appears as a reaction to an actual conflict, which naturally is found just as often among normal people but is solved by them without too much difficulty. The neurotic, however, remains in the grip of the conflict, and his neurosis seems to be more or less the consequence of his having got stuck. We can say, therefore, that the results of the association experiment argue strongly in favour of the regression theory.

THE EVALUATION OF NEUROTIC FANTASIES

409   With the help of the earlier, "historical" conception of neurosis, we thought we could understand why a neurotic with a
powerful parental complex has such great difficulties in adapting himself to life. But now that we know that normal persons
have exactly the same complexes and, in principle, go through
the same psychological development as a neurotic, we can no
longer explain neurosis by the development of certain fantasy
systems. The really explanatory approach now is a prospective
one. We no longer ask whether the patient has a father or
mother complex, or unconscious incest fantasies which tie him
to his parents, for we know today that everybody has them. It
was a mistake to believe that only neurotics have such things.
We ask rather: What is the task which the patient does not
want to fulfil? What difficulty is he trying to avoid?

410   If a person tried always to adapt himself fully to the conditions of life, his libido would always be employed correctly and
adequately. When that does not happen, it gets blocked and
produces regressive symptoms. The non-fulfilment of the demands of adaptation, or the shrinking of the neurotic from difficulties, is, at bottom, the hesitation of every organism in the
face of a new effort to adapt. ⟨The training of animals provides
instructive examples in this respect, and in many cases such an
explanation is, in principle, sufficient. From this standpoint
the earlier mode of explanation, which maintained that the
resistance of the neurotic was due to his bondage to fantasies,
appears incorrect. But it would be very one-sided to take our
stand solely on a point of principle. There is *also* a bondage to
fantasies, even though the fantasies are, as a rule, secondary.
The neurotic's bondage to fantasies (illusions, prejudices, etc.)
develops gradually, as a habit, out of innumerable regressions
from obstacles since earliest childhood. All this grows into a
regular habit familiar to every student of neurosis; we all know
those patients who use their neurosis as an excuse for running
away from difficulties and shirking their duty. Their habitual
evasion produces a habit of mind which makes them take it for
granted that they should live out their fantasies instead of fulfilling disagreeable obligations. And this bondage to fantasy

makes reality seem less real to the neurotic, less valuable and less interesting, than it does to the normal person. As I explained earlier, the fantastic prejudices and resistances may also arise, sometimes, from experiences that were not intended at all; in other words, were not deliberately sought disappointments and suchlike.⟩

411   The ultimate and deepest root of neurosis appears to be the innate sensitiveness,[1] which causes difficulties even to the infant at the mother's breast, in the form of unnecessary excitement and resistance. The apparent aetiology of neurosis elicited by psychoanalysis is actually, in very many cases, only an inventory of carefully selected fantasies, reminiscences, etc., aiming in a definite direction and created by the patient out of the libido he did not use for biological adaptation. Those allegedly aetiological fantasies thus appear to be nothing but substitute formations, disguises, artificial explanations for the failure to adapt to reality. The aforementioned vicious circle of flight from reality and regression into fantasy is naturally very apt to give the illusion of seemingly decisive causal relationships, which the analyst as well as the patient believes in. Accidental occurrences intervene in this mechanism only as "mitigating circumstances." Their real and effective existence must, however, be acknowledged.

412   I must admit that those critics are partly right who get the impression, from their reading of psychoanalytic case histories, that it is all fantastic and artificial. Only, they make the mistake of attributing the fantastic artefacts and lurid, far-fetched symbolisms to the suggestion and fertile imagination of the analyst, and not to the incomparably more fertile fantasy of his patients. In the fantasy material of a psychoanalytic case history there is, indeed, very much that is artificial. But the most striking thing is the active inventiveness of the patient. And the critics are not so wrong, either, when they say that their neurotic patients have no such fantasies. I do not doubt that most of their patients are totally unconscious of having any fantasies at all. When it is in the unconscious, a fantasy is "real" only when it has some demonstrable effect on consciousness, for instance in the form of a dream. Otherwise we can say with a clear conscience that it is

1 ⟨Sensitiveness is naturally only one word for it. We could also say "reactivity" or "lability." As we know, there are many other words in circulation.⟩

not real. So anyone who overlooks the almost imperceptible effects of unconscious fantasies on consciousness, or dispenses with a thorough and technically irreproachable analysis of dreams, can easily overlook the fantasies of his patients altogether. We are therefore inclined to smile when we hear this oft-repeated objection.

413   Nevertheless, we must admit that there is some truth in it. The regressive tendency of the patient, reinforced by the attentions of the psychoanalyst in his examination of the unconscious fantasy activity, goes on inventing and creating even during the analysis. One could even say that this activity is greatly increased in the analytical situation, since the patient feels his regressive tendency strengthened by the interest of the analyst and produces even more fantasies than before. For this reason our critics have often remarked that a conscientious therapy of the neurosis should go in exactly the opposite direction to that taken by psychoanalysis; in other words, that it is the first task of therapy to extricate the patient from his unhealthy fantasies and bring him back again to real life.

414   The psychoanalyst, of course, is well aware of this, but he knows just how far one can go with this extricating of neurotics from their fantasies. As medical men, we should naturally never dream of preferring a difficult and complicated method, assailed by all the authorities, to a simple, clear, and easy one unless for a very good reason. I am perfectly well acquainted with hypnotic suggestion and Dubois' method of persuasion, but I do not use them because they are comparatively ineffective. For the same reason, I do not use "rééducation de la volonté" directly, as psychoanalysis gives me better results.

ACTIVE PARTICIPATION IN THE FANTASY

415   But, if we do use psychoanalysis, we must go along with the regressive fantasies of our patients. Psychoanalysis has a much broader outlook as regards the evaluation of symptoms than have the usual psychotherapeutic procedures. These all start from the assumption that neurosis is an entirely pathological formation. In the whole of neurology hitherto, no one has ever thought of seeing in the neurosis an attempt at healing, or, con-

sequently, of attributing to the neurotic formations a quite special teleological significance. But, like every illness, neurosis is only a compromise between the pathogenic causes and the normal function. Modern medicine no longer considers fever as the illness itself but as a purposive reaction of the organism. Similarly, psychoanalysis does not conceive the neurosis as anti-natural and in itself pathological, but as having a meaning and a purpose.

416   From this follows the inquiring and expectant attitude of psychoanalysis towards neurosis. In all cases it refrains from judging the value of a symptom, and tries instead to understand what tendencies lie beneath that symptom. If we were able to destroy a neurosis in the same way, for instance, as a cancer is destroyed, we would be destroying at the same time a large amount of useful energy. We save this energy, that is, we make it serve the purposes of the drive for recuperation, by pursuing the meaning of the symptoms and going along with the regressive movement of the patient. Those unfamiliar with the essentials of psychoanalysis will certainly have some difficulty in understanding how a therapeutic effect can be achieved when the analyst enters into the "harmful" fantasies of his patients. Not only the opponents of psychoanalysis but the patients themselves doubt the therapeutic value of such a method, which concentrates attention on the very things that the patient condemns as worthless and reprehensible, namely his fantasies. Patients will often tell you that their former doctors forbade them to have any concern with their fantasies, explaining that they could only consider themselves well when they were free, if only temporarily, from this terrible scourge. Naturally they wonder what good it will do when the treatment leads them back to the very place from which they consistently tried to escape.

417   This objection can be answered as follows: it all depends on the attitude the patient takes towards his fantasies. Hitherto, the patient's fantasying was a completely passive and involuntary activity. He was lost in his dreams, as we say. Even his so-called "brooding" was nothing but an involuntary fantasy. What psychoanalysis demands of the patient is apparently the same thing, but only a person with a very superficial knowledge of psychoanalysis could confuse this passive dreaming with the

attitude now required. What psychoanalysis asks of the patient is the exact opposite of what the patient has always done. He is like a man who has unintentionally fallen into the water and sunk, whereas psychoanalysis wants him to act like a diver. It was no mere chance which led him to fall in just at that spot. There lies the sunken treasure, but only a diver can bring it to the surface.

418   That is to say, when the patient judges them from a rational standpoint, he regards his fantasies as worthless and meaningless. In reality, however, they exert their great influence just because they are of such great importance. They are sunken treasures which can only be recovered by a diver; in other words the patient, contrary to his wont, must now deliberately turn his attention to his inner life. Where formerly he dreamed, he must now think, consciously and intentionally. This new way of thinking about himself has about as much resemblance to his former state of mind as a diver has to a drowning man. His former compulsion now has a meaning and a purpose, it has become *work*. The patient, assisted by the analyst, immerses himself in his fantasies, not in order to lose himself in them, but to salvage them, piece by piece, and bring them into the light of day. He thus acquires an objective vantage-point from which to view his inner life, and can now tackle the very thing he feared and hated. Here we have the basic principle of all psychoanalytic treatment.

THE TASK OF ADAPTATION

419   Previously, because of his illness, the patient stood partly or wholly outside life. Consequently he neglected many of his duties, either in regard to social achievement or in regard to his purely human tasks. He must get back to fulfilling these duties if he wants to become well again. By way of caution, I would remark that "duties" are not to be understood here as general ethical postulates, but as duties to himself, by which again I do not mean egocentric interests—for a human being is also a social being, a fact too easily forgotten by individualists. A normal person feels very much more comfortable sharing a common virtue than possessing an individual vice, no matter how seduc-

tive it may be. He must already be a neurotic, or an otherwise unusual person, if he lets himself be deluded by special interests of this kind.

420   The neurotic shrank from his duties and his libido turned away, at least partly, from the tasks imposed by reality. Consequently it became introverted, directed towards his inner life. Because no attempt was made to master any real difficulties, his libido followed the path of regression, so that fantasy largely took the place of reality. Unconsciously—and very often consciously—the neurotic prefers to live in his dreams and fantasies. In order to bring him back to reality and to the fulfilment of his necessary tasks, psychoanalysis proceeds along the same "false" track of regression which was taken by the libido of the patient, so that at the beginning the analysis looks as if it were supporting his morbid proclivities. But psychoanalysis follows the false tracks of fantasy in order to restore the libido, the valuable part of the fantasies, to consciousness and apply it to the duties of the present. This can only be done by bringing up the unconscious fantasies, together with the libido attached to them. Were there no libido attached, we could safely leave these unconscious fantasies to their own shadowy existence. Unavoidably the patient, feeling confirmed in his regressive tendency by the mere fact of having started the analysis, will, amid increasing resistances, lead the analyst's interest down to the depths of his unconscious shadow-world.

421   It will readily be understood that every analyst, as a normal person, will feel in himself the greatest resistances to the regressive tendency of the patient, as he is quite convinced that this tendency is pathological. As a doctor, he believes he is acting quite rightly not to enter into his patient's fantasies. He is understandably repelled by this tendency, for it is indeed repulsive to see somebody completely given up to such fantasies, finding only himself important and admiring himself unceasingly. Moreover, for the aesthetic sensibilities of the normal person, the average run of neurotic fantasies is exceedingly disagreeable, if not downright disgusting. The psychoanalyst, of course, must put aside all aesthetic value-judgments, just like every other doctor who really wants to help his patient. He must not shudder at dirty work. Naturally there are a great many patients who are physically ill and who do recover through

the application of ordinary physical methods, dietetic or suggestive, without closer exploration and radical treatment. But severe cases can be helped only by a therapy based on an exact investigation and thorough knowledge of the illness. Our psychotherapeutic methods hitherto were general measures of this kind; in mild cases they do no harm, on the contrary they are often of real use. But a great many patients prove inaccessible to these methods. If anything helps here, it is psychoanalysis, which is not to say that psychoanalysis is a cure-all. This is a sneer that comes only from ill-natured criticism. We know very well that psychoanalysis fails in certain cases. As everybody knows, we shall never be able to cure all illnesses.

422   The "diving" work of analysis brings up dirty material, piece by piece, out of the slime, but it must first be cleaned before we can recognize its value. The dirty fantasies are valueless and are thrown aside, but the libido attached to them is of value and this, after the work of cleaning, becomes serviceable again. To the professional psychoanalyst, as to every specialist, it will sometimes seem that the fantasies have a value of their own, and not just the libido. But their value is no concern of the patient's. For the analyst these fantasies have only a scientific value, just as it may be of special interest to the surgeon to know whether the pus contains staphylococci or streptococci. To the patient it is all the same, and so far as he is concerned it is better for the analyst to conceal his scientific interest, lest the patient be tempted to take more pleasure than necessary in his fantasies. The aetiological significance which is attributed to these fantasies—incorrectly, to my mind—explains why so much space is given up to the extensive discussion of all forms of fantasy in the psychoanalytic literature. Once one knows that in this sphere absolutely nothing is impossible, the initial estimation of fantasies will gradually wear itself out, and with it the attempt to discover in them an aetiological significance. Nor will the most exhaustive discussion of case histories ever succeed in emptying this ocean. Theoretically the fantasies in each case are inexhaustible.

423   In most cases, however, the production of fantasies ceases after a time, from which one must not conclude that the possibilities of fantasy are exhausted; the cessation only means that no more libido is regressing. The end of the regressive move-

ment is reached when the libido seizes hold of the actualities of life and is used for the solution of necessary tasks. There are cases, and not a few of them, where the patient continues to produce endless fantasies, whether for his own pleasure or because of the mistaken expectations of the analyst. Such a mistake is especially easy for beginners, since, blinded by psychoanalytic case histories, they keep their interest fixed on the alleged aetiological significance of the fantasies, and are constantly endeavouring to fish up more fantasies from the infantile past, vainly hoping to find there the solution of the neurotic difficulties. They do not see that the solution lies in action, in the fulfilment of certain necessary obligations to life. It will be objected that the neurosis is entirely due to the incapacity of the patient to carry out these tasks, and that, by analysing the unconscious, the therapist ought to enable him to do so, or at least give him the means of doing so.

424   Put in this way, the objection is perfectly true, but we have to add that it is valid only when the patient is really conscious of the task he has to fulfil—conscious of it not only academically, in general theoretical outline, but also in detail. It is characteristic of neurotics to be wanting in this knowledge, although, because of their intelligence, they are well aware of the general duties of life, and struggle perhaps only too hard to fulfil the precepts of current morality. But for that very reason they know all the less, sometimes nothing at all, about the incomparably more important duties to themselves. It is not enough, therefore, to follow the patient blindfold on the path of regression, and to push him back into his infantile fantasies by an untimely aetiological interest. I often hear from patients who have got stuck in a psychoanalytic treatment: "My analyst thinks I must have an infantile trauma somewhere, or a fantasy I am still repressing." Apart from cases where this conjecture happened to be true, I have seen others in which the stoppage was caused by the fact that the libido, hauled up by the analysis, sank back again into the depths for want of employment. This was due to the analyst directing his attention entirely to the infantile fantasies and his failure to see what task of adaptation the patient had to fulfil. The consequence was that the libido always sank back again, as it was given no opportunity for further activity.

425   There are many patients who, quite on their own account, discover their life-tasks and stop the production of regressive fantasies fairly soon, because they prefer to live in reality rather than in fantasy. It is a pity that this cannot be said of all patients. A good many of them postpone the fulfilment of their life-tasks indefinitely, perhaps for ever, and prefer their idle neurotic dreaming. I must emphasize yet again that by "dreaming" we do not mean a conscious phenomenon.

426   In consequence of these facts and insights, the character of psychoanalysis has changed in the course of the years. If in its first stage psychoanalysis was a kind of surgery, which removed the foreign body, the blocked affect, from the psyche, in its later form it was a kind of historical method, which tried to investigate the genesis of the neurosis in all its details and to trace it back to its earliest beginnings.

THE TRANSFERENCE

427   There is no doubt that this method owed its existence not only to a strong scientific interest but also to the personal "empathy" of the analyst, traces of which can clearly be seen in the psychoanalytic case material. Thanks to this personal feeling, Freud was able to discover wherein lay the therapeutic effect of psychoanalysis. While this was formerly sought in the discharge of the traumatic affect, it was now found that the fantasies brought out by analysis were all associated with the person of the analyst. Freud called this process the *transference*, because the patient transferred to the analyst the fantasies that were formerly attached to the memory-images of the parents. The transference is not limited to the purely intellectual sphere; rather, the libido that is invested in the fantasies precipitates itself, together with the fantasies, upon the analyst. All those sexual fantasies which cluster round the imago of the parents now cluster round him, and the less the patient realizes this, the stronger will be his unconscious tie to the analyst.

428   This discovery is of fundamental importance in several ways. Above all, the transference is of great biological value to the patient. The less libido he gives to reality, the more exaggerated will be his fantasies and the more he will be cut off from the

world. Typical of neurotics is their disturbed relationship to reality—that is to say, their reduced adaptation. The transference to the analyst builds a bridge across which the patient can get away from his family into reality. He can now emerge from his infantile milieu into the world of adults, since the analyst represents for him a part of the world outside the family.

429   On the other hand, the transference is a powerful hindrance to the progress of the treatment, because the patient assimilates the analyst, who should stand for a part of the extrafamilial world, to his father and mother, so that the whole advantage of his new acquisition is jeopardized. The more he is able to see the analyst objectively, to regard him as he does any other individual, the greater becomes the advantage of the transference. The less he is able to see the analyst in this way, and the more he assimilates him to the father imago, the less advantageous the transference will be and the greater the harm it will do. The patient has merely widened the scope of his family by the addition of a quasi-parental personality. He himself is, as before, still in the infantile milieu and therefore maintains his infantile constellation. In this manner all the advantages of the transference can be lost.

430   There are patients who follow the analysis with the greatest interest without making the slightest improvement, remaining extraordinarily productive in their fantasies although the whole previous history of their neurosis, even its darkest corners, seems to have been brought to light. An analyst under the influence of the historical view might easily be thrown into confusion, and would have to ask himself: What is there in this case still to be analysed? These are just the cases I had in mind before, when I said it is no longer a matter of analysing the historical material, but of action, of overcoming the infantile attitude. The historical analysis would show over and over again that the patient has an infantile attitude to the analyst, but it would not tell us how to alter it. Up to a certain point, this serious disadvantage of the transference applies to every case. It has gradually proved, even, that the part of psychoanalysis so far discussed, extraordinarily interesting and valuable though it may be from a scientific point of view, is in practice far less important than what now has to follow, namely, the analysis of the transference itself.

CONFESSION AND PSYCHOANALYSIS

431   Before I discuss in detail this especially important part of the analysis, I should like to draw attention to a parallel between the first stage of psychoanalysis and a certain cultural institution. By this I mean the religious institution of confession.

432   Nothing makes people more lonely, and more cut off from the fellowship of others, than the possession of an anxiously hidden and jealously guarded personal secret. Very often it is "sinful" thoughts and deeds that keep them apart and estrange them from one another. Here confession sometimes has a truly redeeming effect. The tremendous feeling of relief which usually follows a confession can be ascribed to the readmission of the lost sheep into the human community. His moral isolation and seclusion, which were so difficult to bear, cease. Herein lies the chief psychological value of confession.

433   Besides that, however, it has other consequences: through the transference of his secret and all the unconscious fantasies underlying it, a moral bond is formed between the patient and his father confessor. We call this a "transference relationship." Anyone with psychoanalytic experience knows how much the personal significance of the analyst is enhanced when the patient is able to confess his secrets to him. The change this induces in the patient's behaviour is often amazing. This, too, is an effect probably intended by the Church. The fact that by far the greater part of humanity not only needs guidance, but wishes for nothing better than to be guided and held in tutelage, justifies, in a sense, the moral value which the Church sets on confession. The priest, equipped with all the insignia of paternal authority, becomes the responsible leader and shepherd of his flock. He is the father confessor and the members of his parish are his penitent children.

434   Thus priest and Church replace the parents, and to that extent they free the individual from the bonds of the family. In so far as the priest is a morally elevated personality with a natural nobility of soul and a mental culture to match, the institution of confession may be commended as a brilliant method of social guidance and education, which did in fact perform a tre-

mendous educative task for more than fifteen hundred years. So long as the medieval Church knew how to be the guardian of art and science—a role in which her success was due, in part, to her wide tolerance of worldly interests—confession was an admirable instrument of education. But it lost its educative value, at least for more highly developed people, as soon as the Church proved incapable of maintaining her leadership in the intellectual sphere—the inevitable consequence of spiritual rigidity. The more highly developed men of our time do not want to be guided by a creed or a dogma; they want to understand. So it is not surprising if they throw aside everything they do not understand; and religious symbols, being the least intelligible of all, are generally the first to go overboard. The sacrifice of the intellect demanded by a positive belief is a violation against which the conscience of the more highly developed individual rebels.

435   So far as analysis is concerned, in perhaps the majority of cases the transference to and dependence on the analyst could be regarded as a sufficient end with a definite therapeutic effect, provided that the analyst was a commanding personality and in every way capable of guiding his patients responsibly and being a "father to his people." But a modern, mentally developed person strives, consciously or unconsciously, to govern himself and stand morally on his own feet. He wants to take the helm in his own hands; the steering has too long been done by others. He wants to understand; in other words, he wants to be an adult. It is much easier to be guided, but this no longer suits intelligent people today, for they feel that the spirit of the age requires them to exercise moral autonomy. Psychoanalysis has to reckon with this requirement, and has therefore to reject the demand of the patient for constant guidance and instruction. The analyst knows his own shortcomings too well to believe that he could play the role of father and guide. His highest ambition must consist only in educating his patients to become independent personalities, and in freeing them from their unconscious bondage to infantile limitations. He must therefore analyse the transference, a task left untouched by the priest. Through the analysis the unconscious—and sometimes conscious—tie to the analyst is cut, and the patient is set upon his own feet. That, at least, is the aim of the treatment.[2]

2 [Cf. the "Psychology of the Transference" for a more detailed study.]

ANALYSIS OF THE TRANSFERENCE

436   The transference introduces all sorts of difficulties into the relationship between analyst and patient because, as we have seen, the analyst is always more or less assimilated to the family. The first part of the analysis, the discovery of complexes, is fairly easy, thanks to the fact that everyone likes to unburden himself of his painful secrets. Also, he experiences a particular satisfaction in at last finding someone who has an understanding ear for all those things to which nobody would listen before. For the patient it is a singularly agreeable sensation to be understood and to have a doctor who is determined to understand him at all costs, and is willing to follow him, apparently, through all his devious ways. There are patients who even have a special "test" for this, a special question which the analyst has to go into; if he cannot or will not do this, or if he overlooks it, then he is no good. The feeling of being understood is especially sweet to all those lonely souls who are insatiable in their demand for "understanding."

437   For patients with such an obliging disposition, the beginning of the analysis is, as a rule, fairly simple. The therapeutic effects, often considerable, which may appear about this time are easy to obtain, and for that reason they may seduce the beginner into a therapeutic optimism and analytical superficiality which bear no relation to the seriousness and peculiar difficulties of his task. The trumpeting of therapeutic successes is nowhere more contemptible than in psychoanalysis, for no one should know better than the psychoanalyst that the therapeutic result ultimately depends far more on the co-operation of nature and of the patient himself. The psychoanalyst may legitimately pride himself on his increased insight into the essence and structure of neurosis, an insight that greatly exceeds all previous knowledge in this field. But psychoanalytic publications to date cannot be acquitted of the charge of sometimes showing psychoanalysis in a false light. There are technical publications which give the uninitiated person the impression that psychoanalysis is a more or less clever trick, productive of astonishing results.

438   The first stage of the analysis, when we try to understand, and in this way often relieve, the patient's feelings, is responsi-

ble for these therapeutic illusions. The improvements that may appear at the beginning of an analysis are naturally not really results of the treatment, but are generally only passing alleviations which greatly assist the process of transference. After the initial resistances to the transference have been overcome, it turns out to be an ideal situation for a neurotic. He does not need to make any effort himself, and yet someone comes to meet him more than halfway, someone with an unwonted and peculiar wish to understand, who does not allow himself to get bored and is not put off by anything, although the patient sometimes does his utmost to rile him with his wilfulness and childish defiance. This forbearance is enough to melt the strongest resistances, so that the patient no longer hesitates to set the analyst among his family gods, i.e., to assimilate him to the infantile milieu.

439   At the same time, the patient satisfies another need, that is, he achieves a relationship outside the family and thus fulfils a biological demand. Hence the patient obtains a double advantage from the transference relationship: a personality who on the one hand is expected to bestow on him a loving attention in all his concerns, and to that extent is equated with father and mother, but who, on the other hand, is outside the family and thus helps him to fulfil a vitally important and difficult duty without the least danger to himself. When, on top of that, this acquisition is coupled with a marked therapeutic effect, as not infrequently happens, the patient is fortified in his belief that his new-found situation is an excellent one. We can readily appreciate that he is not in the least inclined to give up all these advantages. If it were left to him, he would prefer to remain united with the analyst for ever. Accordingly, he now starts to produce numerous fantasies showing how this goal might be attained. Eroticism plays a large role here, and is exploited and exaggerated in order to demonstrate the impossibility of separation. The patient, understandably enough, puts up the most obstinate resistance when the analyst tries to break the transference relationship.

440   We must not forget, however, that for a neurotic the acquisition of an extrafamilial relationship is one of life's duties, as it is for everyone, and a duty which till then he has either not fulfilled at all or fulfilled in a very limited way. At this point I

must energetically oppose the view one so often hears that an extrafamilial relationship always means a sexual relationship. ⟨In many cases one would like to say: it is precisely not that. It is a favourite neurotic misunderstanding that the right attitude to the world is found by indulgence in sex. In this respect, too, the literature of psychoanalysis is not free from misrepresentations; indeed there are publications from which no other conclusions can be drawn. This misunderstanding is far older than psychoanalysis, however, and so cannot be laid altogether at its door. The experienced medical man knows this advice very well, and I have had more than one patient who has acted according to this prescription. But when a psychoanalyst recommends it, he is making the same mistake as his patient, who believes that his sexual fantasies come from pent-up ("repressed") sexuality. If that were so, this recipe would naturally be a salutary one. It is not a question of that at all, but of regressive libido which exaggerates the fantasies because it evades the real task and strives back to the infantile level.⟩ If we support this regressive tendency at all points we simply reinforce the infantile attitude from which the neurotic is suffering. He has to learn the higher adaptation which life demands from mature and civilized people. Those who have a decided tendency to sink lower will proceed to do so; they need no psychoanalysis for that.

441   At the same time, we must be careful that we do not fall into the opposite extreme of thinking that psychoanalysis creates nothing but quite exceptional personalities. Psychoanalysis stands outside traditional morality; for the present it should adhere to no general moral standard. It is, and should be, only a means for giving the individual trends breathing-space, for developing them and bringing them into harmony with the rest of the personality. It should be a biological method, whose aim is to combine the highest subjective well-being with the most valuable biological performance. As man is not only an individual but also a member of society, these two tendencies inherent in human nature can never be separated, or the one subordinated to the other, without doing him serious injury.

442   The best result for a person who undergoes an analysis is that he shall become in the end what he really is, in harmony with himself, neither good nor bad, just as he is in his natural state. Psychoanalysis cannot be considered a method of educa-

tion, if by education we mean the topiary art of clipping a tree into a beautiful artificial shape. But those who have a higher conception of education will prize most the method of cultivating a tree so that it fulfils to perfection its own natural conditions of growth. We yield too much to the ridiculous fear that we are at bottom quite impossible beings, that if everyone were to appear as he really is a frightful social catastrophe would ensue. Many people today take "man as he really is" to mean merely the eternally discontented, anarchic, rapacious element in human beings, quite forgetting that these same human beings have also erected those firmly established forms of civilization which possess greater strength and stability than all the anarchic undercurrents. ⟨The strengthening of his social personality is one of the essential conditions for man's existence. Were it not so, humanity would cease to be. The selfishness and rebelliousness we meet in the neurotic's psychology are not "man as he really is" but an infantile distortion. In reality the normal man is "civic-minded and moral"; he created his laws and observes them, not because they are imposed on him from without—that is a childish delusion—but because he loves law and order more than he loves disorder and lawlessness.⟩

RESOLUTION OF THE TRANSFERENCE

443   In order to resolve the transference, we have to fight against forces which are not merely neurotic but have a general significance for normal human beings. In trying to get the patient to break the transference relationship, we are asking of him something that is seldom, or never, demanded of the average person, namely, that he should conquer himself completely. Only certain religions demanded this of the individual, and it is this that makes the second stage of analysis so very difficult.

444   ⟨As you know, it is an habitual prejudice of children to think that love gives them the right to make demands. The infantile conception of loving is getting presents from others. Patients make demands in accordance with this definition, and thus behave no differently from most normal people, whose infantile cupidity is only prevented from reaching too high a pitch by their fulfilling their duties to life and by the satisfaction this

affords the libido, and also because a certain lack of temperament does not incline them from the start to passionate behaviour. The basic trouble with the neurotic is that, instead of adapting himself to life in his own special way, which would require a high degree of self-discipline, he makes infantile demands and then begins to bargain. The analyst will hardly be disposed to comply with the demands the patient makes on him personally, but circumstances may arise in which he will seek to buy his freedom with compromises. For instance, he might throw out hints of moral liberties which, if turned into a maxim, would bring about a general lowering of the cultural level. But in that way the patient merely sinks to the lower level and becomes inferior. Nor is it, in the end, a question of culture at all, but simply of the analyst buying his way out of the constricting transference situation by offering other, alleged advantages. It goes against the real interests of the patient to hold out these compensating advantages so enticingly; at that rate he will never be freed from his infantile cupidity and indolence. Only self-conquest can free him from these.

445   The neurotic has to prove that he, just as much as a normal person, can live reasonably. Indeed, he must do more than a normal person, he must give up a large slice of his infantilism, which nobody asks a normal person to do.

446   Patients often try to convince themselves, by seeking out special adventures, that it is possible to go on living in an infantile way. It would be a great mistake if the analyst tried to stop them. There are experiences which one must go through and for which reason is no substitute. Such experiences are often of inestimable value to the patient.

447   Nowhere more clearly than at this stage of the analysis will everything depend on how far the analyst has been analysed himself. If he himself has an infantile type of desire of which he is still unconscious, he will never be able to open his patient's eyes to this danger. It is an open secret that all through the analysis intelligent patients are looking beyond it into the soul of the analyst, in order to find there the confirmation of the healing formulae—or its opposite. It is quite impossible, even by the subtlest analysis, to prevent the patient from taking over instinctively the way in which his analyst deals with the problems of life. Nothing can stop this, for personality teaches more

than thick tomes full of wisdom. All the disguises in which he wraps himself in order to conceal his own personality avail him nothing; sooner or later he will come across a patient who calls his bluff. An analyst who from the first takes his profession seriously is faced with the inexorable necessity of testing out the principles of psychoanalysis on himself as well. He will be astonished to see how many apparently technical difficulties vanish in this way. Note that I am not speaking of the initial stage of analysis, which might be called the stage of unearthing the complexes, but of this final, extraordinarily tricky stage which is concerned with the resolution of the transference.

448   I have frequently found that beginners look upon the transference as an entirely abnormal phenomenon that has to be "fought against." Nothing could be more mistaken. To begin with we have to regard the transference merely as a falsification, a sexualized caricature, of the social bond which holds human society together and which also produces close ties between people of like mind. This bond is one of the most valuable social factors imaginable, and it would be a cruel mistake to reject absolutely these social overtures on the part of the patient. It is only necessary to purge them of their regressive components, their infantile sexualism. If that is done, the transference becomes a most convenient instrument of adaptation.

449   The only danger—and it is a great one—is that the unacknowledged infantile demands of the analyst may identify themselves with the parallel demands of the patient. The analyst can avoid this only by submitting to a rigorous analysis at the hands of another. He then learns to understand what analysis really means and how it feels to experience it on your own psyche. Every intelligent analyst will at once see how much this must redound to the benefit of his patients. There are analysts who believe that they can get along with a self-analysis. This is Munchausen psychology, and they will certainly remain stuck. They forget that one of the most important therapeutically effective factors is subjecting yourself to the objective judgment of another. As regards ourselves we remain blind, despite everything and everybody. The analyst, of all people, must give up all isolationist tactics and autoerotic mystification if he wants to help his patients to become socially mature and independent personalities.

450   I know that I am also at one with Freud when I set it up as a self-evident requirement that a psychoanalyst must discharge his own duties to life in the proper way. If he does not, nothing can stop his unutilized libido from automatically descending on his patients and in the end falsifying the whole analysis. Immature and incompetent persons who are themselves neurotic and stand with only one foot in reality generally make nothing but nonsense out of analysis. *Exempla sunt odiosa!* Medicine in the hand of a fool was ever poison and death. Just as we demand from a surgeon, besides his technical knowledge, a skilled hand, courage, presence of mind, and power of decision, so we must expect from an analyst a very serious and thorough psychoanalytic training of his own personality before we are willing to entrust a patient to him. I would even go so far as to say that the acquisition and practice of the psychoanalytic technique presuppose not only a specific psychological gift but in the very first place a serious concern with the moulding of one's own character.)

451   The technique for resolving the transference is the same as the one we have already described. The problem of what the patient is to do with the libido he has withdrawn from the person of the analyst naturally occupies a large place. Here too the danger for the beginner is great, as he will be inclined to suggest or to give advice. For the patient the analyst's efforts in this respect are extremely convenient, and therefore fatal. At this important juncture, as everywhere in psychoanalysis, we have to let the patient and his impulses take the lead, even if the path seems a wrong one. Error is just as important a condition of life's progress as truth.

THE PROSPECTIVE FUNCTION OF DREAMS

452   In this second stage of analysis, with its hidden reefs and shoals, we owe an enormous amount to dreams. At the beginning of the analysis, dreams helped us chiefly to discover the fantasies; but here they are often extremely valuable guides to the use of libido. Freud's work laid the foundation for an immense increase in our knowledge in regard to the determination of the manifest dream content by historical material and wish-

ful tendencies. He showed how dreams give access to a mass of subliminal material, mostly memories that have sunk below the threshold. In keeping with his genius for the purely historical method, Freud's procedure is predominantly analytical. Although this method is incontestably of great value we ought not to adopt this standpoint exclusively, as a one-sided historical view does not take sufficient account of the teleological significance of dreams (stressed in particular by Maeder [3]). Unconscious thinking would be quite inadequately characterized if we considered it only from the standpoint of its historical determinants. For a complete evaluation we have unquestionably to consider its teleological or prospective significance as well. If we pursued the history of the English Parliament back to its earliest beginnings, we should undoubtedly arrive at an excellent understanding of its development and the way its present form was determined. But that would tell us nothing about its prospective function, that is, about the tasks it has to accomplish now and in the future.

453   The same is true of dreams, whose prospective function alone was valued in the superstitions of all times and races. There may well be a good deal of truth in this view. Without presuming to say that dreams have prophetic foresight, it is nevertheless possible that we might find, in this subliminal material, combinations of future events which are subliminal simply because they have not yet attained the degree of clarity necessary for them to become conscious. Here I am thinking of those dim presentiments we sometimes have of the future, which are nothing but very faint, subliminal combinations of events whose objective value we are not yet able to apperceive.

454   The future tendencies of the patient are elaborated with the help of these teleological components of the dream. If this work is successful, the patient passes out of the treatment and out of the semi-infantile transference relationship into a life which has been carefully prepared within him, which he has chosen himself, and to which, after mature deliberation, he can declare himself committed.

3 ["Die Symbolik in den Legenden, Märchen, Gebräuchen und Träumen" (1908). —EDITORS.]

FUTURE USES OF PSYCHOANALYSIS

455   As will readily be understood, psychoanalysis can never be used for polyclinical work. It must always remain in the hands of the few who, because of their innate educative and psychological capacities, have a particular aptitude and a special liking for this profession. Just as not every doctor makes a good surgeon, not everyone is fitted to be a psychoanalyst. The predominantly psychological nature of the work will make it difficult for the medical profession to monopolize it. Sooner or later other branches of science will master the method, either for practical reasons or out of theoretical interest. So long as orthodox science excludes psychoanalysis from general discussion as sheer nonsense, we cannot be surprised if other departments learn to master the material before the medical profession does. This is all the more likely as psychoanalysis is a general method of psychological research and a heuristic principle of the first rank in the domain of the humane sciences.

456   It is chiefly the work of the Zurich school that has demonstrated the applicability of psychoanalysis as a method of investigation in mental disease. Psychoanalytic investigation of dementia praecox, for instance, has given us most valuable insights into the psychological structure of this remarkable disease. It would lead me too far afield to go at all deeply into the results of these investigations. The theory of the psychological determinants of this disease is a sufficiently vast territory in itself, and if I were to discuss the symbolistic problems of dementia praecox I would have to put before you a mass of material which I could not hope to deploy within the framework of these lectures, whose purpose is to provide a general survey.

457   The question of dementia praecox has become so extraordinarily complicated because the recent incursion of psychoanalysis into the domains of mythology and comparative religion has afforded us deep insight into ethnological symbolism. Those who were familiar with the symbolism of dreams and of dementia praecox were astounded by the parallelism between the symbols found in modern individuals and those found in the history of the human race. Most startling of all is the parallelism between ethnic and schizophrenic symbols. The complicated

relations between psychology and mythology make it impossible for me to discuss in detail my views on dementia praecox. For the same reason I must refrain from discussing the results of the psychoanalytic investigation of mythology and comparative religion. The principal result of these investigations at present is the discovery of far-reaching parallels between ethnic and individual symbolisms. We cannot yet see what vast perspectives this ethnopsychology may open out. But, from all we know at present, we may expect that psychoanalytic research into the nature of subliminal processes will be enormously enriched and deepened by a study of mythology.

9. A CASE OF NEUROSIS IN A CHILD

458   In these lectures I have had to confine myself to giving you
a general account of the nature of psychoanalysis. Detailed discussion of the method and theory would have required a mass
of case material, exposition of which would have detracted from
a comprehensive view of the whole. But, in order to give you
some idea of the actual process of psychoanalytic treatment,
I have decided to present a fairly short analysis of an eleven-
year-old girl. The case was analysed by my assistant, Miss Mary
Moltzer. I must preface my remarks by saying that this case is
no more typical of the length or course of an ordinary psychoanalysis than one individual is typical of all others. Nowhere is
the abstraction of generally valid rules so difficult as in psychoanalysis, for which reason it is better not to make too many
formulations. We must not forget that, notwithstanding the
great uniformity of conflicts and complexes, every case is unique,
because every individual is unique. Every case demands the
analyst's individual interest, and in every case the course of
analysis is different.

459   In presenting this case, therefore, I am offering but a small
section of the infinitely varied world of the psyche, showing all
those apparently bizarre and arbitrary peculiarities which the
whim of so-called chance scatters into a human life. It is not my
intention to withhold any of the more interesting psychoanalytic details, as I do not want to evoke the impression that
psychoanalysis is a rigidly formalistic method. The scientific
needs of the investigator prompt him always to look for rules
and categories in which the most alive of all living things can
be captured. The analyst and observer, on the other hand, must
eschew formulas and let the living reality work upon him in all
its lawless profusion. Thus I shall try to present this case in its
natural setting, and I hope I shall succeed in showing you how
differently an analysis develops from what might have been expected on purely theoretical grounds.

460   The case in question is that of an intelligent eleven-year-old girl of good family.

ANAMNESIS

461   The clinical history is as follows: She had to leave school several times on account of sudden nausea and headaches, and was obliged to go to bed. In the morning she sometimes refused to get up and go to school. She suffered from bad dreams, was moody and unreliable. I informed the mother, who came to consult me, that these might be the signs of a neurosis, and that something special might be hidden behind them about which one would have to ask the child. This conjecture was not an arbitrary one, for every attentive observer knows that if children are so restless and bad-tempered something is worrying them.

462   The child now confessed to her mother the following story. She had a favourite teacher, on whom she had a crush. During this last term she had fallen behind with her work, and she thought she had sunk in her teacher's estimation. She then began to feel sick during his lessons. She felt not only estranged from her teacher, but even rather hostile to him. She directed all her friendly feelings to a poor boy with whom she usually shared the bread she took to school. She now gave him money as well, so that he could buy bread for himself. Once, in conversation with this boy, she made fun of her teacher and called him a goat. The boy attached himself to her more and more, and considered that he had the right to levy an occasional tribute from her in the form of a little present of money. Then she became afraid that the boy would tell the teacher she had called him a goat, and she promised him two francs if he would give her his solemn word never to say anything to the teacher. From that moment the boy began to blackmail her; he demanded money with threats, and persecuted her with his demands on the way to school. She was in despair. Her attacks of sickness were closely connected with this story; yet, after the affair had been settled as a result of this confession, her peace of mind was not restored as we would have expected.

463   Very often, as I mentioned in the previous lecture, the mere relation of a painful episode has a favourable therapeutic effect.

Generally this does not last very long, although on occasion it may be maintained for a long time. Such a confession is naturally a long way from being an analysis, despite the fact that there are many nerve specialists nowadays who believe that an analysis is only a somewhat more extensive anamnesis or confession.

464   Not long afterwards, the child had a violent attack of coughing and missed school for one day. After that she went back to school for one day and felt perfectly well. On the third day a renewed attack of coughing came on, with pains on the left side, fever and vomiting. She had a temperature of 103° F. The doctor feared pneumonia. But the next day everything had disappeared again. She felt quite well, and there was no trace of fever or nausea.

465   But still our little patient wept the whole time and did not wish to get up. From this strange course of events I suspected a serious neurosis, and I therefore advised analytical treatment.

FIRST INTERVIEW

466   The little girl seemed nervous and constrained, now and then giving a disagreeable forced laugh. She was first of all given an opportunity to talk about what it felt like to be allowed to stay in bed. We learn that it was especially nice then, as she always had company. Everybody came to see her; best of all, she could get herself read to by Mama, from a book with the story in it of a *prince who was ill and only got well again when his wish was fulfilled, the wish being that his little friend, a poor boy, might be allowed to stay with him.*

467   The obvious relation between this story and her own little love-story, as well as its connection with her sickness, was pointed out to her, whereupon she began to weep, saying that she would rather go with the other children and play with them, or they would run away. This was at once allowed, and away she ran, but came back again in no time, somewhat crestfallen. It was explained to her that she had not run away because she was afraid her playmates would run away, but that she herself wanted to run away because of resistances.

468   At the second interview she was less anxious and inhibited. The conversation was led round to the teacher, but she was too embarrassed to speak about him. Finally came the shamefaced admission that she liked him very much. It was explained to her that she need not be ashamed of that; on the contrary, her love was a guarantee that she would do her very best in his lessons. "So then I may like him?" asked the little patient with a happier face.

469   This explanation justified the child in her choice of a love-object. She had, it seemed, been afraid to admit to herself her feelings for the teacher. It is not easy to explain why this should be so. It was previously assumed that the libido has great difficulty in seizing upon a person outside the family because it still finds itself caught in the incestuous bond—a very plausible view indeed, from which it is difficult to withdraw. On the other hand, it must be emphasized that her libido had taken vehement possession of the poor boy, and he too was someone outside the family, so that the difficulty cannot lie in transferring libido to an extra-familial object, but in some other circumstance. Her love for the teacher was for her a more difficult task, it demanded much more from her than her love for the boy, which did not require any moral effort on her part. The hint dropped in the analysis that love would enable her to do her best brought the child back to her real task, which was to adapt to the teacher.

470   Now if the libido draws back from a necessary task, it does so for the very human reason of indolence, which is particularly marked not only in children but also in primitives and animals. Primitive inertia and laziness are the primary reason for not making the effort to adapt. The libido which is not used for this purpose stagnates, and will then make the inevitable regression to former objects or modes of adaptation. The result is a striking activation of the incest complex. The libido withdraws from the object which is so difficult to attain and which demands such great efforts, and turns instead to the easier ones, and finally to the easiest of all, the infantile fantasies, which are then elaborated into real incest fantasies. The fact that, whenever there is a disturbance of psychological adaptation, we always find an

excessive development of these fantasies must likewise be conceived, as I pointed out before, as a regressive phenomenon. That is to say, the incest fantasy is of secondary and not of causal significance, while the primary cause is the resistance of human nature to any kind of exertion. Accordingly, drawing back from certain tasks cannot be explained by saying that man prefers the incestuous relationship, rather he falls back into it because he shuns exertion. Otherwise we would have to say that resistance to conscious effort is identical with preference for the incestuous relationship. This would be obvious nonsense, since not only primitive man but animals too have a mighty dislike of all intentional effort, and are addicted to absolute laziness until circumstances prod them into action. Neither of primitive people nor of animals can it be asserted that preference for incestuous relationships is the cause of their aversion to efforts at adaptation, for, especially in the case of animals, there can be absolutely no question of an incestuous relationship.

471   Characteristically, the child expressed joy not at the prospect of doing her best for the teacher but at being allowed to love him. That was the thing she heard first, because it suited her best. Her relief came from the confirmation that she was justified in loving him—even without making any special effort first.

472   The conversation then went on to the story of the blackmail, which she told again in detail. We learn, furthermore, that she tried to force open her money-box, and when she did not succeed she tried to steal the key from her mother. She also made a clean breast of the other matter: she had made fun of the teacher because he was much nicer to the other girls than to her. But it was true that she had got worse at his lessons, especially in arithmetic. Once she did not understand something, but had not dared to ask for fear of losing the teacher's esteem. Consequently she made mistakes, fell behind, and really did lose it. As a result, she got into a very unsatisfactory position with her teacher.

473   About this time it happened that a girl in her class was sent home because she felt sick. Soon after, the same thing happened to her. In this way, she tried to get away from school, which she no longer liked. The loss of her teacher's esteem led her, on the one hand, to insult him and, on the other, into the affair with the little boy, obviously as a compensation for her lost relation-

ship with the teacher. The explanation she was now given was a simple hint: she would be doing her teacher a good turn if she took pains to understand his lessons by asking questions in time. I may add that this hint had good results; from that moment the little girl became the best pupil and missed no more arithmetic lessons.

474   A point worth stressing in the story of the blackmail is its compulsive character and the lack of freedom it shows in the girl. This is a quite regular phenomenon. As soon as anyone permits his libido to draw back from a necessary task, it becomes autonomous and, regardless of the protests of the subject, chooses its own goals and pursues them obstinately. It is therefore quite common for a person leading a lazy and inactive life to be peculiarly prone to the compulsion of libido, that is, to all kinds of fears and involuntary constraints. The fears and superstitions of primitives furnish the best proof of this, but the history of our own civilization, especially the civilization of antiquity, provides ample confirmation as well. Non-employment of the libido makes it ungovernable. But we must not believe that we can save ourselves permanently from the compulsion of libido by forced efforts. Only to a very limited extent can we consciously set tasks for the libido; other natural tasks are chosen by the libido itself because it is destined for them. If these tasks are avoided, even the most industrious life avails nothing, for we have to consider all the conditions of human nature. Innumerable neurasthenias from overwork can be traced back to this cause, for work done amid internal conflicts creates nervous exhaustion.

THIRD INTERVIEW

475   The girl related a dream she had had when she was five years old, which made an unforgettable impression on her. "I'll never forget the dream as long as I live," she said. I would like to add here that such dreams are of quite special interest. The longer a dream remains spontaneously in the memory, the greater is the importance to be attributed to it. This is the dream: *"I was in a wood with my little brother, looking for strawberries. Then a wolf came and jumped at me. I fled up a staircase, the wolf*

after me. I fell down and the wolf bit me in the leg. I awoke in deadly fear."

476   Before we take up the associations given us by the little girl, I will try to form an arbitrary opinion as to the possible content of the dream, and then see how our results compare with the associations given by the child. The beginning of the dream reminds us of the well-known fairytale of Little Red Ridinghood, which is, of course, known to every child. The wolf ate the grandmother first, then took her shape, and afterwards ate Little Red Ridinghood. But the hunter killed the wolf, cut open the belly, and Little Red Ridinghood sprang out safe and sound.

477   This motif is found in countless myths all over the world, and is the motif of the Bible story of Jonah. The meaning immediately lying behind it is astro-mythological: the sun is swallowed by the sea monster and is born again in the morning. Of course, the whole of astro-mythology is at bottom nothing but psychology—unconscious psychology—projected into the heavens; for myths never were and never are made consciously, they arise from man's unconscious. This is the reason for the sometimes miraculous similarity or identity of myth-forms among races that have been separated from each other in space ever since time began. It explains, for instance, the extraordinary distribution of the cross symbol, quite independently of Christianity, of which America offers specially remarkable examples. It is not possible to suppose that myths were created merely in order to explain meteorological or astronomical processes; they are, in the first instance, manifestations of unconscious impulses, comparable to dreams. These impulses were actuated by the regressive libido in the unconscious. The material which comes to light is naturally infantile material—fantasies connected with the incest complex. Thus, in all these so-called solar myths, we can easily recognize infantile theories about procreation, birth, and incestuous relations. In the fairytale of Little Red Ridinghood it is the fantasy that the mother has to eat something which is like a child, and that the child is born by cutting open the mother's body. This fantasy is one of the commonest and can be found everywhere.

478   From these general psychological considerations we can conclude that the child, in this dream, was elaborating the problem

of procreation and birth. As to the wolf, we must probably put him in the father's place, for the child unconsciously attributed to the father any act of violence towards the mother. This motif, too, is based on countless myths dealing with the violation of the mother. With regard to the mythological parallels, I would like to call your attention to the work of Boas,[1] which includes a magnificent collection of American Indian sagas; then the book by Frobenius, *Das Zeitalter des Sonnengottes;* and finally the works of Abraham, Rank, Riklin, Jones, Freud, Maeder, Silberer, and Spielrein,[2] and my own investigations in *Symbols of Transformation.*

479   After these general reflections, which I give here for theoretical reasons but which naturally formed no part of the treatment, we will go on to see what the child has to tell us about her dream. Needless to say, she was allowed to speak about her dream just as she liked, without being influenced in any way. She picked first on the bite in the leg, and explained that *she had once been told by a woman who had had a baby that she could still show the place where the stork had bitten her.* This expression is, in Switzerland, a variant of the widespread symbolism of copulation and birth. Here we have a perfect parallelism between our interpretation and the association process of the child. For the first association she produced, quite uninfluenced, goes back to the problem we conjectured above on theoretical grounds. I know that the innumerable cases published in the psychoanalytic literature, which were definitely not influenced, have not been able to quash our critics' contention that we suggest our interpretations to the patients. This case, too, will convince no one who is determined to impute to us the crude mistakes of beginners—or, what is worse, falsification.

480   After this first association the little patient was asked what the wolf made her think of. She answered, "I think of my father when he is angry." This, too, coincides absolutely with our theoretical considerations. It might be objected that these considerations were made expressly for this purpose and therefore lack general validity. I think this objection vanishes of itself as soon as one has the requisite psychoanalytic and mythological

1 [The anthropologist Franz Boas (1858–1942); see especially his *Indianische Sagen* (1895).—EDITORS.]   2 [See Bibliography.]

knowledge. The validity of a hypothesis can be seen only on the basis of the right knowledge, otherwise not at all.

481 The first association put the stork in the place of the wolf; the association to the wolf now brings us to the father. In the popular myth the stork stands for the father, for he brings the children. The apparent contradiction between the fairytale, where the wolf is the mother, and the dream, where the wolf is the father, is of no importance for the dream or the dreamer. We can therefore dispense with a detailed explanation. I have dealt with this problem of bisexual symbols in my book.[3] As you know, in the legend of Romulus and Remus both animals, the bird Picus and the wolf, were raised to the rank of parents.

482 Her fear of the wolf in the dream is therefore her fear of the father. The dreamer explained that she was afraid of her father because he was very strict with her. He had also told her that we have bad dreams only when we have done something wrong. She then asked her father, "But what does Mama do wrong? She always has bad dreams."

483 Once her father slapped her because she was sucking her finger. She kept on doing this despite his prohibition. Was this, perhaps, the wrong she had done? Hardly, because sucking the finger was simply a rather anachronistic infantile habit, of little real interest at her age, and serving more to irritate her father so that he would punish her by slapping. In this way she relieved her conscience of an unconfessed and much more serious "sin": *it came out that she had induced a number of girls of her own age to perform mutual masturbation.*

484 It was because of these sexual interests that she was afraid of her father. But we must not forget that she had the wolf dream in her fifth year. At that time these sexual acts had not been committed. Hence we must regard the affair with the other girls at most as a reason for her present fear of her father, but that does not explain her earlier fear. Nevertheless, we may expect that it was something similar, some unconscious sexual wish in keeping with the psychology of the forbidden act just mentioned. The character and moral evaluation of this act are naturally far more unconscious to a child than to an adult. In order to understand what could have made an impression on

---

[3] [Cf. *Symbols of Transformation*, particularly par. 547.]

the child so early, we have to ask what happened in her fifth year. *That was the year in which her younger brother was born.* So even then she was afraid of her father. The associations already discussed show us the unmistakable connection between her sexual interests and her fear.

485   The problem of sex, which nature connects with positive feelings of pleasure, appears in the wolf dream in the form of fear, apparently on account of the bad father, who stands for moral education. The dream was therefore the first impressive manifestation of the sexual problem, obviously stimulated by the recent birth of a younger brother, when as we know all these questions become aired. But because the sexual problem was connected at all points with the history of certain pleasurable physical sensations which education devalues as "bad habits," it could apparently manifest itself only in the guise of moral guilt and fear.

486   This explanation, plausible though it is, seems to me superficial and inadequate. We then attribute the whole difficulty to moral education, on the unproven assumption that education can cause a neurosis. This is to disregard the fact that even people with no trace of moral education become neurotic and suffer from morbid fears. Furthermore, moral law is not just an evil that has to be resisted, but a necessity born from the innermost needs of man. Moral law is nothing other than an outward manifestation of man's innate urge to dominate and control himself. This impulse to domestication and civilization is lost in the dim, unfathomable depths of man's evolutionary history and can never be conceived as the consequence of laws imposed from without. Man himself, obeying his instincts, created his laws. We shall never understand the reasons for the fear and suppression of the sexual problem in a child if we take into account only the moral influences of education. The real reasons lie much deeper, in human nature itself, perhaps in that tragic conflict between nature and culture, or between individual consciousness and collective feeling.

487   Naturally, it would have been pointless to give the child a notion of the higher philosophical aspects of the problem; it would certainly have had not the slightest effect. It was sufficient to remove the idea that she was doing something wrong in being interested in the procreation of life. So it was made clear to her

how much pleasure and curiosity she was bringing to bear on the problem of generation, and how her groundless fear was only pleasure turned into its opposite. The affair of her masturbation met with tolerant understanding, and the discussion was limited to drawing the child's attention to the aimlessness of her action. At the same time, it was explained to her that her sexual actions were mainly an outlet for her curiosity, which she might satisfy in a better way. Her great fear of her father expressed an equally great expectation, which because of the birth of her little brother was closely connected with the problem of generation. These explanations justified the child in her curiosity. With that, a large part of the moral conflict was removed.

FOURTH INTERVIEW

488   The little girl was now much nicer and much more confiding. Her former constrained and unnatural manner had quite disappeared. She brought a dream which she dreamt after the last interview. It ran: *"I am as tall as a church-spire and can see into every house. At my feet are very small children, as small as flowers are. A policeman comes. I say to him, 'If you dare to make any remark, I shall take your sword and cut off your head.'"*

489   In the analysis of the dream she made the following remark: "I would like to be taller than my father, because then he would have to obey me." She at once associated the policeman with her father, who was a military man and had, of course, a sword. The dream clearly fulfils her wish. As a church-spire, she is much bigger than her father, and if he dares to make a remark he will be decapitated. The dream also fulfils the natural wish of the child to be "big," i.e., grown-up, and to have children playing at her feet. In this dream she got over her fear of her father, and from this we may expect a significant increase in her personal freedom and feeling of security.

490   On the theoretical side, we may regard this dream as a clear example of the compensatory significance and teleological function of dreams. Such a dream must leave the dreamer with a heightened sense of the value of her own personality, and this is of great importance for her personal well-being. It does not

matter that the symbolism was not clear to the consciousness of the child, for the emotional effect of symbols does not depend on conscious understanding. It is more a matter of intuitive knowledge, the source from which all religious symbols derive their efficacy. Here no conscious understanding is needed; they influence the psyche of the believer through intuition.

FIFTH AND SIXTH INTERVIEWS

491   The child related the following dream which she had dreamt in the meantime: *"I was standing with my whole family on the roof. The windows of the houses on the other side of the valley shone like fire. The rising sun was reflected in them. Suddenly I saw that the house at the corner of our street was really on fire. The fire came nearer and nearer and took hold of our house. I ran into the street, and my mother threw all sorts of things after me. I held out my apron, and among other things she threw me a doll. I saw that the stones of our house were burning, but the wood remained untouched."*

492   The analysis of this dream presented peculiar difficulties and had to be extended over two sittings. It would lead me too far to describe the whole of the material this dream brought forth; I shall have to limit myself to what is most essential. The salient associations began with the peculiar image of the stones of the house burning but not the wood. It is sometimes worth while, especially with longer dreams, to take the most striking images and analyse them first. This is not the general rule but it may be excused here by the practical need for abbreviation.

493   "It is queer, like in a fairytale," said the little patient about this image. She was shown, with the help of examples, that fairytales always have a meaning. "But not all fairytales," she objected. "For instance, the tale of Sleeping Beauty. What could that mean?" It was explained to her that Sleeping Beauty had to wait for a hundred years in an enchanted sleep until she could be set free. Only the hero whose love overcame all difficulties and who boldly broke through the thorny hedge could rescue her. Thus one often has to wait for a long time before one obtains one's heart's desire.

494   This explanation was suited to the child's understanding,

and on the other hand was perfectly in accord with the history of this fairytale motif. The tale of Sleeping Beauty has obvious connections with an ancient spring and fertility myth, and at the same time contains a problem which has a remarkably close affinity with the psychological situation of a rather precocious little girl of eleven. It belongs to a whole cycle of legends in which a virgin, guarded by a dragon, is rescued by a hero. Without wishing to embark on an interpretation of this myth, I would like to emphasize its astronomical or meteorological components, clearly brought out in the Edda. The earth, in the form of a maiden, is held prisoner by the winter, and is covered with ice and snow. The young spring sun, the fiery hero, melts her out of her frosty prison, where she had long awaited her deliverer.

495   The association given by the little girl was chosen by her simply as an example of a fairytale without a meaning, and not as a direct association to the dream-image of the burning house. About this she only made the remark, "It is queer, like in a fairytale," by which she meant impossible; for to say that stones burn is something completely impossible, nonsensical, and like a fairytale. The explanation she was given showed her that "impossible" and "like a fairytale" are only partly identical, since fairytales do have a great deal of meaning. Although this particular fairytale, from the casual way it was mentioned, seems to have nothing to do with the dream, it deserves special attention because it appeared, as though by chance, while the dream was being analysed. The unconscious came out with just this example, and this cannot be mere chance but is somehow characteristic of the situation at that moment. In analysing dreams we have to look out for these seeming accidents, for in psychology there are no blind accidents, much as we are inclined to assume that these things are pure chance. You can hear this objection as often as you like from our critics, but for a really scientific mind there are only causal relationships and no accidents. From the fact that the little girl chose Sleeping Beauty as an example we must conclude that there was some fundamental reason for this in the psychology of the child. This reason was the comparison or partial identification of herself with Sleeping Beauty; in other words, in the psyche of the child there was a complex which found expression in the Sleeping Beauty motif.

216

The explanation given to the child took account of this inference.

496   Nevertheless, she was not quite satisfied, and still doubted that fairytales have a meaning. As a further example of an incomprehensible fairytale she cited Snow White, who lay enclosed in a glass coffin, in the sleep of death. It is not difficult to see that Snow White belongs to the same cycle of myths as Sleeping Beauty. It contains even clearer indications of the myth of the seasons. The myth material chosen by the child points to an intuitive comparison with the earth, held fast by the winter's cold, awaiting the liberating sun of spring.

497   This second example confirms the first one and the explanation we have given. It would be difficult to maintain that the second example, accentuating as it does the meaning of the first, was suggested by the explanation. The fact that the little girl gave Snow White as another example of a meaningless fairytale proves that she did not realize the identity of Snow White and Sleeping Beauty. We may therefore conjecture that Snow White arose from the same unconscious source as Sleeping Beauty, namely, from a complex concerned with the expectation of coming events. These events may be compared exactly with the deliverance of the earth from the prison of winter and its fertilization by the rays of the spring sun. As you know, from ancient times the fertilizing spring sun was associated with the symbol of the bull, the animal embodying the mightiest procreative power. Although we cannot yet see the connection between these insights and the dream, we will hold fast to what we have gained and proceed with our analysis.

498   The next dream-image shows the little girl catching the doll in her apron. Her first association tells us that her attitude and the whole situation in the dream reminded her of *a picture she knew, showing a stork flying over a village, with little girls standing in the street holding out their aprons and shouting to the stork to bring them a baby.* She added that she herself had long wanted a baby brother or sister. This material, given spontaneously, is clearly related to the myth-motifs already discussed. It is evident that the dream was in fact concerned with the same problem of the awakening reproductive instinct. Of course, nothing of these connections was mentioned to the child.

499   Then, abruptly, after a pause, came the next association:

"Once, when I was five years old, I lay down in the street and a bicycle passed over my stomach." This highly improbable story proved to be, as might be expected, a fantasy, which had become a paramnesia. Nothing of the kind had ever happened, but on the other hand we learn that at school *the little girls used to lie crosswise over each other's bodies and trample with their legs.*

500   Anyone who has read the analyses of children published by Freud and myself [4] will recognize in this childish game the same basic motif of trampling, which we considered must have a sexual undercurrent. This view, demonstrated by our earlier work, was borne out by the next association of our little patient: "I would much rather have a real baby than a doll."

501   All this highly remarkable material brought out by the stork fantasy suggests the typical beginnings of an infantile sexual theory, and at the same time shows us the point round which the little girl's fantasies were revolving.

502   It may be of interest to know that the motif of treading or trampling can be found in mythology. I have documented this in my book on libido.[5] The use of these infantile fantasies in the dream, the paramnesia about the bicyclist, and the tense expectation expressed in the Sleeping Beauty motif all show that the child's inner interest was dwelling on certain problems that had to be solved. Probably the fact that her libido was attracted by the problem of generation was the reason why her interest flagged at school, so that she fell behind in her work. How very much this problem fascinates girls of twelve and thirteen I was able to show in a special case, published in "A Contribution to the Psychology of Rumour." [6] It is the cause of all that smutty talk among children, and of mutual attempts at enlightenment which naturally turn out to be very nasty and often ruin the child's imagination for good. Even the most careful protection cannot prevent them from one day discovering the great secret, and then probably in the dirtiest way. It would be far better for children to learn the facts of life cleanly and in good time, so that they would not need to be enlightened in ugly ways by their playmates.

4 [Cf. "Psychic Conflicts in a Child," pars. 47ff.]
5 [*Symbols of Transformation*, pars. 370, 480.]
6 [Cf. supra, pars. 95ff.]

503   These and other indications showed that the moment had come for a certain amount of sexual enlightenment. The little girl listened attentively to the talk that followed, and then asked very seriously: "So then I really can't have a child?" This question led to an explanation about sexual maturity.

SEVENTH INTERVIEW

504   The little girl began by remarking that she perfectly understood why it was not yet possible for her to have a child; she had therefore renounced all idea of it. But this time she did not make a good impression. It turned out that she had lied to her teacher. She had been late to school, and told the teacher that she had had to go somewhere with her father and had therefore arrived late. In reality, she had been too lazy to get up in time. She told a lie because she was afraid of losing the teacher's favour by confessing the truth. This sudden moral defeat requires an explanation. According to the principles of psychoanalysis, a sudden and striking weakness can only come about when the analysand does not draw from the analysis the conclusions that are necessary at the moment, but still keeps the door open to other possibilities. This means, in our case, that though the analysis had apparently brought the libido to the surface, so that an improvement of personality could occur, for some reason or other the adaptation was not made, and the libido slipped back along its old regressive path.

EIGHTH INTERVIEW

505   The eighth interview proved that this was indeed the case. Our patient had withheld an important piece of evidence in regard to her ideas of sex, and one which contradicted the analyst's explanation of sexual maturity. *She had not mentioned a rumour current in the school that a girl of eleven had got a baby from a boy of the same age.* This rumour was proved to be groundless; it was a fantasy, fulfilling the secret wishes of girls of this age. Rumours often start in this way, as I have tried to show in my paper on the psychology of rumour. They air the

unconscious fantasies, and in this function they correspond to dreams and myths. This rumour kept another way open: she need not wait, she could have a child already at eleven. The contradiction between the accepted rumour and the analyst's explanation created resistances against the latter, as a result of which it was immediately devalued. All the other information and instruction fell to the ground at the same time, giving rise to momentary doubt and uncertainty. The libido then took to its former path and became regressive. This moment was the moment of the relapse.

NINTH INTERVIEW

506   This interview contributed some important details to the history of her sexual problem. First came a significant dream fragment: *"I was with other children in a clearing in a wood, surrounded by beautiful fir-trees. It began to rain, there was thunder and lightning, and it grew dark. Then I suddenly saw a stork in the air."*

507   Before we start analysing this dream, I must mention its parallels with certain mythological ideas. To anyone familiar with the works of Adalbert Kuhn and Steinthal, to which Abraham [7] has recently drawn attention, the curious combination of thunderstorm and stork is not at all surprising. Since ancient times the thunderstorm has had the meaning of an earth-fecundating act, it is the cohabitation of Father Heaven and Mother Earth, where the lightning takes over the role of the winged phallus. The stork in flight is just the same thing, a winged phallus, and its psychosexual meaning is known to every child. But the psychosexual meaning of the thunderstorm is not known to everyone, and certainly not to our little patient. In view of the whole psychological constellation previously described, the stork must unquestionably be given a psychosexual interpretation. The fact that the thunderstorm is connected with the stork and, like it, has a psychosexual meaning seems difficult to accept at first. But when we remember that psychoanalytic research has already discovered a vast number of purely mytholog-

_____
[7] [See *Symbols of Transformation*, index, s.vv.—EDITORS.]

ical connections in the unconscious psychic products, we may conclude that the psychosexual link between the two images is present also in this case. We know from other experiences that those unconscious strata which once produced mythological formations are still active in modern individuals and are unceasingly productive. Only, the production is limited to dreams and to the symptomatology of the neuroses and psychoses, as the correction by reality is so strong in the modern mind that it prevents them from being projected upon the real world.

508 To return to the analysis of the dream: the associations that led to the heart of this image began with the idea of *rain during a thunderstorm*. Her actual words were: "I think of water—my uncle was drowned in the water—it must be awful to be stuck in the water like that, in the dark—but wouldn't the baby drown in the water, too? Does it drink the water that is in the stomach? Queer, when I was ill Mama sent my water to the doctor. I thought he was going to mix something with it like syrup, which babies grow from, and Mama would have to drink it."

509 We see with unquestionable clearness from this string of associations that the child connected psychosexual ideas specifically relating to fertilization with the rain during the thunderstorm.

510 Here again we see that remarkable parallelism between mythology and the individual fantasies of our own day. This series of associations is so rich in symbolical connections that a whole dissertation could be written about them. The symbolism of drowning was brilliantly interpreted by the child herself as a pregnancy fantasy, an explanation given in the psychoanalytic literature long ago.

TENTH INTERVIEW

511 The tenth interview was taken up with the child's spontaneous description of infantile theories about fertilization and birth, which could now be dismissed as settled. The child had always thought that the urine of the man went into the body of the woman, and that from this the embryo would grow. Hence the child was in the water, i.e., urine, from the beginning. Another version was that the urine was drunk with the

doctor's syrup, the child grew in the head, the head was then split open to help the child grow, and one wore hats to cover this up. She illustrated this by a little drawing, showing a child-birth through the head. This idea is archaic and highly mythological. I need only remind you of the birth of Pallas Athene, who came out of her father's head. The fertilizing significance of urine is also mythological; we find excellent proofs of this in the Rudra songs of the Rig-veda.[8] I should also mention something which the mother corroborated, that once the little girl, long before the analysis, declared that she saw a jack-in-a-box dancing on her younger brother's head—a fantasy which may well be the origin of this birth-theory.

512 The drawing had a remarkable affinity with certain artefacts found among the Bataks of Sumatra. They are called magic wands or ancestor-columns, and consist of a number of figures standing one on top of another. The explanation given by the Bataks themselves of these columns, and generally regarded as nonsense, is in remarkable agreement with the mentality of a child, still caught in the infantile bonds. They assert that these superimposed figures are members of a family who, because they committed incest, were entwined by a snake while being bitten to death by another snake. This explanation runs parallel with the assumptions of our little patient, for her sexual fantasies, too, as we saw from the first dream, revolved round her father. Here, as with the Bataks, the primary condition is the incest relationship.

513 A third version was the theory that the child grew in the intestinal canal. This version had its own symptomatic phenomenology thoroughly in accord with Freudian theory. The girl, acting on her fantasy that children were "sicked up," frequently tried to induce nausea and vomiting. She also performed regular pushing-exercises in the water-closet, in order to push the child out. In this situation it was not surprising that the first and most important symptoms in the manifest neurosis were those of nausea.

514 We have now got so far with our analysis that we can cast a glance back at the case as a whole. We found, behind the neurotic symptoms, complicated emotional processes that were un-

8 [Cf. *Symbols of Transformation*, par. 322f.]

doubtedly connected with these symptoms. If we may venture to draw general conclusions from such limited material, we can reconstruct the course of the neurosis somewhat as follows.

515   At the gradual approach of puberty, the libido of the child produced in her an emotional rather than an objective attitude to reality. She developed a crush on her teacher, and this senti- mental indulgence in starry-eyed fantasies obviously played a greater role than the thought of the increased efforts which such a love really demanded. Consequently, her attention fell off, and her work suffered. This upset her former good relationship with the teacher. He became impatient, and the girl, who had been made over-demanding by conditions at home, grew resent- ful instead of trying to improve her work. As a result, her libido turned away from the teacher as well as from her work and fell into that characteristically compulsive dependence on the poor young boy, who exploited the situation as much as he could. For when an individual consciously or unconsciously lets his libido draw back from a necessary task, the unutilized (so-called "repressed") libido provokes all sorts of accidents, within and without—symptoms of every description which force themselves on him in a disagreeable way. Under these conditions the girl's resistance to going to school seized on the first available oppor- tunity, which soon presented itself in the form of the other girl who was sent home because she felt sick. Our patient duly copied this.

516   Once out of school, the way was open to her fantasies. Owing to the libido regression, the symptom-creating fantasies were aroused in real earnest and acquired an influence which they never had before, for previously they had never played such an important role. But now they took on a highly significant con- tent and seemed themselves to be the real reason why the libido regressed to them. It might be said that the child, with her fantasy-spinning nature, saw her father too much in the teacher, and consequently developed incestuous resistances against him. As I explained earlier, I think it is simpler and more probable to assume that it was temporarily convenient for her to see her teacher as the father. Since she preferred to follow the secret promptings of puberty rather than her obligations to the school and her teacher, she allowed her libido to pick on the little boy, from whom, as we saw in the analysis, she promised herself

certain secret advantages. Even if the analysis had proved she really did have incestuous resistances against her teacher owing to the transference of the father-imago, these resistances would only have been secondarily blown-up fantasies. The prime mover would in any case be laziness or convenience, or, to put it in more scientific language, the principle of least resistance.

517   ⟨I think there are cogent reasons for assuming—I mention this only in passing—that it is not always a perfectly legitimate interest in sexual processes and their unknown nature that accounts for the regression to infantile fantasies. For we find the same regressive fantasies even in adults who have long known all about sex, and here there is no legitimate reason. It is also my impression that young people in analysis often try to keep up their alleged ignorance, despite enlightenment, in order to direct attention there rather than to the task of adaptation. Although there is no doubt in my mind that children do exploit their real or pretended ignorance, it must on the other hand be stressed that young people have a right to be sexually enlightened. As I said before, for many children it would be a distinct advantage if this were decently done at home.

518   Through the analysis it became clear that independently of the progressive development of the child's life a regressive movement had set in, which caused the neurosis, the disunion with herself.⟩ By following this regressive tendency, the analysis discovered a keen sexual curiosity, circling round quite certain definite problems. The libido, caught in this labyrinth of fantasies, was made serviceable again as soon as the child was freed from the burden of mistaken infantile fantasies by being enlightened. This also opened her eyes to her own attitude to reality and gave her an insight into her true potentialities. The result was that she was able to look at her immature, adolescent fantasies in an objective and critical way, and to give up these and all other impossible desires, using her libido instead for a positive purpose, in her work and in obtaining the goodwill of her teacher. The analysis brought her great peace of mind, as well as marked intellectual improvement in school; for the teacher himself confirmed that the little girl soon became the best pupil in his class.

519   ⟨In principle, this analysis is no different from that of an adult. Only the sexual enlightenment would be dropped, but its

place would be taken by something very similar, namely, enlightenment concerning the infantilism of his previous attitude to reality and how to acquire a more reasonable one. Analysis is a refined technique of Socratic maieutics, and it is not afraid to tread the darkest paths of neurotic fantasy.⟩

520   I hope that with the help of this very condensed example I may have succeeded in giving you some insight not only into the actual course of treatment, and into the difficulties of technique, but no less into the beauty of the human psyche and its endless problems. I have deliberately stressed certain parallels with mythology in order to indicate some of the uses to which psychoanalytic insights may be put. At the same time, I would like to point out the implications of this discovery. The marked predominance of mythological elements in the psyche of the child gives us a clear hint of the way the individual mind gradually develops out of the "collective mind" of early childhood, thus giving rise to the old theory of a state of perfect knowledge before and after individual existence.

521   ⟨These mythological references which we find in children are also met with in dementia praecox and in dreams. They offer a broad and fertile field of work for comparative psychological research. The distant goal to which these investigations lead is a phylogeny of the mind, which, like the body, has attained its present form through endless transformations. The rudimentary organs, as it were, which the mind still possesses can be found in full activity in other mental variants and in certain pathological conditions.⟩

522   With these hints I have now reached the present position of our research, and have sketched out at least those insights and working hypotheses which define the nature of my present and future work. ⟨I have endeavoured to propound certain views, which deviate from the hypotheses of Freud, not as contrary assertions but as illustrations of the organic development of the basic ideas Freud has introduced into science. It would not be fitting to disturb the progress of science by adopting the most contradictory standpoint possible and by making use of an entirely different nomenclature—that is the privilege of the very few; but even they find themselves obliged to descend from their lonely eminence after a time and once more take part in the slow progress of average experience by which ideas are

evaluated. I hope, also, that my critics will not again accuse me of having contrived my hypotheses out of thin air. I would never have ventured to override the existing ones had not hundreds of experiences shown me that my views fully stand the test in practice. No great hopes should be set on the results of any scientific work; yet if it should find a circle of readers, I hope it will serve to clear up various misunderstandings and remove a number of obstacles which bar the way to a better comprehension of psychoanalysis. Naturally my work is no substitute for lack of psychoanalytic experience. Anyone who wishes to have his say in these matters will have, now as then, to investigate his cases as thoroughly as was done by the psychoanalytic school.⟩

III

GENERAL ASPECTS OF PSYCHOANALYSIS

———

PSYCHOANALYSIS AND NEUROSIS

———

SOME CRUCIAL POINTS IN
PSYCHOANALYSIS

———

PREFACES TO "COLLECTED PAPERS ON
ANALYTICAL PSYCHOLOGY"

GENERAL ASPECTS OF PSYCHOANALYSIS [1]

523   Psychoanalysis today is as much a science as a technique. From the results of the technique there has grown up, in the course of the years, a new psychological science which could be called "analytical psychology." I would willingly use Bleuler's expression "depth psychology" instead, if this kind of psychology were concerned only with the unconscious.

524   Psychologists and doctors in general are by no means conversant with this particular branch of psychology, owing to the fact that its technical foundations are as yet comparatively unknown to them. The main reason for this is that the new method is of an essentially psychological nature, and therefore belongs neither to the realm of medicine nor to that of philosophy. The medical man has, as a rule, but little knowledge of psychology, and the philosopher has no medical knowledge. Consequently, there is a lack of suitable soil in which to plant the spirit of this new method. Furthermore, the method itself appears to many persons so arbitrary that they cannot reconcile its use with their scientific conscience. The formulations of Freud, the founder of the method, laid great stress on the sexual factors; this aroused strong prejudice and repelled many scientific men. I need hardly remark that such an antipathy is not a logical reason for rejecting a new method. In psychoanalysis, moreover, there is much discussion of case-histories, but little discussion of principle. This, too, has naturally led to the method being little understood and therefore to its being regarded as unscientific. For if we do not acknowledge the scientific character of the method, we cannot acknowledge the scientific character of its results.

1 [Originally written in German with the title "Allgemeine Aspekte der Psychoanalyse," translated (anonymously) into English, and read before the Psycho-Medical Society, London, Aug. 5, 1913. With the title "Psycho-Analysis," the translation was published in the *Transactions of the Psycho-Medical Society* (Cockermouth), 1913, and reprinted in *Collected Papers on Analytical Psychology* (London, 1916; 2nd edn., London, 1917, New York, 1920). The present translation is made in consultation with the original German manuscript.—EDITORS.]

525   Before discussing the principles of the psychoanalytic method, I must mention two common prejudices against it. The first is that psychoanalysis is nothing but a rather deep and complicated form of *anamnesis*. Now it is well known that an anamnesis is based on the statements made by the patient's family, and on his own conscious self-knowledge in reply to direct questions. The psychoanalyst naturally makes his anamnesis as carefully as any other specialist. But this is merely the patient's history and must not be confused with analysis. Analysis is the reduction of actual contents of consciousness, ostensibly of a fortuitous nature, to their psychological determinants. This process has nothing to do with the anamnestic reconstruction of the history of the illness.

526   The second prejudice, which is based, as a rule, on a superficial knowledge of psychoanalytic literature, is that psychoanalysis is a *method of suggestion,* by which some kind of systematic teaching is instilled into the patient, thereby effecting a cure in the manner of mental healing or Christian Science. Many analysts, especially those who have practised psychoanalysis for a long time, previously used suggestion therapy, and therefore know very well what suggestion is and what it is not. They know that the psychoanalyst's method of working is diametrically opposed to that of the hypnotist. In direct contrast with suggestion therapy, the psychoanalyst does not attempt to force anything on his patient which the latter does not see for himself and find plausible with his own understanding. Faced with the constant demand of the neurotic for suggestions and advice, the analyst just as constantly endeavours to get him out of this passive attitude and make him use his common sense and powers of criticism in order to equip him for an independent life. We have often been accused of forcing interpretations upon patients, interpretations that are often quite arbitrary. I wish one of these critics would try forcing arbitrary interpretations on my patients, who are very often persons of great intelligence and highly cultured—indeed, not infrequently my own colleagues. The impossibility of such an undertaking would quickly be demonstrated. In psychoanalysis we are entirely dependent on the patient and on his powers of judgment, for the reason that the very nature of analysis consists in leading him to a knowledge of himself. The principles of psycho-

analysis are so utterly different from those of suggestion therapy that on this point the two methods cannot be compared.

527   An attempt has also been made to compare psychoanalysis with the ratiocinative method of Dubois,[2] which is an essentially rational procedure. But this comparison does not hold good, for the psychoanalyst strictly avoids reasoning and arguing with his patients. Naturally he has to listen to their conscious problems and conflicts and take note of them, but not for the purpose of fulfilling their desire to obtain advice or instruction with regard to the conduct of their lives. The problems of a neurotic cannot be solved by advice and conscious reasoning. I do not doubt that good advice at the right time can produce good results, but I do not know how anyone can believe that the psychoanalyst can always give the right advice at the right moment. The neurotic conflict is frequently, indeed usually, of such a nature that advice cannot possibly be given. Furthermore, it is well known that the patient only wants authoritative advice in order to shuffle off the burden of responsibility, referring himself and others to the opinion of a higher authority. So far as reasoning and persuasion are concerned, their effect as a method of therapy is as little to be doubted as that of hypnosis. What I would like to stress here is simply its difference in principle from psychoanalysis.

528   In contradistinction to all previous methods, psychoanalysis endeavours to overcome the disorders of the neurotic psyche through the unconscious, and not from the conscious side. In this work we naturally have need of the patient's conscious contents, for only in this way can we reach the unconscious. The conscious content from which our work starts is the material supplied by the anamnesis. In many cases the anamnesis provides useful clues which make the psychic origin of his symptoms clear to the patient. This, of course, is necessary only when he is convinced that his neurosis is organic in origin. But even in those cases where the patient is convinced from the start of the psychic nature of his illness, a critical survey of the anamnesis can be of advantage, for it discloses a psychological context of which he was unaware before. In this way problems that need special discussion are frequently brought to the surface. This work may occupy many sittings. Finally, the elucidation of the

2 [See par. 41, n. 6, above.—EDITORS.]

conscious material comes to an end when neither the analyst nor the patient can contribute anything further of decisive importance. In the most favourable cases the end comes with the formulation of the problem which, very often, proves insoluble.

529   Let us take the case of a man who was once healthy but developed a neurosis between the ages of thirty-five and forty. His position in life was secure, and he had a wife and children. Parallel with his neurosis he developed an intense resistance to his professional work. He observed that the first symptoms of neurosis became noticeable when he had to overcome a particular difficulty in his career. Later they got worse with each successive difficulty that arose. Passing ameliorations occurred whenever fortune favoured him in his work. The problem that presented itself after a critical discussion of the anamnesis was as follows: the patient knew that he could improve his work and that the satisfaction resulting from this would bring about the much-desired improvement in his neurotic condition. But he was unable to do his work more efficiently because of his great resistance to it. This problem is rationally insoluble. Psychoanalytic treatment must therefore start at the critical point, his resistance to his work.

530   Let us take another case. A woman of forty, mother of four children, became neurotic four years ago after the death of one of them. A new pregnancy, followed by the birth of another child, brought a great improvement in her condition. She now thought that if she could have yet another child she would be helped still further. She knew, however, that she could not have any more children, so she tried to devote her energies to philanthropic interests. But she failed to obtain the least satisfaction from this work. She noticed a distinct alleviation whenever she succeeded in giving real interest to something, however fleetingly, but she felt quite incapable of discovering anything that would bring her lasting interest and satisfaction. The rational insolubility of the problem is clear. Psychoanalytic work must begin with the question of what prevented the patient from developing any interest beyond her longing for a child.

531   Since we cannot pretend that we know from the outset what the solution of such problems is, we have to rely on the clues furnished by the individuality of the patient. Neither conscious questioning nor rational advice can aid us in the discovery of

these clues, for the obstacles which prevent us from finding them are hidden from the patient's consciousness. There is, therefore, no clearly prescribed way of getting at the unconscious obstacles. The only rule that psychoanalysis lays down in this respect is: let the patient talk about anything that comes into his head. The analyst must observe carefully what the patient says and, to begin with, simply take note of it without attempting to force his own opinions upon him. We notice, for instance, that the first-named patient began by talking about his marriage, which we had been told was normal. We now learn that he has difficulties with his wife and does not understand her in the least. This prompts the analyst to remark that evidently the patient's professional work is not his only problem, and that his relation to his wife also needs reviewing. This starts a train of associations all relating to the marriage. Then follow associations about the love-affairs he had before he was married. These experiences, recounted in detail, show that the patient was always rather peculiar in his more intimate relations with women, and that his peculiarity took the form of a childish egoism. This is a new and surprising point of view for him, and explains to him many of his misfortunes with women.

532   We cannot in every case get as far as this on the principle of simply letting the patient talk; few patients have their psychic material so much on the surface. Furthermore, many patients have a real resistance against speaking freely about what occurs to them on the spur of the moment, some because it is too painful for them to tell it to an analyst whom they may not entirely trust, others because apparently nothing occurs to them and they force themselves to talk of things about which they are more or less indifferent. This trick of not talking to the point does not prove that the patient is *consciously* concealing certain painful contents; it can also occur quite unconsciously. In such cases it sometimes helps the patient to tell him that he need not force himself, but need only seize on the very first thoughts that come to him, no matter how unimportant or ridiculous they may seem. In certain cases even these instructions are of no use, and then the analyst has to resort to other measures. One of these is the association experiment, which usually gives apt information concerning the main tendencies of the patient at that moment.

533 A second expedient is the analysis of dreams; this is the real instrument of psychoanalysis. We have already experienced so much opposition to dream analysis that a brief exposition of its principles may not be out of place. The interpretation of dreams, as well as the meaning given to them, is, as we know, in bad odour. It is not long since oneiromancy was practised and believed in; nor is the time long past when even the most enlightened persons were still under the spell of superstition. It is therefore comprehensible that our age should still entertain a lively fear of superstitions that have been only partially overcome. This nervousness in regard to superstition is largely responsible for the opposition to dream-interpretation, but psychoanalysis is in no way to blame for this. We select the dream as an object not because we pay it the homage of superstitious admiration, but because it is a psychic product that is independent of consciousness. We ask for the patient's free associations, but he gives us little or nothing, or else something forced or irrelevant. A dream is a free association, a free fantasy, it is not forced, and is just as much a psychic phenomenon as an association.[3]

534 I cannot disguise the fact that in practice, especially at the beginning of an analysis, we do not under all circumstances make complete and ideal analyses of the dreams. Usually we gather the dream-associations together until the problem which the patient is hiding from us becomes so clear that he can recognize it himself. This problem is then worked through consciously until it is cleared up as far as possible and we are once again confronted with an unanswerable question.

535 You will now ask what is to be done when the patient does not dream at all. I can assure you that hitherto all patients, even those who claimed never to have dreamed before, began to dream when they went through analysis. On the other hand it frequently happens that patients who began by dreaming vividly are suddenly no longer able to remember their dreams. The empirical and practical rule which I have adopted is that the patient, if he does not dream, still has sufficient conscious material which he is keeping back for certain reasons. A common reason is: "I am in the analyst's hands and am quite willing

[3] [The passage which here follows in the original is identical with "The Theory of Psychoanalysis," supra, pars. 324–31.—EDITORS.]

to be treated by him. But the analyst must do the work, I shall remain passive in the matter." Sometimes there are resistances of a more serious nature. For instance, patients who cannot admit certain moral defects in themselves project them upon the analyst, calmly assuming that since he is more or less deficient morally they cannot communicate certain unpleasant things to him.

536   If, then, a patient does not dream from the beginning or ceases to dream, he is keeping back material which would be capable of conscious elaboration. Here the relationship between analyst and patient may be considered one of the chief obstacles. It can prevent them both, the analyst as well as the patient, from seeing the situation clearly. We must not forget that as the analyst shows, and must show, a searching interest in the psychology of his patient, so the patient, if he has an active mind, feels his way into the psychology of the analyst and adopts a corresponding attitude towards him. The analyst is blind to the attitude of his patient to the exact extent that he does not see himself and his own unconscious problems. For this reason I maintain that a doctor must himself be analysed before he practises analysis. Otherwise analysis may easily be a great disappointment to him, because he can, under certain circumstances, get absolutely stuck and then lose his head. He is then readily inclined to assume that psychoanalysis is nonsense, so as to avoid having to admit that he has run his vessel aground. If you are sure of your own psychology you can confidently tell your patient that he does not dream because there is conscious material still to be dealt with. I say you must be sure of yourself at such moments, for the criticisms and unsparing judgments to which you sometimes have to submit can be excessively disturbing to one who is unprepared to meet them. The immediate consequence of the analyst's losing his balance is that he begins to argue with his patient in order to maintain his influence over him. This, of course, renders all further analysis impossible.

537   I have told you that, in the first instance, dreams need be used only as a source of material for analysis. At the beginning of an analysis it is not only unnecessary, but at times unwise, to give a so-called complete interpretation of a dream. A complete and really exhaustive interpretation is very difficult indeed. The interpretations you sometimes come across in the psychoanalytic

literature are very often one-sided and, not infrequently, contestable formulations. I include among these the one-sided sexual reductions of the Viennese school. In view of the myriadsidedness of the dream-material one must beware of all one-sided formulations. The many-sided meaning of a dream, rather than its singleness of meaning, is of the utmost value especially at the beginning of the treatment. Thus, a patient had the following dream not long after her treatment had begun. *She was in a hotel in a strange city. Suddenly a fire broke out. Her husband and her father, who were with her, helped her in the rescue work.*

538 The patient was intelligent, extraordinarily sceptical, and absolutely convinced that dream-analysis was nonsense. I had the greatest difficulty in inducing her to give it even one trial. I selected the fire, the most conspicuous event in the dream, as the starting-point for associations. The patient informed me that she had recently read in the newspapers that a certain hotel in Zurich had been burnt down; that she remembered the hotel because she had once stayed there. At the hotel she had made the acquaintance of a man, and from this a somewhat questionable love-affair developed. In connection with this story the fact came out that she had already had quite a number of similar adventures, all of them decidedly frivolous. This important bit of past history was brought out by the very first association. In her case it would have been pointless to make clear to her the very obvious meaning of the dream. With her frivolous attitude, of which her scepticism was only a special instance, she would have coldly repelled such an attempt. But after the frivolity of her attitude had been recognized and demonstrated to her from the material she herself had furnished, it was possible to analyse the dreams which followed much more thoroughly.

539 It is, therefore, advisable in the beginning to use dreams for getting at the critical material through their associations. This is the best and most cautious procedure, especially for the beginner in psychoanalysis. An arbitrary translation of the dreams is exceedingly inadvisable. That would be a superstitious practice based on the assumption that dreams have well-established symbolic meanings. But there are no fixed symbolic meanings. There are certain symbols that recur frequently, but we are not in a position to get beyond very general statements. For in-

stance, it is quite incorrect to assume that a snake, when it appears in dreams, always has a merely phallic meaning; just as incorrect as it is to deny that it may have a phallic meaning in some cases. Every symbol has at least two meanings. The very frequent sexual meaning of dream-symbols is at most one of them. I cannot, therefore, accept the exclusively sexual interpretations which appear in certain psychoanalytic publications, as little as I can accept the interpretation of dreams as wish-fulfilments, for my experience has led me to regard these formulations as one-sided and inadequate. As an example I will tell you a very simple dream of a young man, a patient of mine. It was as follows: *I was going up a flight of stairs with my mother and sister. When we reached the top I was told that my sister was going to have a baby.*

540   First I will show how, in accordance with the hitherto prevailing point of view, this dream may be translated sexually. We know that incest fantasies play a prominent role in the life of a neurotic, hence the image "with my mother and sister" could be understood as a hint in this direction. "Stairs" are alleged to have a well-established sexual meaning: they represent the sexual act because of the rhythmic climbing. The baby the sister is expecting is nothing but the logical consequence of these premises. Thus translated, the dream would be a clear fulfilment of so-called infantile wishes, which, as you know, are an important part of Freud's dream-theory.

541   I have analysed this dream on the basis of the following reasoning. If I say that stairs are a *symbol* for the sexual act, by what right do I take the mother and sister and baby as *real*, that is, not symbolically? If, on the strength of the assertion that dream-images are symbolic, I assign a symbolic value to certain of these images, what right have I to exempt certain others? If I attach a symbolic value to the ascent of the stairs, I must also attach a symbolic value to the images called mother, sister, and baby. I therefore did not "translate" the dream but really analysed it. The result was surprising. I will give you the patient's associations to the individual dream-images word for word, so that you can form your own opinion of the material. I should say in advance that the young man had finished his studies at the university a few months previously, that he had found the choice of a profession too difficult to make, and that he there-

upon became neurotic. In consequence of this he gave up his work. His neurosis took, among other things, a manifestly homosexual form.

542   His associations to *mother* were as follows: "I have not seen her for a long time, a very long time. I must really reproach myself for this, it is wrong of me to neglect her so."

543   *Mother*, then, stands for something that is neglected in an irresponsible manner. I asked the patient: "What is that?" and he replied, with considerable embarrassment: "My work."

544   Associations to *sister*: "It is years since I have seen her. I long to see her again. Whenever I think of her I always remember the moment I said good-bye. I kissed her with real affection, and at that moment I understood for the first time what love for a woman can mean." It was at once clear to the patient that "sister" stood for "love for a woman."

545   Associations to *stairs*: "Climbing up—getting to the top—making a career—growing up, becoming great."

546   Associations to *baby*: "Newborn—renewal—rebirth—becoming a new man."

547   One has only to hear this material to understand at once that the dream represents not so much the fulfilment of infantile wishes as the fulfilment of biological duties which the patient has neglected because of his neurotic infantilism. Biological justice, which is inexorable, often compels us to make up in dreams for the duties we have neglected in real life.

548   This dream is a typical example of the prospective and finally-oriented function of dreams in general, especially stressed by my colleague Maeder. If we adhered to a one-sided sexual interpretation the real meaning of the dream would escape us. Sexuality in dreams is, in the first instance, a means of expression and by no means always the meaning and aim of the dream. The discovery of its prospective or final meaning is particularly important when the analysis is so far advanced that the eyes of the patient are turned more readily to the future than to his inner world and the past.

549   As regards the handling of the symbolism, we learn from this example that there can be no dream-symbols whose meanings are fixed in every detail, but, at most, a frequent occurrence of symbols with fairly general meanings. So far as the

specifically sexual meaning of dreams is concerned, experience has led me to lay down the following practical rules:

550   If dream-analysis at the beginning of the treatment shows that the dreams have an undoubtedly sexual meaning, this meaning is to be taken realistically; that is, it proves that the sexual problems of the patient need to be subjected to a careful review. For instance, if an incest fantasy is clearly shown to be a latent content of the dream, one must subject the patient's infantile relations with his parents and brothers and sisters, as well as his relations with other persons who are fitted to play the role of father or mother, to a thorough investigation. But if a dream that comes at a later stage of the analysis has, let us say, an incest fantasy as its essential content—a fantasy that we have reason to consider disposed of—concrete value should not under all circumstances be attached to it; it should be regarded as symbolic. The formula for interpretation is: the unknown meaning of the dream is expressed, by analogy, through a fantasy of incest. In this case symbolic and not real value must be attached to the sexual fantasy. If we did not get beyond the real value we should keep reducing the patient to sexuality, and this would arrest the progress of the development of his personality. The patient's salvation does not lie in thrusting him back again and again into primitive sexuality; this would leave him on a low cultural level whence he could never obtain freedom and complete restoration to health. Retrogression to a state of barbarism is no advantage at all for a civilized human being.

551   The above-mentioned formula, according to which the sexuality of a dream is a symbolic or analogical expression of its meaning, naturally applies also to dreams occurring at the beginning of an analysis. But the practical reasons that have impelled us not to take the symbolic value of these sexual fantasies into consideration arise from the fact that a genuine realistic value must be attached to the abnormal sexual fantasies of a neurotic in so far as he allows his actions to be influenced by them. The fantasies not only hinder him in adapting better to his situation, they also lead him to all manner of real sexual acts, and occasionally even to incest, as experience shows. Under these circumstances, it would be of little use to consider the symbolic content only; the concrete aspect must be first dealt with.

552   These statements are based, as you will have observed, on a

different conception of the dream from that put forward by Freud. Indeed, experience has forced a different conception upon me. For Freud, the dream is essentially a symbolic disguise for repressed wishes which would come into conflict with the aims of the personality. I am obliged to regard the structure of a dream from a different point of view. For me the dream is, in the first instance, a subliminal picture of the actual psychological situation of the individual in his waking state. It gives us a résumé of the subliminal associative material constellated by the psychological situation of the moment. The volitional content of the dream, which Freud calls the repressed wish, is for me essentially a means of expression.

553   The activity of consciousness represents, biologically speaking, the individual's struggle for psychological adaptation. Consciousness tries to adjust itself to the necessities of the moment, or, to put it differently: there are tasks ahead which the individual must overcome. In many cases the solution is, in the nature of things, unknown, for which reason consciousness always tries to find the solution by way of analogous experiences. We try to grasp the unknown future on the model of our experience in the past. We have no reason to suppose that the subliminal psychic material obeys other laws than the "supraliminal" material. The unconscious, like the conscious, mobilizes itself round the biological tasks and seeks solutions on the analogy of what has gone before, just as consciousness does. Whenever we wish to assimilate something unknown, we do so by means of analogy. A simple example of this is the well-known fact that when America was discovered by the Spaniards the Indians took the horses of the conquerors, which were unknown to them, for large pigs, because only pigs were familiar in their experience. This is the way we always recognize things, and it is also the essential reason for the existence of symbolism: it is a process of comprehension by means of analogy. The dream is a *subliminal* process of comprehension by analogy. The apparently repressed wishes are volitional tendencies which supply the unconscious dream-thought with a verbal means of expression. On this particular point I find myself in entire agreement with the views of Adler, another pupil of Freud's. As to the fact that the unconscious expresses itself by means of volitional elements or

tendencies, this is due to the archaic nature of dream-thinking, a problem I have discussed elsewhere.[4]

554 Owing to our different conception of the structure of dreams, the further course of analysis assumes a rather different aspect. The symbolic evaluation of sexual fantasies in the later stages necessarily leads, not to a reduction of the personality to primitive tendencies, but to a broadening and continuous development of the patient's attitude; that is, it tends to make his thinking richer and deeper, thus giving him what has always been one of man's most powerful weapons in the struggle for adaptation. By following this new course consistently, I have come to the realization that the religious and philosophical driving forces—what Schopenhauer calls the "metaphysical need" of man—must receive positive consideration during the analytical work. They must not be destroyed by reducing them to their primitive sexual roots, but made to serve biological ends as psychologically valuable factors. In this way these driving forces assume once more the function that has been theirs from time immemorial.

555 Just as primitive man was able, with the help of religious and philosophical symbols, to free himself from his original condition, so too the neurotic can free himself from his illness. It is hardly necessary for me to remark that I do not mean inoculating him with belief in a religious or philosophical dogma; I mean simply that there must be built up in him that same psychological attitude which was characterized by the living belief in a religious or philosophical dogma on earlier levels of culture. A religious or philosophical attitude is not the same thing as belief in a dogma. A dogma is a temporary intellectual formulation, the outcome of a religious and philosophical attitude conditioned by time and circumstances. But the attitude itself is a cultural achievement; it is a function that is exceedingly valuable from a biological point of view, for it gives rise to incentives that drive human beings to do creative work for the benefit of a future age and, if necessary, to sacrifice themselves for the welfare of the species.

556 Thus man attains the same sense of unity and wholeness, the same confidence, the same capacity for self-sacrifice in his

4 [Cf. *Symbols of Transformation*, p. 21, par. 25.—EDITORS.]

conscious existence that belong unconsciously and instinctively to wild animals. Every reduction, every digression from the path that has been laid down for the development of civilization, does nothing more than turn the human being into a crippled animal; it never makes a so-called natural man of him. I have had numerous successes and failures in the course of my analytical practice which have convinced me of the inexorable rightness of this kind of psychological orientation. We do not help the neurotic by relieving him of the demands made by civilization; we can help him only by inducing him to take an active part in the strenuous work of carrying on its development. The suffering he undergoes in performing this service takes the place of his neurosis. But whereas the neurosis and the troubles that attend it are never followed by the pleasant feeling of good work well done, of duty fearlessly performed, the suffering that comes from useful work and from victory over real difficulties brings with it those moments of peace and satisfaction which give the human being the priceless feeling that he has really lived his life.

PSYCHOANALYSIS AND NEUROSIS [1]

557   After many years' experience I now know that it is extremely difficult to discuss psychoanalysis at public meetings and at congresses. There are so many misconceptions of the matter, so many prejudices against certain psychoanalytic views, that it is an almost impossible task to reach mutual understanding in a public discussion. I have always found a quiet conversation on the subject much more useful and fruitful than heated arguments *coram publico*. However, having been honoured by an invitation from the Committee of this Congress to speak as a representative of the psychoanalytic movement, I will do my best to discuss some of the fundamental theoretical problems of psychoanalysis. I must limit myself to this aspect of the subject because I am quite unable to put before my audience all that psychoanalysis means and strives for, and its various applications in the fields of mythology, comparative religion, philosophy, etc. But if I am to discuss certain theoretical problems fundamental to psychoanalysis, I must presuppose that my audience is familiar with the development and the main results of psychoanalytic research. Unfortunately, it often happens that people think themselves entitled to judge psychoanalysis who have not even read the literature. It is my firm conviction that no one is competent to form an opinion on this matter until he has studied the basic writings of the psychoanalytic school.

558   In spite of the fact that Freud's theory of neurosis has been worked out in great detail, it cannot be said to be, on the whole, very clear or easy to understand. This justifies my giving you a short abstract of his fundamental views on the theory of neurosis.

559   You are aware that the original theory that hysteria and the related neuroses have their origin in a trauma or sexual shock

1 [Originally read in English before the 17th International Medical Congress, London, 1913, under the title "On Psychoanalysis." First published in *Collected Papers on Analytical Psychology* (London, 1916; 2nd edn., London, 1917, and New York, 1920), pp. 226–35. The present version is a stylistic revision of this.—EDITORS.]

in early childhood was given up about fifteen years ago. It soon became evident that the sexual trauma could not be the real cause of the neurosis, for the simple reason that the trauma was found to be almost universal. There is scarcely a human being who has not had some sexual shock in early youth, and yet comparatively few develop a neurosis in later life. Freud himself soon realized that many of the patients who related an early traumatic experience had only invented the story of the so-called trauma; it had never occurred in reality, but was a mere creation of fantasy. Moreover, on further investigation it became quite obvious that even if a trauma had actually occurred it was not always responsible for the whole of the neurosis, although it does sometimes look as if the structure of the neurosis depended entirely on the trauma. If a neurosis were the inevitable consequence of the trauma it would be quite incomprehensible why neurotics are not incomparably more numerous than they are.

560   The apparently heightened effect of the shock was clearly due to the exaggerated and morbid fantasy of the patient. Freud also saw that this same fantasy activity manifested itself relatively early in bad habits, which he called infantile perversions. His new conception of the aetiology of neurosis was based on this insight, and he traced the neurosis back to some sexual activity in early infancy. This conception led to his recent view that the neurotic is "fixated" to a certain period of his early infancy, because he seems to preserve some trace of it, direct or indirect, in his mental attitude. Freud also makes the attempt to classify or to differentiate the neuroses, as well as dementia praecox, according to the stage of infantile development in which the fixation took place. From the standpoint of this theory, the neurotic appears to be entirely dependent on his infantile past, and all his troubles in later life, his moral conflicts and his deficiencies, seem to be derived from the powerful influences of that period. Accordingly, the main task of the treatment is to resolve this infantile fixation, which is conceived as an unconscious attachment of the sexual libido to certain infantile fantasies and habits.

561   This, so far as I can see, is the essence of Freud's theory of neurosis. But it overlooks the following important question: What is the cause of this fixation of libido to the old infantile

fantasies and habits? We have to remember that almost everyone has at some time had infantile fantasies and habits exactly corresponding to those of a neurotic, yet he does not become fixated to them; consequently, he does not become neurotic later on. The aetiological secret of the neurosis, therefore, does not lie in the mere *existence* of infantile fantasies but in the so-called *fixation*. The numerous statements of neurotics affirming the existence of infantile sexual fantasies are worthless in so far as they attribute an aetiological significance to them, for the same fantasies can be found in normal individuals as well, a fact which I have often proved. It is only the fixation which seems to be characteristic.

562   It is therefore necessary to demand proof of the reality of this infantile fixation. Freud, an absolutely sincere and painstaking empiricist, would never have evolved this hypothesis had he not had sufficient grounds for it. These grounds are furnished by the results of psychoanalytic investigations of the unconscious. Psychoanalysis reveals the unconscious presence of numerous fantasies which have their roots in the infantile past and are grouped round the so-called "nuclear complex," which in men may be designated as the Oedipus complex, in women as the Electra complex. These terms convey their own meaning exactly. The whole tragic fate of Oedipus and Electra was acted out within the narrow confines of the family, just as a child's fate lies wholly within the family boundaries. Hence the Oedipus complex, like the Electra complex, is very characteristic of an infantile conflict. The existence of these conflicts in infancy has been proved by means of psychoanalytic research. It is in the realm of this complex that the fixation is supposed to have taken place. The extremely potent and effective existence of the nuclear complex in the unconscious of neurotics led Freud to the hypothesis that the neurotic has a peculiar fixation or attachment to it. Not the mere existence of this complex—for everybody has it in the unconscious—but the very strong attachment to it is what is typical of the neurotic. He is far more influenced by this complex than the normal person; many examples in confirmation of this can be found in every one of the recent psychoanalytic histories of neurotic cases.

563   We must admit that this view is a very plausible one, because the hypothesis of fixation is based on the well-known fact that

245

certain periods of human life, and particularly infancy, do sometimes leave determining traces behind them which are permanent. The only question is whether this is a sufficient explanation or not. If we examine persons who have been neurotic from infancy it seems to be confirmed, for we see the nuclear complex as a permanent and powerful agent throughout life. But if we take cases which never show any noticeable trace of neurosis except at the particular time when they break down, and there are many such, this explanation becomes doubtful. If there is such a thing as fixation, it is not permissible to erect upon it a new hypothesis, claiming that at times during certain periods of life the fixation becomes loosened and ineffective, while at others it suddenly becomes strengthened. In these cases we find that the nuclear complex is as active and potent as in those which apparently support the theory of fixation. Here a critical attitude is justifiable, especially when we consider the oft-repeated observation that the moment of the outbreak of neurosis is not just a matter of chance; as a rule it is most critical. It is usually *the moment when a new psychological adjustment, that is, a new adaptation, is demanded.* Such moments facilitate the outbreak of a neurosis, as every experienced neurologist knows.

564   This fact seems to me extremely significant. If the fixation were indeed real we should expect to find its influence constant; in other words, a neurosis lasting throughout life. This is obviously not the case. The psychological determination of a neurosis is only partly due to an early infantile predisposition; it must be due to some cause in the present as well. And if we carefully examine the kind of infantile fantasies and occurrences to which the neurotic is attached, we shall be obliged to agree that there is nothing in them that is specifically neurotic. Normal individuals have pretty much the same inner and outer experiences, and may be attached to them to an astonishing degree without developing a neurosis. Primitive people, especially, are very much bound to their infantility. It now begins to look as if this so-called fixation were a normal phenomenon, and that the importance of infancy for the later mental attitude is natural and prevails everywhere. The fact that the neurotic seems to be markedly influenced by his infantile conflicts shows that it is less a matter of fixation than of the peculiar use which

he makes of his infantile past. It looks as if he exaggerated its importance and attributed to it a wholly artificial value. Adler, a pupil of Freud's, expresses a very similar view.

565   It would be unjust to say that Freud limited himself to the hypothesis of fixation; he was also aware of the problem I have just discussed. He called this phenomenon of reactivation or secondary exaggeration of infantile reminiscences "regression." But in Freud's view it appears as if the incestuous desires of the Oedipus complex were the real cause of the regression to infantile fantasies. If this were the case, we should have to postulate an unexpected intensity of the primary incestuous tendencies. This view led Freud to his recent comparison between what he calls the psychological "incest barrier" in children and the "incest taboo" in primitive man. He supposes that a desire for real incest led primitive man to frame laws against it; while to me it looks as if the incest taboo were only one among numerous taboos of all kinds, and were due to the typical superstitious fear of primitive man—a fear existing independently of incest and its prohibition. I am able to attribute as little strength to incestuous desires in childhood as in primitive humanity. I do not even seek the reason for regression in primary incestuous or any other sexual desires. I must admit that a purely sexual aetiology of neurosis seems to me much too narrow. I base this criticism not on any prejudice against sexuality but on an intimate acquaintance with the whole problem.

566   I therefore suggest that psychoanalytic theory should be freed from the purely sexual standpoint. In place of it I should like to introduce an *energic viewpoint* into the psychology of neurosis.

567   All psychological phenomena can be considered as manifestations of energy, in the same way that all physical phenomena have been understood as energic manifestations ever since Robert Mayer discovered the law of the conservation of energy. Subjectively and psychologically, this energy is conceived as *desire*. I call it *libido,* using the word in its original sense, which is by no means only sexual. Sallust uses it exactly as we do here when he says: "They took more pleasure in handsome arms and war horses than in harlots and revelry." [2]

2 "Magis in armis et militaribus equis quam in scortis et conviviis libidinem habebant." *Catilina*, 7, trans. by Rolfe, pp.14–15.

568   From a broader standpoint libido can be understood as vital energy in general, or as Bergson's *élan vital*. The first manifestation of this energy in the infant is the nutritive instinct. From this stage the libido slowly develops through numerous variants of the act of sucking into the sexual function. Hence I do not consider the act of sucking a sexual act. The pleasure in sucking can certainly not be considered as sexual pleasure, but as pleasure in nutrition, for it is nowhere proved that pleasure is sexual in itself. This process of development is continued into adult life and is accompanied by constantly increasing adaptation to the external world. Whenever the libido, in the process of adaptation, meets an obstacle, an accumulation takes place which normally gives rise to an increased effort to overcome the obstacle. But if the obstacle seems to be insurmountable, and the individual abandons the task of overcoming it, the stored-up libido makes a regression. Instead of being employed for an increased effort, the libido gives up its present task and reverts to an earlier and more primitive mode of adaptation.

569   The best examples of such regressions are found in hysterical cases where a disappointment in love or marriage has precipitated a neurosis. There we find those well-known digestive disorders, loss of appetite, dyspeptic symptoms of all sorts, etc. In these cases the regressive libido, turning back from the task of adaptation, gains power over the nutritive function and produces marked disturbances. Similar effects can be observed in cases where there is no disturbance of the nutritive function but, instead, a regressive revival of reminiscences from the distant past. We then find a reactivation of the parental imagos, of the Oedipus complex. Here the events of early infancy—never before important—suddenly become so. They have been regressively reactivated. Remove the obstacle from the path of life and this whole system of infantile fantasies at once breaks down and becomes as inactive and ineffective as before. But let us not forget that, to a certain extent, it is at work all the time, influencing us in unseen ways. This view, incidentally, comes very close to Janet's hypothesis that the "parties supérieures" of a function are replaced by its "parties inférieures." I would also remind you of Claparède's conception of neurotic symptoms as emotional reflexes of a primitive nature.

570   For these reasons I no longer seek the cause of a neurosis in

the past, but in the present. I ask, what is the necessary task which the patient will not accomplish? The long list of his infantile fantasies does not give me any sufficient aetiological explanation, because I know that these fantasies are only puffed up by the regressive libido, which has not found its natural outlet in a new form of adaptation to the demands of life.

571   You may ask why the neurotic has a special tendency not to accomplish his necessary tasks. Here let me point out that no living creature adjusts itself easily and smoothly to new conditions. The law of inertia is valid everywhere.

572   A sensitive and somewhat unbalanced person, as a neurotic always is, will meet with special difficulties and perhaps with more unusual tasks in life than a normal individual, who as a rule has only to follow the well-worn path of an ordinary existence. For the neurotic there is no established way of life, because his aims and tasks are apt to be of a highly individual character. He tries to go the more or less uncontrolled and half-conscious way of normal people, not realizing that his own critical and very different nature demands of him more effort than the normal person is required to exert. There are neurotics who have shown their heightened sensitiveness and their resistance to adaptation in the very first weeks of life, in the difficulty they have in taking the mother's breast and in their exaggerated nervous reactions, etc. For this peculiarity in the neurotic predisposition it will always be impossible to find a psychological aetiology, because it is anterior to all psychology. This predisposition—you can call it "congenital sensitiveness" or what you like—is the cause of the first resistances to adaptation. As the way to adaptation is blocked, the biological energy we call libido does not find its appropriate outlet or activity, with the result that a suitable form of adaptation is replaced by an abnormal or primitive one.

573   In neurosis we speak of an infantile attitude or of the predominance of infantile fantasies and wishes. In so far as infantile impressions are of obvious importance in normal people they will be equally influential in neurosis, but they have no aetiological significance; they are reactions merely, being chiefly secondary and regressive phenomena. It is perfectly true, as Freud says, that infantile fantasies determine the form and the subsequent development of neurosis, but this is not an aetiology.

Even when we find perverted sexual fantasies whose existence can be demonstrated in childhood, we cannot consider them of aetiological significance. A neurosis is not really caused by infantile sexual fantasies, and the same must be said of the sexualism of neurotic fantasy in general. It is not a primary phenomenon based on a perverted sexual disposition, but merely secondary and a consequence of the failure to apply the stored-up libido in a suitable way. I realize that this is a very old view, but this does not prevent it from being true. The fact that the patient himself very often believes that his infantile fantasies are the real cause of his neurosis does not prove that he is right in his belief, or that a theory based on this belief is right either. It may look as if it were so, and I must admit that very many cases do have that appearance. At all events, it is perfectly easy to understand how Freud arrived at this view. Everyone who has any psychoanalytic experience will agree with me here.

574   To sum up: I cannot see the real aetiology of neurosis in the various manifestations of infantile sexual development and the fantasies to which they give rise. The fact that these fantasies are exaggerated in neurosis and occupy the foreground is a consequence of the stored-up energy or libido. The psychological trouble in neurosis, and the neurosis itself, can be formulated as *an act of adaptation that has failed.* This formulation might reconcile certain views of Janet's with Freud's view that a neurosis is, in a sense, an attempt at self-cure—a view which can be and has been applied to many other illnesses.

575   Here the question arises as to whether it is still advisable to bring to light all the patient's fantasies by analysis, if we now consider them of no aetiological significance. Hitherto psychoanalysis has set about unravelling these fantasies because they were considered aetiologically important. My altered view of the theory of neurosis does not affect the psychoanalytic procedure. The technique remains the same. Though we no longer imagine we are unearthing the ultimate root of the illness, we have to pull up the sexual fantasies because the energy which the patient needs for his health, that is, for adaptation, is attached to them. By means of psychoanalysis the connection between his conscious mind and the libido in the unconscious is re-established. Thus the unconscious libido is brought under the control of the will. Only in this way can the split-off energy

become available again for the accomplishment of the necessary tasks of life. Considered from this standpoint, psychoanalysis no longer appears as a mere reduction of the individual to his primitive sexual wishes, but, if rightly understood, as a highly moral task of immense educational value.

SOME CRUCIAL POINTS IN PSYCHOANALYSIS

A Correspondence between Dr. Jung and Dr. Loÿ [1]

Foreword

A few words may suffice to explain the reasons which led to this correspondence, and the purpose in publishing it.

After being introduced to the theory and practice of suggestion therapy by Professor Forel, I practised it for many years and still use it in suitable cases. When I became aware of the great significance of Freud's psychoanalytic works, I studied them and gradually began to take up analysis myself. I made contact with the nearest centre of psychoanalytic research, which was Zurich. Yet in technical matters I had, in the main, to rely on myself. Hence, when I met with failures, I had to ask myself who or what was to blame, I alone, because I did not know how to apply the "correct psychoanalytic method," or perhaps the method itself, which might not be suitable in all cases. A special stumbling-block for me was the interpretation of dreams: I could not convince myself that there was a generally valid symbolism, and that this symbolism was exclusively sexual, as many psychoanalysts declared. Their interpretations often seemed to me to bear the stamp of arbitrariness.

And so, when I read the following statement by Freud in the *Zentralblatt für Psychoanalyse,* in June 1912, the words seemed to come from my own heart: "Some years ago I gave as an answer to the question of how one can become an analyst: 'By analysing one's own dreams.' This preparation is no doubt enough for many people, but not for everyone who wishes to learn analysis. Nor can everyone succeed in interpreting his own dreams without outside help. I count it as one of the many merits of the Zurich school of analysis that they

---

1 [Originally published as *Psychotherapeutische Zeitfragen; Ein Briefwechsel mit Dr. C. G. Jung,* edited by Dr. R. Loÿ (Leipzig and Vienna, 1914). Translated (except for Dr. Loÿ's foreword) by Mrs. Edith Eder as "On Some Crucial Points in Psychoanalysis," in *Collected Papers on Analytical Psychology* (London, 1916; 2nd edn., London, 1917; New York, 1920). The present translation is based on this. —Editors.]

have laid increased emphasis on this requirement, and have embodied it in the demand that everyone who wishes to carry out analyses on other people shall first himself undergo an analysis by someone with expert knowledge. Anyone who takes up the work seriously should choose this course, which offers more than one advantage; the sacrifice involved in laying oneself open to another person without being driven to it by illness is amply rewarded. Not only is one's aim of learning to know what is hidden in one's own mind far more rapidly attained and with less expense of affect, but impressions and convictions will be gained in relation to oneself which will be sought in vain from studying books and attending lectures." [2]

Dr. Jung declared himself ready to undertake my analysis. A great obstacle arose, however: the distance between us. Thus, many questions which had come up in the analytical interviews and could not be discussed sufficiently thoroughly were settled by correspondence.

When the correspondence reached its present proportions I asked myself whether other colleagues might not find it as stimulating as I had done: psychoanalysts who were just beginning and who needed a guiding thread through the mounting tangle of psychoanalytic literature, practising physicians who perhaps knew of psychoanalysis only through the violent attacks it has had to endure (often from quite unqualified persons who have no experience of it).

I could only answer this question in the affirmative. I asked Dr. Jung to give his consent to my publishing the correspondence, which he readily did.

I do not doubt that the reader will, like me, give him the thanks that are his due; for a more concise and easily understandable account of the psychoanalytic method and of some of the problems it raises does not, to my knowledge, exist.

Dr. R. Loÿ

Sanatorium L'Abri, Montreux-Territet,
14 December 1913

From Dr. Loÿ

12 January 1913

576   What you said at our last interview was extraordinarily stimulating. I was expecting you to throw light on the interpretation of my own and my patients' dreams from the standpoint

---

2 "Recommendations to Physicians Practising Psycho-Analysis" (orig. 1912), pp. 116f.

of Freud's dream interpretation. Instead, you put before me an entirely new conception: the dream as a means, produced by the subconscious, of restoring the moral balance. That is certainly a fruitful thought. But still more fruitful, it seems to me, is your other suggestion. You conceive the tasks of psychoanalysis to be much deeper than I had ever imagined: it is no longer a question of getting rid of troublesome pathological symptoms, but of the analysand learning to know himself completely—not just his anxiety experiences—and on the basis of this knowledge building up and shaping his life anew. But he himself must be the builder; the analyst only furnishes him with the necessary tools.

577 To begin with, I would ask you to consider what justification there is for the original procedure of Breuer and Freud, now entirely given up both by Freud himself and by you, but practised by Frank, for instance, as his only method: the "abreaction of inhibited affects under light hypnosis." Why did you give up the cathartic method? Please explain. More particularly, has light hypnosis in psychocatharsis a different value from suggestion during sleep, long practised in suggestion therapy? That is, has it only the value which the doctor attributes, or says he attributes to it, the value which the patient's faith gives it? In other words, is suggestion in the waking state equivalent to suggestion in the hypnoid state, as Bernheim now asserts, after having used suggestion for many years in hypnosis? You will tell me that we must talk of psychoanalysis, not of suggestion. What I really mean is this: is not the *suggestion* that psychocatharsis in the hypnoid state will produce a therapeutic effect (with limitations, naturally, the age of the patient, etc.) the main factor in the therapeutic effects of psychocatharsis? Frank says in his *Affektstörungen:* "These one-sided attitudes, suggestibility and suggestion, are almost entirely in abeyance in psychocatharsis under light sleep, so far as the content of the ideas reproduced is concerned." [3] Is that really true? Frank himself adds: "How can ruminating on the dreams of youth *in itself* lead to discharge of the stored-up anxiety, whether in the hypnoid state or any other? Must we not rather suppose that ruminating on them would make the anxiety states even

[3] Ludwig Frank, *Affektstörungen: Studien über ihre Aetiologie und Therapie* (1913).

greater?" (I have noticed this myself, far more than I liked.) Of course one says to the patient, "First we must stir up, then afterwards comes peace." And it does come. But does it not come *in spite of the stirring-up process,* because gradually, by means of frequent talks *apart from* light hypnosis, the patient gains such confidence in the analyst that he becomes susceptible to the direct suggestion that an improvement and then a cure will follow? I go still further: in an analysis in the waking state, is not the patient's faith that the method employed will cure him, coupled with his growing confidence in the analyst, a main cause of his cure? And I go still further: in every therapeutic method systematically carried out is not faith in it, confidence in the doctor, a main cause of its success? I won't say the only cause, for one cannot deny that physical, dietetic, and chemical procedures, when properly selected, have their own effect in bringing about a cure, over and above the striking effects produced by indirect suggestion.

From Dr. Jung

28 January 1913

578   With regard to your question concerning the applicability of the cathartic procedure, I can say that I adopt the following standpoint: every procedure is good if it helps. I therefore acknowledge every method of suggestion including Christian Science, mental healing, etc. "A truth is a truth, when it works." It is another question, though, whether a scientifically trained doctor can square it with his conscience to sell little bottles of Lourdes water because this suggestion is at times very helpful. Even the so-called highly scientific suggestion therapy employs the wares of the medicine-man and the exorcising shaman. And why not? The public is not much more advanced either and continues to expect miraculous cures from the doctor. And indeed, we must rate those doctors wise—worldly-wise in every sense—who know how to surround themselves with the aura of a medicine-man. They have not only the biggest practices but also get the best results. This is because, apart from the neuroses, countless physical illnesses are tainted and complicated with psychic material to an unsuspected degree. The medical exorcist betrays by his whole demeanour his full appreciation of

that psychic component when he gives the patient the opportunity of fixing his faith firmly on the mysterious personality of the doctor. In this way he wins the sick man's mind, which from then on helps him to restore his body to health. The cure works best when the doctor himself believes in his own formulae, otherwise he may be overcome by scientific doubt and so lose the proper convincing tone. I myself practised hypnotic suggestion-therapy for a time with enthusiasm. But then there befell me three dubious incidents which I would like to bring to your attention.

579   One day a withered old peasant woman of about 56 came to me to be hypnotized for various neurotic troubles. She was not easy to hypnotize, was very restless, and kept opening her eyes —but at last I did succeed. When I woke her up again after about half an hour she seized my hand and with many words testified to her overflowing gratitude. I told her, "You are by no means cured yet, so keep your thanks till the end of the treatment." "I'm not thanking you for that," she whispered, blushing, "but because you were so *decent*." She looked at me with a sort of tender admiration and departed. I gazed for a long time at the spot where she had stood. So decent? I asked myself, flabbergasted—good heavens, surely she hadn't imagined . . . ? This glimpse made me suspect for the first time that possibly the old reprobate, with the atrocious directness of feminine (at the time I called it "animal") instinct, understood more about the essence of hypnosis than I did with all my knowledge of the scientific profundity of the text-books. My innocence was gone.

580   Next came a pretty, coquettish, seventeen-year-old girl with a very harassed-looking mama. She had suffered since early childhood from *enuresis nocturna* (which she used, among other things, to stop herself being sent to a finishing school in Italy). At once I thought of the old woman and her wisdom. I tried to hypnotize the girl; she went into fits of laughter and held up the hypnosis for twenty minutes. I kept my temper and thought: I know why you laugh, you have already fallen in love with me, but I will give you proof of my decency as a reward for wasting my time with your provocative laughter. At last I put her under. The effect was immediate. The enuresis stopped, and I thereupon informed the young lady that, instead of Wednesday, I would not see her again for hypnosis till the following Satur-

day. On Saturday she arrived with a cross face, boding disaster. The enuresis had come back again. I thought of my wise old woman and asked, "When did it come back?" She (unsuspecting): "Wednesday night." I thought to myself: There we have it, she wants to prove to me that I absolutely must see her on Wednesdays too; not to see me for a whole long week is too much for a tender loving heart. But I did not intend to pander to this annoying romance, so I said, "It would be quite wrong to continue the treatment under these circumstances. We must drop it altogether for three weeks, to give the enuresis a chance to stop. Then come again for treatment." In my malicious heart I knew that I would be away on holiday and the course for hypnotic treatment would be finished. After the holiday my *locum tenens* told me that the young lady had been there with the news that the enuresis had vanished, but her disappointment at not seeing me was very keen. The old woman was right, I thought.

581   The third case gave my joy in suggestion therapy its death-blow. This case really was the limit. A 65-year-old lady came hobbling into the consulting-room on a crutch. She had suffered from pain in the knee-joint for seventeen years, and this at times kept her chained to her bed for many weeks. No doctor had been able to cure her, and she had run through all the cures of present-day medicine. After letting the stream of her narrative pour over me for ten minutes, I said, "I will try to hypnotize you, perhaps that will do you good." "Oh yes, please do!" she said, then leaned her head to one side and fell asleep before ever I said or did a thing. She passed into somnambulism and showed every form of hypnosis you could possibly desire. After half an hour I had the greatest difficulty in waking her; when at last she was awake she jumped up: "I am well, I am all right, you have cured me!" I tried to raise timid objections, but her praises drowned me. She could really walk. I blushed, and said embarrassed to my colleagues: "Behold the marvels of hypnotic therapy!" That day saw the death of my connection with therapy by suggestion; the notoriety aroused by this case shamed and depressed me. When, a year later, the good old lady returned, this time with a pain in her back, I was already sunk in hopeless cynicism; I saw written on her brow that she had just

read in the paper the notice of the reopening of my course on hypnotism. That tiresome romanticism had provided her with a convenient pain in the back so that she might have a pretext for seeing me, and again let herself be cured in the same spectacular fashion. This proved true in every particular.

582   As you will understand, a man possessed of a scientific conscience cannot digest such cases with impunity. I was resolved to abandon suggestion altogether rather than allow myself to be passively transformed into a miracle-worker. I wanted to understand what really goes on in people's minds. It suddenly seemed to me incredibly childish to think of dispelling an illness with magical incantations, and that this should be the sole result of our efforts to create a psychotherapy. Thus the discovery of Breuer and Freud came as a veritable life-saver. I took up their method with unalloyed enthusiasm and soon recognized how right Freud was when, at a very early date, indeed as far back as *Studies on Hysteria,* he began to direct a searchlight on the circumstances of the so-called trauma. I soon discovered that, though traumata of clearly aetiological significance were occasionally present, the majority of them appeared very improbable. Many traumata were so unimportant, even so normal, that they could be regarded at most as a pretext for the neurosis. But what especially aroused my criticism was the fact that not a few traumata were simply inventions of fantasy and had never happened at all. This realization was enough to make me sceptical about the whole trauma theory. (I have discussed these matters in detail in my lectures on the theory of psychoanalysis.) I could no longer imagine that repeated experiences of a fantastically exaggerated or entirely fictitious trauma had a different therapeutic value from a suggestion procedure. It is good if it helps. If only one did not have a scientific conscience and that hankering after the truth! I recognized in many cases, particularly with intelligent patients, the therapeutic limitations of this method. It is merely a rule of thumb, convenient for the analyst because it makes no particular demands on his intellect or his capacity to adapt. The theory and practice are delightfully simple: "The neurosis comes from a trauma. The trauma is abreacted." If the abreacting takes place under hypnotism or with other magical accessories (dark room, special

lighting, etc.), I think at once of my clever old woman, who opened my eyes not only to the magical influence of the mesmeric passes but to the nature of hypnotism itself.

583   What alienated me once and for all from this comparatively effective, indirect method of suggestion, based as it is on an equally effective false theory, was the simultaneous recognition that behind the bewildering and deceptive maze of neurotic fantasies there is a *conflict* which may best be described as a moral one. With this there began for me a new era of understanding. Research and therapy now joined hands in the effort to discover the causes and the *rational* solution of the conflict. For me this meant psychoanalysis. While I was arriving at this insight, Freud had built up his sexual theory of neurosis, thus posing a mass of questions for discussion, all of which seemed worthy of the deepest consideration. I had the good fortune to collaborate with Freud for a long time, and to work with him on the problem of sexuality in neurosis. You know perhaps from some of my earlier works that I was always rather dubious about the significance of sexuality. This has now become the point on which I am no longer altogether of Freud's opinion.

584   I have preferred to answer your questions in a somewhat inconsequential fashion. I will now catch up on the rest: light hypnosis and total hypnosis are simply varying degrees of intensity of unconscious susceptibility to the hypnotist. Who can draw sharp distinctions here? To a critical intelligence it is unthinkable that suggestibility and suggestion can be avoided in the cathartic method. They are present everywhere as general human attributes, even with Dubois[4] and the psychoanalysts, who all think they are working on purely rational lines. No technique and no self-effacement avails here; the analyst works willy-nilly, and perhaps most of all, through his personality, i.e., through suggestion. In the cathartic method, what is of far more importance to the patient than the conjuring up of old fantasies is the experience of being together so often with the analyst, his trust and belief in him personally and in his method. The belief, the self-confidence, perhaps also the devotion with which the analyst does his work, are far more important to the

4 [See supra, par. 41, n. 6.]

patient (imponderabilia though they may be) than the rehearsing of old traumata.[5]

585   It is time we learnt from the history of medicine everything that has ever been of help, then perhaps we shall discover the really necessary therapy—that is, psychotherapy. Did not even the old apothecaries' messes achieve brilliant cures, cures which faded only with the belief in their efficacy?!

586   Because I know that, despite all rational safeguards, the patient does attempt to assimilate the analyst's personality, I have laid it down as a requirement that the psychotherapist must be just as responsible for the cleanness of his hands as the surgeon. I even hold it to be an indispensable prerequisite that the psychoanalyst should first submit himself to the analytical process, as his personality is one of the main factors in the cure.

587   Patients read the analyst's character intuitively, and they should find in him a man with failings, admittedly, but also a man who strives at every point to fulfil his human duties in the fullest sense. Many times I have had the opportunity of seeing that the analyst is successful with his treatment just so far as he has succeeded in his own moral development. I think this answer will satisfy your question.

From Dr. Loÿ

2 February 1913

588   You answer several of my questions in a decidedly affirmative tone, taking it as proved that in cures by the cathartic method the main role is played by faith in the analyst and his method and not by "abreacting" the real or imaginary traumata. I think so too. Equally I agree with your view that the old "apothecaries' messes," as well as the Lourdes cures or those of the mental healers, Christian Scientists, and persuasionists, are to be attributed to faith in the miracle-worker rather than to any of the methods employed.

589   But now comes the ticklish point: the augur can remain an

---

[5] Thus a woman patient, who had been treated by a young colleague without entire success, once said to me: "Certainly I made great progress with him and I am much better than I was. He tried to analyse my dreams. It's true he never understood them, but he took *so much trouble* over them. He is really a good doctor."

augur so long as he himself believes that the will of the gods is made manifest by the entrails of the sacrificial beast. When he no longer believes, he can ask himself: Shall I continue to use my augur's authority to promote the welfare of the State, or shall I make use of my newer, and I hope truer, convictions of today? Both ways are possible. The first is called opportunism, the second the pursuit of truth and scientific honesty. For the doctor, the first way perhaps brings therapeutic success and fame, the second brings the reproach that such a man is not to be taken seriously. What I esteem most highly in Freud and his school is just this passionate desire for truth. On the other hand some people pronounce a different verdict: "It is impossible for a busy practitioner to keep pace with the development of the views of this investigator and his initiates" (Frank, *Affektstörungen*, Introduction, p. 2).

590   One can easily disregard this little quip, but self-criticism needs to be taken more seriously. One can after all ask oneself: Since science is in continual flux, have I the right to ignore on principle any method or combination of methods by which I know I can get therapeutic results?

591   Looking more closely at the fundamental reason for your aversion to the ancillary use of hypnosis (or semi-hypnosis; the degree matters nothing) in treatment by suggestion (which as you say every doctor and every therapeutic method makes use of willy-nilly, no matter what it is called), one must say that what has disgusted you with hypnotism is at bottom nothing but the so-called "transference" to the doctor, which you, with your purely psychoanalytic procedure, can eliminate as little as anybody else, and which actually plays an essential part in the success of the treatment. Your requirement that the psychoanalyst must be responsible for the cleanness of his hands—here I agree unreservedly—is the logical conclusion. But is the possible recourse to hypnosis in a psychotherapeutic procedure any more "augurish" than the unavoidable use of the "transference to the analyst" for therapeutic purposes? In either case we bank on faith as the healing agent. As for the feeling which the patient—whether man or woman—entertains for the analyst, is there never anything in the background save a conscious or unconscious sexual wish? In many cases your impression is certainly correct, and more than one woman has been frank enough

to confess that the beginning of hypnosis was accompanied by a voluptuous sensation. But it is not true in all instances—or how would you explain the underlying feeling in the hypnotizing of one animal by another, e.g., snake and bird? Surely you would say that here the feeling of *fear* prevails, which is an inversion of libido, whereas in the hypnoid state that comes over the female before she succumbs to the male it is the pure *libido sexualis* that predominates, though possibly still mixed with fear.

592   However that may be, from your three cases I cannot draw any ethical distinction between "susceptibility to the hypnotist" and "transference to the analyst" that would condemn a possible combination of hypnosis with psychoanalysis, as an auxiliary. You will ask why I cling so much to the use of hypnosis, or rather of the hypnoid state. It is because I think there are cases that can be cured much more quickly in this way than by a purely psychoanalytic procedure. For example, in no more than five or six interviews I completely cured a fifteen-year-old girl who had suffered from *enuresis nocturna* even since infancy, but was otherwise perfectly sound, gifted, first in her class, etc. Previously she had tried all sorts of treatment without any result.

593   Perhaps I ought to have sought out the psychoanalytic connections between the enuresis and her psychosexual disposition, explained it to her, etc., but I couldn't, the girl had only the short Easter holidays for treatment: so I just hypnotized her and the trouble vanished.

594   In psychoanalysis I use hypnosis to help the patient overcome "resistance."

595   Further, I use semi-hypnosis in conjunction with psychoanalysis to accelerate the "reconstruction" stage.

596   To take an example, a patient afflicted with a washing mania was sent to me after a year's psychocathartic treatment with Dr. X. The symbolic meaning of her washing ceremonies had previously been explained to her, but she became more and more agitated during the "abreaction" of alleged traumata in childhood, because she had persuaded herself by auto-suggestion that she was too old to be cured, that she saw no "images," etc. So I used hypnosis to help her reduce the number of washings—"so that the anxiety feeling would stay away"—and to

train her to throw things on the floor and pick them up again
without washing her hands afterwards, etc.

597   In view of these considerations I should, if you feel disposed
to go further into the matter, be grateful if you would furnish
me with more convincing reasons why the hypnotic procedure
is to be condemned, and explain how to do without it, or what
to replace it with in such cases. Were I convinced, I would give
it up as you have done; but what convinced you has not, so far,
convinced me. *Si duo faciunt idem, non est idem.*

598   I would now like to go on to another important matter to
which you alluded, but only cursorily, and to put one question:
Behind the neurotic fantasies there is almost always (or always)
a moral conflict belonging to the present. That is perfectly clear
to me. Research and therapy coincide; their task is: to seek the
causes and the rational solution of the conflict.

599   Good.—But can the rational solution always be found? "Reasons of expediency" so often bar the way, varying with the type
of patient (children, young girls and women, from "pious"—
hypocritical!—Catholic or Protestant families). Again that ac-
cursed opportunism!—A colleague of mine was perfectly right
when he began to give sexual enlightenment to a young French
boy who was indulging in masturbation. Whereupon, like one
possessed, in rushed a bigoted grandmother, and a disagreeable
scene ensued. How to act in these and similar cases? What to do
in cases where there is a moral conflict between love and duty
(conflicts in marriage)—or in general between instinct and
moral duty? What to do in the case of a girl afflicted with hysterical or anxiety symptoms, who is in need of love and has no
chance to marry, or cannot find a suitable man, and, because she
comes of "good family," wants to remain chaste? Simply try to
get rid of the symptoms by suggestion? But that is wrong as soon
as one knows of a better way.

600   How is one to reconcile one's two consciences: that of the
man who does not want to confine his fidelity to truth *intra
muros,* and that of the doctor who *must* cure, or if he dares not
cure according to his real convictions (owing to opportunist
motives), must at least provide some alleviation? We live in the
present, but with the ideas and the ideals of the future. That is
our conflict. How to resolve it?

From Dr. Jung

4 February 1913

601   . . . You have put me in a somewhat embarrassing position with your question in yesterday's letter. You have rightly guessed the spirit which dictated my last. I am glad you, too, acknowledge this spirit. There are not very many who can boast of such liberalism. I should deceive myself if I thought I was a practising physician. I am above all an investigator, and this naturally gives me a different attitude to many problems. In my last letter I purposely left the practical needs of the doctor out of account, chiefly in order to show you on what grounds one might be moved to give up hypnotic therapy. To anticipate a possible objection, let me say at once that I did not give up hypnosis because I wanted to avoid dealing with the basic forces of the human psyche, but because I wanted to battle with them directly and openly. When once I understood what kind of forces play a part in hypnotism I gave it up, simply to get rid of all the indirect advantages of this method. As we psychoanalysts find to our cost every day—and our patients also—we do not work *with* the "transference to the analyst," [6] but *against it and in spite of it*. Hence we do not bank on the faith of the patient, but on his *criticism*. So much I would say for now about this delicate question.

602   As your letter shows, we are at one in regard to the theoretical aspect of treatment by suggestion. We can therefore apply ourselves to the further task of reaching agreement on practical questions. Your remarks on the doctor's dilemma—whether to be a magician or a scientist—bring us to the heart of the matter. I strive not to be a fanatic—though there are not a few who accuse me of fanaticism. I struggle merely for the recognition of methods of research and their results, not for the application of psychoanalytic methods at all costs. I was a medical practitioner quite long enough to realize that practice obeys, and must obey, other laws than does the search for truth. One might almost say that the practitioner must submit first and foremost

---

[6] Defined in the Freudian sense as the transference to the analyst of infantile and sexual fantasies. A more advanced conception of the transference perceives in it the important process of *empathy*, which begins by making use of infantile and sexual analogies.

to the law of expediency. The investigator would be doing him a great wrong if he accused him of not using the "one true" scientific method. As I said to you in my last letter: "A truth is a truth, when it works." On the other hand, the practitioner must not reproach the investigator if in his search for truth and for new and perhaps better methods he tries out unusual procedures. After all, it is not the practitioner who will have to bear the brunt, but the investigator and possibly his patient. The practitioner must certainly use those methods which he knows how to apply to the greatest advantage and which give him relatively the best results. My liberalism, as you see, extends even to Christian Science. But I deem it most uncalled for that Frank, a practising doctor, should cast aspersions on research in which he cannot participate—the very line of research to which he owes his own method. It is surely high time to stop this running down of every new idea. No one asks Frank and his confrères to be psychoanalysts. We grant them their right to existence, why should they always seek to curtail ours?

603   As my own "cures" show you, I do not doubt the effect of suggestion. I merely had the feeling that I might be able to discover something still better. This hope has been justified. Not for ever shall it be said:

> If ever in this world we reach what's good
> We call what's better just a plain falsehood! [7]

604   I frankly confess that if I were doing your work I should often be in difficulties if I relied on psychoanalysis alone. I can scarcely imagine a general practice, especially in a sanatorium, with no other auxiliaries than psychoanalysis. It is true that at Bircher's sanatorium in Zurich the principle of psychoanalysis has been adopted, at least by several of the assistants, but a whole series of other important educative influences are also brought to bear on the patients, without which things would probably go very badly. In my own purely psychoanalytic practice I have often regretted that I could not avail myself of other methods of re-education that are naturally at hand in an institution—but only, of course, in special cases where one is dealing with particularly uncontrolled, untrained patients. Which of us would

[7] [*Faust, Part I*, The Night Scene.]

assert that he has discovered the panacea? There are cases where psychoanalysis works worse than any other method. But who has ever claimed that psychoanalysis should be used always and everywhere? Only a fanatic could maintain such a view. Patients for whom psychoanalysis is suitable have to be selected. I unhesitatingly send cases I think unsuitable to other doctors. This does not happen often, as a matter of fact, because patients have a way of sorting themselves out. Those who go to a psychoanalyst usually know quite well why they go to him and not to someone else. Moreover there are very many neurotics excellently suited for psychoanalysis. In these matters all schematism is to be abhorred. It is never quite wise to run your head against a brick wall. Whether simple hypnotism, or cathartic treatment, or psychoanalysis shall be used must be determined by the conditions of the case and the preference of the doctor. Every doctor will obtain the best results with the instrument he knows best.

605   But, barring exceptions, I must say definitely that for me, as well as for my patients, psychoanalysis works better than any other method. This is not merely a matter of feeling; from manifold experiences I know many cases can still be helped by psychoanalysis that are refractory to all other methods of treatment. I know many colleagues whose experience is the same, even men engaged exclusively in practical work. It is scarcely credible that an altogether inferior method would meet with so much support.

606   When once psychoanalysis has been applied in a suitable case, it is *imperative* that rational solutions of the conflicts should be found. The objection is at once advanced that many conflicts are intrinsically insoluble. People sometimes take this view because they think only of external solutions—which at bottom are not solutions at all. If a man cannot get on with his wife, he naturally thinks the conflict would be solved if he married someone else. When such marriages are examined they are seen to be no solution whatever. The old Adam enters upon the new marriage and bungles it just as badly as he did the earlier one. A real solution comes only from within, and then only because the patient has been brought to a different attitude.

607   If an external solution is possible no psychoanalysis is necessary; but if an internal solution is sought, we are faced with the

peculiar task of psychoanalysis. The conflict between "love and duty" must be solved on that level of character where "love and duty" are no longer opposites, which in reality they are not. Similarly, the familiar conflict between "instinct and conventional morality" must be solved in such a way that both factors are taken sufficiently into account, and this again is possible only through a change of character. This change psychoanalysis can bring about. In such cases external solutions are worse than none at all. Naturally, expediency determines which road the doctor must ultimately follow and what is then his duty. I regard the conscience-searching question of whether he should remain true to his scientific convictions as a minor one in comparison with the far weightier question of how he can best help his patient. The doctor *must,* on occasion, be able to play the augur. *Mundus vult decipi*—but the curative effect is no deception. It is true that there is a conflict between ideal conviction and concrete possibility. But we should ill prepare the ground for the seed of the future were we to forget the tasks of the present, and sought only to cultivate ideals. That would be but idle dreaming. Do not forget that Kepler once cast horoscopes for money, and that countless artists are condemned to work for a living wage.

From Dr. Loÿ

9 February 1913

608   The same passion for truth possesses us when we think of pure research, and the same wish to cure when we consider therapy. For the researcher, as for the doctor, we desire the fullest freedom in all directions—complete freedom to choose and practise the methods which promise the best fulfilment of their ends at any moment. On this last point we are at one, but it remains a postulate which we must prove to the satisfaction of others if we want recognition for our views.

609   First and foremost there is one question that must be answered, an old question already asked in the Gospels: "What is truth?" I think clear definitions of fundamental ideas are everywhere necessary. How shall we contrive a working definition of the concept "Truth?" Perhaps an allegory may help us.

610   Imagine a gigantic prism in front of the sun, so that its rays

are broken up, but suppose man entirely ignorant of this fact. (I disregard the chemical, invisible, ultra-violet rays.) Men living in the blue-lit region will say, "The sun sends forth blue light only." They are right and yet they are wrong: from their standpoint they are capable of perceiving only a *fragment* of the truth. And so too with the inhabitants of the red, yellow, and intermediate regions. And they will all scourge and slay one another to force their fragmentary truth on the others—until, grown wiser through travelling in each other's regions, they come to the unanimous view that the sun sends out light of different colours. That is a more comprehensive truth, but it is still not *the* truth. Only when a giant lens has recombined the split-up rays, and when the invisible, chemical, and heat rays have given proof of their specific effects, will a view arise more in accordance with the truth, and men will perceive that the sun emits white light which is split up by the prism into different rays with different qualities, and that these rays are recombined by the lens into a beam of white light.

611   This example serves to show that the road to Truth leads through a series of comparative observations, the results of which must be controlled with the help of freely selected experiments until seemingly well-grounded hypotheses and theories can be put forward; but these hypotheses and theories will fall to the ground as soon as a single new observation or a single new experiment contradicts them.

612   The way is toilsome, and in the end all we ever attain is a *relative* truth. But such relative truth suffices for the time being if it serves to explain the most important concatenations of fact in the past, to light up those of the present, and to predict those of the future, so that we are in a position to adapt through our knowledge. Absolute truth, however, would be accessible only to omniscience, having knowledge of all possible concatenations and combinations; but that is not possible for us, because the number of concatenations and combinations is infinite. Accordingly, we shall never know more than an approximate truth. Should new concatenations be discovered, new combinations be built up, the picture changes and with it the whole range of knowledge and action. To what new revolutions in daily life does not every new scientific discovery lead: how absurdly small

was the beginning of the first theory of electricity, how inconceivably great the results!

613   These are commonplaces, but one must continually repeat them when one sees how life is always made bitter for the innovators in every scientific field, and now especially so for the followers of the psychoanalytic school. Everyone admits these commonplaces so long as it is a matter of "academic" discussion, but only so long; as soon as a concrete case has to be considered, sympathies and antipathies rush to the forefront and darken judgment. Therefore the investigator must fight tirelessly, appealing to logic and honesty, for freedom of research in all fields, and must not allow despots of whatever political or religious persuasion to advance "reasons of expediency" in order to destroy or even restrict this freedom. Reasons of expediency may be and are in place elsewhere, but not here. Finally, we must make an end of the dictum of the Middle Ages, *philosophia ancilla theologiae,* as well as the founding of university chairs in favour of this or that political or religious party. All fanaticism is the enemy of science, which above all things must be independent.

614   And when we turn from the search for Truth back to therapeutics, we see immediately that here again we are in agreement. In practice expediency *must* rule: the doctor from the yellow region must adapt himself to the patients in the yellow region, as must the doctor in the blue region to *his* patients; both have the same object in view. And the doctor who lives in the white light must take into consideration the past experiences of patients from the yellow or blue region, in spite or rather because of his wider knowledge. In such cases the way to healing will be long and difficult, may indeed lead more easily to a *cul-de-sac* than in cases where he has to deal with patients who, like himself, have already attained knowledge of the white light, or, in other words, when his patients have already "sorted themselves out." With these sorted-out patients the psychoanalyst is permitted to work exclusively with the methods of psychoanalysis; he can consider himself lucky that he does not need to "play the augur."

615   Now, these methods of psychoanalysis, what are they? If I understand you aright, it is by and large a question of working directly and openly with the fundamental forces of the human

psyche, to the end that the patient, be he sick or sound or in some stage in between—for sickness and health flow into each other imperceptibly—shall have his mental eyes opened to the drama that is being enacted within him. He must learn to know the automatisms that are hostile to the development of his personality, and through this knowledge he must learn gradually to free himself from them; but he must also learn how to exploit and strengthen the favourable automatisms. He must learn to make his self-knowledge real and to control the workings of his mind so that a balance may be struck between feeling and reason. How large a part is played in all this by *suggestion*? I can hardly believe that suggestion can be avoided altogether till the patient feels really freed. This freedom, it goes without saying, is the main thing to strive for, and it must be an *active* freedom. The patient who simply obeys a suggestion obeys it only so long as the "transference to the analyst" remains in force.

616   But in order to adjust himself to all circumstances the patient must have strengthened himself "from within." He should no longer need the crutches of faith but must be capable of tackling all theoretical and practical problems critically and of solving them himself. That is your view, isn't it, or have I not understood you correctly?

617   I next ask, must not every single case be treated differently —within the limits of the psychoanalytic method? For if every case is a case by itself, it must surely require individual treatment.

618   "Il n'y a pas de maladies, il n'y a que des malades," said a French doctor whose name escapes me. But broadly speaking, what course, from a technical point of view, does analysis take, and what deviations occur most frequently? That I would gladly learn from you. I take it for granted that all "augur's tricks," darkened rooms, masks, chloroform, etc., are out of the question.

619   Psychoanalysis—purged so far as is humanly possible of suggestive influence—appears to have one essential difference from psychotherapy à la Dubois. With Dubois, all talk about the past is prohibited from the outset, and "moral reasons for recovery" are placed in the forefront; whilst psychoanalysis uses the subconscious material from the patient's past and present to promote self-knowledge. Another difference lies in the conception

of morality: morals are above all "relative." But what forms (in broad outline) should one give them at times when suggestion cannot be avoided? Expediency must decide, you will say. Agreed, as regards old people or grown-ups who have to live in a not very enlightened milieu. But if one is dealing with children, the seed of the future, isn't it a sacred duty to enlighten them about the shaky foundations of the so-called moral conceptions of the past, which have only a dogmatic basis, and to educate them to full freedom by courageously unveiling the truth? I ask this not so much with respect to the analysing doctor as with respect to the educator. Should not the founding of *progressive schools* be regarded as a task for the psychoanalyst?

From Dr. Jung

11 February 1913

620   The relativity of "truth" has been known for ages and does not stand in the way of anything, and if it did would merely prevent belief in dogmas and authority. But it does not even do that.

621   You ask me—or rather tell me—what psychoanalysis is. Before considering your views, permit me first to try to mark out the territory and give a definition of psychoanalysis.

622   Psychoanalysis is first of all simply a method—but a method complying with all the rigorous requirements which the concept of a "method" implies today. Let me say at once that psychoanalysis is not an *anamnesis,* as those who know everything without learning it are pleased to believe. It is essentially a way of investigating unconscious associations which cannot be got at by exploring the conscious mind. Again, psychoanalysis is not a method of examination in the nature of an intelligence test, though this mistake is common in certain circles. Nor is it a method of catharsis for abreacting, with or without hypnosis, real or imaginary traumata.

623   Psychoanalysis is a method which makes possible the analytical reduction of psychic contents to their simplest expression, and for discovering the line of least resistance in the development of a harmonious personality. In neurosis there is no uniform direction of life because contrary tendencies frustrate and prevent psychological adaptation. Psychoanalysis, so far as we

can judge at present, seems to be the only rational therapy of the neuroses.

624   No programme can be formulated for the technical application of psychoanalysis. There are only general principles, and working rules for individual analysis. (For the latter I would refer you to Freud's work in Vol. I of the *Internationale Zeitschrift für ärztliche Psychoanalyse*.[8]) My only working rule is to conduct the analysis as a perfectly ordinary, sensible conversation, and to avoid all appearance of medical magic.

625   The main principle of psychoanalytic technique is to analyse the psychic contents that present themselves at a given moment. Any interference on the part of the analyst, with the object of forcing the analysis to follow a systematic course, is a gross mistake in technique. So-called chance is the law and order of psychoanalysis.

626   At the beginning of the analysis the anamnesis and diagnosis naturally come first. The subsequent analytic procedure develops quite differently in every case. To give rules is almost impossible. All one can say is that very frequently, right at the beginning, a number of resistances have to be overcome, resistances against both the method and the analyst. Patients who have no notion of psychoanalysis must first be given some understanding of the method. With those who already know something of it there are very often misconceptions to be set right, and also all those objections to be answered which are levelled by scientific criticism. In either case the misconceptions are due to arbitrary interpretations, superficiality, and gross ignorance of the facts.

627   If the patient is himself a doctor his habit of knowing better may prove extremely tiresome. With intelligent colleagues a thorough theoretical discussion is worth while. With the unintelligent and bigoted ones you begin quietly with the analysis. In the unconscious of such folk you have a confederate who never lets you down. The very first dreams demonstrate the wretched inadequacy of their criticism, so that from the whole beautiful edifice of supposedly scientific scepticism nothing remains over but a little heap of personal vanity. I have had very amusing experiences in this respect.

8 ["On Beginning the Treatment (Further Recommendations on the Technique of Psycho-Analysis I)" (1913).—EDITORS.]

628   It is best to let the patients talk freely and to confine yourself to pointing out a connection here and there. When the conscious material is exhausted you go on to dreams, which give you the subliminal material. If people have no dreams, as they allege, or forget them, there is usually still some conscious material that ought to be produced and discussed, but is kept back owing to resistances. When the conscious is emptied then come the dreams, which as you know are the chief object of analysis.

629   How the analysis is to be conducted and what is to be said to the patient depends, first, on the material to be dealt with; second, on the analyst's skill; and third, on the patient's capacity. I must emphasize that no one should undertake an analysis except on the basis of a sound knowledge of the subject, and this means a thorough knowledge of the existing literature. Without this, the work will only be bungled.

630   I do not know what else to tell you beforehand. I must wait for further questions.

631   As to the question of morality and education, let me say that these things belong to a later stage of the analysis, when they find—or should find—their own solution. You cannot make recipes out of psychoanalysis!

From Dr. Loÿ

16 February 1913

632   You write that a sound knowledge of the literature is necessary for an introduction to psychoanalysis. I agree, but with one reservation: the more one reads of it the more clearly one sees how many contradictions there are among the different writers, and less and less does one know—until one has had sufficient personal experience—to which view to give adherence, since quite frequently assertions are made without any proof. For example, I had thought (strengthened in this view by my own experience of suggestion therapy) that the transference to the analyst might be an essential condition of the patient's cure. But you write: "We psychoanalysts do not bank on the patient's *faith,* but on his *criticism.*" As against this Stekel writes ("Ausgänge der psychoanalytischen Kuren," *Zentralblatt für Psychoanalyse,* III, 1912–13, p. 176): "Love for the analyst can become a force conducive to recovery. Neurotics never get well for love

273

of themselves, they get well for love of the analyst. They do it to please him . . ." Here again, surely, the accent is on the power of suggestion? And yet Stekel, too, thinks he is a psychoanalyst pure and simple. On the other hand you remark in your letter of January 28: "The personality of the analyst is one of the main factors in the cure." Should not this be translated as: When the analyst inspires respect in the patient and is worthy of his love, the patient will follow his example in order to please him, and will endeavour to get over his neurosis so as to fulfil his human duties in the widest sense of the word?

633   I think one can only emerge from all this uncertainty when one has gained sufficient personal experience, and then one will also know which procedure is best suited to one's own personality and gives the best therapeutic results. This is another reason for submitting to an analysis oneself, to find out what one is. I am very much in agreement with your definition of psychoanalysis in its negative sense: psychoanalysis is neither an anamnesis nor a method of examination like an intelligence test, nor yet a psychocatharsis. But your definition in the positive sense, that "psychoanalysis is a method for discovering the line of least resistance in the development of a harmonious personality," seems to me to apply only to the laziness of the patient, but not to the releasing of sublimated libido for a new aim in life.

634   You say that in neurosis there is no uniform direction because contrary tendencies prevent psychic adaptation. True, but will not psychic adaptation turn out quite differently according to whether the patient, now cured, re-directs his life simply to the avoidance of pain (line of least resistance) or to the attainment of the greatest pleasure? In the first case he would be more passive, and would simply reconcile himself to the "soberness of reality" (Stekel, p. 187). In the second case he would be "filled with enthusiasm" for something or other, or for some person. But what determines whether he will be more active or more passive in his "second" life? In your opinion, does this determining factor appear spontaneously in the course of analysis, and should the analyst carefully avoid tilting the balance to one side or the other by his influence? Or will he, if he does not refrain from canalizing the patient's libido in a definite direction, have to renounce the right to be called a psychoanalyst at all, and is he to be regarded as a "moderate" or a "radical"? (Fürt-

muller, "Wandlungen in der Freud'schen Schule," *Zentralblatt,* III, p. 191.) But I think you have already answered this question in advance when you write in your letter of February 11: "Any interference on the part of the analyst is a gross mistake in technique. So-called chance is the law and order of psychoanalysis." But, torn from its context, perhaps this sentence does not quite give your whole meaning.

635 With regard to enlightening the patient about the psychoanalytic method before beginning the analysis, you appear to be in agreement with Freud and Stekel: better too little than too much. For knowledge pumped into a patient remains half-knowledge anyway, and half-knowledge begets "wanting to know better," which only impedes progress. So, after a brief explanation, first let the patient talk, pointing out a connection here and there, then, after the conscious material is exhausted, go on to the dreams.

636 But here another obstacle stands in my way, which I have already mentioned at our interview: you find the patient adopting the tone, language, or jargon of the analyst (whether from conscious imitation, transference, or plain defiance, so as to fight the analyst with his own weapons)—how then can you prevent his starting to produce all manner of fantasies as supposedly real traumata of early childhood, and *dreams* which are supposedly spontaneous but in reality, whether directly or indirectly, albeit involuntarily, are *suggested?*

637 I told you at the time that Forel (in *Der Hypnotismus*) made his patients dream just what he wanted, and I myself have easily repeated this experiment. But if the analyst wants to *suggest nothing,* must he keep silent most of the time and let the patient talk—except that, when interpreting the dreams, he may put his own interpretation to the patient?

From Dr. Jung

18 February 1913

638 I cannot but agree with your observation that confusion reigns in psychoanalytic literature. Just at this moment different points of view are developing in the theoretical assessment of analytic results, not to mention the many individual deviations. Over against Freud's almost entirely causal conception there

has developed, apparently in absolute contradiction to Freud, Adler's purely finalist view, though in reality it is an essential complement to Freud's theory. I hold rather to a middle course, taking account of both standpoints. It is not surprising that great disagreement prevails with regard to the ultimate questions of psychoanalysis when you consider how difficult they are. In particular, the problem of the therapeutic effect of psychoanalysis is bound up with the most difficult questions of all, so that it would indeed be astonishing if we had already reached final certitude.

639   Stekel's remark is very characteristic. What he says about love for the analyst is obviously true, but it is simply a statement of fact and not a goal or a guiding principle of analytical therapy. If it were the goal, many cures, it is true, would be possible, but also many failures might result which could be avoided. The goal is to educate the patient in such a way that he will get well for his own sake and by reason of his own determination, and not in order to procure his analyst some kind of advantage—though of course it would be absurd from the therapeutic standpoint not to allow the patient to get well because he simply wants to do his analyst a good turn. The patient should know what he is doing, that's all. It is not for us to prescribe for him the ways by which he should get well. Naturally it seems to me (from the psychoanalytic point of view) an illegitimate use of suggestive influence if the patient is forced to get well out of love for his analyst. This kind of coercion sometimes takes a bitter revenge. The "you must and shall be saved" attitude is no more to be commended in the therapy of the neuroses than in any other department of life. Besides, it contradicts the principles of analytic treatment, which shuns all coercion and tries to let everything grow up from within. I am not opposed, as you know, to suggestive influence in general, but merely to doubtful motivations. If the analyst demands that his patient shall get well out of love for him, the patient may easily reckon on reciprocal services, and will without doubt try to extort them. I can only utter a warning against any such practice. A far stronger motive for recovery—also a far healthier and ethically more valuable one—is the patient's thorough insight into the real situation, his recognition of things as they are and how they should be. If he is worth his salt he will then real-

ize that he can hardly remain sitting in the morass of neurosis.

640   I cannot agree with your interpretation of my remarks on the healing effect of the analyst's personality. I wrote [9] that his personality had a healing effect because the patient *reads* the personality of the analyst, and not that he gets well *out of love for* the analyst. The analyst cannot prevent him from beginning to behave towards his conflicts as he himself behaves, for nothing is finer than the empathy of a neurotic. *But every strong transference serves this purpose too.* If the analyst makes himself amiable to the patient, he simply buys off a lot of resistances which the patient ought to have overcome, and which he will quite certainly have to overcome later on. So nothing is gained by this technique; at most the beginning of the analysis is made easier for the patient, though in certain cases this is not without its uses. To have to crawl through a barbed-wire fence without having some enticing end in view testifies to an ascetic strength of will which you can expect neither from the ordinary person nor from the neurotic. Even Christianity, whose moral demands are set very high, has not scorned to dangle before us the kingdom of heaven as the goal and reward of earthly endeavour. In my view the analyst is entitled to speak of the advantages which follow from the ardours of analysis. Only, he should not represent himself or his friendship, by hints or promises, as a reward, unless he is seriously resolved to make it so.

641   As to your criticism of my tentative definition of psychoanalysis, it must be observed that the road over a steep mountain is the line of least resistance when a ferocious bull awaits you in the pleasant valley road. In other words, the line of least resistance is a compromise with *all* eventualities, not just with laziness. It is a prejudice to think that the line of least resistance coincides with the path of inertia. (That's what we thought when we dawdled over our Latin exercises at school.) Laziness is a temporary advantage only and leads to consequences which involve the worst resistances. On the whole, therefore, it does not coincide with the line of least resistance. Nor is life along the line of least resistance synonymous with the ruthless pursuit of selfish desires. Anyone who lived like that would soon realize with sorrow that he was not following the line of least

9 [Presumably a reference to par. 587, or to an unpublished letter.—EDITORS.]

resistance, because man is also a social being and not just a bundle of egoistic instincts, as some people pretend. You can see this best with primitives and domestic animals, who all have a well-developed social sense. Without some such function the herd could not exist at all. Man as a herd-animal, too, has not by any manner of means to subordinate himself to laws imposed from without; he carries his social imperatives within himself, *a priori,* as an inborn necessity. Here, as you see, I place myself in decided opposition to certain views—quite unjustified, in my opinion—which have been expressed here and there inside the psychoanalytic school.

642 Accordingly the line of least resistance does not signify *eo ipso* the avoidance of pain so much as the just balancing of pain and pleasure. Painful activity by itself leads to no result but exhaustion. A man must be able to enjoy life, otherwise the effort of living is not worth while.

643 What direction the patient's life should take in the future is not ours to judge. We must not imagine that we know better than his own nature, or we would prove ourselves educators of the worst kind. (Fundamental ideas of a similar nature have also been worked out by the Montessori school.[10]) Psychoanalysis is only a means for removing the stones from the path of development, and not a method (as hypnotism often claims to be) of putting things into the patient that were not there before. It is better to renounce any attempt to give direction, and simply try to throw into relief everything that the analysis brings to light, so that the patient can see it clearly and be able to draw suitable conclusions. Anything he has not acquired himself he will not believe in the long run, and what he takes over from authority merely keeps him infantile. He should rather be put in a position to take his own life in hand. The art of analysis lies in following the patient on all his erring ways and so gathering his strayed sheep together. Working to programme, on a preconceived system, we spoil the best effects of analysis. I must therefore hold fast to the sentence you object to: "Any interference on the part of the analyst is a gross mistake in technique. So-called chance is the law and order of psychoanalysis."

644 As you must know, we still cannot give up the pedantic preju-

10 [Dr. Maria Montessori (1870–1952) published *The Montessori Method* in 1912. —Editors.]

278

dice of wanting to correct nature and force our limited "truths" on her. But in the therapy of the neuroses we meet with so many strange, unforeseen and unforeseeable experiences that all hope should vanish of our knowing better and being able to prescribe the way. The roundabout way and even the wrong way are necessary. If you deny this you must also deny that the mistakes of history were necessary. That is the pedant's-eye view of the world. This attitude is no good in psychoanalysis.

645 The question as to how much the analyst involuntarily suggests to the patient is a very ticklish one. It certainly plays a much more important role than psychoanalysis has so far admitted. Experience has convinced me that patients rapidly begin to make use of ideas picked up from psychoanalysis, as is also apparent in their dreams. You get many impressions of this sort from Stekel's book *Die Sprache des Traumes*. I once had a very instructive experience: a very intelligent lady had from the beginning long-drawn-out transference fantasies which appeared in the usual erotic guise. But she absolutely refused to admit their existence. Naturally she was betrayed by her dreams, in which, however, my person was always hidden under some other figure, often rather difficult to make out. A long series of such dreams finally compelled me to remark: "So, you see, it's always like that, the person you are really dreaming about is replaced and masked by someone else in the manifest dream." Till then she had obstinately denied this mechanism. But this time she could no longer evade it and had to admit my working rule—but only to play a trick on me. Next day she brought me a dream in which she and I appeared in a manifestly lascivious situation. I was naturally perplexed and thought of my rule. Her first association to the dream was the malicious question: "It's always true, isn't it, that the person you are really dreaming about is replaced by someone else in the manifest dream?"

646 Clearly, she had made use of her experience to find a protective formula by which she could express her fantasies openly in a quite innocent way.

647 This example shows at once how patients use insights they have gained from analysis. They use them for the purpose of symbolization. You get caught in your own net if you believe ✓ in fixed, unalterable symbols. That has happened to more than one psychoanalyst. It is therefore a fallacious and risky business

to try to exemplify any particular theory with dreams arising from an analysis. Proof can only come from the dreams of demonstrably uninfluenced persons. In such cases one would have to exclude at most telepathic thought-reading. But if you concede this possibility, you would have to subject many other things to a rigorous scrutiny, including judicial verdicts.

648 Although we must pay full attention to the element of suggestion, we should not go too far. The patient is not an empty sack into which we can stuff whatever we like; he brings his own particular contents with him which stubbornly resist suggestion and push themselves again and again to the fore. Analytic "suggestions" merely distort the expression, but not the content, as I have seen countless times. The expression varies without limit, but the content is fixed and can only be got at in the long run, and then with difficulty. Were it not so, suggestion therapy would be in every sense the most effective and rewarding and easiest therapy, a true panacea. Unfortunately it is not, as every honest hypnotist will readily admit.

649 To come back to your question as to whether it is possible for patients to trick the analyst by making deceptive use—perhaps involuntarily—of his mode of expression, this is indeed a very serious problem. The analyst must exercise all possible care and self-criticism not to let himself be led astray by his patient's dreams. One can say that patients almost invariably use in their dreams, to a greater or lesser extent, the mode of expression learnt in analysis. Interpretations of earlier symbols will themselves be used again as fresh symbols in later dreams. It often happens, for instance, that sexual situations which appeared in earlier dreams in symbolic form will appear "undisguised" in later ones—once more, be it noted, in symbolic form—as analysable expressions for ideas of a different nature hidden behind them. Thus the not infrequent dream of incestuous cohabitation is by no means an "undisguised" content, but a dream as freshly symbolic and capable of analysis as all others. You can only arrive at the paradoxical idea that such a dream is "undisguised" if you are pledged to the sexual theory of neurosis.

650 That the patient may mislead the analyst for a longer or shorter time by means of deliberate deception and misrepresentation is possible, as in all other branches of medicine. But

the patient injures himself most, since he has to pay for every deception or subterfuge with an aggravation of his symptoms, or with fresh ones. Deception is so obviously disadvantageous to himself that he can scarcely avoid relinquishing such a course for good.

651 The technique of analysis we can best postpone for oral discussion.

From Dr. Loÿ

23 February 1913

652 From your letter of 18 February I would like first to single out the end, where you so aptly assign the element of suggestion its proper place in psychoanalysis: "The patient is not an empty sack into which we can stuff whatever we like; he brings his own particular contents with him, with which you have always to reckon afresh" [*sic*]. With this I fully agree, as my own experience confirms it. And you add: involuntary analytic suggestions will leave this content intact, but the expression, Proteus-like, can be distorted without limit. Hence it would be a kind of "mimicry," by which the patient seeks to escape the analyst who is driving him into a corner and for the moment seems to him an enemy. Until at last, through the joint work of patient and analyst—the former spontaneously yielding up his psychic content, the latter only interpreting and explaining—the analysis succeeds in bringing so much light into the darkness of the patient's psyche that he can see the true relationships and, without any preconceived plan of the analyst's, draw the right conclusions and apply them to his future life. This new life will follow the line of least resistance—or should we not rather say of least resistances—as a "compromise with all eventualities," in a just balancing of pain and pleasure. It is not for us to decide arbitrarily for the patient how matters stand and what will benefit him; his own nature decides. In other words, we should take over approximately the role of a midwife, who can only bring out into the light of day a child already alive, but who has to avoid a number of mistakes if the child is to remain alive and the mother is not to be injured.

653 All this is very clear to me because it is only an application to psychoanalytic procedure of a principle which should be

generally valid: Never do violence to Nature! Hence I also see that the psychoanalyst must follow his patient's apparently "erring ways" if the patient is ever to arrive at his own convictions and be freed once and for all from infantile reliance on authority. We ourselves as individuals have learnt and can only learn by making mistakes how to avoid them in the future, and mankind as a whole has created the conditions for its present and future stages of development quite as much by following the crooked path as by keeping to the straight one. Have not many neurotics—I do not know if you will agree, but I think so—become ill partly because their infantile faith in authority has gone to pieces? Now they stand before the wreckage of their faith, weeping over it, and terrified because they cannot find a substitute which would show them clearly where they have to turn. So they remain stuck between the infantilisms they are unwilling to renounce and the serious tasks of the present and future (moral conflict). I also see, particularly in such cases, how right you are in saying that it would be a mistake to try to replace their lost faith in authority by another faith in authority, which would be useful only as long as it lasted. This passes a verdict on the deliberate use of suggestive influence in psychoanalysis, and on regarding the "transference to the analyst" as the goal of analytic therapy. I no longer contest your dictum: "Every interference on the part of the analyst is a gross mistake in technique. So-called chance is the law and order of psychoanalysis." Further, I am in entire agreement when you say that altruism [sic] must necessarily be innate in man as a herd-animal. The contrary would be the thing to wonder at.

654   I am very much inclined to assume that not the egoistic but the altruistic instincts are primary. Love and trust of the child for the mother who feeds it, nurses, cherishes and pets it; love of man for wife, regarded as absorption in another's personality; love for offspring, care of them; love for kinsfolk, etc. Whereas the egoistic instincts owe their existence only to the desire for exclusive possession of the object of love, the desire to possess the mother exclusively, in opposition to the father and brother and sisters, the desire to have a woman for oneself alone, the desire for jewellery, clothes, etc. . . . But perhaps you will say I am being paradoxical and that the instincts, whether altruistic or egoistic, arise together in the heart of man, and that every

instinct is ambivalent by nature. But I ask: are our feelings and instincts really ambivalent? Are they perhaps bipolar? Can the qualities of emotions be compared at all? Is love really the opposite of hate?

655   Be that as it may, it is lucky that man carries his social imperatives within himself as an inborn necessity, otherwise our civilized humanity would be in a bad way, having to submit to laws imposed only from without: when the earlier religious faith in authority died out we would rapidly and infallibly fall into complete anarchy. We would then have to ask ourselves whether it would not be better to try to maintain by force an exclusively religious belief in authority, as the Middle Ages did. For the benefits of civilization, which strives to grant every individual as much outward freedom as is consistent with the freedom of others, would be well worth such a sacrifice as the sacrifice of free research. But the age of this use of force against nature is past, civilized mankind has abandoned these erroneous ways, not out of caprice, but obeying an inner need, and therefore we may look forward with joyful anticipation to the future. Mankind, advancing in knowledge and obeying its own law, will find its way across the ruins of faith in authority to the moral autonomy of the individual.

From Dr. Jung

March 1913

656   At various places in your letters it has struck me that the problem of the "transference" seems to you particularly critical. Your feeling is entirely justified. The transference is indeed at present the central problem of analysis.

657   You know that Freud regards the transference as a projection of infantile fantasies upon the analyst. To that extent it is an infantile-erotic relationship. However, seen from outside, and superficially, the thing does not always look like an infantile-erotic relationship by any means. So long as it is a case of a so-called positive transference, you can as a rule recognize the infantile-erotic content of the transference without much difficulty. But if it is a so-called negative transference, you see nothing but violent resistances which sometimes disguise themselves in theoretical, seemingly critical or sceptical forms. In a certain

sense the determining factor in these relationships is the patient's relationship to authority, that is, in the last resort, to his father. In both forms of transference the analyst is treated as if he were the father—either with affection or with hostility. According to this view of the transference it acts as a resistance as soon as the question arises of resolving the infantile attitude. But this form of transference must be destroyed in so far as the aim of analysis is the patient's moral autonomy.

658   A lofty aim, you will say. Lofty indeed, and far off, but still not altogether so remote, since it actually corresponds to one of the predominating trends of our stage of civilization—the urge towards individualization, which might serve as a motto for our whole epoch. (Cf. Müller-Lyer, *The Family*.) Anyone who does not believe in this ultimate aim but still adheres to the old scientific causalism will naturally tend to take only the hostile element out of the transference and let the patient remain in a positive relationship to the father, in accordance with the ideals of a past epoch. As we know, the Catholic Church is one of the most powerful organizations based on this tendency. I do not venture to doubt that there are very many people who feel happier under the coercion of others than when forced to discipline themselves (see Shaw's *Man and Superman*). None the less, we would be doing our neurotic patients a grievous wrong if we tried to force them all into the category of the coerced. Among neurotics, there are not a few who do not require any reminders of their social duties and obligations, but are born and destined rather to be bearers of new cultural ideals. They are neurotic as long as they bow down before authority and refuse the freedom to which they are destined. As long as we look at life only retrospectively, as is the case in the psychoanalytic writings of the Viennese school, we shall never do justice to these persons and never bring them the longed-for deliverance. For in this way we train them only to be obedient children and thereby strengthen the very forces that made them ill—their conservative backwardness and submission to authority. Up to a point this is the right way to take with people suffering from an infantile insubordination who cannot *yet* adapt to authority. But the impulse which drives the others out of their conservative father-relationship is by no means an infantile wish for insubordination; it is a powerful urge to develop

their own personality, and the struggle for this is for them an imperative duty. Adler's psychology does much greater justice to this situation than Freud's.

659 For one type of person (called the infantile-rebel) a positive transference is, to begin with, an important achievement with a healing significance; for the other (the infantile-obedient) it is a dangerous backsliding, a convenient way of evading life's duties. For the first a negative transference denotes increased insubordination, hence a backsliding and an evasion of life's duties, for the second it is a step forward with a healing significance. (For the two types see Adler, "Trotz und Gehorsam," *Monatshefte für Pädagogik und Schulpolitik,* VIII, 1910.)

660 So the transference must, as you see, be evaluated quite differently according to the type of case.

661 The psychological process of transference—whether negative or positive—consists in a "libidinal investment" of the personality of the analyst, that is to say he stands for an emotional value. (As you know, by libido I mean very much what the ancients meant by the cosmogonic principle of Eros, or in modern language, "psychic energy.") The patient is bound to the analyst by ties of affection or resistance and cannot help following and imitating his psychic attitude. By this means he feels his way along (empathy). And with the best will in the world and for all his technical skill the analyst cannot prevent it, for empathy works surely and instinctively in spite of conscious judgment, be it never so strong. If the analyst himself is neurotic and insufficiently adapted to the demands of life or of his own personality, the patient will copy this defect and reflect it in his own attitudes: with what results you can imagine.

662 Accordingly I cannot regard the transference merely as a projection of infantile-erotic fantasies. No doubt that is what it is from one standpoint, but I also see in it, as I said in an earlier letter, a process of empathy and adaptation. From this standpoint, the infantile-erotic fantasies, in spite of their undeniable reality, appear rather as a means of comparison or as analogical images for something not yet understood than as independent wishes. This seems to me the real reason why they are unconscious. The patient, not knowing the right attitude, tries to grasp at the right relationship to the analyst by way of comparison and analogy with his infantile experiences. It is not

surprising that he gropes back to just the most intimate relationships of his childhood in the attempt to discover the appropriate formula for his relationship to the analyst, for this relationship is very intimate too but differs from the sexual relationship as much as does that of a child to its parents. This latter relationship—child to parent—which Christianity has everywhere set up as a symbolic formula for human relationships in general, serves to restore to the patient that direct feeling of human fellowship of which he has been deprived by the incursions of sexual and social valuations (valuations from the standpoint of power, etc.). The purely sexual and other more or less primitive and barbaric valuations militate against a direct, purely human relationship, and this creates a damming up of libido which may easily give rise to neurotic formations. Through analysis of the infantile content of the transference fantasies the patient is brought back to a remembrance of the childhood relationship, which, stripped of its infantile qualities, gives him a clear picture of a direct human relationship over and above merely sexual valuations, etc. I can only regard it as a misconception to judge the child-relationship retrospectively as a merely sexual one, even though a certain sexual content cannot be denied.

663   Recapitulating, I would like to say this of the positive transference:

The patient's libido fastens on the person of the analyst in the form of expectation, hope, interest, trust, friendship, and love. The transference first produces a projection of infantile fantasies, often with a predominantly erotic tinge. At this stage it is, as a rule, of a decidedly sexual character, even though the sexual component remains relatively unconscious. But this emotional process serves as a bridge for the higher aspect of empathy, whereby the patient becomes conscious of the inadequacy of his own attitude through recognition of the analyst's attitude, which is accepted as being adapted to life's demands and as normal. Through remembrance of the childhood relationship with the help of analysis the patient is shown the way which leads out of the subsidiary, purely sexual or power values acquired in puberty and reinforced by social prejudice. This road leads to a purely human relationship and to an intimacy based not on the existence of sexual or power factors but on the value of personality. That is the road to freedom which the analyst should show his patient.

664   I ought not to conceal from you at this point that the stubborn assertion of sexual values would not be maintained so tenaciously if they did not have a profound significance for that period of life in which propagation is of primary importance. The discovery of the value of human personality is reserved for a riper age. For young people the search for personality values is very often a pretext for evading their biological duty. Conversely, the exaggerated longing of an older person for the sexual values of youth is a short-sighted and often cowardly evasion of a duty which demands recognition of the value of personality and submission to the hierarchy of cultural values. The young neurotic shrinks back in terror from the expansion of life's duties, the old one from the dwindling of the treasures he has attained.

665   This view of the transference is, as you will have observed, closely connected with the acceptance of biological "duties." By this I mean the tendencies or determinants that produce culture in man with the same logic as in the bird they produce the artfully woven nest, and antlers in the stag. The purely causal, not to say materialistic views of the last few decades seek to explain all organic formation as the reaction of living matter, and though this is undoubtedly a heuristically valuable line of inquiry, as far as any real explanation goes it amounts only to a more or less ingenious postponement and apparent minimizing of the problem. I would remind you of Bergson's excellent criticism in this respect. External causes can account for at most half the reaction, the other half is due to the peculiar attributes of living matter itself, without which the specific reaction formation could never come about at all. We have to apply this principle also in psychology. The psyche does not merely *react,* it gives its own specific answer to the influences at work upon it, and at least half the resulting formation is entirely due to the psyche and the determinants inherent within it. Culture can never be understood as reaction to environment. That shallow explanation can safely be left to the past century. It is just these determinants that appear as psychological imperatives, and we have daily proof of their compelling power. What I call "biological duty" is identical with these determinants.

666   In conclusion, I must take up one point which seems to have caused you uneasiness. That is the *moral* question. Among our patients we observe so many so-called immoral impulses that the thought involuntarily forces itself on the psychotherapist how it would be if all these desires were gratified. You will have seen from my earlier letters that these desires should not be taken too seriously. Mostly they are boundlessly exaggerated demands which are thrust to the forefront by the patient's dammed-up libido, usually against his will. The canalizing of libido for the fulfilment of life's simple duties is in most cases sufficient to reduce the pressure of these desires to zero. But in certain cases it is a recognized fact that "immoral" tendencies are not got rid of by analysis, but appear more and more clearly until it becomes evident that they belong to the biological duties of the individual. This is particularly true of certain sexual demands aiming at an individual evaluation of sexuality. This is not a question for pathology, it is a social question of today which imperatively demands an ethical solution. For many it is a biological duty to work for a solution of this question, i.e., to find some sort of practical solution. (Nature, as we know, is not satisfied with theories.) Nowadays we have no real sexual morality, only a legalistic attitude to sexuality; just as the Middle Ages had no real morality of money-making but only prejudices and a legalistic point of view. We are not yet far enough advanced to distinguish between moral and immoral behaviour in the realm of free sexual activity. This is clearly expressed in the customary treatment, or rather ill-treatment, of unmarried mothers. All the repulsive hypocrisy, the high tide of prostitution and of venereal diseases, we owe to the barbarous, wholesale legal condemnation of certain kinds of sexual behaviour, and to our inability to develop a finer moral sense for the enormous psychological differences that exist in the domain of free sexual activity.

667   The existence of this exceedingly complicated and significant contemporary problem may serve to make clear to you why we so often find among our patients people who, because of their spiritual and social gifts, are quite specifically called to take an active part in the work of civilization—that is their biological destiny. We should never forget that what today seems to us a moral commandment will tomorrow be cast into the

melting-pot and transformed, so that in the near or distant future it may serve as a basis for new ethical formations. This much we ought to have learnt from the history of civilization, that the forms of morality belong to the category of transitory things. The finest psychological tact is needed with these sensitive natures if they are to turn the dangerous corner of infantile irresponsibility, indolence, or licentiousness, and to give the patient a clear and unclouded vision of the possibility of morally autonomous behaviour. Five per cent on money lent is fair interest, twenty per cent is despicable usury. We have to apply this view to the sexual situation as well.

668   So it comes about that there are many neurotics whose inner decency prevents them from being at one with present-day morality and who cannot adapt themselves so long as the moral code has gaps in it which it is the crying need of our age to fill. We deceive ourselves greatly if we think that many married women are neurotic merely because they are unsatisfied sexually or because they have not found the right man or because they have an infantile sexual fixation. The real reason in many cases is that they cannot recognize the cultural task that is waiting for them. We all have far too much the standpoint of the "nothing but" psychology, that is, we still think that the new future which is pressing in at the door can be squeezed into the framework of what is already known. And so these people see only the present and not the future. It was of profound psychological significance when Christianity first proclaimed that the orientation to the future was the redeeming principle for mankind. In the past nothing can be altered, and in the present little, but the future is ours and capable of raising life's intensity to the highest pitch. A little span of youth belongs to us, all the rest belongs to our children.

669   Thus your question about the significance of the loss of faith in authority answers itself. The neurotic is ill not because he has lost his old faith, but because he has not yet found a new form for his finest aspirations.

PREFACES TO "COLLECTED PAPERS ON ANALYTICAL PSYCHOLOGY"[1]

First Edition

670   This volume contains a selection of articles and pamphlets on analytical psychology written at intervals during the past fourteen years.[2] These years have seen the development of a new discipline and, as is usual in such a case, have involved many changes of viewpoint, conception, and formulation.

671   It is not my intention to present the fundamental concepts of analytical psychology in this book. The volume does, however, throw some light on a certain line of development which is especially characteristic of the Zurich school of psychoanalysis.

672   As is well known, the merit of discovering the new analytical method of general psychology belongs to Professor Freud of Vienna. His original views have had to undergo many important modifications, some of them owing to the work done at Zurich, in spite of the fact that he himself is far from agreeing with the standpoint of this school.

673   I cannot here explain the fundamental differences between

1 [Published in *Collected Papers on Analytical Psychology*, edited by Dr. Constance E. Long (London, 1916; 2nd edn., London, 1917, and New York, 1920). The prefaces were probably written in German and translated by Dr. Long; they are published here with minor revisions.—EDITORS.]

2 [Contents of 1st edition and location in the Coll. Works: "On the Psychology and Pathology of So-called Occult Phenomena" (Vol. 1); "The Association Method": Lecture I, untitled, and Lecture II, "The Familial Constellations" (Vol. 2); Lecture III, "The Psychic Life of the Child" (Vol. 16, as "Psychic Conflicts in a Child"); "The Significance of the Father in the Destiny of the Individual," "A Contribution to the Psychology of Rumour," and "On the Significance of Number Dreams" (Vol. 4); "A Criticism of Bleuler's 'Theory of Schizophrenic Negativism'" (Vol. 3); "Psychoanalysis" and "On Psychoanalysis" (Vol. 4, as "Concerning Psychoanalysis" and "Psychoanalysis and Neurosis"); "On Some Crucial Points in Psychoanalysis" (Vol. 4); "On the Importance of the Unconscious in Psychopathology" (Vol. 3); "A Contribution to the Study of Psychological Types" (Vol. 6); "The Psychology of Dreams" (Vol. 8, as "General Aspects of Dream Psychology"); "The Content of the Psychoses" (Vol. 3); and "New Paths in Psychology" (Vol. 7, appendix; see n. 4, infra).—EDITORS.]

the two schools but would mention only the following: The Viennese School adopts an exclusively sexualistic standpoint while that of the Zurich School is symbolistic. The Viennese School interprets the psychological symbol semiotically, as a sign or token of certain primitive psychosexual processes. Its method is analytical and causal. The Zurich School recognizes the scientific possibility of such a conception but denies its exclusive validity, for it does not interpret the psychological symbol semiotically only but also symbolistically, that is, it attributes a positive value to the symbol.

674   The value of the symbol does not depend merely on historical causes; its chief importance lies in the fact that it has a meaning for the actual present and for the future, in their psychological aspects. For the Zurich School the symbol is not merely a sign of something repressed and concealed, but is at the same time an attempt to comprehend and to point the way to the further psychological development of the individual. Thus we add a prospective meaning to the retrospective value of the symbol.

675   The method of the Zurich School, therefore, is not only analytical and causal but synthetic and prospective, in recognition of the fact that the human mind is characterized by *fines* (aims) as well as by *causae*. This deserves particular emphasis, because there are two types of psychology, the one following the principle of hedonism, the other the power principle. The philosophical counterpart of the former type is scientific materialism and of the latter the philosophy of Nietzsche. The principle of the Freudian theory is hedonism, while the theory of Adler (one of Freud's earliest personal pupils) is founded on the power principle.

676   The Zurich School, recognizing the existence of these two types (also remarked by the late Professor William James), considers that the views of Freud and Adler are one-sided and valid only within the limits of their corresponding type. Both principles exist in every individual though not in equal proportions.

677   Thus, it is obvious that every psychological symbol has two aspects and should be interpreted in accordance with both principles. Freud and Adler interpret in the analytical and causal way, reducing to the infantile and primitive. Thus with Freud the conception of the "aim" is the fulfilment of the wish, while

with Adler it is the usurpation of power. In their practical analytical work both authors take the standpoint which brings to light only infantile and grossly egoistic aims.

678   The Zurich School is convinced that within the limits of a diseased mental attitude the psychology is such as Freud and Adler describe. It is, indeed, just on account of such an impossible and childish psychology that the individual is in a state of inner dissociation and hence neurotic. The Zurich School, therefore, in agreement with them so far, also reduces the psychological symbol (the fantasy-products of the patient) to his fundamental infantile hedonism or infantile desire for power. Freud and Adler content themselves with the result of mere reduction, which accords with their scientific biologism and naturalism.

679   But here a very important question arises. Can man obey the fundamental and primitive impulses of his nature without gravely injuring himself or his fellow beings? He cannot assert either his sexual desire or his desire for power unlimitedly in the face of limits which are very restrictive. The Zurich School has in view the end-result of analysis, and it regards the fundamental thoughts and impulses of the unconscious as symbols, indicative of a definite line of future development. We must admit, however, that there is *no scientific justification* for such a procedure, because our present-day science is based wholly on causality. But causality is only one principle, and psychology cannot be exhausted by causal methods only, because the mind lives by aims as well. Besides this controversial philosophical argument we have another of much greater value in favour of our hypothesis, namely that of *vital necessity*. It is impossible to live according to the promptings of infantile hedonism or according to a childish desire for power. If these are to be given a place they must be taken symbolically. Out of the symbolic application of infantile trends there evolves an attitude which may be termed philosophic or religious, and these terms characterize sufficiently well the lines of the individual's further development. The individual is not just a fixed and unchangeable complex of psychological facts; he is also an extremely variable entity. By an exclusive reduction to causes the primitive trends of a personality are reinforced; this is helpful only when these primitive tendencies are balanced by a recognition of their symbolic value. Analysis and reduction lead to causal truth; this by

itself does not help us to live but only induces resignation and hopelessness. On the other hand, the recognition of the intrinsic value of a symbol leads to constructive truth and helps us to live; it inspires hopefulness and furthers the possibility of future development.

680   The functional importance of the symbol is clearly shown in the history of civilization. For thousands of years the religious symbol proved a most efficacious device in the moral education of mankind. Only a prejudiced mind could deny such an obvious fact. Concrete values cannot take the place of the symbol; only new and more effective symbols can be substituted for those that are antiquated and outworn and have lost their efficacy through the progress of intellectual analysis and understanding. The further development of the individual can be brought about only by means of symbols which represent something far in advance of himself and whose intellectual meanings cannot yet be grasped entirely. The individual unconscious produces such symbols, and they are of the greatest possible value in the moral development of the personality.

681   Man almost invariably has philosophic and religious views concerning the meaning of the world and of his own life. There are some who are proud to have none. But these are exceptions outside the common path of mankind; they lack an important function which has proved itself to be indispensable to the human psyche.

682   In such cases we find in the unconscious, instead of modern symbolism, an antiquated, archaic view of the world and of life. If a necessary psychological function is not represented in the sphere of consciousness it exists in the unconscious in the form of an archaic or embryonic prototype.

683   This brief résumé may show the reader what he may expect *not* to find in this collection of papers. The essays are stations on the way toward the more general views developed above.

Küsnacht/Zurich, January 1916

Second Edition

684   In agreement with my honoured collaborator, Dr. C. E. Long, I have made certain additions to the second edition of

this book. It should especially be noted that a new chapter on "The Concept of the Unconscious" [3] has been added. This is a lecture I gave early in 1916 to the Zurich Society for Analytical Psychology. It provides a general survey of a most important problem in practical analysis, namely the relation of the ego to the psychological non-ego. Chapter XIV, "The Psychology of the Unconscious Processes," [4] has been fundamentally revised, and I have taken the opportunity to incorporate an article [5] that describes the results of more recent researches.

685   In accordance with my usual method of working, my description is as generalized as possible. My habit in daily practice is to confine myself for some time to studying the human material. I then abstract as general a formula as possible from the data collected, obtaining from it a point of view and applying it in my practical work until it has been either confirmed, modified, or else abandoned. If it is confirmed, I publish it as a general viewpoint without giving the empirical material. I introduce the material amassed in the course of my practice only in the form of example or illustration. I therefore beg the reader not to consider the views I present as mere fabrications of my brain. They are, as a matter of fact, the results of extensive experience and ripe reflection.

686   These additions will enable the reader of the second edition to familiarize himself with the recent views of the Zurich School.

687   As regards the criticism encountered by the first edition of this work, I was pleased to find my writings were received with

[3] [This was a translation of the original version of "The Relations between the Ego and the Unconscious." Later in 1916 the German original was translated into French under the title "La Structure de l'inconscient." See *Two Essays on Analytical Psychology*, pp. 121ff. and 263ff.—EDITORS.]

[4] [A revised and expanded version of "New Paths in Psychology" (orig. in *Raschers Jahrbuch für Schweizer Art und Kunst*, Zurich, 1912). In 1926 it was again expanded and published under the title *Das Unbewusste im normalen und kranken Seelenleben*. A revised and expanded version of this appeared in 1942 as *Über die Psychologie des Unbewussten*. See *Two Essays on Analytical Psychology*, pp. 3ff. and 243ff.—EDITORS.]

[5] [Part II, untitled, of "The Content of the Psychoses," Ch. XIII in the *Collected Papers*. This was originally written in English and published as "On Psychological Understanding," *Journal of Abnormal Psychology* (Boston), IX (1915). Later in 1914, translated into German and published as a supplement to *Der Inhalt der Psychose*. See *The Psychogenesis of Mental Disease*, pp. 179ff.—EDITORS.]

much more open-mindedness among English critics than was the case in Germany, where they are met with the silence born of contempt. I am particularly grateful to Dr. Agnes Savill for an exceptionally understanding criticism in the *Medical Press.* My thanks are also due to Dr. T. W. Mitchell for an exhaustive review in the *Proceedings of the Society for Psychical Research.*[6] This critic takes exception to my heresy respecting causality. He considers that I am entering upon a perilous, because unscientific, course when I question the sole validity of the causal viewpoint in psychology. I sympathize with him, but in my opinion the nature of the human mind compels us to take the finalistic view. It cannot be disputed that, psychologically speaking, we are living and working day by day according to the principle of directed aim or purpose as well as that of causality. A psychological theory must necessarily adapt itself to this fact. What is plainly directed towards a goal cannot be given an exclusively causalistic explanation, otherwise we should be led to the conclusion expressed in Moleschott's famous dictum: "Man ist was er isst" (Man *is* what he eats). We must always bear in mind that *causality is a point of view.* It affirms the inevitable and immutable relation of a series of events: *a-b-c-z.* Since this relation is fixed, and according to the causal point of view must necessarily be so, looked at logically the order may also be reversed. *Finality is also a point of view,* and it is empirically justified by the existence of series of events in which the causal connection is indeed evident *but the meaning of which only becomes intelligible in terms of end-products (final effects).* Ordinary life furnishes the best instances of this. The causal explanation must be mechanistic if we are not to postulate a metaphysical entity as first cause. For instance, if we adopt Freud's sexual theory and assign primary importance psychologically to the function of the genital glands, the brain is seen as an appendage of the genital glands. If we approach the Viennese concept of sexuality, with all its vague omnipotence, in a strictly scientific manner and reduce it to its physiological basis, we shall arrive at the first cause, according to which psychic life is for the most, or the most important part, tension and relaxation of the genital glands. If we assume for the moment that this mechanistic

6 [Savill, "Psychoanalysis" (1916); Mitchell (1916).—EDITORS.]

explanation is "true," it would be the sort of truth which is exceptionally tiresome and rigidly limited in scope. A similar statement would be that the genital glands cannot function without adequate *nourishment,* the inference being that sexuality is a subsidiary function of nutrition. The truth of this forms an important chapter in the biology of the lower forms of life.

688   But if we wish to work in a really psychological way we shall want to know the *meaning* of psychological phenomena. After learning what kinds of steel the various parts of a locomotive are made of, and what iron-works and mines they come from, we do not really know anything about the locomotive's *function,* that is to say its *meaning.* But "function" as conceived by modern science is by no means exclusively a causal concept; it is especially a final or "teleological" one. For it is impossible to consider the psyche from the causal standpoint only; we are obliged to consider it also from the final point of view. As Dr. Mitchell remarks, it is impossible to think of causal determination as having at the same time a finalistic reference. That would be an obvious contradiction. But the theory of cognition does not need to remain on a pre-Kantian level. It is well known that Kant showed very clearly that the mechanistic and the teleological viewpoints are not *constituent* (objective) principles—as it were, qualities of the object—but that they are purely *regulative* (subjective) principles of thought, and, as such, not mutually inconsistent. I can, for example, easily conceive the following thesis and antithesis:

> *Thesis:* Everything came into existence according to mechanistic laws.
>
> *Antithesis:* Some things did not come into existence according to mechanistic laws only.

Kant says to this: Reason cannot prove either of these principles because *a priori* the purely empirical laws of nature cannot give us a determinative principle regarding the potentiality of events.

689   As a matter of fact, modern physics has necessarily been converted from the idea of pure mechanism to the finalistic concept of the conservation of energy, because the mechanistic explanation recognizes only reversible processes whereas the actual truth is that the processes of nature are irreversible. This fact led to the concept of an energy that tends towards relief of tension and hence towards a definitive final state.

690   Obviously, I consider both these points of view necessary, the causal as well as the final, but would at the same time stress that since Kant's time we have come to realize that the two viewpoints are not antagonistic if they are regarded as regulative principles of thought and not as constituent principles of the process of nature itself.

691   In speaking of the reviews of this book I must mention some that seem to me wide of the mark. I was once again struck by the fact that certain critics cannot distinguish between the theoretical explanation given by the author and the fantastic ideas produced by the patient. One of my critics is guilty of this confusion when discussing "On the Significance of Number Dreams." The associations to the quotation from the Bible in this paper are, as every attentive reader will perceive, not arbitrary explanations of my own but a cryptomnesic conglomeration emanating not from my brain at all but from that of the patient. Surely it is not difficult to see that this conglomeration of numbers corresponds exactly to the unconscious psychological function from which the whole mysticism of numbers originated, Pythagorean, cabalistic, and so forth, back to very early times.

692   I am grateful to my serious reviewers, and should like here to express my thanks also to Mrs. Harold F. McCormick for her generous help in the production of this book.

June 1917

IV

THE SIGNIFICANCE OF THE FATHER IN THE DESTINY OF THE INDIVIDUAL

———

INTRODUCTION TO KRANEFELDT'S "SECRET WAYS OF THE MIND"

———

FREUD AND JUNG: CONTRASTS

THE SIGNIFICANCE OF THE FATHER IN THE DESTINY OF THE INDIVIDUAL [1]

Foreword to the Second Edition

This little essay, written seventeen years ago, ended with the words: "It is to be hoped that experience in the years to come will sink deeper shafts into this obscure territory, on which I have been able to shed but a fleeting light, and will discover more about the secret workshop of the daemon who shapes our fate." Experience in later years has indeed altered and deepened many things; some of them have appeared in a different light, and I have seen how the roots of the psyche and of fate go deeper than the "family romance," and that not only the children but the parents, too, are merely branches of one great tree. While I was working on the mother-complex in my book *Wandlungen und Symbole der Libido*,[2] it became clear to me what the deeper causes of this complex are; why not only the father, but the mother as well, is such an important factor in the child's fate: not because they themselves have this or that human failing or merit, but because they happen to be—by accident, so to speak—the human beings who first impress on the childish mind those mysterious and mighty laws which govern not only families but entire nations, indeed the whole of humanity. Not laws devised by the wit of man, but the laws and forces of nature, amongst which man walks as on the edge of a razor.

I am letting this essay appear in unaltered form. There is nothing in it that is actually wrong—merely too simple, too naïve. The

1 [First published as "Die Bedeutung des Vaters für das Schicksal des Einzelnen," *Jahrbuch für psychoanalytische und psychopathologische Forschungen* (Leipzig), I (1909), 155–73. This was translated by M. D. Eder under the present title and published in *Collected Papers on Analytical Psychology* (London, 1916; 2nd edn., London, 1917, and New York, 1920). The German original was reprinted (1909) as a pamphlet, and a second edition in this form appeared (Vienna, 1927) with a brief foreword. A third edition, much revised and expanded, with a new foreword, was published in 1949 (Zurich). The present version is a translation of the third edition. Passages which the author added to that version are given in pointed brackets ⟨ ⟩ in the text, while any of significance which they replaced, or which were omitted, are given in square brackets [ ] in the footnotes (as translated from the 1909 version).—EDITORS.]

2 [Revised (1952) and translated as *Symbols of Transformation*.—EDITORS.]

Horatian verse, which I then placed at the end, points to that deeper, darker background:

> "Scit Genius natale comes qui temperat astrum,
> Naturae deus humanae, mortalis in unum,
> Quodque caput, vultu mutabilis, albus et ater." [3]

C. G. J.

Küsnacht, December 1926

Foreword to the Third Edition

This essay was written nearly forty years ago, but this time I did not want to publish it in its original form. Since that time so many things have changed and taken on a new face that I felt obliged to make a number of corrections and additions to the original text. It was chiefly the discovery of the collective unconscious that raised new problems for the theory of complexes. Previously the personality appeared to be unique and as if rooted in nothing; but now, associated with the individually acquired causes of the complex, there was found to be a general human precondition, the inherited and inborn biological structure which is the instinctual basis of every human being. From it proceed, as throughout the whole animal kingdom, determining forces which inhibit or strengthen the more or less fortuitous constellations of individual life. Every normal human situation is provided for and, as it were, imprinted on this inherited structure, since it has happened innumerable times before in our long ancestry. At the same time the structure brings with it an inborn tendency to seek out, or to produce, such situations instinctively. A repressed content would indeed vanish into the void were it not caught and held fast in this pre-established instinctual substrate. Here are to be found those forces which offer the most obstinate resistance to reason and will, thus accounting for the conflicting nature of the complex.

I have tried to modify the old text in accordance with these discoveries and to bring it, in some degree, up to the level of our present knowledge.

C. G. J.

October 1948

[3] "[(Why this should be so) only the Genius knows—that companion who rules the star of our birth, the god of human nature, mortal though he be in each single life, and changeful of countenance, white and black."—Horace, *Epistles*, II, ii, 187–89.—TRANS.]

> The Fates lead the willing,
> but drag the unwilling.
>
> CLEANTHES

693   Freud has pointed out that the emotional relationship of the child to the parents, and particularly to the father, is of a decisive significance in regard to the content of any later neurosis. This relationship is indeed the infantile channel along which the libido [4] flows back when it encounters any obstacles in later years, thus reactivating the long-forgotten psychic contents of childhood. It is ever so in life when we draw back before too great an obstacle, say the threat of some severe disappointment or the risk of some too far-reaching decision. The energy stored up for the solution of the task flows back and the old river-beds, the obsolete systems of the past, are filled up again. A man disillusioned in love falls back, as a substitute, upon some sentimental friendship [5] or false religiosity; if he is a neurotic he regresses still further back to the childhood relationships he has never quite forsaken, and to which even the normal person is fettered by more than one chain—the relationship to father and mother.

694   Every analysis carried out at all thoroughly shows this regression more or less plainly. One peculiarity which stands out in the works of Freud is that the relationship to the father seems to possess a special significance. ⟨This is not to say that the father always has a greater influence on the moulding of the child's fate than the mother. His influence is of a specific nature and differs typically from hers.[6]⟩

695   The significance of the father in moulding the child's psyche may be discovered in quite another field—the study of the family.[7] The latest investigations show the predominating influence of the father's character in a family, often lasting for centuries.

4 [Orig. footnote: Libido is what earlier psychologists called "will" or "tendency." The Freudian expression is a *denominatio a potiori*. *Jahrbuch*, I (1909), 155.]

5 [*In orig., also:* masturbation.]

6 ⟨I have discussed this question on two occasions: *Symbols of Transformation* (in regard to the son), and "Psychological Aspects of the Mother Archetype" (in regard to the daughter).⟩

7 Sommer, *Familienforschung und Vererbungslehre* (1907); Joerger, "Die Familie Zero" (1905); Ziermer, "Genealogische Studien über die Vererbung geistiger Eigenschaften" (1908).

The mother seems to play a less important role. If this is true of heredity, we may expect it to be true also of the psychological influences emanating from the father.[8] The scope of the problem has been widened by the researches of my pupil, Dr. Emma Fürst, on the similarity of reaction-type within families.[9] She conducted association tests on 100 persons coming from 24 families. From this extensive material, so far only the results for nine families and 37 persons (all uneducated) have been worked out and published. But the calculations already permit some valuable conclusions. The associations were classified on the Kraepelin-Aschaffenburg scheme as simplified and modified by me, and the difference was then calculated between each group of qualities in a given subject and the corresponding group in every other subject. We thus get mean figures of the differences in reaction-type.

Non-related men	5.9
Non-related women	6.0
Related men	4.1
Related women	3.8

696   Relatives, especially if they are women, therefore have on average a similar reaction-type. This means that the psychological attitude of relatives differs but slightly. Examination of the various relationships yielded the following results:

697   The mean difference for husband and wife amounts to 4.7%. But the dispersion value for this mean figure is 3.7, which is high, indicating that the mean of 4.7 is composed of a very wide range of figures: there are married couples with great similarity in reaction-type and others with less.

698   On the whole, fathers and sons, mothers and daughters, stand closer together:

| Difference for fathers and sons: | 3.1 |
| Difference for mothers and daughters: | 3.0 |

[8] [Orig.: These experiences, and those gained more particularly in an analysis carried out conjointly with Dr. Otto Gross, have impressed upon me the soundness of this view.] [For Gross, cf. Jones, Freud: Life and Work, II, p. 33.—Editors.]
[9] "Statistical Investigations on Word-Associations and on Familial Agreement in Reaction Type among Uneducated Persons" (orig. 1907).

699   Except for a few cases of married couples (where the difference dropped to 1.4), these are among the lowest figures. Fürst even had one case where a 45-year-old mother and her 16-year-old daughter differed by only 0.5. But it was just in this case that the mother and daughter differed from the father's reaction-type by 11.8. The father was a coarse, stupid man and a drinker; the mother went in for Christian Science. In accordance with this, mother and daughter exhibited an extreme value-predicate type of reaction,[10] which in my experience is an important sign of a conflicting relationship to the object. Value-predicate types show excessive intensity of feeling and thus betray an unadmitted but nonetheless transparent desire to evoke answering feelings in the experimenter. This view agrees with the fact that in Fürst's material the number of value-predicates increases with the age of the subject.

700   The similarity of reaction-type in children and parents provides matter for thought. For the association experiment is nothing other than a small segment of the psychological life of a man, and everyday life is at bottom an extensive and greatly varied association experiment; in principle we react in one as we do in the other. Obvious as this truth is, it still requires some reflection—and limitation. Take the case of the 45-year-old mother and her 16-year-old daughter: the extreme value-predicate type of the mother is without doubt the precipitate of a whole life of disappointed hopes and wishes. One is not in the least surprised at a value-predicate type here. But the 16-year-old daughter had not really lived at all; she was not yet married, and yet she reacted as if she were her mother and had endless disillusions behind her. She had her mother's attitude, and to that extent was identified with her mother. The mother's attitude was explained by her relationship to the father. But the daughter was not married to the father and therefore did not need this attitude. She simply took it over from the environmental influences and later on will try to adapt herself to the world under the influence of this family problem. To the extent that an ill-assorted marriage is unsuitable, the attitude resulting from it will be unsuitable too. In order to adapt, the girl in later

10 By this I mean reactions where the response to the stimulus-word is always a subjectively toned predicate instead of an objective relationship, e.g., *flower / nice, frog / horrible, piano / frightful, salt / bad, singing / sweet, cooking / useful.*

life will have to overcome the obstacles of her family milieu; if she does not, she will succumb to the fate to which her attitude predisposes her.

701   Clearly such a fate has many possibilities. The glossing over of the family problem and the development of the negative of the parental character may take place deep within, unnoticed by anyone, in the form of inhibitions and conflicts which she herself does not understand. Or, as she grows up, she will come into conflict with the world of actualities, fitting in nowhere, until one stroke of fate after another gradually opens her eyes to her own infantile, unadapted qualities. The source of the infantile disturbance of adaptation is naturally the emotional relation to the parents. It is a kind of psychic contagion, caused, as we know, not by logical truths but by affects and their physical manifestations.[11] In the most formative period between the first and fifth year all the essential characteristics, which fit exactly into the parental mould, are already developed, for experience teaches us that the first signs [12] of the later conflict between the parental constellation and the individual's longing for independence occur as a rule before the fifth year.

702   I would like to show, with the help of a few case-histories, how the parental constellation hinders the child's adaptation.[13]

Case 1

703   A well-preserved woman of 55, dressed poorly but carefully, with a certain elegance, in black; hair carefully arranged; a polite, rather affected manner, fastidious in speech, devout. The patient might be the wife of a minor official or shopkeeper. She informed me, blushing and dropping her eyes, that she was the divorced wife of a common peasant. She had come to the clinic on account of depression, night terrors, palpitations, and nervous twitches in the arms—typical features of a mild climacteric neurosis. To complete the picture, the patient added that she suffered from severe anxiety-dreams; some man was pursuing her, wild animals attacked her, and so on.

11 Vigouroux and Juquelier, *La Contagion mentale* (1904), ch. 6.
12 [*Orig.:* . . . of the struggle between repression and libido (Freud) . . .]
13 [*Orig.:* It must suffice to present only the chief events, i.e., those of sexuality.]

704   Her anamnesis began with the family history. (So far as possible I give her own words.) Her father was a fine, stately, rather
corpulent man of imposing appearance. He was very happily
married, for her mother worshipped him. He was a clever man,
a master craftsman, and held a dignified position. There were
only two children, the patient and an elder sister. The sister
was the mother's and the patient the father's favourite. When
she was five years old her father suddenly died of a stroke at the
age of forty-two. She felt very lonely, and also that from then on
she was treated by her mother and sister as the Cinderella. She
noticed clearly enough that her mother preferred her sister to
herself. The mother remained a widow, her respect for her husband being too great to allow her to marry a second time. She
preserved his memory "like a religious cult" and taught her
children to do likewise.

705   The sister married relatively young; the patient did not
marry till she was twenty-four. She had never cared for young
men, they all seemed insipid; her mind turned always to more
mature men. When about twenty she became acquainted with
a "stately" gentleman of over forty, to whom she was much
drawn, but for various reasons the relationship was broken off.
At twenty-four she got to know a widower who had two children. He was a fine, stately, rather corpulent man, with an
imposing presence, like her father; he was forty-four. She married him and respected him enormously. The marriage was
childless; his children by the first marriage died of an infectious
disease. After four years of married life her husband died of a
stroke. For eighteen years she remained his faithful widow. But
at forty-six (just before the menopause) she felt a great need of
love. As she had no acquaintances she went to a matrimonial
agency and married the first comer, a peasant of about sixty
who had already been twice divorced on account of brutality
and perverseness; the patient knew this before marriage. She
remained five unbearable years with him, then she also obtained
a divorce. The neurosis set in a little later.

706   For the reader with psychological [14] experience no further
elucidation is needed; the case is too obvious. I would only emphasize that up to her forty-sixth year the patient did nothing

14 [Orig.: psychanalytical.]

but live out a faithful copy of the milieu of her early youth. The exacerbation of sexuality at the climacteric led to an even worse edition of the father-substitute, thanks to which she was cheated out of the late blossoming of her sexuality. The neurosis reveals, flickering under the repression, the eroticism of the aging woman who still wants to please (affectation).[15]

Case 2

707 A man of thirty-four, of small build, with a clever, kindly expression. He was easily embarrassed, blushed often. He had come for treatment on account of "nervousness." He said he was very irritable, readily fatigued, had nervous stomach-trouble, was often so deeply depressed that he sometimes thought of suicide.

708 Before coming to me for treatment he had sent me a circumstantial autobiography, or rather a history of his illness, in order to prepare me for his visit. His story began: "My father was a very big and strong man." This sentence awakened my curiosity; I turned over a page and there read: "When I was fifteen a big lad of nineteen took me into a wood and indecently assaulted me."

709 The numerous gaps in the patient's story induced me to obtain a more exact anamnesis from him, which led to the following disclosures: The patient was the youngest of three brothers. His father, a big, red-haired man, was formerly a soldier in the Swiss Guard at the Vatican; later he became a policeman. He was a stern, gruff old soldier, who brought up his sons with military discipline; he issued commands, did not call them by name, but whistled for them. He had spent his youth in Rome, and during his gay life there had contracted syphilis, from the consequences of which he still suffered in old age. He was fond of talking about his adventures in early life. His eldest son (considerably older than the patient) was exactly like him, a big, strong man with red hair. The mother was an ailing woman, prematurely aged. Exhausted and tired of life, she died at forty when the patient was eight years old. He preserved a tender and beautiful memory of his mother.

15 [*Orig.:* . . . but dares not acknowledge her sexuality.]

710   At school he was always the whipping-boy and always the object of his schoolfellows' mockery. He thought his peculiar dialect might be to blame. Later he was apprenticed to a strict and unkind master, with whom he stuck it out for over two years, under conditions so trying that all the other apprentices ran away. At fifteen the assault already mentioned took place, together with several other, milder homosexual experiences. Then fate packed him off to France. There he made the acquaintance of a man from the south, a great boaster and Don Juan. He dragged the patient to a brothel; he went unwillingly and out of fear, and found he was impotent. Later he went to Paris, where his eldest brother, a master-mason and the replica of his father, was leading a dissolute life. The patient stayed there a long time, badly paid and helping his sister-in-law out of pity. The brother often took him along to a brothel, but he was always impotent.

711   One day his brother asked him to make over to him his inheritance, 6,000 francs. The patient consulted his second brother, who was also in Paris, and who urgently tried to dissuade him from handing over the money, because it would only be squandered. Nevertheless the patient went and gave his inheritance to his brother, who naturally ran through it in the shortest possible time. And the second brother, who would have dissuaded him, was also let in for 500 francs. To my astonished question why he had so light-heartedly given the money to his brother without any guarantee he replied: well, he asked for it. He was not a bit sorry about the money, he would give him another 6,000 francs if he had it. The eldest brother afterwards went to the bad altogether and his wife divorced him.

712   The patient returned to Switzerland and remained for a year without regular employment, often suffering from hunger. During this time he made the acquaintance of a family and became a frequent visitor. The husband belonged to some peculiar sect, was a hypocrite, and neglected his family. The wife was elderly, ill, and weak, and moreover pregnant. There were six children, all living in great poverty. For this woman the patient developed a warm affection and shared with her the little he possessed. She told him her troubles, saying she felt sure she would die in childbed. He promised her (although he possessed nothing) that he would take charge of the children and bring them up. The

woman did die in childbed, but the orphanage interfered and allowed him only one child. So now he had a child but no family, and naturally could not bring it up by himself. He thus came to think of marrying. But as he had never yet fallen in love with a girl he was in great perplexity.

713   It then occurred to him that his elder brother was divorced from his wife, and he resolved to marry her. He wrote to her in Paris, saying what he intended. She was seventeen years older than he, but not averse to his plan. She invited him to come to Paris to talk matters over. But on the eve of the journey fate willed that he should run an iron nail into his foot, so that he could not travel. After a while, when the wound was healed, he went to Paris and found that he had imagined his sister-in-law, now his fiancée, to be younger and prettier than she really was. The wedding took place, however, and three months later the first coitus, on his wife's initiative. He himself had no desire for it. They brought up the child together, he in the Swiss and she in the Parisian fashion, as she was a French woman. At the age of nine the child was run over and killed by a cyclist. The patient then felt very lonely and dismal at home. He proposed to his wife that they should adopt a young girl, whereupon she broke out into a fury of jealousy. Then, for the first time in his life, he fell in love with a young girl, and simultaneously the neurosis started with deep depression and nervous exhaustion, for meanwhile his life at home had become a hell.

714   My suggestion that he should separate from his wife was dismissed out of hand, on the ground that he could not take it upon himself to make the old woman unhappy on his account. He obviously preferred to go on being tormented, for the memories of his youth seemed to him more precious than any present joys.

715   This patient, too, moved all through his life in the magic circle of the family constellation. The strongest and most fateful factor was the relationship to the father; its masochistic-homosexual colouring is clearly apparent in everything he did. Even the unfortunate marriage was determined by the father, for the patient married the divorced wife of his elder brother, which amounted to marrying his mother. At the same time, his wife was the mother-substitute for the woman who died in childbed. The neurosis set in the moment the libido was withdrawn from

the infantile relationship and for the first time came a bit nearer to an individually determined goal. In this as in the previous case, the family constellation proved to be by far the stronger, so that the narrow field of neurosis was all that was left over for the struggling individuality.

Case 3

716   A 36-year-old peasant woman, of average intelligence, healthy appearance, and robust build, mother of three healthy children. Comfortable economic circumstances. She came to the clinic for the following reasons: for some weeks she had been terribly wretched and anxious, slept badly, had terrifying dreams, and also suffered by day from anxiety and depression. She stated that all these things were without foundation, she herself was surprised at them, and had to admit that her husband was quite right when he insisted that it was all "stuff and nonsense." Nevertheless, she simply could not get over them. Often strange thoughts came into her head; she was going to die and would go to hell. She got on very well with her husband.

717   Examination of the case yielded the following results. Some weeks before, she happened to take up some religious tracts which had long lain about the house unread. There she was informed that people who swore would go to hell. She took this very much to heart, and ever since then had been thinking that she must stop people swearing or she would go to hell too. About a fortnight before she read these tracts her father, who lived with her, had suddenly died of a stroke. She was not actually present at his death, but arrived only when he was already dead. Her terror and grief were very great.

718   In the days following his death she thought much about it all, wondering why her father had to die so suddenly. During these meditations she suddenly remembered that the last words she had heard her father say were: "I am one of those who have got into the devil's clutches." This memory filled her with trepidation, and she recalled how often her father had sworn savagely. She also began to wonder whether there was really a life after death, and whether her father was in heaven or hell. It was during these musings that she came across the tracts and

311

began to read them, until she came to the place where it said that people who swore would go to hell. Then great fear and terror fell upon her; she covered herself with reproaches, she ought to have stopped her father's swearing and deserved to be punished for her negligence. She would die and would be condemned to hell. From that hour she was filled with sorrow, grew moody, tormented her husband with her obsessive ideas, and shunned all joy and conviviality.

719   The patient's life-history was as follows: She was the youngest of five brothers and sisters and had always been her father's favourite. Her father gave her everything she wanted if he possibly could. If she wanted a new dress and her mother refused it, she could be sure her father would bring her one next time he went to town. Her mother died rather early. At twenty-four she married the man of her choice, against her father's wishes. The father flatly disapproved of her choice although he had nothing particular against the man. After the wedding she made her father come and live with them. That seemed the obvious thing, she said, since the others had never suggested having him with them. He was, as a matter of fact, a quarrelsome, foulmouthed old drunkard. Husband and father-in-law, as may easily be imagined, did not get on at all. There were endless squabbles and altercations, in spite of which the patient would always dutifully fetch drink for her father from the inn. All the same, she admitted her husband was right. He was a good, patient fellow with only one failing: he did not obey her father enough. She found that incomprehensible, and would rather have seen her husband knuckle under to her father. When all's said and done, a father is still a father. In the frequent quarrels she always took her father's part. But she had nothing to say against her husband, and he was usually right in his protests, but even so one must stand by one's father.

720   Soon it began to seem to her that she had sinned against her father by marrying against his will, and she often felt, after one of these incessant wrangles, that her love for her husband had died. And since her father's death it was impossible to love him any more, for his disobedience had usually been the cause of her father's fits of raging and swearing. At one time the quarrelling had become too much for the husband, and he induced his wife to find a room for her father elsewhere, where he lived

312

for two years. During this time husband and wife lived together peaceably and happily. But by degrees she began to reproach herself for letting her father live alone; in spite of everything he was her father. And in the end, despite her husband's protests, she fetched her father home again because, as she said, at bottom she loved her father better than her husband. Scarcely was the old man back in the house than the strife broke out again. And so it went on till the father's sudden death.

721   After this recital she broke into a string of lamentations: she must get a divorce from her husband, she would have done so long ago but for the children. She had committed a great wrong, a grievous sin, when she married her husband against her father's wishes. She ought to have taken the man her father wanted her to have; he, certainly, would have obeyed her father, and then everything would have been all right. Oh, she wailed, her husband was not nearly as nice as her father, she could do anything with her father, but not with her husband. Her father had given her everything she wanted. And now she wanted most of all to die, so that she could be with her father.

722   When this outburst was over, I asked curiously why she had refused the husband her father had proposed?

723   It seems that the father, a small peasant on a lean little holding, had taken on as a labourer, just at the time when his youngest daughter was born, a wretched little boy, a foundling. The boy developed in a most unpleasant fashion: he was so stupid that he could not learn to read or write, or even to speak properly. He was an absolute blockhead. As he approached manhood a series of ulcers developed on his neck, some of which opened and continually discharged pus, giving this dirty, ugly creature a truly horrible appearance. His intelligence did not grow with his years, so he stayed on as a farm-labourer without any recognized wage.

724   To this oaf the father wanted to marry his favourite daughter.

725   The girl, fortunately, had not been disposed to yield, but now she regretted it, for this idiot would unquestionably have been more obedient to her father than her good man had been.

726   Here, as in the foregoing case, it must be clearly understood that the patient was not at all feeble-minded. Both possessed normal intelligence, although the blinkers of the infantile

constellation kept them from using it. That appears with quite remarkable clearness in this patient's life-story. The father's authority is never even questioned. It makes not the least difference to her that he was a quarrelsome old drunkard, the obvious cause of all the bickering and dissension; on the contrary, her husband must bow down before this bogey, and finally our patient even comes to regret that her father did not succeed in completely destroying her life's happiness. So now she sets about destroying it herself, through her neurosis, which forces on her the wish to die so that she may go to hell—whither, be it noted, her father has already betaken himself.

727   If ever we are disposed to see some demonic power at work controlling mortal destiny, surely we can see it here in these melancholy, silent tragedies working themselves out, slowly and agonizingly, in the sick souls of our neurotics. Some, step by step, continually struggling against the unseen powers, do free themselves from the clutches of the demon who drives his unsuspecting victims from one cruel fatality to another; others rise up and win to freedom, only to be dragged back later to the old paths, caught in the noose of the neurosis. You cannot even maintain that these unhappy people are always neurotics or "degenerates." If we normal people examine our lives,[16] we too perceive how a mighty hand guides us without fail to our destiny, and not always is this hand a kindly one.[17] Often we call it the hand of God or of the devil, (thereby expressing, unconsciously but correctly, a highly important psychological fact: that the power which shapes the life of the psyche has the character of an autonomous personality. At all events it is felt as such, so that today in common speech, just as in ancient times, the source of any such destiny appears as a daemon, as a good or evil spirit.

16 [*Orig.:* . . . from the psychanalytic standpoint . . .]
17 "Throughout we believe ourselves to be the masters of our deeds. But reviewing our lives, and chiefly taking our misfortunes and their consequences into consideration, we often cannot account for our doing this act and omitting that, making it appear as if our steps had been guided by a power foreign to us. Therefore Shakespeare says:

'Fate show thy force: ourselves we do not owe;
What is decreed must be, and be this so!' "

—Schopenhauer, "On Apparent Design in the Fate of the Individual," *Parerga and Paralipomena* (trans. by Irvine, p. 26).

728   ⟨The personification of this source goes back in the first place to the father, for which reason Freud was of the opinion that all "divine" figures have their roots in the father-imago. It can hardly be denied that they do derive from this imago, but what we are to say about the father-imago itself is another matter. For the parental imago is possessed of a quite extraordinary power; it influences the psychic life of the child so enormously that we must ask ourselves whether we may attribute such magical power to an ordinary human being at all. Obviously he possesses it, but we are bound to ask whether it is really his property. Man "possesses" many things which he has never acquired but has inherited from his ancestors. He is not born as a *tabula rasa*, he is merely born unconscious. But he brings with him systems that are organized and ready to function in a specifically human way, and these he owes to millions of years of human development. Just as the migratory and nest-building instincts of birds were never learnt or acquired individually, man brings with him at birth the ground-plan of his nature, and not only of his individual nature but of his collective nature. These inherited systems correspond to the human situations that have existed since primeval times: youth and old age, birth and death, sons and daughters, fathers and mothers, mating, and so on. Only the individual consciousness experiences these things for the first time, but not the bodily system and the unconscious. For them they are only the habitual functioning of instincts that were preformed long ago. "You were in bygone times my wife or sister," says Goethe, clothing in words the dim feelings of many.

729   ⟨I have called this congenital and pre-existent instinctual model, or pattern of behaviour, the *archetype*. This is the imago that is charged with the dynamism we cannot attribute to an individual human being. Were this power really in our hands and subject to our will, we would be so crushed with responsibility that no one in his right senses would dare to have children. But the power of the archetype is not controlled by us; we ourselves are at its mercy to an unsuspected degree. There are many who resist its influence and its compulsion, but equally many who identify with the archetype, for instance with the *patris potestas* or with the queen ant. And because everyone is

315

in some degree "possessed" by his specifically human preforma-
tion, he is held fast and fascinated by it and exercises the same
influence on others without being conscious of what he is doing.
The danger is just this unconscious identity with the archetype:
not only does it exert a dominating influence on the child by
suggestion, it also causes the same unconsciousness in the child,
so that it succumbs to the influence from outside and at the
same time cannot oppose it from within. The more a father
identifies with the archetype, the more unconscious and irresponsible, indeed psychotic, both he and his child will be. In
the case we have discussed, it is almost a matter of "folie à
deux.") [18]

730   In our case, it is quite obvious what the father was doing,
and why he wanted to marry his daughter to this brutish creature: he wanted to keep her with him and make her his slave
for ever. What he did is but a crass exaggeration of what is done
by thousands of so-called respectable, educated parents, who
nevertheless pride themselves on their progressive views. The
fathers who criticize every sign of emotional independence in
their children, who fondle their daughters with ill-concealed
eroticism and tyrannize over their feelings, who keep their sons
on a leash or force them into a profession and finally into a "suitable" marriage, the mothers who even in the cradle excite their
children with unhealthy tenderness, who later make them into
slavish puppets and then at last ruin their love-life out of jealousy: they all act no differently in principle from this stupid,
boorish peasant. ⟨They do not know what they are doing, and
they do not know that by succumbing to the compulsion they
pass it on to their children and make them slaves of their parents
and of the unconscious as well. Such children will long continue
to live out the curse laid on them by their parents, even when

18 [Orig.: . . . for the power of the infantile constellation has provided highly
convincing material for the religions in the course of the millennia.

[All this is not to say that we should cast the blame for original sin upon our
parents. A sensitive child, whose sympathies are only too quick to reflect in his
psyche the excesses of his parents, bears the blame for his fate in his own character. But, as our last case shows, this is not always so, for the parents can (and
unfortunately only too often do) instil the evil into the child's soul, preying
upon his ignorance in order to make him the slave of their complexes.]

the parents are long since dead. "They know not what they do." ✓
Unconsciousness is the original sin.) [19]

Case 4

731   An eight-year-old boy, intelligent, rather delicate-looking,
brought to me by his mother on account of enuresis. During the
consultation the child clung all the time to his mother, a pretty,
youthful woman. The marriage was a happy one, but the father
was strict, and the boy (the eldest child) was rather afraid of
him. The mother compensated for the father's strictness by a
corresponding tenderness, to which the boy responded so much
that he never got away from his mother's apron-strings. He
never played with his school-fellows, never went alone into the
street unless he had to go to school. He feared the boys' rough-
ness and violence and played thoughtful games at home or
helped his mother with the housework. He was extremely jealous of his father, and could not bear it when the father showed
tenderness to the mother.

19 [*Orig.*: It will be asked, wherein lies the magic power of the parents to bind
their children to themselves, often for the whole of their lives? The psychoanalyst
knows that it is nothing but sexuality on both sides.

[We are always trying not to admit the child's sexuality. But this is only because of wilful ignorance, which happens to be very prevalent again just now.*

[I have not given any real analysis of these cases. We therefore do not know
what happened to these puppets of fate when they were children. A profound
insight into the living soul of a child, such as we have never had before, is given
in Freud's contribution to the present semi-annual volume of the *Jahrbuch*
["Analysis of a Phobia in a Five-year-old Boy"]. If I venture, after Freud's mas-
terly presentation, to offer another small contribution to the study of the child-
psyche, it is because psychoanalytic case-histories seem to me always valuable.

[* *Orig. footnote:* This was seen at the Amsterdam Congress in 1907 [First
International Congress of Psychiatry and Neurology; cf. the second paper in this
vol.—EDITORS], when an eminent French savant assured us that Freud's theory
was nothing but "une plaisanterie." This gentleman had evidently read neither
Freud's latest writings nor mine, and knew far less about the subject than a little
child. This pronouncement, so admirably grounded, met with the approbation
of a well-known German professor in his report to the Congress. One can but
bow before such thoroughness. At the same Congress a noted German neurologist immortalized his name with the following brilliant argument: "If in Freud's
view hysteria really does rest on repressed affects, then the whole German army
must be hysterical."]

317

732   I took the boy aside and asked him about his dreams. Very often he dreamt of a *black snake that wanted to bite his face.* Then he would cry out, and his mother had to come to him from the next room and stay by his bedside.

733   In the evening he would go quietly to bed. But when falling asleep it seemed to him that a *wicked black man with a sword or a gun was lying on his bed, a tall thin man who wanted to kill him.* The parents slept in the next room. The boy often dreamt that something dreadful was going on in there, as if there were *great black snakes or evil men who wanted to kill Mama.* Then he would cry out, and Mama came to comfort him. Every time he wet his bed he called his mother, who would then have to change the bedclothes.

734   The father was a tall thin man. Every morning he stood naked at the wash-stand in full view of the boy, to perform a thorough ablution. The boy also told me that at night he often started up from sleep at the sound of strange noises in the next room; then he was always horribly afraid that something dreadful was going on in there, a struggle of some kind, but his mother would quiet him and say it was nothing.

735   It is not difficult to see what was happening in the next room. It is equally easy to understand the boy's aim in calling out for his mother: he was jealous and was separating her from the father. He did this also in the daytime whenever he saw his father caressing her. Thus far the boy was simply the father's rival for his mother's love.

736   But now comes the fact that the snake and the wicked man threaten him as well: the same thing happens to him as happens to his mother in the next room. To that extent he identifies with his mother and thus puts himself in a similar relationship to the father. This is due to his homosexual component, which feels feminine towards the father. ⟨The bed-wetting is in this case a substitute for sexuality. Pressure of urine in dreams and also in the waking state is often an expression of some other pressure, for instance of fear, expectation, suppressed excitement, inability to speak, the need to express an unconscious content, etc. In our case the substitute for sexuality has the significance of a premature masculinity which is meant to compensate the inferiority of the child.

737   ⟨Although I do not intend to go into the psychology of

dreams in this connection, the motif of the black snake and of the black man should not pass unmentioned. Both these terrifying spectres threaten the dreamer as well as his mother. "Black" indicates something dark, the unconscious. The dream shows that the mother-child relationship is menaced by unconsciousness. The threatening agency is represented by the mythological motif of the "father animal"; in other words the father appears as threatening. This is in keeping with the tendency of the child to remain unconscious and infantile, which is decidedly dangerous. For the boy, the father is an anticipation of his own masculinity, conflicting with his wish to remain infantile. The snake's attack on the boy's face, the part that "sees," represents the danger to consciousness (blinding).⟩ [20]

738   This little example shows what goes on in the psyche of an eight-year-old child who is over-dependent on his parents, the blame for this lying partly on the too strict father and the too tender mother. ⟨The boy's identification with his mother and fear of his father are in this individual instance an infantile neurosis, but they represent at the same time the original human situation, the clinging of primitive consciousness to the unconscious, and the compensating impulse which strives to tear consciousness away from the embrace of the darkness. Because man has a dim premonition of this original situation behind his individual experience, he has always tried to give it generally valid expression through the universal motif of the divine hero's fight with the mother dragon, whose purpose is to deliver man from the power of darkness. This myth has a "saving," i.e., therapeutic significance, since it gives adequate expression to the dynamism underlying the individual entanglement. The myth is not to be causally explained as the consequence of a personal father-complex, but should be understood teleologically, as an attempt of the unconscious itself to rescue consciousness from the danger of regression. The ideas of "salvation" are not subsequent rationalizations of a father-complex; they are, rather,

---

20 [Orig.: It is not difficult to see, from the Freudian standpoint, what the bed-wetting means in this case. Micturition dreams give us the clue. Here I would refer the reader to an analysis of this kind in my paper "The Analysis of Dreams" (cf. supra, pars. 82f.). Bed-wetting must be regarded as an infantile sexual substitute, and even in the dream-life of adults it is easily used as a cloak for the pressure of sexual desire.]

archetypally preformed mechanisms for the development of consciousness.) [21]

739   What we see enacted on the stage of world-history happens also in the individual. The child is guided by the power of the parents as by a higher destiny. But as he grows up, the struggle between his infantile attitude and his increasing consciousness begins. The parental influence, dating from the early infantile period, is repressed and sinks into the unconscious, but is not eliminated; by invisible threads it directs the apparently individual workings of the maturing mind. Like everything that has fallen into the unconscious, the infantile situation still sends up dim, premonitory feelings, feelings of being secretly guided by otherworldly influences. (Normally these feelings are not referred back to the father, but to a positive or negative

21 [Orig.: The infantile attitude, it is evident, is nothing but infantile sexuality. If we now survey all the far-reaching possibilities of the infantile constellation, we are obliged to say that in essence our life's fate is identical with the fate of our sexuality. If Freud and his school devote themselves first and foremost to tracing out the individual's sexuality, it is certainly not in order to excite piquant sensations but to gain a deeper insight into the driving forces that determine the individual's fate. In this we are not saying too much, but rather understating the case. For, when we strip off the veils shrouding the problems of individual destiny, we at once widen our field of vision from the history of the individual to the history of nations. We can take a look, first of all, at the history of religion, at the history of the fantasy systems of whole peoples and epochs. The religion of the Old Testament exalted the paterfamilias into the Jehovah of the Jews, whom the people had to obey in fear and dread. The patriarchs were a stepping-stone to the Deity. The neurotic fear in Judaism, an imperfect or at any rate unsuccessful attempt at sublimation by a still too barbarous people, gave rise to the excessive severity of Mosaic law, the compulsive ceremonial of the neurotic.* Only the prophets were able to free themselves from it; for them the identification with Jehovah, complete sublimation, was successful. They became the fathers of the people. Christ, the fulfiller of their prophecies, put an end to this fear of God and taught mankind that the true relation to the Deity is love. Thus he destroyed the compulsive ceremonial of the law and was himself the exponent of the personal loving relationship to God. Later, the imperfect sublimations of the Christian Mass resulted once again in the ceremonial of the Church, from which only those of the numerous saints and reformers who were really capable of sublimation were able to break free. Not without cause, therefore, does modern theology speak of the liberating effect of "inner" or "personal" experience, for always the ardour of love transmutes fear and compulsion into a higher, freer type of feeling.

[* Orig. footnote: Cf. Freud, Zeitschrift für Religionspsychologie (1907).] [I.e., "Obsessive Acts and Religious Practices."—EDITORS.]

deity. This change is accomplished partly under the influence of education, partly spontaneously. It is universal. Also, it resists conscious criticism with the force of an instinct, for which reason the soul (*anima*) may fittingly be described as *naturaliter religiosa*. The reason for this development, indeed its very possibility, is to be found in the fact that the child possesses an inherited system that anticipates the existence of parents and their influence upon him. In other words, behind the father stands the archetype of the father, and in this pre-existent archetype lies the secret of the father's power, just as the power which forces the bird to migrate is not produced by the bird itself but derives from its ancestors.

740   It will not have escaped the reader that the role which falls to the father-imago in our case is an ambiguous one. The threat it represents has a dual aspect: fear of the father may drive the boy out of his identification with the mother, but on the other hand it is possible that his fear will make him cling still more closely to her. A typically neurotic situation then arises: he wants and yet does not want, saying yes and no at the same time.

741   This double aspect of the father-imago is characteristic of the archetype in general: it is capable of diametrically opposite effects and acts on consciousness rather as Yahweh acted towards Job—ambivalently. And, as in the Book of Job, man is left to take the consequences. We cannot say with certainty that the archetype always acts in this way, for there are experiences which prove the contrary. But they do not appear to be the rule.) [22]

742   An instructive and well-known example of the ambivalent behaviour of the father-imago is the love-episode in the Book of Tobit.[23] Sara, the daughter of Raguel, of Ecbatana, desires to marry. But her evil fate wills it that seven times, one after the

22 [*Orig.:* These are the roots of the first religious sublimations. In the place of the father with his constellating virtues and faults there appears on the one hand an altogether sublime deity, and on the other hand the devil, who in modern times has been largely whittled away by the realization of one's own moral responsibility. Sublime love is attributed to the former, low sexuality to the latter. As soon as we enter the field of neurosis, this antithesis is stretched to the limit. God becomes the symbol of the most complete sexual repression, the devil the symbol of sexual lust. Thus it is that the conscious expression of the father-constellation, like every expression of an unconscious complex when it appears in consciousness, acquires its Janus face, its positive and its negative components.]
23 Chs. 3 : 7ff. and 8 : 1ff.

other, she chooses a husband who dies on the wedding-night. It is the evil spirit Asmodeus, by whom she is persecuted, that kills these men. She prays to Yahweh to let her die rather than suffer this shame again, for she is despised even by her father's maid-servants. The eighth bridegroom, her cousin Tobias, the son of Tobit, is sent to her by God. He too is led into the bridal chamber. Then old Raguel, who had only pretended to go to bed, goes out and thoughtfully digs his son-in-law's grave, and in the morning sends a maid to the bridal chamber to make sure that he is dead. But this time Asmodeus' role is played out, for Tobias is alive.

743 ⟨The story shows father Raguel in his two roles, as the in-consolable father of the bride and the provident digger of his son-in-law's grave. Humanly speaking he seems beyond re-proach, and it is highly probable that he was. But there is still the evil spirit Asmodeus and his presence needs explaining. If we suspect old Raguel personally of playing a double role, this malicious insinuation would apply only to his sentiments; there is no evidence that he committed murder. These wicked deeds transcend the old man's daughter-complex as well as Sara's father-complex, for which reason the legend fittingly ascribes them to a demon. Asmodeus plays the role of a jealous father who will not give up his beloved daughter and only relents when he remembers his own positive aspect, and in that capacity at last gives Sara a pleasing bridegroom. He, significantly enough, is the eighth: the last and highest stage.[24] Asmodeus stands for the negative aspect of the father archetype, for the archetype is the genius and daemon of the personal human being, "the god of human nature, changeful of countenance, white and black." [25] The legend offers a psychologically correct explanation: it does not attribute superhuman evil to Raguel, it distinguishes between man and daemon, just as psychology must distinguish between what the human individual is and can do and what must be ascribed to the congenital, instinctual system, which the individual has not made but finds within him. We would be doing the gravest injustice to Raguel if we held

[24] ⟨Cf. the axiom of Maria and the discussion of 3 and 4, 7 and 8, in *Psychology and Alchemy,* pars. 201ff. and 209.⟩
[25] ⟨Horace, *Epistles,* II, 2, 187–89.⟩

him responsible for the fateful power of this system, that is, of the archetype.

744   ⟨The potentialities of the archetype, for good and evil alike, transcend our human capacities many times, and a man can appropriate its power only by identifying with the daemon, by letting himself be possessed by it, thus forfeiting his own humanity. The fateful power of the father complex comes from the archetype, and this is the real reason why the *consensus gentium* puts a divine or daemonic figure in place of the father. The personal father inevitably embodies the archetype, which is what endows his figure with its fascinating power. The archetype acts as an amplifier, enhancing beyond measure the effects that proceed from the father, so far as these conform to the inherited pattern.⟩ [26]

26 [*Orig.*: Unfortunately medical etiquette forbids me to report a case of hysteria which fits this pattern exactly, except that there were not seven husbands but only three, unluckily chosen under all the ominous signs of an infantile constellation. Our first case, too, belongs to this category, and in our third case we see the old peasant at work, preparing to dedicate his daughter to a like fate.

[As a pious and dutiful daughter (cf. her prayer in Tobit, ch. 3), Sara has brought about the usual sublimation and splitting of the father-complex, on the one hand elevating her infantile love into the worship of God, and on the other turning the obsessive power of the father into the persecuting demon Asmodeus. The story is beautifully worked out and shows father Raguel in his two roles, as the inconsolable father of the bride and the provident digger of his son-in-law's grave, whose fate he foresees.

[This pretty fable has become a classic example in my analytical work, for we frequently meet with cases where the father-demon has laid his hand upon his daughter, so that her whole life long, even when she does marry, there is never a true inward union, because her husband's image never succeeds in obliterating the unconscious and continually operative infantile father-ideal. This is true not only of daughters, but also of sons. An excellent example of this kind of father-constellation can be found in Brill's recently published "Psychological Factors in Dementia Praecox" (1908).

[In my experience it is usually the father who is the decisive and dangerous object of the child's fantasy, and if ever it happened to be the mother I was able to discover behind her a grandfather to whom she belonged in her heart.

[I must leave this question open, because my findings are not sufficient to warrant a decision. It is to be hoped that experience in the years to come will sink deeper shafts into this obscure territory, on which I have been able to shed but a fleeting light, and will discover more about the secret workshop of the demon who shapes our fate, of whom Horace says:

> "Scit Genius natale comes qui temperat astrum,
> Naturae deus humanae, mortalis in unum,
> Quodque caput, vultu mutabilis, albus et ater."]

323

INTRODUCTION TO KRANEFELDT'S
"SECRET WAYS OF THE MIND" [1]

745　　At the present time, one can well say, it is still quite impossible to draw up a comprehensive and hence a proper picture of all that commonly goes by the much abused name "psychoanalysis." What the layman usually understands by "psychoanalysis"—a medical dissection of the soul for the purpose of disclosing hidden causes and connections—touches only a small part of the phenomena in question. Even if we regard psychoanalysis from a wider angle—in agreement with Freud's conception of it—as essentially a medical instrument for the cure of neurosis, this broader point of view still does not exhaust the nature of the subject. Above all, psychoanalysis in the strictly Freudian sense is not only a therapeutic method but a psychological theory, which does not confine itself in the least to the neuroses and to psychopathology in general but attempts also to bring within its province the normal phenomenon of the dream and, besides this, wide areas of the humane sciences, of literature and the creative arts, as well as biography, mythology, folklore, comparative religion, and philosophy.

746　　It is a somewhat curious fact in the history of science—but one that is in keeping with the peculiar nature of the psychoanalytic movement—that Freud, the creator of psychoanalysis (in the narrower sense), insists on identifying the method with his sexual theory, thus placing upon it the stamp of dogmatism. This declaration of "scientific" infallibility caused me, at the time, to break with Freud, for to me dogma and science are incommensurable quantities which damage one another by mutual contamination. Dogma as a factor in religion is of ines-

1 [Originally published in W. M. Kranefeldt's *Die Psychoanalyse* (Berlin and Leipzig, 1930). Translated by Ralph M. Eaton in the English version of the volume, *Secret Ways of the Mind* (New York, 1932; London, 1934). The present translation is of the original, but reference was made to the Eaton version. —EDITORS.]

timable value precisely because of its absolute standpoint. But when science dispenses with criticism and scepticism it degenerates into a sickly hot-house plant. One of the elements necessary to science is extreme uncertainty. Whenever science inclines towards dogma and shows a tendency to be impatient and fanatical, it is concealing a doubt which in all probability is justified and explaining away an uncertainty which is only too well founded.

747   I emphasize this unfortunate state of affairs not because I want to make a critical attack on Freud's theories, but rather to point out to the unbiased reader the significant fact that Freudian psychoanalysis, apart from being a scientific endeavour and a scientific achievement, is a psychic symptom which has proved to be more powerful than the analytical art of the master himself. As Maylan's book on "Freud's tragic complex"[2] has shown, it would not be at all difficult to derive Freud's tendency to dogmatize from the premises of his own personal psychology —indeed, he taught this trick to his disciples and practised it more or less successfully himself—but I do not wish to turn his own weapons against him. In the end no one can completely outgrow his personal limitations; everyone is more or less imprisoned by them—especially when he practises psychology.

748   I find these technical defects uninteresting and believe it is dangerous to lay too much stress on them, as it diverts attention from the one important fact: that even the loftiest mind is most limited and dependent just at the point where it seems to be freest. In my estimation the creative spirit in man is not his personality at all but rather a sign or symptom of a contemporary movement of thought. His personality is important only as the mouthpiece of a conviction arising out of an unconscious, collective background—a conviction that robs him of his freedom, forces him to sacrifice himself and to make mistakes which he would criticize mercilessly in others. Freud is borne along by a particular current of thought which can be traced back to the Reformation. Gradually it freed itself from innumerable veils and disguises, and it is now turning into the kind of psychology which Nietzsche foresaw with prophetic insight—the discovery of the psyche as a new fact. Some day we shall be able to

2 [*Freuds tragischer Komplex: Eine Analyse der Psychoanalyse* (1929).—EDITORS.]

see by what tortuous paths modern psychology has made its way from the dingy laboratories of the alchemists, via mesmerism and magnetism (Kerner, Ennemoser, Eschimayer, Baader, Passavant, and others), to the philosophical anticipations of Schopenhauer, Carus, and von Hartmann; and how, from the native soil of everyday experience in Liébeault and, still earlier, in Quimby (the spiritual father of Christian Science),[3] it finally reached Freud through the teachings of the French hypnotists. This current of ideas flowed together from many obscure sources, gaining rapidly in strength in the nineteenth century and winning many adherents, amongst whom Freud is not an isolated figure.

749   What is designated today by the catchword "psychoanalysis" is not in reality a uniform thing, but comprises in itself many different aspects of the great psychological problem of our age. Whether or not the public at large is conscious of this problem does not alter the fact of its existence. In our time the psyche has become something of a problem for everyone. Psychology has acquired a power of attraction which is really astounding. It explains the surprising, world-wide spread of Freudian psychoanalysis, which has had a success comparable only to that of Christian Science, theosophy, and anthroposophy—comparable not only in its success but also in its essence, for Freud's dogmatism comes very close to the attitude of religious conviction that characterizes these movements. Moreover, all four movements are decidedly psychological. When we add to this the almost unbelievable rise of occultism in every form in all civilized parts of the Western world, we begin to get a picture of this current of thought, everywhere a little taboo yet nonetheless compelling. Similarly, modern medicine shows significant leanings towards the spirit of Paracelsus, and is becoming increasingly aware of the importance of the psyche in somatic diseases. Even the traditionalism of criminal law is beginning to yield to the claims of psychology, as we can see from the suspension of sentences and the more and more frequent practice of calling in psychological experts.

750   So much for the positive aspects of this psychological move-

3 [Phineas Parkhurst Quimby (1802–66), American hypnotist and mental healer, consulted by Mary Baker Eddy, whose ideas he is thought to have influenced. —EDITORS.]

ment. But these aspects are balanced on the other side by equally characteristic negative ones. Already at the time of the Reformation the conscious mind had begun to break away from the metaphysical certainties of the Gothic age, and this separation became more acute and widespread with every passing century. At the beginning of the eighteenth century the world saw the truths of Christianity publicly dethroned for the first time, and at the beginning of the twentieth the government of one of the largest countries on earth is making every effort to stamp out the Christian faith as if it were a disease. Meanwhile, the intellect of the white man as a whole has outgrown the authority of Catholic dogma, and Protestantism has succeeded in splitting itself into more than four hundred denominations through the most trivial quibbles. These are obvious negative aspects, and they explain why people increasingly flock to any movement from which they expect a helpful truth to come.

751   Religions are the great healing systems for the ills of the soul. Neuroses and similar illnesses arise, one and all, from psychic complications. But once a dogma is disputed and questioned, it has lost its healing power. A person who no longer believes that a God who knows suffering will have mercy on him, will help and comfort him and give his life a meaning, is weak and a prey to his own weakness and becomes neurotic. The innumerable pathological elements in the population constitute one of the most powerful factors that lend support to the psychological tendencies of our time.

752   Another and by no means unimportant contingent is formed by all those who, after a period of belief in authority, have awakened with a kind of resentment and find a satisfaction mixed with self-torture in advocating a so-called new truth which is destructive of their old, still-smouldering convictions. Such people can never keep their mouths shut and, because of the weakness of their conviction and their fear of isolation, must always flock together in proselytizing bands, thus at least making up in quantity for their doubtful quality.

753   Finally, there are those who are earnestly searching for something, who are thoroughly convinced that the soul is the seat of all psychic sufferings and at the same time the dwelling-place of all the healing truths that have ever been announced as glad tidings to suffering humanity. From the soul come the most

327

senseless conflicts, yet we also look to it for a solution or at least a valid answer to the tormenting question: why?

754   One does not have to be neurotic to feel the need of healing, and this need exists even in people who deny with the deepest conviction that any such healing is possible. In a weak moment they cannot help glancing inquisitively into a book on psychology, even if only to find a recipe for adroitly bringing a refractory marriage partner to reason.

755   These entirely different interests on the part of the public are reflected in the variations on the theme of "psychoanalysis." The Adlerian school, which grew up side by side with Freud, lays particular stress on the social aspect of the psychic problem and, accordingly, has differentiated itself more and more into a system of social education. It denies, not only in theory but in practice, all the essentially Freudian elements of psychoanalysis, so much so that with the exception of a few theoretical principles the original points of contact with the Freudian school are almost unrecognizable. For this reason Adler's "individual psychology" can no longer be included in the concept of "psychoanalysis." It is an independent system of psychology, the expression of a different temperament and a wholly different view of the world.

756   No one who is interested in "psychoanalysis" and who wants to get anything like an adequate survey of the whole field of modern psychiatry should fail to study the writings of Adler. He will find them extremely stimulating, and in addition he will make the valuable discovery that exactly the same case of neurosis can be explained in an equally convincing way from the standpoint of Freud or of Adler, despite the fact that the two methods of explanation seem diametrically opposed to one another. But things that fall hopelessly apart in theory lie close together without contradiction in the paradoxical soul of man: every human being has a power instinct as well as a sexual instinct. Consequently, he displays both of these psychologies, and every psychic impulse in him has subtle overtones coming from the one side as much as the other.

757   Since it has not been established how many primary instincts exist in man or in animals, the possibility at once arises that an ingenious mind might discover a few more psychologies, apparently contradicting all the rest and yet productive of highly

satisfactory explanations. But these discoveries are not just a simple matter of sitting down and evolving a new psychological system out of, shall we say, the artistic impulse. Neither Freud's nor Adler's psychology came into existence in this way. Rather, as if they were fated by an inner necessity, both investigators confessed their ruling principle, putting on record their own personal psychology and hence also their way of observing other people. This is a question of deep experience and not an intellectual conjuring-trick. One could wish that there were more confessions of this sort; they would give us a more complete picture of the psyche's potentialities.

758   My own views and the school I have founded are equally psychological, and are therefore subject to the same limitations and criticisms that I have allowed myself to urge against these other psychologists. So far as I myself can pass judgment on my own point of view, it differs from the psychologies discussed above in this respect, that it is not monistic but, if anything, dualistic, being based on the principle of opposites, and possibly pluralistic, since it recognizes a multiplicity of relatively autonomous psychic complexes.

759   It will be seen that I have deduced a theory from the fact that contradictory and yet satisfactory explanations are possible. Unlike Freud and Adler, whose principles of explanation are essentially reductive and always return to the infantile conditions that limit human nature, I lay more stress on a constructive or synthetic explanation, in acknowledgment of the fact that tomorrow is of more practical importance than yesterday, and that the Whence is less essential than the Whither. For all my respect for history, it seems to me that no insight into the past and no re-experiencing of pathogenic reminiscences—however powerful it may be—is as effective in freeing man from the grip of the past as the construction of something new. I am of course very well aware that, without insight into the past and without an integration of significant memories that have been lost, nothing new and viable can be created. But I consider it a waste of time and a misleading prejudice to rummage in the past for the alleged specific causes of illness; for neuroses, no matter what the original circumstances from which they arose, are conditioned and maintained by a wrong attitude which is present all the time and which, once it is recognized, must be

corrected *now* and not in the early period of infancy. Nor is it enough merely to bring the causes into consciousness, for the cure of neurosis is, in the last analysis, a moral problem and not the magic effect of rehearsing old memories.

760   My views differ further from those of Freud and Adler in that I give an essentially different value to the unconscious. Freud, who attributes an infinitely more important role to the unconscious than Adler (this school allows it to disappear completely into the background), has a more religious temperament than Adler and for this reason he naturally concedes an autonomous, if negative, function to the psychic non-ego. In this respect I go several steps further than Freud. For me the unconscious is not just a receptacle for all unclean spirits and other odious legacies from the dead past—such as, for instance, that deposit of centuries of public opinion which constitutes Freud's "superego." It is in very truth the eternally living, creative, germinal layer in each of us, and though it may make use of age-old symbolical images it nevertheless intends them to be understood in a new way. Naturally a new meaning does not come ready-made out of the unconscious, like Pallas Athene springing fully-armed from the head of Zeus; a living effect is achieved only when the products of the unconscious are brought into serious relationship with the conscious mind.

761   In order to interpret the products of the unconscious, I also found it necessary to give a quite different reading to dreams and fantasies. I did not reduce them to personal factors, as Freud does, but—and this seemed indicated by their very nature—I compared them with the symbols from mythology and the history of religion, in order to discover the meaning they were trying to express. This method did in fact yield extremely interesting results, not least because it permitted an entirely new reading of dreams and fantasies, thus making it possible to unite the otherwise incompatible and archaic tendencies of the unconscious with the conscious personality. This union had long seemed to me the end to strive for, because neurotics (and many normal people, too) suffer at bottom from a dissociation between conscious and unconscious. As the unconscious contains not only the sources of instinct and the whole prehistoric nature of man right down to the animal level, but also, along with these, the creative seeds of the future and the

roots of all constructive fantasies, a separation from the unconscious through neurotic dissociation means nothing less than a separation from the source of all life. It therefore seemed to me that the prime task of the therapist was to re-establish this lost connection and the life-giving co-operation between conscious and unconscious. Freud depreciates the unconscious and seeks safety in the discriminating power of consciousness. This approach is generally mistaken and leads to desiccation and rigidity wherever a firmly established consciousness already exists; for, by holding off the antagonistic and apparently hostile elements in the unconscious, it denies itself the vitality it needs for its own renewal.

762   Freud's approach is not always mistaken, however, for consciousness is not always firmly established. This presupposes a good deal of experience of life and a certain amount of maturity. Young people, who are very far from knowing who they really are, would run a great risk if they obscured their knowledge of themselves still further by letting the "dark night of the soul" pour into their immature, labile consciousness. Here a certain depreciation of the unconscious is justified. Experience has convinced me that there are not only different temperaments ("types"), but different stages of psychological development, so that one can well say that there is an essential difference between the psychology of the first and the second half of life. Here again I differ from the others in maintaining that the same psychological criteria are not applicable to the different stages of life.

763   If, to all these considerations, one adds the further fact that I distinguish between extraverts and introverts, and again distinguish each of them by the criterion of its most differentiated function (of which I can clearly make out four), it will be evident that hitherto my main concern as an investigator in the field of psychology has been to break in rudely upon a situation which, seen from the other two standpoints, is simple to the point of monotony, and to call attention to the inconceivable complexity of the psyche as it really is.

764   Most people have wanted to ignore these complexities, and have frankly deplored their existence. But would any physiologist assert that the body is simple? Or that a living molecule of albumen is simple? If the human psyche is anything, it must be of unimaginable complexity and diversity, so that it cannot

331

possibly be approached through a mere psychology of instinct. I can only gaze with wonder and awe at the depths and heights of our psychic nature. Its non-spatial universe conceals an untold abundance of images which have accumulated over millions of years of living development and become fixed in the organism. My consciousness is like an eye that penetrates to the most distant spaces, yet it is the psychic non-ego that fills them with non-spatial images. And these images are not pale shadows, but tremendously powerful psychic factors. The most we may be able to do is misunderstand them, but we can never rob them of their power by denying them. Beside this picture I would like to place the spectacle of the starry heavens at night, for the only equivalent of the universe within is the universe without; and just as I reach this world through the medium of the body, so I reach that world through the medium of the psyche.

765   Thus I cannot regret the complications introduced into psychology by my own contributions, for scientists have always deceived themselves very thoroughly when they thought they had discovered how simple things are.

766   In this introduction I hope I have conveyed to the reader that the psychological endeavours summed up in the layman's idea of "psychoanalysis" ramify very much further historically, socially, and philosophically than the term indicates. It may also become clear that the field of research presented in this book is far from being a distinct, easily delimited territory. On the contrary it is a growing science, which is only just beginning to leave its medical cradle and become a psychology of human nature.

767   The exposition that now follows is not intended to describe the whole range of present-day psychological problems. It confines itself to surveying the beginnings of modern psychology and the elementary problems which fall chiefly within the province of the physician. I have included in my introduction a number of wider considerations so as to give the reader a more general orientation.

FREUD AND JUNG: CONTRASTS[1]

768   The difference between Freud's views and my own ought
really to be dealt with by someone who stands outside the orbit
of those ideas which go under our respective names. Can I be
credited with sufficient impartiality to rise above my own ideas?
Can any man do this? I doubt it. If I were told that someone
had rivalled Baron Munchausen by accomplishing such a feat,
I should feel sure that his ideas were borrowed ones.

769   It is true that widely accepted ideas are never the personal
property of their so-called author; on the contrary, he is the
bondservant of his ideas. Impressive ideas which are hailed as
truths have something peculiar about them. Although they come
into being at a definite time, they are and have always been
timeless; they arise from that realm of creative psychic life
out of which the ephemeral mind of the single human being
grows like a plant that blossoms, bears fruit and seed, and then
withers and dies. Ideas spring from something greater than the
personal human being. Man does not make his ideas; we could
say that man's ideas make him.

770   Ideas are, inevitably, a fatal confession, for they bring to
light not only the best in us, but our worst insufficiencies and
personal shortcomings as well. This is especially the case with
ideas about psychology. Where should they come from except from our most subjective side? Can our experience of the
objective world ever save us from our subjective bias? Is not
every experience, even in the best of circumstances, at least
fifty-per-cent subjective interpretation? On the other hand, the
subject is also an objective fact, a piece of the world; and what

1 [Originally published as "Der Gegensatz Freud und Jung," *Kölnische Zeitung*
(Cologne), May 7, 1929, p. 4. Reprinted in *Seelenprobleme der Gegenwart* (Zurich,
1931), and translated by W. S. Dell and Cary F. Baynes, under the present title,
in *Modern Man in Search of a Soul* (London and New York, 1933). The original
German text is retranslated here, though reference has been made to the 1933
translation.—EDITORS.]

comes from him comes, ultimately, from the stuff of the world itself, just as the rarest and strangest organism is none the less supported and nourished by the earth which is common to all. It is precisely the most subjective ideas which, being closest to nature and to our own essence, deserve to be called the truest. But: "What is truth?"

771   For the purposes of psychology, I think it best to abandon the notion that we are today in anything like a position to make statements about the nature of the psyche that are "true" or "correct." The best that we can achieve is true expression. By true expression I mean an open avowal and detailed presentation of everything that is subjectively observed. One person will stress the *forms* into which he can work this material, and will therefore believe that he is the creator of what he finds within himself. Another will lay most weight on *what* is observed; he will therefore speak of it as a phenomenon, while remaining conscious of his own receptive attitude. The truth probably lies between the two: true expression consists in giving form to what is observed.

772   The modern psychologist, however ambitious, can hardly claim to have achieved more than this. Our psychology is the more or less successfully formulated confession of a few individuals, and so far as each of them conforms more or less to a type, his confession can be accepted as a fairly valid description of a large number of people. And since those who conform to other types none the less belong to the human species, we may conclude that this description applies, though less fully, to them too. What Freud has to say about sexuality, infantile pleasure, and their conflict with the "reality principle," as well as what he says about incest and the like, can be taken as the truest expression of his personal psychology. It is the successful formulation of what he himself subjectively observed. I am no opponent of Freud's; I am merely presented in that light by his own short-sightedness and that of his pupils. No experienced psychiatrist can deny having met with dozens of cases whose psychology answers in all essentials to that of Freud. By his own subjective confession, Freud has assisted at the birth of a great truth about man. He has devoted his life and strength to the construction of a psychology which is a formulation of his own being.

773   Our way of looking at things is conditioned by what we are. And since other people have a different psychology, they see things differently and express themselves differently. Adler, one of Freud's earliest pupils, is a case in point. Working with the same empirical material as Freud, he approached it from a totally different standpoint. His way of looking at things is at least as convincing as Freud's, because he too represents a psychology of a well-known type. I know that the followers of both schools flatly assert that I am in the wrong, but I may hope that history and all fair-minded persons will bear me out. Both schools, to my way of thinking, deserve reproach for over-emphasizing the pathological aspect of life and for interpreting man too exclusively in the light of his defects. A convincing example of this in Freud's case is his inability to understand religious experience, as is clearly shown in his book *The Future of an Illusion*.

774   For my part, I prefer to look at man in the light of what in him is healthy and sound, and to free the sick man from just that kind of psychology which colours every page Freud has written. I cannot see how Freud can ever get beyond his own psychology and relieve the patient of a suffering from which the doctor himself still suffers. It is the psychology of neurotic states of mind, definitely one-sided, and its validity is really confined to those states. Within these limits it is true and valid even when it is in error, for error also belongs to the picture and carries the truth of a confession. But it is not a psychology of the healthy mind, and—this is a symptom of its morbidity—it is based on an uncriticized, even an unconscious, view of the world which is apt to narrow the horizon of experience and limit one's vision. It was a great mistake on Freud's part to turn his back on philosophy. Not once does he criticize his assumptions or even his personal psychic premises. Yet to do so was necessary, as may be inferred from what I have said above; for had he critically examined his own foundations he would never have been able to put his peculiar psychology so naïvely on view as he did in *The Interpretation of Dreams*. At all events, he would have had a taste of the difficulties I have met with. I have never refused the bitter-sweet drink of philosophical criticism, but have taken it with caution, a little at a time. All too little, my opponents will say; almost too much, my own feeling

335

tells me. All too easily does self-criticism poison one's naïveté, that priceless possession, or rather gift, which no creative person can do without. At any rate, philosophical criticism has helped me to see that every psychology—my own included—has the character of a subjective confession. And yet I must prevent my critical powers from destroying my creativeness. I know well enough that every word I utter carries with it something of myself—of my special and unique self with its particular history and its own particular world. Even when I deal with empirical data I am necessarily speaking about myself. But it is only by accepting this as inevitable that I can serve the cause of man's knowledge of man—the cause which Freud also wished to serve and which, in spite of everything, he has served. Knowledge rests not upon truth alone, but upon error also.

775   It is perhaps here, where the question arises of recognizing that every psychology which is the work of one man is subjectively coloured, that the line between Freud and myself is most sharply drawn.

776   A further difference seems to me to consist in this, that I try to free myself from all unconscious and therefore uncriticized assumptions about the world in general. I say "I try," for who can be sure that he has freed himself from all of his unconscious assumptions? I try to save myself from at least the crassest prejudices, and am therefore disposed to recognize all manner of gods provided only that they are active in the human psyche. I do not doubt that the natural instincts or drives are forces of propulsion in psychic life, whether we call them sexuality or the will to power; but neither do I doubt that these instincts come into collision with the spirit, for they are continually colliding with something, and why should not this something be called "spirit"? I am far from knowing what spirit is in itself, and equally far from knowing what instincts are. The one is as mysterious to me as the other; nor can I explain the one as a misunderstanding of the other. There are no misunderstandings in nature, any more than the fact that the earth has only one moon is a misunderstanding; misunderstandings are found only in the realm of what we call "understanding." Certainly instinct and spirit are beyond my understanding. They are terms which we posit for powerful forces whose nature we do not know.

777   My attitude to all religions is therefore a positive one. In their symbolism I recognize those figures which I have met with in the dreams and fantasies of my patients. In their moral teachings I see efforts that are the same as or similar to those made by my patients when, guided by their own insight or inspiration, they seek the right way to deal with the forces of psychic life. Ceremonial ritual, initiation rites, and ascetic practices, in all their forms and variations, interest me profoundly as so many techniques for bringing about a proper relation to these forces. My attitude to biology is equally positive, and to the empiricism of natural science in general, in which I see a herculean attempt to understand the psyche by approaching it from the outside world, just as religious gnosis is a prodigious attempt of the human mind to derive knowledge of the cosmos from within. In my picture of the world there is a vast outer realm and an equally vast inner realm; between these two stands man, facing now one and now the other, and, according to temperament and disposition, taking the one for the absolute truth by denying or sacrificing the other.

778   This picture is hypothetical, of course, but it offers a hypothesis which is so valuable that I will not give it up. I consider it heuristically and empirically justified and, moreover, it is confirmed by the *consensus gentium*. This hypothesis certainly came to me from an inner source, though I might imagine that empirical findings had led to its discovery. Out of it has grown my theory of types, and also my reconciliation with views as different from my own as those of Freud.

779   I see in all that happens the play of opposites, and derive from this conception my idea of psychic energy. I hold that psychic energy involves the play of opposites in much the same way as physical energy involves a difference of potential, that is to say the existence of opposites such as warm and cold, high and low, etc. Freud began by taking sexuality as the only psychic driving force, and only after my break with him did he take other factors into account. For my part, I have summed up the various psychic drives or forces—all constructed more or less *ad hoc*—under the concept of energy, in order to eliminate the almost unavoidable arbitrariness of a psychology that deals purely with power-drives. I therefore speak not of separate

drives or forces but of "value intensities." [2] By this I do not
mean to deny the importance of sexuality in psychic life, though
Freud stubbornly maintains that I do deny it. What I seek is to
set bounds to the rampant terminology of sex which vitiates all
discussion of the human psyche, and to put sexuality itself in its
proper place.

780   Common-sense will always return to the fact that sexuality
is only one of the biological instincts, only one of the psycho-
physiological functions, though one that is without doubt very
far-reaching and important. But—what happens when we can no
longer satisfy our hunger? There is, quite obviously, a marked
disturbance today in the psychic sphere of sex, just as, when a
tooth really hurts, the whole psyche seems to consist of nothing
but toothache. The kind of sexuality described by Freud is that
unmistakable sexual obsession which shows itself whenever a
patient has reached the point where he needs to be forced or
tempted out of a wrong attitude or situation. It is an over-
emphasized sexuality piled up behind a dam, and it shrinks at
once to normal proportions as soon as the way to development
is opened. Generally it is being caught in the old resentments
against parents and relations and in the boring emotional tan-
gles of the "family romance" that brings about the damming
up of life's energies, and this stoppage unfailingly manifests itself in the form of sexuality called "infantile." It is not sexuality
proper, but an unnatural discharge of tensions that really belong to quite another province of life. That being so, what is
the use of paddling about in this flooded country? Surely,
straight thinking will grant that it is more important to open
up drainage canals, that is, to find a new attitude or way of life
which will offer a suitable gradient for the pent-up energy.
Otherwise a vicious circle is set up, and this is in fact what
Freudian psychology appears to do. It points no way that leads
beyond the inexorable cycle of biological events. In despair we
would have to cry out with St. Paul: "Wretched man that I am,
who will deliver me from the body of this death?" And the spiritual man in us comes forward, shaking his head, and says in
Faust's words: "Thou art conscious only of the single urge,"
namely of the fleshly bond leading back to father and mother or

2 Cf. "On Psychic Energy," pars. 14ff.

forward to the children that have sprung from our flesh—"incest" with the past and "incest" with the future, the original sin of perpetuation of the "family romance." There is nothing that can free us from this bond except that opposite urge of life, the spirit. It is not the children of the flesh, but the "children of God," who know freedom. In Ernst Barlach's tragedy *The Dead Day,* the mother-daemon says at the end: "The strange thing is that man will not learn that God is his father." That is what Freud would never learn, and what all those who share his outlook forbid themselves to learn. At least, they never find the key to this knowledge. Theology does not help those who are looking for the key, because theology demands faith, and faith cannot be made: it is in the truest sense a gift of grace. We moderns are faced with the necessity of rediscovering the life of the spirit; we must experience it anew for ourselves. It is the only way in which to break the spell that binds us to the cycle of biological events.

781   My position on this question is the third point of difference between Freud's views and my own. Because of it I am accused of mysticism. I do not, however, hold myself responsible for the fact that man has, always and everywhere, spontaneously developed a religious function, and that the human psyche from time immemorial has been shot through with religious feelings and ideas. Whoever cannot see this aspect of the human psyche is blind, and whoever chooses to explain it away, or to "enlighten" it away, has no sense of reality. Or should we see in the father-complex which shows itself in all members of the Freudian school, and in its founder as well, evidence of a notable release from the fatalities of the family situation? This father-complex, defended with such stubbornness and oversensitivity, is a religious function misunderstood, a piece of mysticism expressed in terms of biological and family relationships. As for Freud's concept of the "superego," it is a furtive attempt to smuggle the time-honoured image of Jehovah in the dress of psychological theory. For my part, I prefer to call things by the names under which they have always been known.

782   The wheel of history must not be turned back, and man's advance toward a spiritual life, which began with the primitive rites of initiation, must not be denied. It is permissible for science to divide up its field of inquiry and to operate with

limited hypotheses, for science must work in that way; but the human psyche may not be so parcelled out. It is a whole which embraces consciousness, and it is the mother of consciousness. Scientific thought, being only one of the psyche's functions, can never exhaust all its potentialities. The psychotherapist must not allow his vision to be coloured by pathology; he must never allow himself to forget that the ailing mind is a human mind and that, for all its ailments, it unconsciously shares the whole psychic life of man. He must even be able to admit that the ego is sick for the very reason that it is cut off from the whole, and has lost its connection not only with mankind but with the spirit. The ego is indeed the "place of fears," as Freud says in *The Ego and the Id,* but only so long as it has not returned to its "father" and "mother." Freud founders on the question of Nicodemus: "How can a man be born when he is old? Can he enter the second time into his mother's womb, and be born?" (John 3:4). History repeats itself, for—to compare small things with great—the question reappears today in the domestic quarrel of modern psychology.

783 For thousands of years, rites of initiation have been teaching rebirth from the spirit; yet, strangely enough, man forgets again and again the meaning of divine procreation. Though this may be poor testimony to the strength of the spirit, the penalty for misunderstanding is neurotic decay, embitterment, atrophy, and sterility. It is easy enough to drive the spirit out of the door, but when we have done so the meal has lost its savour—the salt of the earth. Fortunately, we have proof that the spirit always renews its strength in the fact that the essential teaching of the initiations is handed on from generation to generation. Ever and again there are human beings who understand what it means that God is their father. The equal balance of the flesh and the spirit is not lost to the world.

784 The contrast between Freud and myself goes back to essential differences in our basic assumptions. Assumptions are unavoidable, and this being so it is wrong to pretend that we have no assumptions. That is why I have dealt with fundamental questions; with these as a starting-point, the manifold and detailed differences between Freud's views and my own can best be understood.

BIBLIOGRAPHY

BIBLIOGRAPHY

A. LIST OF PERIODICALS CITED, WITH ABBREVIATIONS

Amer. J. Psychol. = American Journal of Psychology. Baltimore.

Arch. Psychol. Suisse rom. = Archives de psychologie de la Suisse romande. Geneva.

Arch. Rass. u. GesBiol. = Archiv für Rassen- und Gesellschaftsbiologie. Leipzig and Berlin.

Berl. klin. Wschr. = Berliner klinische Wochenschrift. Berlin.

J. abnorm. Psychol. = Journal of Abnormal Psychology. Boston.

Jb. psychoanal. psychopath. Forsch. = Jahrbuch für psychoanalytische und psychopathologische Forschungen. Vienna and Leipzig.

Med. Klinik = Medizinische Klinik. Vienna and Berlin.

Med. Pr. = Medical Press. London.

Münch. med. Wschr. = Münchener medizinische Wochenschrift. Munich.

Monatshefte für Pädagogik und Schulpolitik. Vienna.

Proc. Soc. psych. Res., Lond. = Proceedings of the Society for Psychical Research. London.

Psychiat.-neurol. Wschr. = Psychiatrisch-neurologische Wochenschrift. Halle.

Z. ReligPsychol. = Zeitschrift für Religionspsychologie. Halle.

Z. Völkerpsychol. Sprachw. = Zeitschrift für Völkerpsychologie und Sprachwissenschaft. Berlin.

Zbl. Nervenheilk. = Zentralblatt für Nervenheilkunde und Psychiatrie. Berlin.

Zbl. Psychoan. = Zentralblatt für Psychoanalyse. Wiesbaden.

B. GENERAL BIBLIOGRAPHY

ABRAHAM, KARL. *Dreams and Myths.* Translated by William Alanson White. (Nervous and Mental Disease Monograph Series, 15.) New York, 1913.

——. "The Psycho-Sexual Differences between Hysteria and Dementia Praecox." In: *Selected Papers.* Translated by Douglas Bryan and Alix Strachey. (International Psycho-Analytical Library, 13.) London, 1927.

ADLER, ALFRED. *The Neurotic Constitution.* Translated by B. Glueck and J. E. Lind. London, 1921. (Original: *Über den nervösen Charakter.* 1912.)

——. "Trotz und Gehorsam," *Monatshefte für Pädagogik und Schulpolitik* (Vienna), VIII (1910). Also in: ADLER and FURTMÜLLER, CARL (eds.). *Heilen und Bilden.* Munich, 1914.

ASCHAFFENBURG, GUSTAV. "Die Beziehungen des sexuellen Lebens zur Entstehung von Nerven- und Geisteskrankheiten," *Münch. med. Wschr.*, LIII (1906), 1793–98.

BARLACH, ERNST. *Der Tote Tag.* Berlin, 1912; 2nd edn., 1918.

BINET, ALFRED. *Alterations of Personality.* Translated by Helen Green Baldwin. London, 1896. (Original: *Les Altérations de la personnalité.* 1892.)

BINSWANGER, OTTO LUDWIG. "Freud'sche Mechanismen in der Symptomatologie von Psychosen," *Psychiat.-neurol. Wschr.*, VIII (1906).

——. *Die Hysterie.* (Specielle Pathologie und Therapie, edited by Herman Nothnagel et al., 12, First Half, Part 2.) Vienna, 1904.

BLEULER, EUGEN. "Die Psychoanalyse Freuds," *Jb. psychoanal. psychopath. Forsch.*, II (1910), 623–730.

BOAS, FRANZ. *Indianische Sagen von der Nord-pacifischen Küste Amerikas.* Berlin, 1895.

BREUER, JOSEF, and FREUD, SIGMUND. *Studies on Hysteria.* Translated by James and Alix Strachey. (Complete Psychological Works of Sigmund Freud, Standard Edition, 2.) London, 1955. (Original: *Studien über Hysterie.* 1895.)

BRILL, A. A. "Psychological Factors in Dementia Praecox: an Analysis," *J. abnorm. Psychol.*, III (1908), 219.

FLOURNOY, THÉODORE. *From India to the Planet Mars.* Translated by

D. B. Vermilye. New York, 1900. (Original: *Des Indes à la planète Mars.* 1900.)

——. "Nouvelles observations sur un cas de somnambulisme avec glossolalie," *Arch. Psychol. Suisse rom.,* I (1901), 101–255.

FOREL, AUGUSTE. *Hypnotism: or, Suggestion and Psychotherapy.* Translated from the 5th German edn. by H. W. Armit. London and New York, 1906. (Original: *Der Hypnotismus.* 1889.)

FRANK, LUDWIG. *Affektstörungen. Studien über ihre Ätiologie und Therapie.* (Monographien aus dem Gesamtgebiete der Neurologie und Psychiatrie, 4.) Berlin, 1913.

FREUD, SIGMUND. "Character and Anal Erotism." Translated by R. C. McWatters. In: Standard Edn.,* 9. 1959. (Original: "Charakter und Analerotik," *Psychiat.-neurol. Wschr.,* IX (1907).)

——. *Collected Papers.* (International Psycho-Analytical Library, 7–10, 37.) London, 1924–50. 5 vols.

——. "The Defence Neuro-Psychoses." Translated by John Rickman. In *Collected Papers,* q.v., 1. (To appear in the Standard Edn.,* 3.) (Original: *Die Abwehrneuropsychosen.* 1894.)

——. *The Ego and the Id.* Translated by Joan Riviere. (International Psycho-Analytical Library, 12.) London, 1927. (To appear in the Standard Edn.,* 19.) (Original: *Das Ich und das Es.* 1923.)

——. "Five Lectures on Psycho-Analysis." (Delivered on the Occasion of the Celebration of the Twentieth Anniversary of the Foundation of Clark University, Worcester, Mass., September 1909.) Translated by James Strachey. In: Standard Edn.,* 11. 1957. (Original: *Ueber Psychoanalyse.* 1910.)

——. "Fragment of an Analysis of a Case of Hysteria." Translated by Alix and James Strachey. In: Standard Edn.,* 7. 1953. (Original: "Bruchstücke einer Hysterie-Analyse." 1905.)

——. "Freud's Psycho-Analytic Procedure." Translated by J. Bernays. In: Standard Edn.,* 7. 1953. (Original: "Die Freud'sche Psychoanalytische Methode." 1904.)

——. *The Future of an Illusion.* Translated by W. D. Robson-Scott. London, 1928. (International Psycho-Analytical Library, 15.) (To appear in the Standard Edn.,* 21.) (Original: *Die Zukunft einer Illusion.* 1927.)

* The Standard Edition of the Complete Psychological Works of Sigmund Freud, translated under the general editorship of James Strachey. London.

——. *The Interpretation of Dreams*. Translated by James Strachey. Standard Edn.,* 4, 5. 1953. (Original: *Die Traumdeutung*. 1900.)

——. *Jokes and Their Relation to the Unconscious*. Standard Edn.,* 8. 1960. (Original: *Der Witz und seine Beziehung zum Unbewussten*. 1905.)

——. "Obsessive Acts and Religious Practices." Translated by R. C. McWatters. In: Standard Edn.,* 9. 1959. (Original: "Zwangshandlungen und Religionsübung," *Z. ReligPsychol.*, I (1907).)

——. "On Beginning the Treatment (Further Recommendations on the Technique of Psycho-Analysis I)." In: Standard Edn.,* 12. 1958.

——. "On Psychotherapy." Translated by J. Bernays. In: Standard Edn.,* 7. 1953. (Original: "Über Psychotherapie." 1904.)

——. "The Origin and Development of Psychoanalysis." See "Five Lectures on Psycho-Analysis."

——. "Psycho-Analytic Notes on an Autobiographical Account of a Case of Paranoia (Dementia Paranoides)." Translated by Alix and James Strachey. In: Standard Edn.,* 12. 1958. (Original: "Psychoanalytische Bemerkungen über einen autobiographisch beschriebenen Fall von Paranoia (Dementia Paranoides)." 1911.)

——. *The Psychopathology of Everyday Life*. Translated by A. A. Brill. In: *Basic Writings of Sigmund Freud*. New York, 1938. (To appear in Standard Edn.,* 6.) (Original: *Zur Psychopathologie des Alltagslebens*. 1901.)

——. "Recommendations to Physicians Practising Psycho-Analysis." Translated by Joan Riviere. In: Standard Edn.,* 12. 1958. (Original: "Ratschläge für den Arzt bei der psychoanalytischen Behandlung." 1912.)

——. *Sammlung kleiner Schriften zur Neurosenlehre*. Vienna, 1906–22. 5 vols. (Mostly translated in *Collected Papers*, q.v.)

——. "Three Essays on the Theory of Sexuality." Translated by James Strachey. Standard Edn.,* 7. 1953. (Original: *Drei Abhandlungen zur Sexualtheorie*. 1905.)

FROBENIUS, LEO. *Das Zeitalter des Sonnengottes*. Vol. I (no more published). Berlin, 1904.

FÜRST, EMMA. "Statistical Investigations on Word-Associations and on Familial Agreement in Reaction Type among Uneducated Persons." In: C. G. JUNG (ed.). *Studies in Word-Association*. Translated by M. D. Eder. London, 1918; New York, 1919.

FURTMÜLLER, CARL. "Wandlungen in der Freud'schen Schule," *Zbl. Psychoan.*, III (1912–13), 189–201.

GOETHE, JOHANN WOLFGANG VON. *Faust: Part One*. Translated by Philip Wayne. (Penguin Classics.) Harmondsworth, 1956.

———. *Werke*. (Gesamtausgabe.) Edited by Ernst Beutler. Zurich, 1948–54. 24 vols. (For the poem quoted on p. 315, see Vol. II, p. 43.)

HARTMANN, CARL ROBERT EDUARD VON. *Philosophy of the Unconscious*. Translated by W. C. Coupland. London, 1931.

HASLEBACHER, J. A., "Psychoneurosen und Psychoanalyse," *Correspondenzblatt für Schweizer Ärzte* (Basel), XL:7 (Mar. 1, 1910).

HOCHE, ALFRED E. "Eine psychische Epidemie unter Aerzten," *Med. Klinik*, VI (1910), 1007–10.

HORACE. *Satires, Epistles, and Ars Poetica*. With an English translation by H. Rushton Fairclough. (Loeb Classical Library.) London and New York, 1929.

JAMES, WILLIAM. *Pragmatism*. London and Cambridge (Mass.), 1907.

JANET, PIERRE. *Les Névroses*. Paris, 1898. Later edn., 1909.

JONES, ERNEST. "Freud's Theory of Dreams," *Amer. J. Psychol.*, XXI (1910), 283–308.

———. *On the Nightmare*. (International Psycho-Analytical Library, 20.) London, 1931.

———. "Remarks on Dr Morton Prince's article 'The Mechanism and Interpretation of Dreams.' " *J. abnorm. Psychol.*, V (1910–11), 328–36.

———. *Sigmund Freud: Life and Work*. London, 1953–57. 3 vols. (Also pub. New York separately. Refs. are to the London edn.)

JÖRGER, J. "Die Familie Zero," *Arch. Rass. u. GesBiol.* (Leipzig and Berlin), II (1905), 494–559.

JUNG, CARL GUSTAV. "The Association Method." In: *Experimental Researches*. (Collected Works, 2.*) (Alternative source: *Collected Papers on Analytical Psychology*, q.v.)

———. *Collected Papers on Analytical Psychology*. Edited by Con-

* For details of the Collected Works of C. G. Jung (especially volumes yet unpublished, cited here without date) see the end of this volume.

stance Long, translated by various persons. London, 1916; 2nd edn., London, 1917, New York, 1920.

———. "The Familial Constellations." In: *Experimental Researches.* (Collected Works, 2.*) (Alternative source: *Collected Papers on Analytical Psychology,* q.v.)

———. "New Paths in Psychology." In: *Two Essays on Analytical Psychology,* q.v.

———. "On Psychic Energy." In: *The Structure and Dynamics of the Psyche.* (Collected Works, 8.) 1960.

———. "On Psychological Understanding." In: *The Psychogenesis of Mental Disease,* q.v.

———. "Psychic Conflicts in a Child." In: *The Development of Personality.* (Collected Works, 17.) 1954.

———. *The Psychogenesis of Mental Disease.* (Collected Works, 3.) 1960.

———. "Psychological Aspects of the Mother Archetype." In: *The Archetypes and the Collective Unconscious.* (Collected Works, 9, part i.) 1959.

———. *Psychological Types.* (Collected Works, 6.*) (Alternative source: translation by H. G. Baynes, London and New York, 1923.)

———. *Psychology and Alchemy.* (Collected Works, 12.) 1953.

———. "The Psychology of Dementia Praecox." In: *The Psychogenesis of Mental Disease,* q.v.

———. "Psychology of the Transference." In: *The Practice of Psychotherapy.* (Collected Works, 16.) 1954.

———. *Studies in Word-Association.* In: *Experimental Researches.* (Collected Works, 2.*) (Alternative source: *Studies in Word-Association. . . .* under the direction of C. G. Jung. Translated by M. D. Eder. London, 1918; New York, 1919.)

———. *Symbols of Transformation.* (Collected Works, 5.) 1956.

———. *Two Essays on Analytical Psychology.* (Collected Works, 7.) 1953.

———. *Wandlungen und Symbole der Libido.* Leipzig and Vienna, 1912.

KUHN, FRANZ FELIX ADALBERT. *Mythologische Studien.* Gütersloh, 1886–1912. 2 vols.

MAEDER, ALFRED. "Contributions à la psychologie de la vie quotidienne," *Arch. Psychol. Suisse rom.*, VI (1906–7), 148 ff., and VII (1907–8), 283 ff.

———. "Essai d'interprétation de quelques rêves," *Arch. Psychol. Suisse rom.*, VI (1906–7), 354 ff.

———. "Die Symbolik in den Legenden, Märchen, Gebräuchen und Träumen," *Psychiat.-neurol. Wschr.* (Halle), X (1908).

MAYLAN, CHARLES E. *Freuds tragischer Komplex: Eine Analyse der Psychoanalyse.* Munich, 1929.

MITCHELL, T. WEIR. Review of "Collected Papers on Analytical Psychology," *Proc. Soc. psych. Res., Lond.*, XXIX (1916), 191–95.

MÜLLER-LYER, FRANZ. *The Family.* Translated by F. W. Stella Browne. London, 1931. (Original: *Die Familie.* 1912.)

OPPENHEIM, H. "Thatsächliches und Hypothetisches über das Wesen der Hysterie," *Berl. klin. Wschr.*, XXVII (1890), 553.

PAGE, H. W. "Shock from Fright." In: HACK TUKE. *Dictionary of Psychological Medicine.* London, 1892.

———. *Injuries of the Spine and Spinal Cord without Apparent Mechanical Lesions, and Nervous Shock—Their Surgical and Medico-Legal Aspects.* London and Philadelphia, 1883.

PETERS, WILHELM. "Gefühl und Erinnerung." In: EMIL KRAEPELIN. *Psychologische Arbeiten.* Leipzig and Berlin, 1914. (Vol. 6, pt. 2, pp. 197–260.)

PRINCE, MORTON. *The Dissociation of a Personality.* New York and London, 1906.

———. "The Mechanism and Interpretation of Dreams," *J. abnorm. Psychol.*, V (1910–11), 139–95.

PUTNAM, JAMES J. "Personal Impressions of Sigmund Freud and His Work, with special reference to His Recent Lectures at Clark University," *J. abnorm. Psychol.*, IV (1909–10), 293, 372.

———. "Persönliche Erfahrungen mit Freud's psychoanalytischer Methode," *Zbl. Psychoan.*, I (1910–11), 533–48.

RANK, OTTO. *The Myth of the Birth of the Hero.* Translated by William Alanson White. (Nervous and Mental Disease Monograph Series, 18.) New York, 1914.

———. "Ein Traum, der sich selbst deutet," *Jb. psychoanal. psychopath. Forsch.*, II (1910), 465–540.

RIKLIN, FRANZ. *Wishfulfilment and Symbolism in Fairy Tales.* Trans-

349

lated by William Alanson White. (Nervous and Mental Disease Monograph Series, 21.) New York, 1915.

SADGER, ISIDOR. "Analerotik und Analcharakter," *Die Heilkunde* (Vienna), Feb. 1910.

SALLUST (C. Sallustius Crispus). [*Works.*] With an English translation by J. C. Rolfe. (Loeb Classical Library.) London and New York, 1921.

SAVILL, AGNES. "Psychoanalysis," *Med. Pr.*, CLII (1916), 446–48.

SCHOPENHAUER, ARTHUR. *Transcendent Speculations on the Apparent Design in the Fate of the Individual*. Translated by David Irvine. London, 1913. (Original: "Über die anscheinende Absichtlichkeit im Schicksale des Einzelnen," *Sämmtliche Werke*, ed. Julius Frauenstadt, 2nd edn., Leipzig, 1877, Vol. V [*Parerga und Paralipomena*, Vol. II], 222–23.)

SHAW, GEORGE BERNARD. *Man and Superman*. London, 1903.

SILBERER, HERBERT. "Phantasie und Mythos," *Jb. psychoanal. psychopath. Forsch.*, II (1910), 541–622.

———. *Problems of Mysticism and Its Symbolism*. Translated by Smith Ely Jelliffe. New York, 1917.

SOMMER, ROBERT. *Familienforschung und Vererbungslehre*. Leipzig, 1907.

SPIELMEYER, WALTER. Untitled note in *Zbl. Nervenheilk.*, XXIX (1906), 322–24.

SPIELREIN, SABINA. "Über den psychologischen Inhalt eines Falls von Schizophrenie," *Jb. psychoanal. psychopath. Forsch.*, III (1912), 329–400.

STEINTHAL, HEYMANN. "Die Sage von Simson," *Z. Völkerpsychol. Sprachw.*, II (1861), 129–78.

STEKEL, WILHELM. "Ausgänge der psychoanalytischen Kuren," *Zbl. Psychoan.*, III (1912–13), 175–88.

———. *Die Sprache des Traumes*. Wiesbaden, 1911.

VIGOUROUX, A., and JUQUELIER, P. *La Contagion mentale*. (Bibliothèque internationale de psychologie.) Paris, 1904.

ZIERMER, MANFRED. "Genealogische Studien über die Vererbung geistiger Eigenschaften," *Arch. Rass.- u. GesBiol.*, V (1908), 178–220, 327–63.

INDEX

INDEX

A

abasia, 5

Abraham, Karl, 100, 122, 211, 220

abreaction, 11, 14, 90, 254, 258, 262

accidents, 223; apparent, 216; and emotional development, 177, 179; hysteria and, 90

activity, and passivity, 274

Acts of the Apostles, 53

adaptation, 137, 182, 186ff, 248; abnormal, 249; failure in, 250; infantile, 137; new, and neurosis, 246; psychological, 271, 274; reduced, in neurotics, 191; resistance to, infantile, 249; transference and, 199, 285

Adler, Alfred, 48, 87, 240, 247, 276, 285, 291f, 328, 335

advice, 231

affection, need for, 114

affects: aetiological significance in hysteria, 10f; blocking of, 12, 90; children's, intensity of, 152; displacement of, 13; effects of traumatic, 12f; in normal persons, 11; retardation of development of, 130

affluxes, libidinal, 126

Agamemnon, 154

aims, and causes, 291f

albumen, 331

alchemists, 326

altruism, 282

ambivalence: of father-imago, 321; of instincts, 283

America: cross symbol in, 210; psychoanalysis in, 88

amnesia: of childhood/infantile, 117, 163f; neurotic, 164

Amsterdam Congress (1907), 317n

anal eroticism, 20, 21, 76

analogy, 240

analysis, 250; fantasy invention during, 184; first stage, 194f; second stage, 197, 200; of transference, 194ff; see also dream-analysis; psychanalysis; psychoanalysis

analyst: analysis of, 198f, 235, 253, 260, 274; fear of loss of, 63; interference by, 272, 275; loss of balance by, 235; personality of, 198ff, 260, 274, 277; possibility of deceiving, 280; procedure of, 272; relation to patient, 193, 235, 285; requirements for, 202; resistances of, 187; transference relation to, 191, see also transference

analytical psychology, 229

anamnesis, 97; and psychoanalysis, 230f, 271

anarchy, 283

ancestor-columns, 222

anchorite, 121

Andermatt, 35ff

animals, 242; artistic impulse in, 123; gradual change in reproductive principles, 123; hypnosis in, 262; laziness in, 208; and remembered impressions, 179; social sense in, 278; training of, 182

Annunciation, 54

ant, queen, 315

anthroposophy, 326

antlers, 287

anxiety attacks, 162

apathy, neurotic, 113

aphonia, 5, 69, 70

"apothecaries' messes," 260

353

sanatoria, 265; as science, 229; and other sciences, 202; scope of, 324; and self-knowledge, 48; and sexuality, 79; suggestion in, 280, 281; suitability for, 266; and symptoms, 184; technical application, 272; therapeutic effect, 190, 276; *see also* analysis; psychanalysis
Psychoanalytical Society, 79
psychocatharsis, 274; *see also* catharsis
psychology, 229; two types, 291; *see also* analytical psychology; depth psychology; individual psychology
psychoneuroses, sexuality and, 3*ff*
puberty: and development of hysterical psychosis, 21*f*; libido and, 114; and objectification of sexual goal, 19; reactivation of childhood traumata at, 13
puppy, 104
purposiveness, 161
Putnam, James J., 56, 57

Q

Quimby, Phineas P., 326 & *n*

R

Raguel, 321*f*, 323*n*
Raimann, Emil, 13 & *n*
Rank, Otto, 145, 211
Rascher's Yearbook, 79
ratiocinative method, 231
reactions, value-predicate, 305
reaction-types, similarity in families, 304
reactivation, of parental images, 248
reactivity, 183*n*
reality: adaptation to, enhanced, 126; —, loss of, 119, 120; disappearance of, 121; flight from, 183; neurotics and, 191; no loss of in neuroses, 121; soberness of, 274
reality function, and sexuality, 122*ff*
reality principle, 334
reconstruction stage, 262

recovery, motives for, 276
reduction, 292
rééducation de la volonté, 184
reflexes, emotional, 248
Reformation, 325, 327
regression, 121–22*n*, 181, 207, 224, 247, 303; conditions of, 169*f*; effect of, 178; end of, 188*f*; of libido, 162*ff*, 187, 248; teleological significance, 179*f*
relapse, 63*f*
relationship: analyst-patient, 193, 235, 285, *see also* transference; extra-familial, 195*f*; parent-child, 137, 286, *see also* parents; transference, *see* transference
relatives, and association reactions, 304
religion, 330; in analysis, 241; comparative, 324; —, psychoanalysis and, 202, 203; and dogma, 324; Freud and, 335; history of, and fantasies, 320*n*; infantile constellations and, 316*n*; sacrifice in, 155; symbolism of, 337; unconscious fantasies and, 151; *see also* symbol, religious
reminiscences, 11, 14, 134, 162, 168, 248; and dreams, 145, 149; excited by hypnosis, 92; transformation into fantasies, 175
repetition, significance of, 40
repression, 12, 91*ff*, 99, 126; conscious, 93; and dreams, 28*f*; and hysteria, 19, 21; of Oedipus complex, 156; sexual, God and, 321*n*
reproduction, evolutionary change in principles, 123, 125*f*
reproductive organs, development of, 104
resistance(s), 110, 174, 235, 283*f*; of analyst, 187; to complex, 16, 154*f*; in dreams, 28*ff*; hypnosis and, 262; to hysterical fantasies, 19; initial, in analysis, 195, 272; to sexual problem, 172; to wish-fulfilment, 68; to work, 232
retrogression, 239

THE COLLECTED WORKS OF
C. G. JUNG

THE PUBLICATION of the first complete collected edition, in English, of the works of C. G. Jung has been undertaken by Routledge and Kegan Paul, Ltd., in England and by the Bollingen Foundation, through Pantheon Books Inc., in the United States. The edition contains revised versions of works previously published, such as *Psychology of the Unconscious,* which is now entitled *Symbols of Transformation;* works originally written in English, such as "Psychology and Religion"; works not previously translated, such as *Aion;* and, in general, new translations of the major body of Professor Jung's writings. The author has supervised the textual revision, which in some cases is extensive. Sir Herbert Read, Dr. Michael Fordham, and Dr. Gerhard Adler compose the Editorial Committee; the translator is R. F. C. Hull.

Every volume of the Collected Works contains material that either has not previously been published in English or is being newly published in revised form. In addition to *Aion,* the following volumes will, entirely or in large part, be new to English readers: *Psychiatric Studies; The Archetypes and the Collective Unconscious; Alchemical Studies; Mysterium Coniunctionis; The Spirit in Man, Art, and Literature;* and *The Practice of Psychotherapy.*

The volumes are not being published in strictly consecutive order; but, generally speaking, works of which translations are lacking or unavailable are given precedence. The price of the volumes varies according to size; they are sold separately, and may also be obtained on standing order. Several of the volumes are extensively illustrated. Each volume contains an index and, in most cases, a bibliography; the final volumes will contain a complete bibliography of Professor Jung's writings and a general index of the entire edition. Subsequent works of the author's are being added in due course.

*1. PSYCHIATRIC STUDIES
  On the Psychology and Pathology of So-Called Occult Phenomena
  On Hysterical Misreading
  Cryptomnesia   (*continued*)
* Published 1957.

1. (continued):

On Manic Mood Disorder
A Case of Hysterical Stupor in a Prisoner in Detention
On Simulated Insanity
A Medical Opinion on a Case of Simulated Insanity
A Third and Final Opinion on Two Contradictory Psychiatric Diagnoses
On the Psychological Diagnosis of Facts

2. EXPERIMENTAL RESEARCHES

STUDIES IN WORD ASSOCIATION

The Associations of Normal Subjects (by Jung and Riklin)
Experimental Observations on Memory
On the Determination of Facts by Psychological Means
An Analysis of the Associations of an Epileptic
The Association Method
Reaction-Time in Association Experiments
On Disturbances in Reproduction in Association Experiments
The Significance of Association Experiments for Psychopathology
Psychoanalysis and Association Experiments
Association, Dream, and Hysterical Symptoms

PSYCHOPHYSICAL RESEARCHES

On Psychophysical Relations of the Association Experiment
Psychophysical Investigations with the Galvanometer and Pneumograph in Normal and Insane Individuals (by Peterson and Jung)
Further Investigations on the Galvanic Phenomenon and Respirations in Normal and Insane Individuals (by Ricksher and Jung)

*3. THE PSYCHOGENESIS OF MENTAL DISEASE

The Psychology of Dementia Praecox
The Content of the Psychoses
On Psychological Understanding
A Criticism of Bleuler's Theory of Schizophrenic Negativism
On the Importance of the Unconscious in Psychopathology
On the Problem of Psychogenesis in Mental Disease
Mental Disease and the Psyche
On the Psychogenesis of Schizophrenia
Recent Thoughts on Schizophrenia
Schizophrenia

* Published 1960.

* Published 1961.
† Published 1956.

* Published 1953.
† Published 1960.

(continued)

* Published 1959.

* Published 1958.

(*continued*)

* Published 1953.   † Published 1954.